D0550554

SUZANNE HEYWOOD was born in the [...] hood sailed around the world with her [...] formal education. She came back to the UK aged seventeen and won a place to study at Oxford University. After her PhD at Cambridge University, she joined McKinsey and Company, where she became a senior partner. She is now a managing director of Exor and chair of CNH Industrial. She married Jeremy in 1997 and they have three children.

The *Sunday Times* bestseller

'I just couldn't put it down. A fabulous book'   IAIN DALE, *LBC*

'This is an astonishing book … She captures a remarkable sweep of recent UK political history and the central part that her late husband – a brilliant product and architect of the UK civil service and arguably the most influential cabinet secretary of modern times – played in making it work better'   *Financial Times*

'An intimate personal memoir that is in places very moving and a fascinating political history that is at times revelatory … The book brilliantly captures the way in which the personal and political are inextricably entwined'   *The Times*

'A fitting tribute to an important public servant and a valuable insider account for political junkies … She has succeeded hands down in justifying her belief that her husband was a worthy subject'   *Sunday Times*

'This book should be read in a similar spirit to Mantel's masterpieces – as a portrait of an exceptional man who was always at the centre of events … *What Does Jeremy Think?* will be invaluable as a source for scholars and historians both as to how, when, why and by whom certain decisions were taken, and to what the decision-making process within government looks like up close'   JONATHAN PORTES, *Guardian*

SUZANNE HEYWOOD

WHAT DOES JEREMY THINK?

Jeremy Heywood and
the Making of Modern Britain

**WILLIAM
COLLINS**

William Collins
An imprint of HarperCollins*Publishers*
1 London Bridge Street
London SE1 9GF

WilliamCollinsBooks.com

HarperCollins*Publishers*
1st Floor, Watermarque Building, Ringsend Road
Dublin 4, Ireland

First published in Great Britain in 2021 by William Collins
This William Collins paperback edition published in 2022

1

A catalogue record for this book is
available from the British Library

ISBN 978-0-00-835316-2

Typeset in Adobe Garamond Pro
Printed and bound in the UK using 100%
renewable electricity at CPI Group (UK) Ltd

MIX
Paper from
responsible sources
FSC™ C007454

This book is produced from independently certified FSC™ paper
to ensure responsible forest management.

For more information visit: www.harpercollins.co.uk/green

For Jeremy,
civil servant, husband and father

'Some heroes wear capes – mine wore a cardigan.'
Jonathan Heywood

'It may safely be asserted that, as matters now stand, the
Government of the country could not be carried on
without the aid of an efficient body of permanent officers,
occupying a position duly subordinate to that of the
Ministers who are directly responsible to the Crown and to
Parliament, yet possessing sufficient independence,
character, ability, and experience to be able to advise,
assist, and to some extent, influence, those who are from
time to time set over them.'
Northcote-Trevelyan Report, 1854

Contents

Illustrations

Meeting with David Cameron and Nick Clegg (*Shutterstock*)

Jeremy with David Cameron in his Downing Street office (*Tom Stoddart Archive/Getty Images*)

Receiving the knighthood in 2012 (*John Stillwell/WPA Pool/Getty Images*)

With the twins in 2003

Jeremy and Jonny in 2002

The family in Santa's Grotto

A Cabinet meeting with David Cameron (*Neil Hall/AFP/Getty Images*)

Welcoming Theresa May to Downing Street in 2016 (*Andrew Parsons*)

Becoming Baron Heywood of Whitehall, 2018

The family in Malta, 2017

UK Prime Ministers speaking at Jeremy's memorial service (*Shutterstock*)

Seated at the memorial service (*Shutterstock*)

(All pictures from the author's personal collection unless otherwise stated)

Foreword

I will always be grateful for the year that I spent talking to Jeremy about this book. And I know Jeremy felt the same way. The last time we spoke about it was in the hospital shortly before he died. By that point, Jeremy was rarely awake, and I was sitting by his side, talking to him, or maybe to myself, and watching him breathe. The news had been full of reports of his retirement as Cabinet Secretary, and I feared would soon be full of news of his death. But for then it was just the two of us, the beeping of the hospital instruments and the rumble of cars on the Marylebone Road.

During one of those afternoons, Jeremy opened his eyes. 'Your book,' he said, his voice faint and raspy though still clear. 'We have to put our names on it. Jeremy and Suzanne. So all our descendants will know. They'll be amazed.'

'They will indeed,' I said, though his eyes were closed again. 'I'll make sure they know. Grandad Jeremy and all you did.'

I'd begun writing this book a year before, in October 2017. That was six months after Jeremy had been diagnosed with lung cancer, but while he was still working as Cabinet Secretary, trying to help Theresa May deliver Brexit. The process had started with a series of interviews, sitting on the sofa in our children's playroom where we discussed everything from Black Wednesday to the financial crisis and multiple attempts to reform the public sector.

'It's like Rosencrantz and Guildenstern, isn't it?' Jeremy said with a smile at the end of one of these sessions.

I'd laughed at this, remembering when we had gone to see Tom Stoppard's play, which tells the story of those two minor characters from *Hamlet*, and Jeremy leaning over in the darkness to whisper that it made no sense at all since he'd never seen Shakespeare's original. But it was also typically modest. Yes, Jeremy's story is like Rosencrantz and Guildenstern, who witnessed so much. But Jeremy saw several Hamlets rise and fall. And unlike Rosencrantz and Guildenstern, he was on stage throughout, though determined not to catch the spotlight. Indeed, it's partly Jeremy's punctiliousness about minimising his visibility that explains why, until now, he's barely left a mark on the endless pages dedicated to those years.

So this is my account of the role that Jeremy played in the making of modern Britain. It's the tale of a man who evolved from being a specialist economist in the outskirts of the Civil Service into someone whom many considered the consummate insider, though he never stopped challenging the system.

Some people have questioned why I have written a biography of a civil servant, and why Jeremy agreed to let me interview him for it. The fundamental reason is that we both believed that this is a story that has historical value and that the Civil Service will be better defended if it is understood than if it hides itself away. Ideally Jeremy would have shared his memories and learnings from almost thirty years of service in interviews and speeches after leaving office as his predecessors have done, perhaps followed by a biography several years later, as has also been done before. However, fate did not give him that option and instead forced us to decide whether to tell his tale in this way or to allow his memories to be lost.

This story emerged from many hours of talking to Jeremy, who found it difficult to escape his biographer. We began by discussing each story in outline so that I understood his perspective on it and I then researched each one in detail. Over the course of writing the book this meant interviewing almost two hundred eyewitnesses, including all the prime ministers whom Jeremy served, together with many of the other ministers, civil servants and special advisers with whom he worked, as well as his business contacts, family and friends.*

---

* The list of interviewees and other contributors is in the appendix.

Many interviewees also shared personal papers and diaries and later commented on draft chapters. Jeremy sent me texts giving me his view of what I needed to cover in these interviews, unable to resist a little back-seat driving, and would quiz me on my findings when I returned from each one. His text before my interview with David Cameron is a good example of his interventions – and while perhaps not typical of those sent between spouses, it was very useful. It read as follows:

> For DC. Early days with Lamont. Black Wednesday. JH/DC relationship, first few days as PM. Role of JH and Gus, decision to keep JH, initial decisions on fiscal consolidation, constructive challenge to HMT on pace of cuts. Worries about monetary tightness, Leveson, appointment as Cab Sec. NHS pause, why did we get it so wrong? Pfizer/AZ. BAE/Airbus, aircraft carriers, decision to call referendum and failure to talk about immigration, Bob Kerslake decision, reflections on Civil Service, no contingency planning on Scotland and Brexit, Snowden, DRIPA etc.

In doing my research I also drew on my journals, Jeremy's personal documents and letters and some of the books published about these years. Once this work was done, Jeremy reviewed each section of the draft text, which inevitably led to further questions and iterations.

Given that the purpose of this narrative is to share what Jeremy thought and what it was like to play his role, I've allowed the story to unfold over time rather than packaging it into themes. It also doesn't attempt to cover in detail issues in which he was only peripherally involved, even if they were of national importance.

I've tried, where I can, to tell this tale through conversations. These, though as accurate as possible – with the exception of removing the profanities common in political life – are, of course, recreated. But they were all reviewed by Jeremy, and many were also checked by the other participants. To avoid dizzying the reader with names, I haven't attempted to list in the text all the people who worked alongside Jeremy on each issue and I've also largely dispensed with titles, since they were rarely used in daily dialogue; I hope I will be forgiven for all of this.

Some have noted that this book is kind, at least compared to many political biographies. This, however, reflects how Jeremy thought. In all our conversations, he rarely criticised his colleagues or the politicians he served. Jeremy's focus was instead always on the policy – developing it in line with ministers' aims and getting it delivered. Occasionally these stories came with a raised eyebrow or a slight smile, as he described the behaviours he had to manage, but never more.

Other people have pointed out that a biography written by a spouse is unusual, and indeed it is. One eminent biographer even told me there should 'probably be a law against it'. My response to this was to write faster and more furiously. Yes, there are biases – as there are in any autobiography – though I assured Jeremy this would be no hagiography. Our relationship also means that I have left it to others to judge Jeremy's contribution to our country during his time in office and indeed what difference he might have made to later crises, such as the coronavirus epidemic in 2020. There are, however, insights included here that only a spouse could have, particularly one who once worked in the same place and who, through most of the period concerned, was discussing these events daily with her subject.

There are many questions that I pondered as this book evolved. How much should the Civil Service change to accommodate different administrations? When is it right for leaders to defend their staff and when should they let them go? What role should special advisers play and how should the Civil Service be protected from politicisation? In particular, this narrative may fuel the debate about how much power a civil servant should have. But although Jeremy created policy, he only ever did so with his ministers' permission and he was always clear that it was the elected government, not the Civil Service, that took decisions and was accountable to the people.

Writing this book brought many joyous moments, laughing over stories with Jeremy and discovering, through the access I was privileged to have, new insights into Britain's recent history. At times it was also incredibly sad because, although I'd wanted to write it for years, Jeremy only agreed to let me begin after he became seriously ill and realised that this would be the only way to tell his story. I, therefore, wrote the first draft chased by time, asking questions I knew I could never ask again. We think memories last forever, but they don't; not unless we make an effort to capture them.

Postscript. I am grateful to Alastair Campbell for the title, which was a frequently asked question in Whitehall. On the cover Jeremy is standing in front of a painting in his office called *Glass* by David Austen. The chapter titles come from Jeremy's beloved playlist (*Jeremy1961* by azureseal on Spotify).

Note for the paperback edition: I have included a new chapter on the Greensill scandal, something that erupted after the publication of the hardback edition of this book. In this, I record the attempt that was made to scapegoat Jeremy – someone who could no longer defend himself – to distract attention from a ministerial lobbying scandal, and my fight to defend him.

'The words "civil servant" seem too dry to describe greatness. But Jeremy was a great man whom I look back upon with a sense of pride in what he achieved and a sense of privilege in having achieved at least some of it together'
Tony Blair

'A collapsing pound, stock exchange crash, leaks, scandals, sackings, banks going under, capital flight, sometimes all in the same morning. Jeremy didn't need crisis, but crisis needed him'
Gordon Brown

'His was a confidence born of genuine ability, talent and brain. We were so lucky to have him'
David Cameron

'Jeremy's tenacity, that semi-permanent half-smile he always used to have, his svelte intellect, and his preternatural appetite for finding agreement in a sea of disputes were, in many ways, qualities that were tailor made for Coalition Government'
Nick Clegg

'Surely the legend of our brilliant Civil Service should no longer be the fictional story of Sir Humphrey but the true story of Sir Jeremy. The greatest public servant of our time'
Theresa May

Prologue

The Treasury, 1994

'I don't know why you're thinking of doing it,' Stephen Webb, one of the Treasury's other fast-stream trainees, said shaking his head at me in the canteen. 'He's the scariest person in the building. That's why I'm not applying and nor is anyone else I know.'

A crowd of people had gathered by the counter to stare at the pies and chips through the glass. In the middle, I could see a pair of scuffed, brown-suede shoes.

I refocused on Stephen. 'Why is he scary?'

'He's phenomenally clever. And he works all the time.'

Two tables away, the Chancellor sat down. A tall, thin man walked by, ripping open a bag of crisps.

'Hey Jeremy,' Ken Clarke said.

'Hi.' Jeremy took a chair facing the Chancellor, and they began a conversation, their heads close together.

Stephen looked at me and raised his eyebrows. We returned our trays and headed back to our offices.

But the job nagged at me. 'A Fundamental Review of the Treasury,' the posting said. 'Administrative Trainee wanted to help on a small team led by Jeremy Heywood.' Maybe Jeremy was the scariest person in the Treasury, but I'd never run away from a challenge. That's why, a few days later, on 12 May 1994, I found myself standing outside Allington Towers near Victoria Station. The name sounded like something from a children's novel, but the reality was a grimy tower block, home to the Treasury's many support functions. It was also, somewhat oddly, the headquarters of the newly created Fundamental Expenditure Review team.

I looked up, counting floors. The window ten storeys above me looked into Jeremy's office where I was due to have my interview and we were to meet for the first time.

1

'Money':
The UK's failure in Bath

Two years previously

On 5 September 1992, Jeremy Heywood, the Chancellor of the Exchequer's principal private secretary, followed his boss, Norman Lamont, and Robin Leigh-Pemberton, the governor of the Bank of England, into the Georgian Assembly Rooms in Bath. Jeremy lowered his angular frame into a back-row seat next to Nigel Wicks, who oversaw international finance issues in the Treasury, and Paul Gray, who led on monetary policy. Looking up, he saw Helmut Schlesinger, the fiercely independent, silver-haired president of the German Bundesbank, sitting on the other side of the negotiating table staring back at the UK delegation through wire-framed glasses.

Jeremy placed his pad of paper on the table by his chair and fiddled with his pen. His hands were clammy. This informal meeting of European Finance Ministers, or ECOFIN, which the UK was chairing, was Britain's best, and possibly its only, opportunity to get the Germans to reduce their interest rate. The stakes were high even though the meeting was supposed to be informal. If the Germans moved, it would take the pressure off the pound. If they didn't, sterling could fall out of the Exchange Rate Mechanism (ERM), causing chaos for the UK and the rest of Europe.

After the meeting began, Lamont, his bushy eyebrows drawn together and his voice slightly raised, pressed Schlesinger to act. From his seat in the back row, Jeremy willed his boss on as the focus tightened on the embattled British Chancellor, arguing in the face of Schlesinger's unblinking stare.

At 11.15 a.m., following a whispered conversation with Nigel Wicks, Jeremy snuck out of the door at the back of the room. With the Chancellor getting nowhere, it was time to call Terry Burns, the Treasury's ever-optimistic permanent secretary. While the Treasury switchboard searched for Terry, who was playing golf on this sunny Saturday, Jeremy paced the floor. He hoped Terry would know how to turn the meeting around, but though only thirty, he had enough knowledge of international negotiations to fear that solving this was beyond even Terry.

Most of the experience that was making Jeremy so pessimistic had been gained during his secondment to the International Monetary Fund (IMF) in Washington DC from 1988 to 1990. His toughest challenge there – apart from avoiding alcohol poisoning at the Fox and Hounds on 16th Street – had been haggling over the size of the UK's IMF shareholding. The UK had again held a weak hand in that negotiation because, although it was the second largest shareholder after the United States, this position wasn't justified by its GDP. Everyone knew Britain would have to yield, the only question was whether it became the IMF's fourth largest shareholder behind Japan and Germany, but ahead of France, or fifth behind France.

In preparation for this battle, Jeremy had built a spreadsheet on the IMF's shareholder structure and become an expert on its history. He'd fed this knowledge into his briefs for his boss, Frank Cassell, while trying to calm Frank's fury at this attack on the UK's international status. The fight had raged unchecked through the autumn of 1989. But when, in an entirely separate discussion, President François Mitterrand of France proposed the creation of a new bank, the European Bank for Reconstruction and Development (EBRD), Jeremy spotted a potential compromise.

'What if we loan France enough of our IMF quota for us to share fourth place in exchange for them agreeing to Mrs Thatcher's request to put the EBRD's headquarters in London?' he asked Frank.

Frank scraped back his hair and looked at Jeremy.

Jeremy smiled. He was pleased with this idea – as was Whitehall when Frank later suggested it. And after many further discussions, the deal was concluded at a meeting of forty nations in Paris in May

1990. The EBRD's offices would be in London, and its first president would be a Frenchman, Jacques Attali. The parallel deal on IMF shareholding was also agreed although this was kept secret since it would have been frowned on by the IMF's board. So it was written up by Nigel Wicks and his French counterpart in a separate memorandum and filed in the Treasury's basement.*

Although the UK's position had been weak during that Washington negotiation, in Bath in 1992 the situation was far worse because the UK's European partners didn't seem to care if the pound fell out of the ERM. And this time Jeremy couldn't think of anything they could trade in return for their help, apart from the avoidance of chaos.

The phone rang. 'I've finished eight holes,' Terry said.

'Great,' Jeremy said. 'But I'm afraid you'll have to stop there. We need you here in Bath.'

When the ECOFIN meeting broke for lunch, the Chancellor bolted his food before rushing back to his hotel with Jeremy, Paul and Nigel to call the Prime Minister.

'Terry, is that you making all that noise?' John Major asked when they were all on the line.

'Yes. I'm driving down to Bath.'

'Well pull over, then.'

'I can't. I'm on the motorway. I hope the police don't catch me.'

Terry wasn't the only one speaking against a barrage of background noise. Sarah Hogg, the head of the Prime Minister's Policy Unit, was dialling in from a police station at the Braemar Games. She had her hand over the receiver, but deep Scottish voices still kept leaking into the conversation.

Norman Lamont ignored all this and launched into an update. The view of the group when he finished was clear: the Chancellor needed to keep pressing Schlesinger either to reduce Germany's interest rates or to realign the Deutsche Mark upwards within the ERM.

---

* The existence of this memo, which says that, during any future IMF quota round, either the UK or France, whichever had the larger calculated share, would loan the other enough to keep their allocations equal, was confirmed to me by Nigel Wicks.

'But you can't trust the Germans on this,' Sarah said, which generated a background chorus of hearty Scottish police voices: 'Absolutely, love, you can't trust the Germans.'

The informal ECOFIN was under way again by the time Terry reached Bath.

'The Chancellor is still battling it out,' Jeremy said when he emerged from the Assembly Rooms, 'and he's incredibly frustrated that the Italians and Spanish aren't doing more to help – after all, they're in as much trouble as we are.'

Terry frowned. 'What can I do?'

'I don't think we can change the outcome of the meeting but we are going to need a communiqué. God knows what we're going to say in it, but the reporters will be demanding a conclusion. And we don't have long to put one together since we are going to be thrown out of the Assembly Rooms at seven to make way for a dance.'

Jeremy and Terry spent some time after that trying to create some text out of nothing. But by the time the UK team filed into the hall next door to face the world's press, this was still threadbare and Jeremy was feeling nauseous and in desperate need of a cigarette.

'In present circumstances,' Norman Lamont told the reporters, his words barely audible in a room that seemed to suck the strength from his voice, 'the Bundesbank has no intention to increase rates.'

On his way back to London later that evening in the Chancellor's car, Jeremy leaned back in his seat and half-closed his eyes. John Major had convinced Margaret Thatcher to let the UK join the ERM just before the Conservative Party conference in October 1990. This was a time that Jeremy remembered well since he'd spent most of the conference holed up in Norman's hotel room in Bournemouth, helping the then Chief Secretary conclude his spending review negotiations with other Cabinet ministers.

It had been hoped that having the pound in the ERM would help control inflation because it would give the markets more certainty about exchange rates. Over time, the argument went, this would bring the UK's inflationary expectations, and ultimately its inflation rate, into line with Germany's, the anchor of the system.

Given that Britain's membership of the ERM was central to John Major's political vision of being at the heart of Europe, it wasn't surprising that, when he succeeded Margaret Thatcher as Prime Minister a month later, he'd been determined to maintain it. What was perhaps more surprising was his decision to appoint his campaign manager, Norman Lamont, as his Chancellor, since Norman was far more cautious about the whole European project.

All that had led them to that day, 5 September 1992, which Lamont had spent fighting to try to keep sterling in a mechanism he'd never wanted to join. The problem was that, in addition to facing intransigent colleagues in Europe, the Chancellor was also under pressure at home. While the Bundesbank wanted to keep German interest rates high to try to dampen down inflation post-reunification, the UK had the opposite need – with unemployment soaring and its economy contracting, it needed to lower its interest rates, but couldn't do this because it would weaken sterling.

Over the preceding weeks, Jeremy had written two notes to the Chancellor about this economic trap. Neither of these, he recalled with a twinge of guilt, had he shared with Terry Burns even though they'd both argued against the Treasury's official view that, if the pound didn't stay strong within the ERM, inflation would rise, and living standards would fall. Instead, in his first note back in June 1992, Jeremy had suggested that, if the Germans weren't willing to reduce their rates, the best option might be for sterling to devalue, possibly together with the lira. This would then allow the UK to lower its domestic rates, at least in the short term.

By the time Jeremy had written his second note in August 1992, a summer holiday in Turkey had given him time to harden his opinion. The UK's membership of the ERM was no longer sustainable, he told the Chancellor, unless German rates came down or the dollar strengthened. If neither happened, the UK should pull out, allow sterling to find its own level and rejoin when domestic economic conditions made it more appropriate.

The notes had been persuasive, at least with the Chancellor. But despite several attempts, Lamont had failed to weaken John Major's commitment to the ERM. So the pound was still in, and they still needed the Germans to lower their interest rates. Their attempt to persuade them to do this in Bath had failed, but the Chancellor couldn't have tried any harder. Indeed, at one point, Jeremy had thought Schlesinger was about to walk out of the Assembly Rooms and suspected it was only the intervention of Theo Waigel, the German finance minister, who'd leaned over to talk to Schlesinger, that had prevented him from doing so.

But one thing was at least clear, Jeremy concluded as the Chancellor's car turned into Whitehall – with no sign of Europe's strongest economy being willing to help, Britain was on its own in trying to solve this crisis.

2
'All Along the Watchtower': The pound flatlines

September 1992

Jeremy spent much of Tuesday 8 September 1992 watching the Reuters screen on his desk. It wasn't good news: sterling was weakening after Finland, which had tagged the markka to the euro's predecessor, the ecu, had stopped trying to prop it up and the markka had fallen by 14 per cent. Next door in Sweden, where they were still defending the krona, the overnight interest rate had hit 500 per cent.

'It makes it clear to speculators that the same thing could happen to us,' Jeremy told Jonathan Portes, the Chancellor's speechwriter.

Jonathan, an old friend who was known both for his intelligence and for sharing Jeremy's love of a good party, nodded. 'They're picking us off one by one.'

'What we need is an orderly devaluation,' Jeremy said. The way this was playing out was reminiscent of what he'd seen with the French West African countries like Mauritania and Côte d'Ivoire during his time at the IMF. Those countries had all used the CFA franc, which was pegged to the French franc. This had given them stability but had also prevented them from devaluing to boost their exports, leaving them with permanent austerity as the only way of managing their budgets. However, despite orchestrating a campaign to change this in both the IMF's board and – with the help of his fellow UK delegation member, Suma Chakrabarti – also in the World Bank, Jeremy had failed to get the French to move.

Back in London, Jeremy kept watching the lira through the rest of that week as it slid to the bottom of its permitted exchange rate band, the fluctuation allowed against a weighted average of the other ERM currencies. The Italian and German central banks intervened to help, but there was widespread speculation that the Italians would eventually have to give in and devalue, moving the lira to a lower exchange rate band.

On Saturday evening, with the markets at last closed, Jeremy was back at home, discussing the week's events with his flatmate Philip Barton, when Terry Burns rang.

'Nigel Wicks called,' Terry said. 'I told him I couldn't talk because I was on a squidgy line.'

'What?'

'I was standing in a pavilion at a twenty-fifth wedding anniversary party.'

'Okay. So, what did he say?'

'He said "our sick friend is going to have an operation tomorrow. And our strong friend shows signs of moving".'

This news meant that Jeremy spent a less than relaxing Sunday morning back in the Treasury clustered with Norman Lamont, Terry Burns and Nigel Wicks around one end of the long table in the Chancellor's office.

'The Italians are planning to devalue by 7 per cent,' Nigel said, 'and, if they do, the Bundesbank may reduce its discount rate by 0.5 per cent.'

The Chancellor smiled at this long-awaited news. 'What made them change their minds?'

'Apparently it took Helmut Kohl having a row with Schlesinger,' Nigel Wicks said.

Jeremy glanced at Norman Lamont. The pressure the Chancellor had applied in Bath must also have played a role in this decision.

The question they then debated was whether, if the Italians did move the lira, then the UK should also devalue the pound. There was no consensus in the room though Jeremy thought they should – after all, the UK needed to do something given sterling's vulnerability. But John Major took a different view when the Italian Prime Minister rang later that day to ask him the same question.

'He told Giuliano that the only politically feasible solution was to realign all the currencies within the ERM rather than just the lira and the pound,' Barry Potter, the Prime Minister's private secretary, told Jeremy. 'But since the French referendum is only a week away, something more widespread doesn't seem to be on offer.'

Jeremy was disappointed by this, though not surprised. After all it was the calling of the French referendum, which had followed the Danish rejection of the Maastricht Treaty, that had triggered the current turbulence. Pacifying the population of one European nation was hard enough, but if the French also lost their vote, the treaty was probably dead. That possibility had in turn weakened a whole series of other assumptions. For a start, it made the adoption of the euro, which had a chapter within the treaty, less likely, and thus removed one reason for the ERM's existence. And, if the ERM wasn't needed, then speculators might be able to push down the value of the weaker currencies within it, forcing them out while making a fortune by betting against them. But while the speculators' logic was clear, the reverse was presumably also true – if the French voted 'oui' the ERM should strengthen, and there might be no need for further devaluations.

Jeremy had missed the first few months of the tortuous Maastricht Treaty negotiations the previous year because, after Norman had been promoted from Chief Secretary to Chancellor in November 1990, Jeremy had waited before moving to join him, keen to avoid displacing his colleague John Gieve. So, while Norman had settled into his huge new room overlooking the Foreign Office on the far side of the Treasury, Jeremy had stayed in the Chief Secretary's office.

But despite the impeccable music taste of his new minister, David Mellor, Jeremy had missed working for Norman. It wasn't just that he was itching to help the Chancellor tackle his new agenda; it was also because, over many years, he'd built a close working relationship with Norman Lamont. Some of this was due to the multiple trips they'd taken together while Norman had been financial secretary and had wanted to share the UK's privatisation experience with the world. This had meant days of often dull meetings in foreign cities, punctuated by evenings during which Norman had insisted on exploring their more exotic districts while Jeremy had tried to keep them both out of trouble – including one trip to Morocco which had culminated in an evening in Marrakesh drinking gin and listening to Shirley Bassey tapes with the consul general and five bunny girls.

As a result, when John Gieve had been ready to move on, Jeremy was keen to succeed him and begin working for Norman again. The Treasury mandarins were less enthusiastic, but in the end, gave in – presumably deciding that, despite his relative youth and inexperience, this chain-smoking, hard-partying 29-year-old could still be relied on to head up the Chancellor's office.

After Jeremy took possession of John's desk in April 1991, complete with its word processor, a Reuters screen and green-shaded lamp, he'd begun to focus on the Maastricht negotiations. The meetings to negotiate the financial chapter of the treaty took place in a large, dark-brown conference room in the Charlemagne Building in Brussels where Lamont had again been flanked by Nigel Wicks on one side – his face often creased into a broad, gap-toothed smile at one of the Chancellor's dry remarks – with the all-seeing, bespectacled John Kerr, the UK's ambassador to the EU on the other. Jeremy, meanwhile, spent most of these meetings hanging around outside, staying in touch with issues back in the office, eating cheese baguettes, drinking coffee and occasionally popping in to contribute bits of text or a joke to keep the Chancellor's spirits up.

Norman Lamont's focus in these discussions, in contrast to that of the ministers from the other eleven member states, was on obtaining an opt-out from the final stage of Economic and Monetary Union (EMU). However, while the Chancellor was willing to debate the principle of this opt-out throughout 1991, he was determined not to share the draft legal text until the last minute because he was worried that, once it was agreed, the UK might be excluded from the rest of the discussions. While this was understandable, it meant that, when Jeremy walked into the negotiating chamber in Maastricht for the final day of discussions on 9 December 1991, and stacked copies of the text on the table in front of the UK delegation, nothing had been decided. He felt nervous, but the Chancellor still seemed unperturbed, informing his team that he'd told the chair of the meeting, Wim Kok, the Dutch finance minister, that the opt-out was non-negotiable.

Part way through the meeting, at the Chancellor's signal, the UK team walked around the room distributing the opt-out, a brilliant piece of drafting by Mark Blythe, the Treasury's lawyer, and John Arrowsmith from the Bank of England, that detailed all the things Britain wanted to avoid. However, despite its elegance, Wim Kok frowned when he received his copy. He flipped through it before looking up.

'We will need to review this line by line,' he intoned into his microphone.

The Chancellor shook his head. 'It's non-negotiable,' he muttered before pushing his chair back, getting to his feet and walking around the oval table. After a pause, he pushed the door open and walked out, leaving it flapping behind him.

Jeremy, Nigel and the other UK officials glanced at each other.

'He's probably gone to the bathroom,' Jeremy told the officials sitting in the delegation next to him.

A few minutes later, Wim Kok paused the meeting and also disappeared out the door. Nigel Wicks followed. It was, Jeremy decided, getting up himself, a good time to get another coffee and a cheese baguette.

Two espressos later, Nigel reappeared. 'The Prime Minister has talked to Helmut Kohl and Ruud Lubbers,' he said, 'and they've told Wim Kok that he should accept our EMU opt-out.'

Jeremy blinked. This was an unexpectedly helpful intervention by the German and Dutch leaders. It seemed, from Nigel's debrief, that they'd decided that the UK had made enough of a concession by agreeing to a UK-specific opt-out rather than pressing for a more general provision. But whatever the reason, the deal was done – with a little brinkmanship, the Chancellor had secured Britain's position.

The rest of the finance ministers' meeting was, from the UK's point of view, relatively straightforward. Meanwhile, the Prime Minister's focus in the parallel heads of government meeting was on ensuring the UK also wasn't subject to the Social Chapter of the treaty, which included new rules on working hours, worker consultation and equal treatment of men and women in the labour market. The overall outcome was, Major declared at the end of the Maastricht negotiation, 'game, set and match' to the UK.

From a political perspective, this was true – they had ensured that the UK could avoid the bits of the treaty it disliked while enjoying the things it liked, such as the single market. But it was only a partial victory because other parts of the treaty had increased the power of the European Parliament and given the EU more rights on asylum and immigration. And though Jeremy didn't know this then, the increase in British Euroscepticism that would be nurtured by these powers would echo throughout the rest of his career.

After the Italians devalued the lira on Sunday 13 September 1992, and the Germans at last reduced their interest rates, Jeremy spent Monday morning willing the pound upwards. It strengthened a little, though he'd hoped for more – after all, this was the first move in German rates in almost five years.

Terry felt the same way. 'We need to give the pound another boost by increasing the UK's interest rates,' he told the Chancellor when they met. But when Terry joined the Chancellor for his meeting with the Prime Minister later that day, John Major disagreed.

'He's worried an increase might flatten the economy, so he wants to postpone any decision,' the Chancellor told Jeremy when they returned.

On Tuesday 15 September the pound weakened further. Jeremy felt hopeless watching it. In their four years of working together, he'd helped Norman Lamont navigate many crises. These had included the sale of the government's shareholding in BP during which, after the government had arranged for paratroopers to abseil down the front of BP's headquarters unfurling a huge banner with the price printed on it, the stock market had crashed in the middle of a UK hurricane. But unlike the BP share sale, where the next step – making sure that the banks underwriting the deal didn't pull out – had been clear, this crisis had no clear resolution.

That evening Robin Leigh-Pemberton, the governor of the Bank of England, Eddie George, the deputy governor, and Terry Burns, together with various other officials and advisers, gathered in the Chancellor's office to discuss what to do next to support the pound.

'It's been a rough day,' Eddie said, his round face creased with worry. 'The Deutsche Mark has actually strengthened despite their rate cut.'

'We need to put our rates up,' Terry said again.

'But first we need to show we've tried to intervene,' Eddie said. 'We've sold almost 500 million Deutsche Marks today to try to keep the pound at 2.78 Deutsche Marks, and we've borrowed another $14 billion that we can use for more overt intervention if we need it.'

Owen Barder, the Chancellor's private secretary, stuck his head around the door. 'I have a call from your office, Mr Governor.'

Robin Leigh-Pemberton nodded, unfurled himself from his seat and walked out. A few minutes later, he burst back in. 'Schlesinger has told reporters from *Handelsblatt* and the *Wall Street Journal* that a wider realignment of currencies than just the move in the lira would have been a good thing,' he said.

The Chancellor gaped. 'What?'

'It's going to be on the front page of tomorrow's *Financial Times*.'

'You need to speak to Schlesinger,' the Chancellor told the governor, his voice sharp. 'He needs to retract his words. If he doesn't, speculators will go mad shorting the pound.'

Norman Lamont was right, Jeremy thought. Talking of a comprehensive realignment was tantamount to telling the markets that the pound and the other weak currencies were about to be devalued. If the traders believed that, it would become a self-fulfilling prophecy.

The response from Schlesinger, which Jeremy relayed to the Chancellor later that evening, was apologetic but not particularly helpful. The reporters shouldn't have shared his comments before he'd approved them, and he was doing his best to sort it out.

'He clearly has a different approach to dealing with the press than we do,' Jeremy said. 'Whether or not he intended it, he's torpedoed the pound, in the middle of all this uncertainty over the French referendum, and now seems surprised that journalists want to print his words.'

On 16 September 1992, a day later dubbed 'Black Wednesday', Jeremy spent his journey into the Treasury worrying about what would happen when the market opened. When the bell rang at nine, the answer was as bad as he had feared – for the first time, sterling dropped below the floor of its ERM band and the Bank of England began intervening, as it was required to do, selling other currencies to buy the pound.

At 8.30 a.m., Terry appeared. 'The Bank has completed two interventions, spending £300 million each time,' he told Norman Lamont. 'The pound rallied but has since fallen back, so they're about to try another burst of £400 million.'

Jeremy was finding it hard to visualise these sums. He also knew that the Bank's actions were probably pointless since the money they were throwing into the currency market was almost certainly sliding straight into the hands of the traders betting against sterling. He lit a cigarette with shaking fingers and looked at the Chancellor.

'What's the Bank's advice?' Norman Lamont asked.

'They think we should put up interest rates in a way that catches the market off guard,' Terry said.

This made sense to Jeremy although, with rates already at 10 per cent, it would only work if the speculators believed the government could stomach such an extraordinarily high interest rate politically.

'Goodness knows what the Prime Minister will say,' Norman said. 'What does the governor think we should do if that doesn't work?'

'He thinks we should let the pound find its own level. But we would still have to raise interest rates and would probably have to leave the ERM for a while.'

'I need to talk to the Prime Minister,' the Chancellor said.

Jeremy placed a call through to Admiralty House, where the Prime Minister was based while Number 10 was being repaired after being hit by an IRA mortar bomb the previous year. When the call came through, he remained on the line to take notes. Again, the Chancellor tried to convince John Major to increase rates, and again the Prime Minister resisted, saying he was worried this might aggravate unemployment.

When the governor and deputy governor arrived in the Chancellor's office at 9 a.m., however, they were clear that there was no other option.

'Even if we spend all we can defending the pound,' Eddie George said, 'and others also spend vast amounts, it's unlikely to cut the mustard without a move on rates.'

After another debate, the Chancellor spoke to the Prime Minister again at 10.30, telling him that the Bank and the Treasury both also supported a substantial increase in rates. And this time, much to Jeremy's relief, the Prime Minister agreed, though only to a 2 per cent increase.

Everyone gathered around the Reuters screen on Jeremy's desk just before the rate increase was announced at 11 a.m. The top of the hour came and went.

'The pound's not moving,' Jeremy said.

'It was too little, too late,' the Chancellor said, shaking his head. 'The markets have been open for hours.'

The conversation about what to do next swirled around after that with no consensus emerging. But just before midday when they heard that, despite the Bank spending another £2 billion, the pound was still flatlining, opinions hardened.

'We need to suspend our membership of the ERM,' the governor declared, and everyone nodded.

'I need to talk to the Prime Minister about this in person,' the Chancellor said. 'This is an enormous decision both for the government and for him personally.'

Jeremy called Admiralty House again.

'The Prime Minister is busy, I'm afraid,' said Barry Potter.

'How can he be busy?' Jeremy said. 'We're spending millions every minute supporting the pound and the Chancellor wants to discuss suspending our ERM membership.'

'I know, I'll do what I can.'

Jeremy replaced the handset and shook his head at the Chancellor before wiping his hands on his trousers and picking up his box of Silk Cuts. Again he pictured rows of traders hunched over their desks, phones glued to their ears, buying back billions of pounds from the speculators on the Bank of England's behalf for more than they were worth.

A few minutes passed.

'Well, I'm going over there,' the Chancellor said. He gathered up his papers and swept out of the door with Terry Burns, the governor and the deputy governor following in his wake.

Jeremy took a step forward to follow them before pausing. If the situation deteriorated, someone would need to help handle things in the Treasury. 'Go with them,' he told Owen Barder. 'And take the mobile phone with you,' he added, pointing at the office's much-prized Motorola Microtac handset.

Minutes passed. Jeremy visualised the Chancellor marching up Whitehall. At 12.30 p.m., the phone rang.

'We're sitting on the sofas outside the Prime Minister's office,' Owen said in a low voice. 'We're being told he's still too busy to see us though it's not clear that anyone else is in with him.'

'This is incredible,' Jeremy said. 'Tell me when you go in.'

The phone rang again about twenty minutes later.

'The meeting has just started,' Owen said. 'Terry has asked me to stick my head around the door to tell them each time the Bank spends another billion pounds.'

Jeremy paced the floor, watching the Reuters screen and fielding calls from the Treasury's press office.

Owen rang once more. 'Douglas Hurd, Ken Clarke and Michael Heseltine have just gone in.'

Jeremy shook his head. 'The Prime Minister clearly wants more of his Cabinet involved in this decision. But they need to hurry up.'

Shortly before two, the Chancellor swept back into the Treasury with Terry and the others still in tow. 'I argued for a temporary suspension of the UK's membership,' he told Jeremy, 'but Ken wanted to try raising interest rates again first and Douglas and Michael were pressing for a realignment. It was unbelievable. As if we haven't already tried those options.'

'What did you decide?'

There was a pause. 'The Prime Minister sided with Ken,' the Chancellor said.

Jeremy stared at Norman. The Prime Minister's hesitation was understandable – after all, this threatened to bring the government down. But it was still extraordinary for him to overrule his Chancellor on such a major economic decision.

At 2.15 p.m. a crowd regathered around the Reuters screen on Jeremy's desk. Taking the interest rate up by a further 3 per cent to an eye-watering 15 per cent would surely kick-start sterling, Jeremy thought. But again, when the announcement came, the line on the screen remained flat.

'It's like watching the heart rate monitor of a dead patient,' the Chancellor said.

When the market closed at 4 p.m., the Bank of England stopped intervening to support the pound having sold $28 billion of reserves trying to do so during the day.* They had done what they could but the patient had indeed been impossible to revive. With its life support removed, sterling fell through its ERM floor while the Chancellor made his way back up Whitehall to Admiralty House. Again Douglas Hurd, Ken Clarke and Michael Heseltine joined his meeting with the Prime Minister and again the different arguments were rehearsed. But this time the Chancellor returned with the news that Britain would suspend its ERM membership.

Jeremy helped Terry Burns and Gus O'Donnell, the head of the Prime Minister's press office, draft a statement for the Chancellor to make announcing this decision. Gus had been Jeremy's first boss in the Treasury and was one of the cleverest economists Jeremy knew.

'The real reason I'm here is to make sure the Chancellor sticks to his promise not to resign,' Gus told Jeremy in a low voice before going down to the Treasury's central courtyard to check on the arrangements for the press conference.

'Okay,' Jeremy said, though he didn't think Gus needed to worry since Norman Lamont had already shown him the note he'd received from the Prime Minister. This made it clear that John Major had no intention of resigning and didn't want his Chancellor to either.

'Everything is ready,' Gus said when he returned, 'although we need to thank Alastair Campbell from the *Mirror* for suggesting we should cover up the open drain behind the Chancellor's podium so we would avoid the easy headlines.'

A few minutes later, the Chancellor went down with Gus and his special adviser, David Cameron, to deliver his statement. It wasn't long – only 137 words – but that didn't make it any less humiliating. The latest interest rate increase would be cancelled, Norman Lamont

---

* The Treasury later estimated the cost of the Bank's interventions in the run-up to sterling leaving the ERM to be around £3.3 billion.

told the assembled press, and Britain would suspend its membership of the ERM. While the reporters started shouting questions, Jeremy, who was sitting at his desk up in the Chancellor's office, took another bite of his takeaway pizza and wondered what the hell they were going to do next.

3

'Life in the Fast Lane':
The importance of economics

September–November 1992

On Friday 18 September 1992, the Concorde hurtled down the runway at Heathrow. Once above the ocean, it accelerated to supersonic speed, forcing Jeremy back into his seat.

When the motion steadied, Jeremy leaned forward to join a shouted conversation with the Chancellor, Nigel Wicks and Alan Budd, the Treasury's chief economic adviser. There were many implications of the week's events to dissect, including the surge in British Euroscepticism and the Prime Minister's determination to cut interest rates now that Britain had been released from the ERM's shackles. More personal were the attacks on the 'devalued' Chancellor that had filled the newspapers after Black Wednesday.

'They think this was a British crisis caused by stupid British politicians and particularly by me,' Norman Lamont had told Jeremy.

Which was, Jeremy had assured him, wrong – after all, the Chancellor hadn't chosen to enter the ERM and other countries had also struggled within it. Hadn't the newspapers noticed the difficulties faced by the Italians and Spanish?

But for the Chancellor and his team, the main topic to discuss above the Concorde's howling engine was what the UK's monetary policy framework should be outside the ERM. Developing this would take weeks, but if they knew its likely shape, they could hint at it in Washington to help the UK regain credibility ahead of the French referendum in two days' time. The overall objective of this framework, they agreed, should continue to be low inflation. But if that were to be achieved outside the ERM, they needed a new way of demonstrating to the markets that interest rate decisions were being taken for economic rather than political reasons.

Two days later, when Jeremy woke up in the British ambassador's palatial residence in Washington, stretching out his legs in the massive bed, he felt far more relaxed. The Chancellor's statements in the G7 and IMF interim committee meetings had gone well and Jeremy had secretly enjoyed being part of the pomp and cavalcades. The only issue had been Norman Lamont's comment in his press conference on Saturday morning about singing in his bath after Black Wednesday. Once again, the press had mocked the Chancellor and Jeremy had spent a good part of the rest of the day assuring the Treasury's press office that Norman hadn't meant to imply that Britain's costly exit from the ERM had been a good thing.

The other thing that hadn't gone as smoothly as Jeremy had hoped was the ambassador's drinks party on Saturday evening. He'd had high hopes for this because his girlfriend Reyahn had been coming down from Boston where she was studying art history to join it. However, despite the idyllic setting on a terrace overlooking acres of manicured embassy gardens, all that anyone had wanted to talk about – Jeremy included – was Black Wednesday and its economic repercussions.

Jeremy's relationship with Reyahn, an archive assistant in the National Portrait Gallery, had started earlier that year in the glamorous surroundings of the Chancellor's fiftieth birthday party at 11 Downing Street. Jeremy had invited the Treasury manager responsible for export credit policy to this but soon decided he was more interested in Reyahn, who was there with Jonathan Portes.

The four of them had swept into the state rooms of Number 11 past politicians, businesspeople and civil servants eating canapés and sipping champagne. They'd collected their drinks from David Mellor, who was serving at the bar, and wandered around sipping these while chatting and occasionally dancing. Some way through the evening, just before the kedgeree arrived, the whole party was marched outside by the Chancellor's wife, Rosemary Lamont, to hear a nightingale call.

'It's one of the Chancellor's favourite sounds,' the guest standing next to Jeremy said, 'though it's actually coming from a tape recorder hidden under that bush.'

Jeremy had laughed at this before going back inside to dance with Reyahn while the journalist Petronella Wyatt twirled David Cameron around the floor and then sang 'Happy Birthday' to the Chancellor in a husky, Marilyn Monroe voice. It had been a perfect evening, Jeremy thought, particularly since, judging by the smiles of the Treasury mandarins, it seemed they were at last accepting him despite his youth and closeness to the Chancellor.

By the time Jeremy arrived back in London from Washington, the result of the French referendum was at last in: they'd voted 'oui' by a tiny margin and were continuing with Maastricht despite the upsets of the summer. However, the news from Reyahn was less positive – the letter that chased him back across the Atlantic accused him of ignoring her at the ambassador's drinks party and complained that he'd forgotten to introduce her to the Chancellor.

Jeremy felt bad about this – her accusations were fair though his behaviour hadn't been intentionally hurtful. But since there was little he could do beyond sending an apology by return post, he distracted himself at work, where they were beginning to detail the UK's new monetary framework.

For years, as Jeremy who had studied history and economics at university knew well, the UK had been dogged by high inflation, which undermined living standards for those on fixed incomes, reduced competitiveness and destabilised industrial relations. Between 1972 and 1982, the UK's average retail inflation rate had been 14 per cent, occasionally soaring to 27 per cent. Various methods had been used to try to control this – including an attempt by Nigel Lawson, while he had been Chancellor, to tackle the problem by controlling different measures of the money supply.

Jeremy had played a small part in this effort when he'd moved to the Treasury in 1984 after realising that his first department – the Health and Safety Executive – was not the place to be if he wanted to get on in the Civil Service. Jeremy's first job after he'd arrived in the Treasury had been helping to tend its economic model, which spewed out the data on the money supply that Nigel Lawson needed. Although his numbers on the assets held by the UK's building societies were hardly the most critical part of this, Jeremy was still part of the debates that took place between some of the leading civil servants and economists of the day as they tried to interpret the figures emerging from the model. These included Rachel Lomax, the dynamic assistant secretary in charge of monetary policy, with whom Jeremy was somewhat infatuated, and Tim Lankester, who'd been Margaret Thatcher's first economic private secretary.

Despite Jeremy's enthusiasm, however, it soon became clear to Nigel Lawson that trying to control inflation this way was hard, if not impossible. The Chancellor, therefore, changed tack, this time trying to borrow Germany's anti-inflationary credibility by shadowing the Deutsche Mark at 3 DM to the pound. This approach, unlike many of its predecessors, had worked – at least it had until Margaret Thatcher discovered what Nigel was up to and demanded that he should stop.

After the more recent failed experiment of the ERM, which had proved that, in any event under current economic conditions, exchange rate targeting was also flawed, the government now needed a new way to swing the same cat. After many discussions with his officials, his fingers gesticulating back and forth through clouds of cigarette smoke in his office, Norman Lamont concluded that the best way to do this was by targeting inflation itself rather than any secondary measure, mirroring the approach being used in New Zealand and Canada.

Jeremy was enthusiastic about this, though he also agreed with the Chancellor's view that, because the new policy would require judgements to be made based on a wide range of monetary indicators, decisions had to become more transparent, which in turn would encourage decision-makers to be more predictable. This transparency would be achieved through a range of measures including publishing a monthly monetary report detailing the basis for the government's judgements and quarterly updates from the Bank of England on its pursuit of the inflation target. The Chancellor even considered going further and releasing, after a time lag, the minutes of his meetings with the governor to review monetary conditions – notes that had, until then, been classified as secret. However, in the end he decided against this because it would have made it clear when the Bank disagreed with the government, which might have increased rather than decreased market uncertainty.

Jeremy sat on Norman Lamont's left at the long oval table in the Chancellor's office during their discussions about these changes, taking spidery notes and sharing an ashtray. As the pieces slid into place, he felt a sense of satisfaction – out of the ruins of the ERM they were creating a new mechanism for controlling inflation and starting the next chapter of the UK's economic history.

There was though, Lamont told Jeremy at the end of one of these debates, one thing missing from the new approach. Jeremy nodded since he knew what this was – they both believed that the Bank of England should become independent, as had many others over the years including Jeremy's university hero, John Maynard Keynes. Based on another Jeremy memo the previous autumn, the Chancellor had also tried to persuade the Prime Minister of this view, pointing out that an independent Bank would reinforce the UK's commitment to low inflation ahead of its move into the narrow bands of the ERM. With sterling outside the ERM, that argument was, of course, no longer relevant – but when he drafted a new note for the Chancellor to send to the Prime Minister, Jeremy argued that making the Bank independent would still be beneficial since it would take the politics out of interest rate decisions.

When he finished his draft of this memo, Jeremy went through it with Terry Burns. Terry still didn't know about the two notes that Jeremy had written to the Chancellor on the ERM but when he'd found out about his previous note on making the Bank of England independent, Terry had come storming into the private office. He was worried about how an independent Bank would be held accountable to Parliament, he'd told Jeremy – but more fundamentally he objected to not being consulted.

Jeremy had, until that discussion, always felt justified going around the system if he'd felt he was pursuing something that was intellectually correct. He was still proud of the paper he'd written while he'd been at the Health and Safety Executive, for example, in which he'd pointed out that there was no correlation between the number of times inspectors visited a factory and that factory's level of compliance with the health and safety legislation. This conclusion had unsurprisingly generated considerable irritation. For once the different groupings that made up the Health and Safety Executive – the remnants of five different Whitehall departments – had an issue around which they could unite: who was this fresh-faced 21-year-old and what right did he have to cast doubt on their profession?

Back then Jeremy had been amused by this reaction, partly because he doubted he would ever be a mandarin himself. Indeed, in one of his letters to his friend Carrie, he'd told her that he doubted he had the 'ability or the ruthlessness' to get to the top and anyway didn't care for it 'because it seems that, with greater seniority, one just gets embroiled in more paperwork and more functions and speeches'.

But that had been almost a decade ago. Now, though he still wasn't sure he had the ability to reach the top, he was more minded to play the game to see where it went. And part of that – as Terry had made clear – meant working with his colleagues. He also had to admit that Terry's input had significantly improved the text of his draft memo on the Bank of England.

It didn't, however, change the outcome.

'The Prime Minister isn't willing to decide this now,' the Chancellor said when he returned from Admiralty House, 'though he's content for us to keep thinking about it.'

Jeremy was disappointed but not surprised by this. The Prime Minister's response to the first memo had also been 'no' because he hadn't wanted to give away the power to set interest rates. Now he was probably also worried that, despite Britain's exit from the ERM, making the Bank of England independent might look like a step towards monetary union, which could in turn make it even more challenging for him to convince the Eurosceptics in his party to back the Maastricht Bill in the House of Commons.

By early October, with the Prime Minister getting anxious about reports of the pound being in 'free fall', the Chancellor agreed to share part of his new monetary policy framework with John Watts, the chair of the Treasury and Civil Service Committee in the House of Commons. Jeremy and Terry, therefore, decamped to Brighton to finalise his letter to John during the Tory Party conference. For

Jeremy, sitting with his pen poised while Terry negotiated the final wording with the Chancellor and Prime Minister, this discussion felt historic. For years he'd debated economic theory and practice – at university, within the Civil Service, during his master's degree at the London School of Economics and in meetings of the Apostates, the economics discussion group he'd created a few years earlier with his similarly obsessed friends and named in honour of John Maynard Keynes. But in all those discussions, he'd never dreamt he would play a role in helping to define and document how a new monetary policy for the UK would work.

The final letter to John Watts, which was sent on 8 October 1992, summarised this thinking. It also set a target for inflation in the long term of 2 per cent or less and an ambition of keeping it between 1 and 4 per cent during that Parliament – something that had required multiple last-minute calls with the deputy governor, who worried this range was too narrow. The Chancellor then set out the detail of the UK's new policy under the barrel-vaulted ceiling of Mansion House on Thursday 29 October, only six weeks after Britain had left the ERM. His new measures were, he said, all about 'clear policies, steadily pursued. Sound money, low inflation, [and] a firm approach to public expenditure.'

With this announcement made, and relatively well received, the Chancellor turned his attention to bringing about this 'firm approach to public expenditure'. During the 1990 spending round, which had culminated in the smoky final negotiations with spending ministers that Jeremy had joined in Norman's hotel room in Bournemouth, it had become clear that what the government spent each year didn't actually reflect the Treasury's judgement about what the country could afford. Instead, total spending was the sum of the outcomes of these individual negotiations with departments with a bunch of other line items added on top, including debt interest, local author-ity spending and various accounting adjustments. The Treasury did set a top-down aspiration for overall spending each year, but in real-ity, this had little effect on the negotiations – and in any case, because the target was a ratio of public spending to GDP, it changed as the economic conditions evolved.

To address this issue, the Chancellor decided to separate the Budget into cyclically adjusted spending, like unemployment benefits, which was largely determined by the economic cycle, and non-cyclical spending, which was under departments' direct control. For non-cyclical spending they would then set, for the first time, an absolute top-down target. The Chancellor also persuaded the Prime Minister to create a new Cabinet committee, EDX, to oversee the allocation of public spending. Given the Prime Minister's political caution, they hoped that bringing the most senior members of Cabinet together in EDX would make it easier to get decisions made on difficult issues like child benefit or defence spending.

Jeremy was pleased with these changes, and hoped that with them agreed he might get a few quiet weeks and uninterrupted weekends. But instead he returned to his desk to find his in-tray full of papers on privatisation from the financial secretary, a scheme to train young Russians in finance, which the Chancellor had promised Boris Yeltsin during a Russian state visit to London in early November, the financial implications of Michael Heseltine's proposal to close thirty-one coal mines and the latest twists in the progress of the Maastricht Treaty through the House of Commons. This meant that he was still slumping out of the Treasury at 10 or 11 p.m. most evenings, the guards at the front door rustling around to find the keys to lock up the building as he came past.

In early November 1992, Jeremy pushed all this to one side again so that he could focus on the Autumn Statement. The run-up to this became fraught after ministers started using EDX to defend their own budgets while making unrealistic suggestions for cuts elsewhere. This frustrated the Chancellor so much that he stormed out of one meeting early, declaring that the government didn't have the capacity to make tough decisions, an incident that was again widely reported in the press.

More productive was the thinking Jeremy was helping to prepare on measures to strengthen the UK's economy outside the ERM. Having grown up during a period of soaring unemployment, Jeremy was fascinated by the challenge of trying to stimulate the economy to create jobs. This was why, though he'd enjoyed his undergraduate tutorials at Oxford on microeconomics with the quietly spoken, but opinionated, Roger van Noorden, he'd found those with the younger, bearded George Yarrow on economic organisation, during which they'd applied those principles to the real world, more engaging. Of course, Jeremy's university years had consisted of far more than these economic debates, including several relationships, numerous parties and the launch of a new student paper: '*Crux* – The World's Only Humorous Magazine'. But Jeremy's interest in increasing productivity to reduce unemployment was a more lasting legacy of his university years – particularly since *Crux* only managed a single edition.

After his first two years in the Civil Service – one at the Health and Safety Executive annoying the bosses of the factory inspectors and one at the Treasury tending its economic model – Jeremy had again focused on employment and productivity during his master's degree at the London School of Economics in 1985. By that point Britain was seven years into Thatcherism, and the Chicago School of macroeconomic thinking – which argued that markets were the best allocators of resources – was in the ascendancy. But in the years since then it had become clear, at least to Jeremy, that this pure free market approach, though intellectually attractive, wouldn't address the UK's high unemployment rate. His view, therefore, was far more Keynesian – free markets needed to be tempered by government stimuli, particularly during a recession – and this belief would influence the advice he gave ministers throughout his career.

Back in 1992, this economic perspective also underpinned the package Jeremy helped create for the Autumn Statement. This included a £1.8 billion extension of the Jubilee Line, more road building and a £750 million fund to buy empty properties. The Chancellor also launched the Private Finance Initiative, which was designed to attract private funding for new public infrastructure in exchange for ongoing lease payments.

The Autumn Statement was well received when it was published on 12 November. Even Reyahn, who after a series of difficult calls had forgiven Jeremy for his behaviour in Washington, was enthusiastic, sending Jeremy her thoughts on the photo of him that appeared on the front page of the *Independent* the following day. 'We have here,' she said, 'the archetypal image of the public servant: overworked in his efforts to defend policy.'

When Jeremy again returned to his in-tray after the Autumn Statement, he found that it was full of a new set of issues including deciding who the next governor of the Bank of England should be after Robin Leigh-Pemberton's scheduled retirement the following July. The office fell back into a more normal rhythm after all the drama of the year. Each evening, the private office loaded piles of submissions on various policy questions, many accompanied by one of Jeremy's pithy handwritten covering notes, into Norman Lamont's red boxes for him to read overnight. And most mornings Jeremy would be found in the Chancellor's office going through the pile again, finding the papers either untouched or with the words 'J, please refer' scribbled on them, which meant he had the baleful task of trying to extract a decision in person.

Overall though, things at last felt easier. For the first time in months, Jeremy wasn't always the last person to leave the building each evening. And the mandarins seemed happy to seek his views on submissions they were writing or meetings they were due to attend – coming in to see him, sitting in his shirtsleeves wreathed in smoke at his desk outside the Chancellor's office. Yes, all in all work was at last feeling manageable again. But then, as they say, things can change fast in politics.

4

'Shot by Both Sides': Losing a minister

November 1992–May 1993

On Thursday 26 November, two weeks after the Autumn Statement, Jeremy was sitting reading at his desk. But rather than consuming the latest juicy privatisation update from the financial secretary's office, or a thick missive from the Inland Revenue on some newly discovered tax loophole, he was poring over a copy of the *Sun* newspaper. And he was shaking his head.

'They're claiming the Chancellor has exceeded his credit-card limit twenty-two times in the previous eight years and is overdrawn again,' he told Mridul Hegde, who'd taken over from Jonathan Portes as the Chancellor's speechwriter. 'How can they possibly know that – even if it's true?'

'And it's hardly helpful coming just after the "champagne and large breakfasts" story,' Mridul said.

Jeremy frowned. 'The Chancellor told me he'd always intended to pay his bill from the Tory Party conference when the hotel sent it on. The papers just seem determined to bring him down.'

Dealing with the salacious stories that swirled around Norman Lamont was nothing new. In fact, alongside coming to grips with the Maastricht negotiations, Jeremy's first few weeks in the Chancellor's office had been dominated by another scandal. The first indication of trouble then had been a call from Dick Saunders, the Treasury's press secretary. The *News of the World* was claiming that the Chancellor's basement flat in Notting Hill was being rented to a 'Miss Whiplash' who was offering 'correctional services', Dick told

Jeremy. That had led to a week during which Miss Whiplash was all the Chancellor could think about, pacing the floor while debating the emerging evidence that the entire story was a set-up by the newspapers. And what Jeremy learned from that experience – in addition to a few sordid details about 'correctional services' – was the need to get the facts of a scandal clear early on and use them to correct any press misunderstandings before the story mushroomed.

This is why, in November 1992, Jeremy pushed the *Sun* to one side when the Chancellor arrived in the office and began quizzing him about his credit-card statements.

'I never received them,' the Chancellor said, his voice clipped. 'They must have got lost under the doormat while the builders were in Number 11.'

This explanation was passed on to the press, but within hours, the *Evening Standard* was running with another story, this time about Lamont paying £17.47 for champagne and Raffles cigarettes at a branch of Threshers in Praed Street, a seedy area of Paddington. The question was, they said, since the Chancellor smoked cigars, and his wife didn't smoke, who was he buying the cigarettes for?

The following day, when Jeremy embarked on a new set of questions, he found the Chancellor in no mood to talk. Norman remembered buying wine at a branch of Threshers, but he couldn't recall which street it had been on, and he didn't want to spend any more time on the matter. This meant that the Treasury's press office had little to say when the story escalated after a Mr Onanugna came forward to claim that he'd served the Chancellor when he'd gone in to Threshers to buy his champagne and cigarettes.

At this point Jeremy decided to intervene again, this time to ask Mridul if she could go and look for any newly bought bottles of alcohol in Number 11.

A while later, Mridul reappeared. She'd found three bottles of wine, she told Jeremy, so she'd decided to go back to Threshers to repeat the purchase.

'Can you guess what they cost?' she asked, placing the bottles on his desk.

Jeremy smiled. 'Tell me.'

'£17.47,' she said, flourishing the receipt. 'And look, this doesn't show what I bought, or which branch of Threshers I visited, only the postal code.'

By Friday evening, they'd unravelled the story. After David Cameron convinced the Chancellor to talk him through his route home on the night in question, they'd discovered that he'd gone past another branch of Threshers in Connaught Street. Since that branch had the same postal code as the one in Praed Street, it was almost certainly where Norman had bought his wine.

While Andrew Hudson, who was by then head of the Treasury's press office, agreed a statement with Threshers, Jeremy headed home. He was hoping for a quiet evening, but late on Friday night Andrew was back on the phone reporting yet another crisis: this time the press had discovered that the Treasury had paid part of the Chancellor's legal bill for sorting out the Miss Whiplash affair the previous year and were claiming that this was a misuse of taxpayers' money.

Jeremy picked up the phone to call Terry. While the other stories, though upsetting for the Chancellor, were relatively trivial, this one, if handled badly, threatened both the Chancellor and the Treasury's integrity. Jeremy and Terry, therefore, spent several hours working through the facts and agreeing a statement with everyone concerned. It was reasonable, this argued, for the government to have paid a small amount, £4,000 plus VAT, towards Norman's £23,000 bill because his role as Chancellor had increased his legal costs – an argument that, while inevitably somewhat arbitrary, was at least logical.

Putting this statement out and allowing a copy of the Threshers receipt to be shown on live television meant that by the time the Chancellor rang Jeremy on Sunday morning, he was sounding far more cheerful. The Prime Minister had agreed the newspapers were out to get him on trivial matters, he said, and the press had at last backed away.

That winter everyone managed a Christmas break, including Jeremy, who flew to Central America to celebrate New Year's Eve with Reyahn. They walked through ancient ruins in the rainforest in Guatemala, and went on from there to Flores, dazzled by the luminous red-brick buildings, painted doors, mopeds and cobblestone streets. Jeremy enjoyed it all, but he was so exhausted that, when they reached Ambergris Caye in Belize, a beautiful, white sand-ringed island, he went to bed for a day. The year had caught up with him and all he wanted to do was sleep.

In January, Jeremy returned to London reinvigorated and ready to help the Chancellor refocus on normal Treasury business. The importance of this was underlined by the latest economic figures, which showed unemployment inching towards three million and public sector borrowing heading towards an estimated £35 billion by the end of 1993, and £50 billion by the end of 1994.

Jeremy reviewed these figures on his way down to Dorneywood, the Chancellor's country mansion in Buckinghamshire, for their first substantial discussion about the spring Budget. Debt levels hadn't reached such figures since 1976, when Prime Minister James Callaghan had felt forced to ask the IMF to loan Britain $3.9 billion. The recession, the recent over-generous spending round, for which Jeremy felt partly responsible after those negotiations in Bournemouth, and an overestimate of tax revenues, had all left the UK drowning in debt.

As a committed sound-money Conservative, it was no surprise that Norman Lamont was determined to bring the deficit back under control. Jeremy, though his politics weren't defined by party allegiance, agreed – if the debt wasn't reduced, the UK risked having its credit rating cut, which would raise its debt interest payments and potentially push it into a negative spiral.

Part of the solution to this was getting public spending under control, but since that wouldn't be enough on its own, the primary focus of the Dorneywood discussion was on potential tax increases. What the Chancellor wanted were a few bold changes rather than many small increases, each requiring separate Finance Bill legislation. And after hearing the options, he felt the least unattractive was an increase in National Insurance – partly because this was less visible than an increase in income tax – combined with an increase in fuel duty and the imposition of VAT on fuel.

Like Jeremy, the senior Treasury officials in the room supported the need for tax increases but several, including Terry, worried that imposing so many simultaneously would depress the economy. It would be better, they argued, to phase them in, but it was unclear how they could do that while also making sure they would still be implemented.

'But what about,' someone said, 'if we legislate for all these measures in this Finance Bill but implement them over time?'

The room went quiet before exploding into discussion. Passing legislation for future tax rises was novel but there was no obvious reason why it couldn't be done. And if it was possible, everyone felt more comfortable about putting in place a tough set of tax increases.

In Dorneywood's genteel drawing room this all made sense, but in the car back up to London, the Chancellor worried about the potential political fallout from the Budget. Over the following days he, therefore, tested his thinking with the Prime Minister and asked David Cameron to set up meetings with groups of Tory backbenchers in which he explained the Budget context, while not revealing the specific tax changes that he had in mind.

While the tea-trays rattled back and forth, fuelling these discussions in the Chancellor's office, Jeremy sat in the private office outside with Mridul and Owen working through drafts of the Budget speech. These last few days before a Budget were always frenetic as they tried to stitch together dozens of announcements into a flowing narrative and made sure each tax change was correctly and consistently described, not only in the speech but also in the accompanying press releases and the Red Book, which summarised the Budget measures and their impact. While he did this, Jeremy also watched out for any 'smelly rats' that had snuck into the text. This was the term that Gus O'Donnell had taught him to use to describe innocuous-looking proposals – like changing the taxation of Jaffa Cakes to bring them in line with other biscuits – that the Inland Revenue was keen to implement, but which came at a high political cost.

There was also the annual challenge of coming up with one or two jokes, and the equally predictable struggle to take on board the Prime Minister's last-minute drafting changes. But it all came together, as it always did, enabling the Chancellor to stand up in the House of Commons on 16 March 1993 to announce a flood of tax increases including the freezing of most allowances, a reduction in the tax

relief on mortgage interest payments and an increase in taxes on
cigarettes and alcohol – though not on whisky or other spirits, mind-
ful of the Scottish lobby. It would be exaggerating to describe
Norman Lamont as environmentally conscious, but he was happy to
include the fuel price escalator, which would raise the cost of fuel
annually by 3 per cent above inflation, and he imposed VAT on
domestic fuel and power, starting at 8 per cent in April 1994 and
rising to 17.5 per cent from April 1995.

When the Chancellor announced this last change, the House
became rowdy and the Deputy Speaker had to call MPs to order.
After a pause, Norman continued, saying the government would
take these additional fuel costs into account when uprating benefits
the following year.

The headlines the following day were painful. The *Daily Express*
called the budget Lamont's 'Tax Time Bomb', while other papers
claimed that putting VAT on fuel would cause people to freeze
during the winter. Much to Jeremy and the Chancellor's frustration,
the green lobby said nothing, despite having pointed out for decades
that exempting fuel from VAT was both un-environmental and
almost unique to Britain.

Admiralty House was soon on the phone. The Prime Minister
wanted to announce extra help for pensioners and others on low
incomes, his office reported, something that he did the following
day. This reduced the outcry, but when fully in place, would forfeit
nearly half of the tax being raised by putting VAT on fuel. And, of
course, it also led to further reports of divisions between the
Chancellor and the Prime Minister.

All in all it had been a painful Budget, but despite the outcry, the
poor handling of some of the measures and the fair-weather
friendship of the lobby groups, Jeremy still believed Norman had
been right to take tough action on the deficit.

Jeremy returned from a short break in the spring of 1993 hoping to
find the Chancellor's mood improved. But, if anything, it was worse,
partly because, when Norman had been asked by a reporter during
the Newbury by-election what he regretted most – claiming to see
the green shoots of economic recovery back in October 1991 or

singing in the bath after Black Wednesday – he'd quipped, '*Je ne regrette rien.*' With the press howling again, Norman told Terry during one of their bilaterals he was certain he would be sacked, though Terry assured him this was unlikely.

Jeremy also hoped the Chancellor was mistaken, but when, on Tuesday 27 May, Mary Francis rang from the Prime Minister's office to ask the Chancellor to come over, it felt ominous.

On his return, Norman beckoned Jeremy into his office. 'Well that's it,' he said, slumping into his chair. 'I'm being forced to resign.'

'Resign?' Jeremy gawped at the Chancellor.

'The Prime Minister offered to make me environment minister. But that would be an insult. And I really don't understand why he's doing this when we're at last beginning to see results. Inflation is below 2 per cent for the first time in a generation, unemployment has peaked, and the economy is recovering. Moving me now makes it look like none of this is due to our actions.'

Jeremy said nothing. What could he say? The Chancellor was right about his achievements. And he had often been blamed for the consequences of things he hadn't chosen to do, like joining the ERM. But he did have an uncanny ability to attract poor press, even if many of the stories were made up.

Jeremy helped Norman pack his personal items while the office filled up with special advisers and officials. The Treasury didn't lose its Chancellor every day, and for all his idiosyncrasies, Norman was respected for his determination to act in the country's best interests and his courage under fire.

After Norman left, Jeremy lolled in his chair. He picked up a submission and put it back down. It was the end of an era. He remembered the day at the end of the summer of 1986 when Jonathan de Berker, the avuncular head of the Economist Management Unit, had rung him to say that the financial secretary needed a new private secretary, and most unusually, was looking for an economist. A multi-year partnership and friendship had followed that had lasted through multiple crises, scandals and exotic foreign trips. Now all that was over, and Norman's successor might have entirely different views – and want an entirely different private secretary.

5

'I Got the Blues':
Serving multiple masters

May 2003–January 1994

It wasn't long until the identity of the new Chancellor was revealed. It was Ken Clarke, the home secretary who, despite their difficult meetings during the ERM crisis, remained a close friend of Norman Lamont's.

Terry Burns came to see Jeremy later that afternoon, finding him still sitting at his desk, sorting papers and smoking. 'Come on,' Terry said, 'we've been summoned to meet the new Chancellor to give him a briefing.'

Jeremy jumped up, relieved to be taking some action. On their way over to the Home Office in Terry's car, they discussed how Ken Clarke might want to change various Treasury policies. Terry didn't, however, mention Norman Lamont, which felt odd until Jeremy realised it was deliberate – their loyalty as civil servants, whatever their personal feelings, was to the new Chancellor.

They arrived at the Home Office's concrete bunker in Queen Anne's Gate full of anticipation, but when they made their way into the home secretary's vast office, they found it deserted. Terry and Jeremy exchanged glances – Ken's private secretary had assured them he was in here.

'Maybe he's …' Jeremy began before hearing scuffling.

A door in the corner of the office burst open, and Ken Clarke appeared. 'Sorry,' their new Chancellor said cheerily. 'I was just going to the loo.'

Jeremy grinned while Terry nodded. 'We're here to take you through your diary for the rest of the week,' Terry said.

'Luckily I'm free,' Ken said, 'since I was supposed to be at a ministerial meeting in Denmark. So, if you send over some red boxes, I'll get started on the paperwork.'

Jeremy glanced at Terry, who raised an eyebrow. This was a new regime.

On Thursday afternoon they held a small farewell party for Norman Lamont in the Chancellor's office. Terry gave a short speech in which he said what a sad day it was to lose someone who'd been a Treasury minister for seven years.

'I can still remember,' Terry said, 'when you came to say goodbye to me before the 1992 election, and I said you might win.'

'I remember,' Norman said.

'Well, that was at least one forecast the Treasury got right,' Terry said, and everyone laughed.

Norman came over to see Jeremy before he left, handing him a folded note. Jeremy gave Norman a smile, though in reality he was struggling with a jumble of emotions – loss, certainly, and sadness. But also guilt, or at least a wish that he could somehow have prevented this ending. He opened the letter when he got home later that evening. 'No one could have been better supported than I was, and what little I achieved was much due to you. We also did have some hilarious times together. I don't think you'll ever go through anything like it again!'

When he read this, Jeremy smiled. But he also felt anxious because, while they were kind, Norman's words also neatly captured Jeremy's fear that he might never again work with a minister who trusted him so much and that, like Norman's, his career may have peaked in the aftermath of Black Wednesday.

Jeremy tried to ignore this worry in the days after Ken Clarke's arrival in the Treasury. After all, there were plenty of other things to focus on, including deciding how to address the continuing discontent about the imposition of VAT on domestic fuel and power, which was being stoked by the Labour Party – when it wasn't busy digging out the promises made by each Conservative Member of Parliament in 1992 and pointing out those that had been breached. But despite these distractions, Jeremy's mind kept coming back to the moment before the April 1992 election when Brian Fox, the Treasury's head of people, had called him into his office to tell him he would probably have to move out of the Chancellor's office if Labour won because he was seen as being too close to the Tories – and far too close to Norman Lamont. That discussion had made Jeremy conscious that his role depended not only on how well he did his job but also on the relationship he had with his minister – the question, therefore, was whether a new minister, who knew him far less well, would be willing to keep him on.

Luckily this period of uncertainty was soon over because, a few days after his appointment, Ken Clarke told Jeremy that he saw no need to change his private office. In fact the only adjustment he wanted to make was to bundle out David Cameron to go to work with the new home secretary, Michael Howard, so he could replace him with his own special advisers from the Home Office, Tessa Keswick and David Ruffley. Jeremy was relieved – though he was sorry to see David go because he'd enjoyed debating the events and policies of the day with a special adviser who was close to his own age. They were, however, to work together again.

While there wasn't much change in personnel after Ken Clarke's arrival, there was a change of style. Unlike his predecessor, the new Chancellor was keen to be involved in the government's broader dramas, including its ongoing war of attrition with its backbenchers to get the Maastricht Bill approved. Here Jeremy was in luck because his flatmate Philip Barton was leading the work on the bill in the Foreign Office, which meant that Jeremy could get the inside scoop on its progress over dinner in their local pizzeria. The news, though, wasn't good: in fact it was so bad that, after the government lost a motion on the social chapter of the treaty on 22 July 1993, the Prime Minister was forced to call a confidence motion. This would have brought the government down if it had been lost, though in the end it was won by forty votes.

But however great the drama of the day, Ken Clarke was always relaxed. He was meticulous about going through his papers and was willing to take advice from Jeremy and other Treasury officials, particularly if they were willing to debate the issues with him over a lunchtime pint and a cigar at The Colonies pub in Victoria or a curry at the Pimlico Tandoori. He was also a keen birdwatcher, although his attempts to do a bit of bird spotting during his official trips, including during his visit to Japan to attend the G7 with Jeremy in early July 1993, were often frustrated by the over-zealous security guards.

Towards the end of July, the currency markets again became turbulent with the franc hovering at the bottom of its ERM band. Although sterling was no longer threatened, the Chancellor was concerned about the state of the markets and the stability of the UK's EU partners and was, therefore, keen to attend the emergency meeting of EU finance ministers and central bank governors that was held in early August in Brussels. It was, Jeremy reflected on their flight out to this, incredible how much had changed in a year. Although the informal ECOFIN in Bath the previous year had also taken place in the middle of an ERM crisis – and had involved a similar cast list – then the UK had been chairing the meeting and the debate had been critical to sterling's future. Now they would be merely observing a debate about a system they'd already left.

Ken Clarke was, however, in no mood to be a bystander. When the meeting began, he threw himself into the discussion, arguing that the Deutsche Mark and Dutch guilder should be allowed to float above their ERM bands to take pressure off the weaker currencies. After objecting to this, the chair of the meeting, Philippe Maystadt – who as Belgium's finance minister was perhaps conscious of the political consequences of allowing the Belgian franc to sink beneath the Dutch guilder – adjourned the discussion, saying he wanted to hold bilateral meetings with the main ERM members.

Since this move excluded the UK from these discussions, Jeremy, the Chancellor and Nigel Wicks spent the next few hours hanging around outside the meeting room, knocking back glasses of wine, eating bread rolls and trying to pick up gossip from the other delegations.

'No agreement has been reached,' Maystadt said when everyone filed back into the meeting room at 10 p.m. that evening, 'so I propose that we should suspend the ERM for a temporary, but indefinite, period.'

After a moment of silence, Maystadt looked around. 'Does anyone see any other solution?' he demanded.

Ken Clarke leant forwards. 'Suspending the ERM would be catastrophic,' he said. 'People would see it as a total political failure on the part of the Community.'

'I agree,' said Mogens Lykketoft, the Danish finance minister.

'So do I,' declared Portugal's finance minister, Jorge Braga de Macedo.

The German and French finance ministers were also nodding.

Maystadt scrutinised the room. 'Then we'll make one more effort,' he conceded.

After that, the mood changed, and less than thirty minutes later, the group agreed to widen the ERM bands from 3 per cent to 15 per cent.

Jeremy smiled at the Chancellor when they reached this conclusion. If a similar decision had been made a year before, Black Wednesday might never have happened.

It turned out that Jeremy wasn't Ken Clarke's only admirer. Jorge Braga de Macedo approached them during the final handshakes at nearly one in the morning. 'So, will the UK rejoin the ERM?' he asked the Chancellor. 'After all, you're within the 15 per cent band.'

Ken Clarke laughed. 'The time isn't right.'

In fact, the only person who seemed disappointed by the outcome of the emergency meeting was the Prime Minister, whom the Chancellor rang on their way back to London. The Eurosceptics would probably have been happier, John Major said, if the ERM had collapsed.

But regardless of whether people liked it, the ERM had survived another day. However, this further exposure of its fragility had underlined for many Europeans the need to progress towards full monetary union without delay. This, of course, also meant that the mighty Bundesbank – which had failed to support the ERM during its troubles – had brought forward the day when it would be forced to hand over some of its own powers to the European Central Bank.

* * *

Jeremy shared the Chancellor's good mood in the days after they returned from Brussels, but for a different reason – he was increasingly sure that Ken Clarke trusted him and respected his advice. Jeremy's colleagues, many of whom saw him as the Treasury's 'golden boy' after his early promotion to become the Chancellor's principal private secretary, would have been surprised by his insecurity. It partly stemmed from the fact that he'd started his career in the backwaters of the Health and Safety Executive, and his status as an economist hadn't helped, since at the time these specialists were managed separately from – and rather looked down on by – the Civil Service generalists who led on policy.

Jeremy's lack of security had also been increased by Brian Fox's comment about his future if Labour had won the 1992 election. And Jonathan de Berker, who managed the Treasury's economists, had compounded this when he'd suggested, after Jeremy's second lung collapse in 1987, that he was too sickly to return to private office. These collapses, which tend to afflict tall, thin men, had been excruciatingly painful because the cure at the time was to insert talcum through tubes into the chest to inflame the lung tissue and make it reattach to the chest wall. This procedure was followed by several weeks of recuperation during which Jeremy lay in hospital reading obscure books like Raymond Roussel's *Impressions of Africa* while dosed up on morphine. Jeremy's second lung collapse had been so unpleasant that, after it, he'd considered stopping smoking. If he'd done so, this story might have ended differently, but he abandoned the idea after his doctor said that, though advisable, his lung collapses hadn't made it any more essential.

With all this history, it wasn't surprising that Jeremy felt nervous about his position within the Civil Service. However, after his trip to Brussels with Ken Clarke, this feeling faded because he realised that the people who had the most reason to doubt him were the ones who had taken the biggest risks on his behalf. Terry Burns had forgiven the secret memos that he had drafted for Norman Lamont to send to the Prime Minister, and rather than holding a grudge, had become his mentor. And Ken Clarke, despite knowing how close Jeremy had been to his predecessor, had kept him in post after becoming Chancellor.

The Chancellor confirmed his view of Jeremy not long afterwards in a note that he penned on the latest iteration of the forthcoming Budget speech:

> If I may say so your re-draft is brilliant. I do not know if:
>   (1) you and I are completely agreed on macro-economic policy;
>   (2) you really seek to set out my views in a clearer way than I usually manage; or
>   (3) you have subtly influenced my views over the last four months so that they have changed without my realising it and now coincide with your own.
>   I think I shall not be troubled with an answer!

When the Chancellor got up to present his Budget on 30 November 1993, he started by saying that he felt like a lion-tamer trying out his act for the first time. Luckily, the big cats behaved while the Chancellor explained the extra compensation he was putting in place to counter the impact of VAT on fuel and ramped up the annual increase in road fuel duty from Norman Lamont's 3 per cent to 5 per cent in real terms.

After the Budget, Jeremy decided that it was time to start considering his own next move. After all, apart from his two-year secondment to the IMF in Washington, he'd been working directly for ministers ever since 1986. Most of that time he'd worked long hours, rolling from crisis to crisis, his sleeves pushed up and wreathed in cigarette smoke. Now he knew that his success wasn't just due to his relationship with Norman Lamont, he was ready to try something new. And since his relationship with Reyahn had come to an end the previous autumn after they'd both accepted the difficulty of maintaining it at long distance, he was free to move anywhere. So, when Terry said that, partly as a thank you for all those hours in private office, the Treasury would pay for Jeremy to attend a short course to build his management skills, Jeremy chose Harvard's three-month management development programme, attracted by the idea of living somewhere new and studying a series of real-life case studies.

Before Jeremy could leave for America, however, he joined Terry, the Chancellor and the Chancellor's wife Gillian for one last ministerial trip. This time they were off to the Far East on a journey that was intended to create new links for British businesses, although happily it also promised some terrific birdwatching opportunities.

When they landed in Hong Kong in late December 1993, they were met by Ed Llewellyn, the governor's chief of staff – someone else who would play a role in Jeremy's later life. Dinner in Government House and a game of carpet bowls followed, during which Chris Patten – a friend and political ally of the Chancellor's – briefed them on Hong Kong's political situation. The next day they took the governor's boat, the *Lady Maureen*, out to Lantau Island, where the Chancellor and Gillian birdwatched while Ed, Jeremy, Terry and Chris Patten climbed the peak. Two more days of business discussions were combined with a visit to a bird sanctuary, a few games of table tennis, lunch on a junk in Aberdeen harbour, an evening at a jazz club and a helicopter ride around the island, which Jeremy spent curled up in a ball, trying not to look out of the window.

On New Year's Eve they flew over the giant Buddha on Lantau Island to Jakarta, arriving in time to welcome in 1994 while listening to an Indonesian group play a passable version of 'Auld Lang Syne'. More meetings with business leaders followed, together with earnest discussions about how to ship home the horse that the Chancellor had been given. After final stops in Indonesia and the Philippines, Jeremy paused outside the airport terminal in Manila to throw his two half-empty packets of cigarettes into a bin. He'd smoked for over ten years, and had been lucky enough to work for two similarly addicted Chancellors, but it was becoming so frowned on that it was getting difficult to get pleasure from it. He was, therefore, determined to make the next phase of his life tobacco-free.

On their flight back to London, Jeremy talked to Terry about what he might do when he returned from Harvard. The Bank of England had offered him a job, he said, but ideally, he wanted to do something that took him away from economics and from working closely with ministers, at least for a while. 'Maybe I can succeed John MacAuslan as the head of HR,' he mused. 'I'd find it interesting to sort out our personnel policies.'

'Perhaps,' Terry said, 'but if you're interested in organisation then

I have a better idea – would you be willing to lead the review of the Treasury that I'm going to launch in the spring?'

They explored this idea while the plane flew on across India and the Middle East. It had been years since the Treasury had last examined itself, and after all the criticism following Black Wednesday, it seemed a good time to do it again. And Jeremy felt that, from his lofty vantage point in the Chancellor's office, he'd already spotted a few things that could be made a lot better.

Back in London, Jeremy handed over his private office responsibilities to Nick Macpherson, whom he'd strongly supported as his successor. After that it was time to pack for Boston, with only two items marked as essential: his new portable stereo system and a box of his favourite CDs. These included the great Bob Dylan of course, but also Louis Prima's greatest hits, which had been stuck in Jeremy's head ever since he'd gone to watch *Mad Dog and Glory* on his first cigarette-free social evening.

Going to Harvard was, he knew, a defining moment in his career. He'd proven himself at the IMF and at the Treasury. Now he would be joining a class of international students at Harvard. This might prove that he was unwise to stray too far from his economist roots – or it might demonstrate that there were few limitations to the direction of his future career.

6

'Light My Fire':
Needing a zoologist

January 1994–May 1997

Jeremy's first shock after arriving in Massachusetts was the spartan dorm he was expected to share with the six other students who made up his study group. The second was the cold, which crawled beneath his skin – though this did at least remove any temptation to sneak outside for a cigarette. And since smoking was banned inside most of the buildings, it was the perfect environment in which to reinvent himself as a clean-living, non-smoking English gentleman from the British government.

But the real oddity of Harvard wasn't the dorm or the freezing wind – it was how seriously everyone, including Jeremy, was soon taking it, even though it didn't lead to a formal qualification. Each evening Jeremy had to prepare three cases, talking them over with his study group in preparation for a morning discussion in which the professors would fire questions at the class. Most of the papers focused on mysterious topics like pricing, marketing and accounting. But a few covered incidents such as the Maastricht Treaty negotiations that Jeremy knew well. This gave him the satisfaction of highlighting to the professors any errors he found – something he did with some relish given the delight they took in exposing students who hadn't done their overnight reading.

By the second half of the course it was clear that Jeremy's economic background was no handicap – in fact he was often leading the debates in his study group and in the wider class, even when the topics were unfamiliar. The pace relaxed a little and many of the US participants began heading home to see their families for part of each weekend. Jeremy even hosted a few visitors himself including Isabel, a fey and enigmatic Swiss artist friend of Reyahn's with whom he'd somewhat inconveniently started a relationship on his last evening in Britain before flying out to the US.

Jeremy's final visitor at Harvard was Terry who, as Jeremy's sponsor, was expected to spend a day on campus. Terry attended various of the Harvard sessions, including one in which he found out to his delight that he could access the *Wall Street Journal* through the internet.

'So, are you still happy to lead the Treasury's review?' he asked Jeremy over breakfast on his final morning.

Jeremy nodded. Harvard had increased his interest in how organisations worked, a topic that many people overlooked. 'Yes,' he said. 'I can't wait to get started.'

Back in London in early May 1994, Jeremy became the Treasury's Head of Corporate and Management Change, a convoluted title for the job of leading the Treasury's Fundamental Expenditure Review (FER). His team consisted of a policy official, Richard Thomas, a secretary, Anna Molloy, and a part-time chair, Colin Southgate from Thorn EMI. To complete his squad, Jeremy told Terry he needed a fast-stream trainee. Finding someone should be straightforward he added – after all, having been head of the Chancellor's office through a tumultuous period, he was well known across the department. But when the job was advertised, only two people applied and one of them, against all the advice of my fast-stream friends, was me.

After staring up at the window into Jeremy's office in Allington Towers from the pavement outside, I appeared on the tenth floor in my best burgundy jacket, complete with shiny gold buttons and shoulder pads, my hair pulled back into a French braid. Jeremy lounged in his chair peering at me over piles of papers, twisting a pen between restless fingers, a multi-coloured thread bracelet tied around his narrow wrist.

We talked for a while about the need to make the Treasury more focused on the things that mattered.

'It's a chance to change the organisation,' Jeremy said, 'and nothing is predetermined.'

'We also need to make it easier for women to work here,' I said. 'Have you noticed how few there are?'

'And what other views do you have?'

'I have lots,' I said and we both grinned.

The next day Jeremy called to tell me I'd got the job. He later said, whenever asked, that he'd been looking for a zoologist to complete his team and I was the only one that had applied.

We launched the Fundamental Expenditure Review in front of the assembled Treasury at the QEII Centre on 6 June 1994 on the same stage where, nearly two years before, Norman Lamont had defended the UK's membership of the ERM at the European Policy Forum. However, this time it was Jeremy who was in the spotlight, standing alongside Terry Burns and Paul Gray, the Treasury's head of HR, encouraging people to share their views and assuring them that the review wouldn't just be an exercise in headcount reduction.

Jeremy found this a daunting experience. It was the first time he'd led a major piece of work himself, and standing in front of hundreds of his colleagues, he knew he'd be the one they blamed if it went wrong. But darting around in the aisles handing out microphones, I felt far more warmth from the audience because, although the review was threatening, Jeremy's self-deprecation and honesty seemed to be reassuring people that it would be conducted in good faith.

After the launch, Jeremy sat with Richard and me laying out our next steps – consulting staff, understanding what work the department was already doing and asking the rest of Whitehall what it thought of the Treasury. Jeremy worked fast, filling pages of paper with scribbled notes, pausing to sip strong black instant coffee from a glass beaker. But when we met Terry later that day to go through our plan, Terry said that the Chancellor and Colin Southgate had a different view of how the project should be run. They wanted to work top-down, first identifying the department's objectives and then working out how they would be delivered.

'I understand,' Jeremy said, 'but I don't think that's enough on its own. By the way,' he added, 'I am thinking of setting up an electronic bulletin board to gather input on the review.'

'Really?' Terry asked. 'How would it work?'

Jeremy smiled – Terry's obsession with new technology was well known. In fact, when they had been preparing to introduce the Council Tax to replace the much-hated Poll Tax three years previously, Terry – then the Treasury's chief economic adviser – had built his own Excel model of how it might operate. Though simple, this model was far more effective than the Department of the Environment's massive version, which could only churn out a single set of figures each day. 'People will send their comments to my secretary Anna and she'll input them manually,' Jeremy said.

'Okay,' Terry said. 'I'll give you a month. But the Chancellor will want some top-down thinking done at the same time. And I need you to find out how I can download the bulletin board onto my computer.'

Jeremy spent most of the following few weeks striding around the Treasury with me following along in the wake of his swirling dark coat. Our aim was to interview every team in the building to find out what they were doing, though it often felt more like we were an invading force. I thought this was only my imagination until one morning when we bumped into Robin Fellgett, one of the Treasury's senior officials, who accused us of circling the building, looking for a kill.

There was a lot to unpick in those meetings because there was no consistency in how the Treasury's work was organised. Many teams, like the one we found at the back of the building setting daylight saving times, were doing work it was hard to see fitting into any version of the Treasury's objectives. Some jobs were also missing. For example, no one below Terry was responsible for making sure the Budget balanced. And there were teams of specialists, including whole divisions of microeconomists, shadowing what everyone else was doing.

Jeremy spent hours writing notes, reading papers and scribbling questions. What should the Treasury do about pay, grading and training, all of which had been neglected for years? Could we live with only one layer of management between the work being done and it going to ministers? And, if the Treasury's structure was flatter, how would gurus be retained, those people who knew a huge amount but were often poor at managing staff?

Richard Thomas and I sat in the office next to Jeremy's, which though bigger than his, was in the middle of the building so had no windows and was permeated by a grinding noise from the lift shaft. While Richard, who was a grade senior to me and owned an impressive collection of braces and stripy shirts with white collars, focused on organising the staff surveys, I worried about managing the flood of queries, written in almost unintelligible, tiny script, that was pouring out of Jeremy's door. After a while, I developed a system. The most interesting questions I followed up on in detail. Those with potential, I dumped in the battered grey metal filing cabinet behind my desk, where they stayed until they were raised a second time. The rest I binned.

At the end of our first month of work the Chancellor approved the Treasury's new objectives after adding 'and the outlook for jobs' to the intention of strengthening 'the long-term performance of the economy'. After that we began designing an organisation that could deliver these. I felt overwhelmed, and so did Jeremy. Each solution raised more issues, and everyone wanted to be consulted and to know what we were recommending.

We both felt passionate about some of the changes that were emerging from our thinking – like getting the Treasury to spend more time on policy issues that cut across departmental boundaries, to think more strategically and to build more knowledge. Jeremy spent hours finessing the arguments for each of our proposals, lecturing me on the importance not only of lucid thinking, but also of clear prose, annotating endless drafts with trails of amendments in fine, red ink.

While Jeremy did that, he asked me to take on other responsibilities, like telling the Treasury's typing pool – a room full of ladies who spent their days typing out memos on sheets of paper interleaved with multiple layers of carbon paper – that their roles were likely to disappear. This was a daunting task, standing on a podium in a vast meeting room at the top of the Treasury's marble staircase, though I told my audience that I hoped they would all choose to become personal secretaries, and almost all of them did.

In September 1994 we completed the first draft of the report. After that, our days became absorbed in a series of negotiations.

Without losing the essence of what we wanted, Jeremy adjusted wording or added more details to our thinking until most of the Treasury's senior mandarins were, if not happy, at least more comfortable with the recommendations.

Towards the end of this writing frenzy, the role of private secretary to the financial secretary became free and I decided to throw myself into the competition.

'But why – we haven't finished the review?' Jeremy asked when I told him.

'But the main thinking is finished. And in any case, this is the best job in the Treasury for someone at my grade. Didn't you start your private office career in the same role?'

Jeremy didn't say much in response to this – and his mood didn't improve when the financial secretary, George Young, appointed me to the post a few days later. Rather grudgingly, Jeremy prepared my final performance review – giving me the top rating while adding in a scrawl at the bottom that I'd 'deserted' the review before it had concluded.

Despite his annoyance, Jeremy started inviting me to join him occasionally for lunch after I left the FER so we could discuss his ongoing consultations with the Treasury's unions, and he could advise me on the challenges I was facing in private office.

Seeing Jeremy like this wasn't unusual. Jeremy had lunch, and often dinner, most days with a friend or colleague. If something was going on in the Treasury, Jeremy knew about it, and many people turned to him for advice. I, therefore, didn't read any ulterior motive into our meetings, particularly because he'd told me during the review that he was going out with an exotic-sounding artist called Isabel and I'd said I was dating an Australian theoretical physicist called Lloyd.

The final FER report was published in October 1994. In a rush of pride, Jeremy wrote again to his friend Carrie:

So far, so good. Even in the disputatious Treasury no one has really managed to mount a challenge to its logic, even though the human consequences of the changes are deeply uncomfortable (ignoring the ludicrous generosity of the redundancy programme). Once the current consultation period comes to its silent conclusion, I will have to find another job, which will be a bit like Norman Lamont trying to find a new seat following the boundary changes and doing his best to assassinate John Major.

Completing the FER and finding a new role did end up taking Jeremy a while, though not because of his attempted assassination of the mandarin class. The issue, Jeremy told me over one of our lunches, was that the senior Treasury officials, including Terry, were keen for Jeremy's next job to be a 'proper one' and Jeremy didn't want to look like he'd benefited from the FER. The obscure position he accepted in the end, as head of securities and markets policy, therefore, made perfect sense.

Jeremy began this new role in May 1995, taking over responsibility for overseeing the UK's securities exchanges and leading the Treasury's efforts to curb fraud. This meant that he was soon busy working on the Crest Project, a troubled attempt to digitise the settlement of share transactions, attending the Financial Action Task Force, an international group that met three times a year in Paris to coordinate efforts to reduce financial crime and negotiating new EU directives on money laundering.

I found all of this interesting when Jeremy told me about it, though rather technical. What I found more intriguing was how Jeremy was approaching these new challenges. Over yet another lunch, which by that point were often taking place at Jeremy's instigation in the uber-cool Institute of Contemporary Arts off the Mall, he told me that he'd spent several days on the trading floors of various banks getting input on issues such as how to reform the stamp duty on share sales.

'It's only when you get out of Whitehall that you really understand what's going on,' he told me. 'You need to get external views before your thinking is settled or all you get is bland, trade association inputs.'

This was to become, I later realised, one of the defining characteristics of how Jeremy operated.

By early June 1995, after I'd broken up with Lloyd and Jeremy had stopped mentioning Isabel, we started mixing our lunches with an occasional evening drink. Our conversations also changed. We still began by discussing Treasury topics, perhaps the latest privatisation that I was working on with George Young, or the most recent twist in Jeremy's fight against financial crime, but we then moved on to discuss other things like the types of people we liked or places we wanted to visit.

We were also sharing more of our own stories. Jeremy told me he'd always loved history, inspired by his mother Brenda, an archaeologist who'd done her thesis on the Vallum, an earthwork running along the south side of Hadrian's Wall. At university he'd combined this with economics, a choice that he also attributed to Brenda, who'd taken him to Brussels, aged fifteen, to meet his cousin Alan who was living an enviable bachelor lifestyle while working for the European Economic Commission.

With a schoolteacher father, Peter, and one younger brother, Simon, making up the rest of the family, Jeremy's childhood had been comfortable, though hardly posh. He'd gone to a Quaker school, Bootham in York, and though he wasn't a Quaker himself, he admired their sense of duty, tolerance and modesty. He'd excelled academically at both school and university, scooping up all the available prizes and scholarships. But he also had an unconventional side, telling me how, after trying and failing to dye his white-blond hair black after he'd reached Oxford, he'd worn the thin plastic glove that came with the kit for weeks afterwards, convincing his friends that the skin on his hand would wither away if he allowed it to be exposed to the air.

As for his political beliefs, Jeremy told me he'd written his own 'manifesto' back in 1985, just after moving to the Treasury. In it he'd proposed a series of measures to reduce inherited wealth which, he'd argued, served to reinforce inequality. His other policies included abolishing inheritance rights except between spouses, preventing transfers of capital and requiring the wealthiest in society to buy government annuities to pay for their pensions.

'But I soon lost interest in trying to codify my views,' Jeremy told me at the end of this short political rant, the only one I ever heard him give. 'The fact was that I was loving life as a Treasury civil servant. I was doing work that stretched me and my thinking was occasionally, through multiple management clearance levels and endless trips down to the typing pool to collect corrected memos, even beginning to find its way up to Treasury ministers.'

In mid-June 1995 the Treasury offered me a place on a six-week economics course in Oxford.

'I want to do it,' I told Jeremy. 'After all, you've always said that understanding economics is fundamental to working in the Treasury.'

'Sure,' he said, 'but who else is going?'

'They sent me the list,' I said, trying to restrain a smile, 'and it seems to be almost all men.'

It was a few days before Jeremy made the next move, asking me if I would like to join him for an evening of jazz before going up to Oxford. After I agreed, we arranged to meet at his flat in Clapham. It seemed a reasonable plan, but when I reached his apartment on the top floor of a building on Cavendish Road, I found that several people were already there.

'This is Isabel and her parents,' Jeremy said waving towards them. 'They're just giving me a plant.'

I decided to play it cool, so I didn't ask why Isabel was visiting, or the reason for the fern. Instead, while he finished his conversation, I hung around on the outskirts of the group, examining the rug hung on the wall of Jeremy's lounge, the nipple-shaped light switches and the hunk of dark wood framing the gas meter.

'I co-own the flat with my friend Philip Barton,' Jeremy said a while later after the others had left and we were in our cab. 'It's a big improvement over some of the places I've lived in.'

'What were they like?'

Jeremy grimaced and took me through his housing journey – starting with his damp, smoke-filled basement room in Hurst Street during his second year in Oxford, feeding 10p coins into the electricity meter. His housing highlight had been a party-heavy period that had come a few years later while he'd been studying at the London School of Economics and renting Gus O'Donnell's pad in Clapham – though Gus remembered it less favourably after he'd returned from his posting in Washington to find his wooden floor needed re-polishing and his vacuum cleaner full of burst balloons.

At the end of the second jazz set in the darkened basement of the 606 Club on Lots Road in Chelsea, we stumbled out and stood on the pavement.

I looked at Jeremy. 'Do you want to come back to my place for a drink?'

'Sure,' he said.

We took a cab to Maida Vale with me wondering what I was doing. First, the practicalities – all I could offer was tap water. And second, I wasn't sure why I'd invited him, apart from the fact that he made me laugh. But once we were there, it made more sense. Jeremy sat on a hard-backed chair while I showed him my collection of South Pacific carvings and woven baskets of seashells, describing the decade I'd spent as a child sailing around the world.

Jeremy listened to my story, his water barely touched. My parents had loaded me, aged seven, and my brother Jon, aged six, onto a schooner called *Wavewalker* before setting sail from Plymouth to recreate Captain Cook's third and final voyage around the world. The tale of the next ten years had then become one that could be told in two different ways. What could be more romantic, many thought – my parents and brother included – than life on the ocean, seeing the world?

But Jeremy was more interested in how I'd experienced my childhood. So I described the frustration I'd felt at being trapped on a boat with limited access to schooling or friends, a feeling that had intensified in my later teens, after my pleas to return to England had been overruled, and my relationship with my mother had deteriorated into weeks of silences.

It was, Jeremy said, one of the strangest tales he'd ever heard. But it didn't seem to discourage him because, just before heading back to south London at 4 a.m., he told me he thought we could become more than friends.

I gave him a hug, but my answer was 'maybe' because I was genuinely unsure. After all, he was older than me and far more experienced. We also worked in the same place, though not together anymore. But our conversations were always fascinating, funny and warm. And I missed him when he wasn't around.

My economics course was short-lived – on 5 July 1995, the day after I arrived in Oxford, John Major reshuffled his Cabinet, moving George Young to Transport and appointing the Minister for Agriculture, Fisheries and Food, Michael Jack, as the new financial secretary. I was called back to London, and that evening, Jeremy took me out for dinner at the Royal Festival Hall by the Thames to advise me on how to handle a ministerial transition.

'I didn't like you going away,' he said at the end of his sermon.

I laughed. 'Maybe that's because I told you who else was on the course.'

That night Jeremy invited me to stay over at his flat and I accepted, sleeping prudishly on the far side of the bed. We were woken in the early hours by the phone ringing, followed by the sound of a wild woman's voice on the answering machine demanding that Jeremy should ring her back.

'Don't worry,' he said, reaching out in the darkness to hold my hand, 'it's only one of my ex-girlfriends.'

So I didn't, though the calls continued at regular intervals through the night.

A few weeks after we started going out, having discovered that Jeremy couldn't drive, I hired a car and drove us down to the south coast to stay in a lighthouse for the weekend. We spent most of our time there walking along the clifftops while Jeremy told me irreverent stories about everyone, himself included, and I laughed.

On our way back up to London, while I was still still basking in the after-glow of our weekend away, Jeremy announced that he was due to go to Italy for two weeks at the start of the summer.

'Sure,' I said, focused on the traffic.

'With an ex-girlfriend,' he added.

'The one who was screaming into your answerphone?'

'No.'

'Okay, a different one. Well I don't mind – so long as she is an "ex".'

'Of course she is. But she'll get upset if I ring you. So, you don't mind if I don't, do you? It will only be for two weeks.'

Yes, I did mind. I'd been prepared to be generous but an ex who objected to phone calls was not an ex, at least by my definition. When we reached Cavendish Road, I packed my bag and headed north. The phone rang shortly after I walked back into my flat in Maida Vale.

'We need to talk.'

'Other girls may have tolerated your ambiguous relationships,' I told him, 'but I won't.'

After some further debate, we agreed the terms of trade. Since the holiday had already been booked, he would still go. But he would ring me every day.

The following morning, Jeremy sent me a card. 'Our conversation last night was important – very important. Not only did it make it clear to me how my other relationships have to evolve, it also underlined how much I love you.'

It was, I realised when I calmed down, the first time he'd told me that he loved me.

After Jeremy returned from his break – which he said had been 'very difficult' – we went on holiday ourselves, flying out to Prague in the Czech Republic and making our way south to Český Krumlov, a town full of medieval houses curving down to meet small brick squares. We walked around the town while I took black and white photos, giggling at Jeremy's chatter and amused by his multi-coloured woollen waistcoats, which he seemed to think were trendy. Back in our hotel room, he produced a small pair of speakers from his bag and placed them on a cupboard.

'I need to introduce you to my favourite music,' he told me. 'It goes back a long way. I had the best music system at college – a turntable, NAD amplifier and speakers that my parents gave me for my eighteenth birthday. Then I was listening to "Hotel California" and "Firth of Fifth", but by the time I reached the Health and Safety Executive, I'd discovered Bob's brilliant *Blood on the Tracks*.'

So we listened to Portishead, Eurythmics and Bob Dylan, and we kept playing Jeremy's records while we made our way on to Hungary. A few days later in Budapest, we sat outside a fourteenth-century church under a deepening blue sky.

I took a deep breath. 'I know about some of your ex-girlfriends, but perhaps you should tell me about the rest.'

'Okay. But you go first.'

So I did. It didn't take long. Three loves, all still cared for, but none right at the time.

'Now it's your turn.'

Jeremy started talking. After a while, I found an envelope in my bag and began writing names down, filling the white oblong. Jeremy kept talking and my writing became smaller. But when we got up to walk again, I threw the envelope into a bin – I'd decided that I cared about the music, but not about the old romances.

Back in London, Jeremy was determined to keep our relationship quiet. Even after I moved into his flat in Clapham, we still split up at Embankment Underground station each morning before changing onto the Circle Line so that we would arrive separately at the Treasury's door.

In the evenings and on the weekends he would amuse me with stories of trying to catch people manipulating the prices on the London Metal Exchange and tried to instil in me his passion for Manchester United, the football team he'd followed since he was a boy. The day our satellite recorder broke, only hours before the start of a match, was one of the few times I ever saw him run. While Jeremy talked, I cleared a decade of debris out of the flat, including a hideous pink dinner service, washed the towels in the bathroom – something he claimed was unnecessary since he only used them after he showered – and got to know his dry-humoured and utterly reliable flatmate, Philip.

I thought Jeremy might propose in the spring of 1996 when we visited Paris and sat on the steps of the Sacré-Coeur overlooking the city, but he didn't. We were, I felt, caught in a trap – Jeremy wouldn't ask until he was sure of my answer and I only wanted to accept once I'd been asked. So I was still waiting for a proposal when we went on holiday that summer to Poland. Halfway across Rynek Główny, the main square in Krakow, we stopped to hear a trumpeter play.

'Will you marry me?' Jeremy asked in the silence that followed the final note.

'Yes, of course,' I said, smiling at the fact that, after so many weeks of waiting, the question had emerged seemingly impromptu, leaving Jeremy looking almost as surprised as I was.

My answer was, however, already prepared. Jeremy was quirky and impractical, and would probably never be able to drive a car or change a lightbulb, but I wanted to be with him and knew I could rely on him. And having been left fending for myself and my younger brother at sixteen after my parents had sailed back up through the Pacific leaving us behind in New Zealand, that's what I needed – together, of course, with his humour and love.

Despite our joy, it was October before Jeremy was prepared to share our news with anyone else because, he told me, he hated the idea of people prying into our lives. For me those weeks were frustrating and disconcerting as I interpreted and misinterpreted his reluctance to reveal our engagement. But eventually, at a dinner with his old friend Suma, Jeremy confessed our secret. A few days later, we spent a Saturday afternoon in Hatton Garden in Holborn buying a ring – though the romance of that long-awaited trip was lost when the shopkeeper offered us a discount for cash and Jeremy started quizzing him about his money-laundering arrangements.

I was content after that to keep our news quiet, at least for a while. Then the Christmas 1996 edition of *Chequerboard*, the Treasury's in-house magazine, landed on my desk.

Those of you who were unsure that anything really good had come out of the FER will be delighted to hear of the engagement of two of its principal authors, Jeremy Heywood and Suzanne Cook. The Treasury's very own Thin Man and Thin Woman are refusing to comment, beyond making the very apt point that 'this is all very expensive'. Makes one ask if they did a proper cost-benefit analysis before they took this step.

7

'Close to Me':
Outside the inner circle

May 1997–January 1998

Jeremy placed a bet in the Treasury's sweepstake, which was set up using Nick Macpherson's odds, that Labour would win the 1997 election with a 125-seat majority while I was more cautious, betting only on 60.

On 1 May 1997 our election night party in Clapham began with the discovery that we were both wrong. To the rousing strains of 'Things Can Only Get Better', the exit polls suggested that, after eighteen years of Conservative rule, the rebranded 'New Labour' party, which was committed to both public service and enterprise, was on its way to a far bigger win than anyone had expected. By the early hours of the morning, most of our friends had left but Jeremy, Philip and I were still huddled on the sofa watching the results come in, confirming the new prime minister's whopping 179-seat majority.

Across the country, euphoria was in the air as Tony Blair made his way into Downing Street. And in the Treasury, Jeremy and I were in the crowd of officials applauding Gordon Brown when he climbed the Treasury's sweeping staircase to his new office. Three days later, Gordon made the change that Norman Lamont had argued so hard for – giving the Bank of England the right to make independent decisions on interest rates.

Jeremy and I were enthralled by this political landslide and the changes it might bring, even though the immediate consequences of it for us were limited. By that time I'd been promoted into a new job, in which I was responsible for the Chancellor's briefings for his

ECOFIN meetings with other European finance ministers. But despite doing most of the work on these, in those heady days after the election I was considered too junior to join the meetings with the new Chancellor to discuss them. On Jeremy's side of the Treasury, where he was still focused on financial crime, almost nothing had changed and he felt shut out of the discussions about the new government's policies – indeed we only heard about the plan to move banking supervision away from the Bank of England when we read about it in the *Evening Standard*.

While we both found it frustrating to be excluded from all of this, we were distracted by our impending wedding and the purchase of our first house – a neat, yellow three-bedroom end-of-terrace property only a few hundred yards away from Jeremy's flat in Clapham. But when Jeremy also found out that he wasn't being considered for promotion, even though Terry Burns had become chief economist at a similar age, he became even more fed up and began talking about leaving the Civil Service. He would speak again to Clive Hollick about joining United News and Media, he told me, though he wasn't in any hurry to decide.

On 2 August 1997 we were married in St Cyr's Church in Stinchcombe, a small village on the western edge of the Cotswolds. When I entered the small honey-yellow stone chapel, Jeremy turned to smile at me. We glided through the rest of the day, though the moment that we kept coming back to afterwards was our drive to Berkeley Castle for our reception in a 1931 blue Durant. The sun was shining, we held hands and we giggled the whole way.

We started our honeymoon at the Grand Hotel Serbelloni, an old villa fronted by gardens drifting down to Lake Como in northern Italy. We spent our time there exploring old villas and castles, while Jeremy chortled at my frequent mispronunciations, which I blamed on having barely entered a schoolroom during my childhood.

'Please read this word again,' he kept saying one afternoon standing by the lake, pointing to 'Goethe' in the guidebook, wiping away tears of laughter.

But there were also more romantic moments, like the evening when we sat on a low wall outside the Hotel Villa Giulia by Lake Garda watching the lights flickering across the water.

'Each light,' Jeremy said, 'represents a lifetime of love, and if you add them together, that's how much I love you.'

I smiled and held his hand. By that time I was about to start a new job as a management consultant at McKinsey, having become frustrated both by my continuing exclusion from ministerial meetings and the Treasury's lingering sexism, underlined by a comment in my most recent performance report that I should become more 'fluffy'. With Jeremy also restless in his job, we knew our lives would continue to change. But that no longer mattered because the most important part had been forever settled.

We returned to London that autumn in the aftermath of the emotional outpouring triggered by Princess Diana's death. A few days afterwards, Jeremy received a call from Jonathan Powell, Tony Blair's chief of staff.

'Alex and Moira are both leaving Number 10, so do you want to join Tony's private office?' Jonathan asked.

Jeremy had already heard about these departures. Alex Allan, the principal private secretary, was due to become high commissioner to Australia and Moira Wallace, the Treasury private secretary, was taking over as head of the Social Exclusion Unit. He took a deep breath. 'In principle, yes. But what job would I do?'

'You would be the "domestic supremo" – the senior private secretary on the domestic policy side – while John Holmes continues to cover foreign and Northern Ireland issues.'

'But who will be principal private secretary?'

'Robin Butler thought I might want to do it, which he was getting ready to resist since I'm a special adviser rather than a civil servant. But I don't – I'm happy being chief of staff. So John Holmes will take the title for now, in addition to looking after the foreign side of the office, though he's going to be busy covering both the Northern Irish ceasefire and the Hong Kong handover.'

Jeremy felt a twinge of disappointment at the news that he wasn't being considered for the top role, though it didn't surprise him that Robin Butler, the Cabinet Secretary, would be concerned about Jonathan taking it on since it involved a number of sensitive issues including liaising with the Opposition in the run-up to an election and with the Palace in the case of a hung Parliament. 'Well, I'm interested in doing the domestic policy job,' he said.

'Great,' Jonathan said. 'Though the process might be a little tricky because the Chancellor has put forward his own candidate – Martin Donnelly. But my brother Charles, who used to work for Mrs Thatcher, has warned me not to take the Treasury's person. And several people have recommended you. So I'll see what I can do.'

'I know I could do the job,' Jeremy told me that evening after recounting this conversation, 'though we shouldn't kid ourselves that it will be easy – there's a lot of work to be done to get a grip on the Prime Minister's domestic policy agenda. I've also told Terry that I would like to get it agreed that I will be principal private secretary when John Holmes moves on.'

'That would be good,' I said.

'But many of these suggestions come to nothing so we shouldn't get too excited.'

'Of course.'

Jeremy grinned. 'But if I get the job, I'll be working for a prime minister determined to reform the public sector – and for one who has a big enough majority to make things happen.'

I returned his smile. 'But you're not going to get too excited, are you?'

Jeremy continued leading the Treasury's fight against financial crime for several more weeks after that conversation, while at home, more reluctantly, he helped strip the internal wooden doors of our new house. It was early October before Jonathan rang again, this time to ask Jeremy to come in to meet the Prime Minister.

'He's in here,' Jonathan said when Jeremy arrived in Downing Street on Thursday 9 October. He was holding open the door to the left of the stone hallway at the back of Number 10.

Jeremy paused, conscious he was about to meet the person everyone expected to transform the country. Then he walked in to find Tony Blair leaning back in his chair peeling an orange. The Prime Minister stood up to shake Jeremy's hand before sitting back down to quiz him on what he thought of the housing market in south

Clapham, my new job at McKinsey, whether that was where William Hague had worked and where Jeremy's parents lived.

'We'll be in touch,' Blair said, giving Jeremy a broad smile, and less than half an hour after it began, the interview was over.

'That was it?' I asked when Jeremy described this to me.

'Yes,' Jeremy said. 'I think he already knows who he wants. And I gather that the Chancellor is still pushing for Martin because he's believed to be pro-European.'

Two days later, while Jeremy was having lunch with one of his City contacts in Rules, trying to pick up a new bit of City insight on financial crime, his phone rang. Derry Irvine – Tony Blair's old pupil master and mentor, who was by then the Lord Chancellor – wanted to see him in the House of Lords.

Jeremy abandoned lunch, his guest, and his second glass of wine to arrive hot and flustered in Derry's office. This second interview was far tougher – a 45-minute grilling that covered everything from his class of degree to his views on how the policy and administrative roles of the Cabinet Secretary should be split. But again, Jeremy came home with no sense of whether it had gone well and when he might hear any news.

On Monday 20 October, while he was still waiting for a smoke signal from Number 10, Jeremy joined the Chancellor when he went to open the new trading system at the London Stock Exchange – a rare moment when his job took him back into ministerial orbit. The timing wasn't ideal since the Friday before, Charlie Whelan, the Chancellor's pugnacious spokesman, had briefed that Britain was unlikely to join EMU before the next election. In the kerfuffle that followed, it emerged that Charlie had done this while standing outside the Red Lion pub on Whitehall, and without any clear agreement from Number 10.

But whatever the background to the story, it left the Chancellor opening the new trading system while the market turned the boards behind him into a sea of red. Combined with a row over Bernie Ecclestone, the head of Formula 1 motor racing, from whom Labour had accepted a cash donation before doing an impressive U-turn to exempt the sport from a ban on tobacco advertising, it also marked the first difficult period for New Labour, though the party still retained much of its post-election glow.

On 6 November 1997 Jonathan Powell called Jeremy again. 'I'm sorry we've taken so long – it's been a busy time. But one of the consequences of the last few days is that it has convinced Tony that he needs you in Number 10.'

Jeremy breathed out, only at that moment accepting how disappointed he would have been if the Prime Minister hadn't chosen him. 'Great,' he said, keeping his voice measured, 'though I do have one condition. I've heard that Moira hasn't been allowed to join the Prime Minister's bilaterals with the Chancellor despite being the Treasury private secretary. For me to do the job effectively it's essential that I join those.'

'Okay. I'll confirm that with Tony.'

On 17 November 1997 Jeremy started work in Number 10. The week leading up to this had been difficult after Jeremy discovered that he'd been given a desk in the outer private office rather than in the one Jonathan shared with John Holmes on the right-hand side of the Cabinet Room. Where his desk was located might seem like a trivial issue, he'd told me, but he knew he'd struggle to be effective if he was in a different room. Luckily, Robin Butler had backed him up – after all, Jeremy was going to be the most senior member of the home Civil Service in Number 10. And in the end, it was resolved happily enough, with Jonathan keeping his slot with his back towards the double doors into the Cabinet Room and a new desk being shoved in for Jeremy alongside John Holmes on the opposite side of the room.

Jeremy found adjusting to the role itself easier because, although the scope was far broader, it was similar to the one he'd played for Norman Lamont and Ken Clarke. Each day he read through the papers coming in from departments on domestic policy issues, provided advice to the Prime Minister on them and attended the meetings where they were discussed. Following his request to Jonathan Powell, he also joined the Prime Minister's weekly bilaterals with the Chancellor. The two leaders were close, Jeremy told me and they respected each other's judgement. But when they fell out, the rows were fierce, and Jeremy and Ed Balls, the Chancellor's special adviser, were often asked to leave the room.

As Jeremy had suspected, attending these bilaterals was essential because they were the moments when the two sides of New Labour came together and agreed – or disagreed – on the way forward. It also meant that Jeremy could minute the things they discussed. This innovation was greeted with particular enthusiasm by the Treasury because, unlike Norman Lamont or Ken Clarke, Gordon Brown did much of his policy thinking with his two special advisers, Ed Balls and Ed Miliband, his press secretary Charlie Whelan and the paymaster general, Geoffrey Robinson, in Geoffrey's suite at the Grosvenor House Hotel.

After a few weeks, Jeremy suggested to Ed that they could make the bilaterals even more effective if they met beforehand to identify the major political judgements required.

'Sure,' Ed said. 'But not in Number 10.'

'Okay, but not in the Treasury. Have you tried Café Churchill?'

These pre-meetings, which David Miliband, the head of the Number 10 Policy Unit, and Tom Scholar, the Chancellor's principal private secretary, also joined, soon became a Tuesday morning institution. Jeremy had suggested Churchill's because of its location in the no-man's-land of Whitehall. It had little else to recommend it, but it worked because, while sipping the mediocre coffee – or eating the bacon sandwiches Ed ordered each time it was Jeremy's turn to pay – it gave them a place to talk. In fact, it was only when they needed to go through detailed numbers, for example in the run-up to the Budget, that they abandoned its Formica tables for the wooden grandeur of Ed's office in the Treasury.

Jeremy's relationship with Ed made it easier to resolve Treasury issues, like the scandal that exploded shortly after his arrival in Downing Street over Geoffrey Robinson's multi-million-pound trust fund in Guernsey. However, to make progress on domestic policy, he knew he also needed to get close to the Prime Minister's tight-knit and fiercely loyal group of political advisers in Downing Street. Each of these had a specific job, like Alastair Campbell's role as chief press secretary or Anji Hunter's as director of government relations. But they also spent a lot of time hanging out with the Prime Minister, chewing the fat during breaks in the working day. In part this was necessary downtime; but Tony Blair also found it valuable to mull over political strategy in an unstructured way. Later on this informal style of government became criticised, but back then, Jeremy saw no reason to try to change it, even if he could have done so, since the Prime Minister found these conversations useful and it allowed the rest of the office to get on with their work.

It took time for Jeremy to gain the trust of this inner circle, particularly after their early row with Robin Butler, which had led to Robin insisting on an order being laid in Privy Council before he would allow Alastair and Jonathan to 'direct' civil servants. In any case, Jeremy knew he would always be outside their group because he hadn't been with them during their dark days in opposition. But he started gaining their confidence once they realised that he understood their priorities, could weed out policy proposals that wouldn't work politically and was able to cajole Whitehall, and sometimes even the Treasury, into serving up acceptable alternatives.

'I used to wonder who you were when I saw you walking behind Norman Lamont,' Alastair said a few weeks after Jeremy joined Number 10. 'You reminded me of the guy who always appeared in the background of Gorbachev's press photos. Though he was big and dark-haired while you looked emaciated and about eighteen years old.'

Jeremy smiled – being included in Alastair's banter showed that he was being accepted. 'Ah yes – that was probably when you were working for Eddie Shah,' he retorted, Eddie being the somewhat thuggish proprietor of the *Today* newspaper with its motto 'propa truth, not propaganda'.

Alongside building these relationships, Jeremy was also becoming accustomed to Number 10's weekly rhythm. Each Sunday evening the Prime Minister wrote a note setting out the things that were on his mind, including reflections on what had been in the press, how to deliver New Labour's priorities, or the latest results from his pollster, Philip Gould. These streams of consciousness, which sometimes ran to ten or more pages, were written out in longhand before being transcribed by one of the garden room team posted at Chequers, the

Prime Minister's official country residence in Buckinghamshire, where Tony spent most of his weekends.

At 9 a.m. each Monday morning, Jeremy would join the Number 10 special advisers to go through this note with the Prime Minister, and to discuss any other topics that Jonathan Powell or anyone else wanted to raise. The first part of this meeting was usually spent on domestic policy because New Labour's first Budget was approaching and they needed to turn the plethora of policy documents that the party had drawn up in opposition into legislation, including signing up to the European Social Chapter and new policies on law and order. The discussions were brisk and business-like, and after each discussion, Jeremy would minute out the conclusions to Whitehall.

After this, the group turned to political issues, which usually meant pondering matters of party positioning – debates that, from Jeremy's perspective, went on interminably, not least because the conversation usually ended where it started. After all, the Prime Minister's view of how New Labour should present itself was unlikely to be changed by a Monday morning debate among fellow travellers – particularly when Gordon Brown, its other key architect, wasn't present.

When he became Cabinet Secretary in January 1998, Richard Wilson asked to attend these Monday morning office meetings. The Prime Minister agreed, but after the first few, decided this wasn't the right way to engage the Civil Service because it pulled the discussion into procedural issues. Therefore, they created a new meeting, the Dep Secs meeting at 9.45 a.m., which included Richard and the heads of the Cabinet Office secretariats. This second discussion, like the first, was crowded with people keen to talk to this new Prime Minister who'd just swept into power. And since Richard's bolder secretariat heads liked to take this opportunity to raise interesting or sensitive issues directly with Blair, the conversation could cover almost anything.

Monday mornings concluded with a bilateral between the Prime Minister and Richard to cover more sensitive personnel or intelligence issues – after which Jeremy would stumble out to face the tottering stack of papers in his in-tray. But while this jamboree of meetings often felt inefficient to Jeremy, who attended them all, it did mean that by lunchtime everyone knew what the Prime Minister's priorities were for the week ahead, and anyone in Whitehall waiting for a signal from Number 10 could get to work.

Jeremy was full of enthusiasm about his new job when we went to Sicily after Christmas that year, telling me about his determination to make progress on the Prime Minister's health, education and crime priorities. This all changed, however, in early 1998 after an article by Andrew Rawnsley in the *Observer* claimed that the Prime Minister thought Gordon Brown had 'psychological flaws'. Alastair Campbell was accused of being the 'close Blair ally' who'd said this – and later admitted he'd probably inspired it. But whoever the source was, the harm was done, with counter-briefing soon appearing in *The Times* describing Brown as the government's 'Chief Executive' to Tony Blair's 'Chairman'. Jeremy tried to stay out of the firing line, though this was made more difficult by another *Times* article in mid-February, which claimed that the Prime Minister had recruited him to gain more control over his Chancellor.

What was frustrating, Jeremy told me, was that the Rawnsley article completely changed the dynamic between Number 10 and the Treasury. After it came out, he and Ed Balls were often asked to leave the Prime Minister's bilaterals with the Chancellor. Ed also became reluctant to share papers with Jeremy, even the draft Budget documents, which made it almost impossible for the Prime Minister to provide input. Unless things got better, Jeremy couldn't see how the government would function, let alone how it would achieve all of Tony Blair's ambitions.

8

'Fix You':
Changing Number 10

January 1998–February 1999

For Tony Blair, the early months of 1998 were dominated by the immense effort required to negotiate the Good Friday Agreement in Northern Ireland. But for Jeremy and David Miliband, the big policy events of the first part of the year were always going to be the government's first Budget in March and the Comprehensive Spending Review in July, both of which would test the newly strained relationship between Number 10 and the Treasury.

In addition to preparing for these set-piece events, the Prime Minister also started asking Jeremy to help mediate ministerial disputes. One of these was the row over the much-anticipated welfare Green Paper being prepared by the minister for welfare reform, Frank Field. When the first draft of this had landed in Number 10 the previous autumn, Jeremy had gone through it with Sharon White, the welfare adviser in the Number 10 Policy Unit.

'I hope this hasn't gone anywhere near the Treasury,' he'd told her, flipping through the document. After examining the history of the welfare state as far back as the 1500s, the paper argued that welfare payments should be based on contributions to a social insurance scheme and shouldn't be means tested. This would, however, result in enormous costs, particularly if the government provided credits for those too poor to contribute or whose careers were interrupted, for example to care for children.

'I know,' Sharon had said, 'and I'm not an expert on the Elizabethan Poor Laws. So, if that section is going to stay in, we'll need to find a historian to help us.'

This storm had been building for a while – ever since the Prime Minister had appointed Frank and invited him to 'think the unthinkable'. The idea was that, while the Chancellor put in place a windfall tax on the privatised utilities and used the resulting £5 billion to fund the New Deal, a series of initiatives to get people back into work, Frank would help the Prime Minister think about radical ways of reshaping the welfare state, one of Tony Blair's key political objectives.

For a while, Frank's patch had seemed quiet. In part this was because everyone was focused on Frank's boss, Harriet Harman. Harriet had the job Frank wanted – Secretary of State for Social Security – although this came with its own challenges. Despite arriving in government wanting to reform childcare, Harriet had instead been told that her first task was to persuade Labour backbenchers to support the £300 million a year reduction in lone parent benefits that Labour had inherited from the Conservatives.

The Chancellor could, of course, have used some of his windfall taxes to help Harriet. But both he and the Prime Minister thought that backing down on the promise they'd made to implement the Conservative Party's cuts would signal weakness to the markets and voters. So, instead, Harriet was sent into battle, and despite widespread backbench unease, got the reduction agreed in mid-December 1997 with only forty-seven Labour MPs voting against it. It was a remarkable achievement, though it came at significant reputational cost – with one militant disabled rights group even daubing the gates of Downing Street with red paint. And later, of course, the Treasury would buy Harriet's hard-won cuts back out through the introduction of child tax credits.

Given all this, it wasn't until Frank's draft text was circulated in the autumn of 1997 that it became clear how radical his thinking was. Jeremy was used to policy disagreements between government departments. But if you added in the fact that Gordon Brown and Frank didn't get on, and that the Chancellor was in favour of means testing rather than social insurance and wanted to lead on welfare reform himself, it was clear disaster loomed. And little of this was being moderated by Harriet Harman given her preoccupation with lone parent benefits and her own corrosive working relationship with Frank.

'The best way to sort this out is to set up a Cabinet committee,' Richard Wilson told the Prime Minister when they discussed the issue during one of their bilaterals.

'Okay,' the Prime Minister said – much to Jeremy's surprise, given Tony Blair's well-known dislike of formal committees – 'let's give it a go.'

Richard was smiling when he left, but after the door closed, Tony turned to Jeremy. 'Anything is worth trying,' he said, 'but I doubt Richard's committee will work. I need you to sort this out.'

'Okay,' Jeremy said because, of course, he would try to do so. But he felt queasy at the prospect since there seemed little chance of either Frank Field or Gordon Brown changing their minds.

Over the following weeks, therefore, while Harriet and Frank bickered through sessions of Richard's Cabinet Committee on Welfare Reform, and Gordon Brown glowered, Jeremy and Sharon spent hours in other meetings listening to Frank. When Frank paused, Sharon shared her examination of his thinking with gentle charm and Jeremy – while assuring Frank that the Prime Minister was broadly sympathetic to his thinking – suggested small amendments to his text and emphasised the need to bring Harman and the Chancellor along. Alastair Campbell, who joined some of these discussions, took a more direct approach – telling Frank what needed to change, and going to see Harriet to give her equally blunt feedback.

Through this process, which Jeremy and Sharon debated daily back in the office with David Miliband, Ed Balls and Ed Miliband, the paper morphed from describing specific policies to outlining a set of welfare principles that simultaneously meant everything and nothing. When the final version of *New Ambitions For Our Country: A New Contract for Britain* was published on 26 March 1998, Frank Field described it as 'a Third Way: not an end of the welfare state or a defence of the status quo, but a welfare state to meet modern needs'. Iain Duncan Smith, the shadow social security secretary, however, described it as 'vacuous' – which was a pity, Jeremy observed to Sharon, after they'd worked so hard to develop those welfare principles.

Jeremy's negotiations with the Treasury on the 1998 Budget that March were more forthright than those with Frank Field, and less civil.

When Ed Balls at last shared the papers, Jeremy discovered that the main policy being proposed was a working families tax credit which, with no expense spared, would guarantee a basic income of £180 a week for families where at least one person worked full time. After Harriet Harman's lone parent trauma and Frank Field's Green Paper, the Chancellor was about to put in place the first plank of his own welfare programme that would be based on encouraging paid work and extending means-tested benefits.

Despite its cost, Jeremy knew he had little chance of influencing the Chancellor's tax credit. He was, however, able to make some changes to the spending side of the Budget. Here, although the government remained committed to working for two years within the ceilings inherited from the Conservatives, he pushed for more money to be allocated to the Prime Minister's education and health priorities. In addition, the Treasury decided to take the annual real-terms increase in road fuel duty up to 6 per cent – twice the size of Norman Lamont's original increase. This, of course, later turned out to be a mistake.

Overall, it had been a hectic start to the year, though it helped that I was also working long hours in my new job at McKinsey. Jeremy and I often shared a cab home in the evenings, having dinner together before he settled down to write up minutes of meetings or read documents while I reviewed PowerPoint decks. We were also still finding time to get away, escaping for a week to Greece after the Budget before coming home to paint our living room beige with dark blue skirting boards.

Paintbrushes were also being primed in Number 10 after the Prime Minister decided to move out of the small room off the hall where he'd interviewed Jeremy. He wanted his office to be on the first floor, he told Jeremy and Jonathan Powell, which was where Margaret Thatcher's study had been.

Jeremy frowned at this. He'd been surprised coming into Downing Street how inefficient it was compared to the Treasury. Memos were still being typed out in triplicate, people worked in silos and everything was done on paper to avoid the prehistoric IT system that was unable to communicate with the rest of Whitehall. He was itching to apply some of our thinking from the Fundamental Expenditure Review, but since John Holmes was the principal private secretary, and, therefore, had responsibility for such matters, and Jonathan chaired the Number 10 staff meetings, he'd been holding back to avoid causing offence.

This inefficiency was made worse by the location of the Prime Minister's office. Because Tony Blair's office was on the opposite side of the Cabinet Room from Jeremy, John and Jonathan, they often didn't know who he was meeting and they found it difficult to pop in to get his informal view on issues. If he moved into the admittedly beautiful White Room on the first floor, with its large sash windows and ornate plasterwork ceiling, the situation would be even worse because then they wouldn't even be on the same floor.

Over the following days, Jeremy enlisted Jonathan's help in convincing the Prime Minister that, despite the allure of the White Room, their own office on the right-hand side of the Cabinet Room had its own, more subtle, charms, and was far more practical. After this was agreed – partly, Jeremy suspected, because Blair became sick of the argument – Jeremy, Jonathan and John shuffled one room further over to the right and David Miliband closed the circle by grabbing the Prime Minister's old office off the hall.

This last move pleased Jeremy since by then he was spending hours working with David on the Comprehensive Spending Review ahead of its publication in July. This analysis, which would set out the government's three-year spending plans from 1999 to 2002, was the first opportunity for New Labour to loosen the reins because it extended beyond the Conservatives' two-year spending ceiling. Jeremy initially thought this would make the negotiations between Number 10 and the Treasury easier, but it soon became clear that having more money to allocate was in fact making them harder because there was more to fight over.

Where Number 10 and the Treasury were aligned, however, was in their determination to ensure the new money wasn't frittered away. To prevent this, the Treasury was working on a new performance framework for departments – or at least that's what Jeremy thought until Terry Burns called him on 1 July 1998, two weeks before the review was finalised. The Chancellor had decided to scrap the performance framework, Terry said, and to replace it with a new system of Public Service Agreements (PSAs) more closely linked to the government's pledges. While it was hard to object to this, Jeremy couldn't help being alarmed at such a last-minute change in direction. He was, however, reassured to hear that Suma Chakrabarti, his old friend from Washington, was developing the new PSAs, with the results due to be published that autumn.

While Suma began work, Jeremy focused on a more immediate issue – trying to settle the 1998 Strategic Defence Review, which was due to form part of the Comprehensive Spending Review. The Prime Minister had asked Jeremy to spend time on this because he was convinced that there was scope to reduce the Ministry of Defence's budget without undermining the UK's defence capabilities – a view Jeremy shared based on what he'd seen during Norman Lamont's spending review negotiations in 1990. In particular, Jeremy had been struck then by how much duplication there was across the army, navy and air force – if the forces worked more closely together, they would surely be more efficient and possibly more effective. After a tense series of meetings, this debate stimulated the creation of a new Joint Rapid Reaction Force, staffed from all three services. The Royal Navy and Royal Air Force also agreed to merge their Sea Harrier and Harrier GR7 aircraft fleets, both of which would operate from the UK's three small aircraft carriers.

These aircraft carriers then became the subject of a second debate since the defence secretary was keen to replace them with two new carriers, which would cost £3 billion and come into service in 2012 and 2014. Jeremy questioned this decision, given its huge price tag, but the department insisted that they still needed carriers to provide air cover for distant battles like the Falklands War. And the huge new carriers, each similar in length to the Palace of Westminster and taller than Nelson's Column, would be a significant upgrade they argued, since they would have far greater range and more flexibility in what they could carry.

* * *

Although this work, the first of Jeremy's many reviews of the Ministry of Defence's budget, was interesting, the topic he was most excited about that autumn was the introduction of the national minimum wage. This was something that had been official Labour Party policy since 1985, and included in their 1992 manifesto, but had been seen for years by many economists, and most on the political right, as a mad, job-destroying intervention. However, by this time the principle of a minimum wage was broadly accepted – including by Jeremy, who, having been reassured by the detailed analysis of its potential impact on the labour market, also saw it as a moral imperative.

The final hurdle before the wage could be announced was to decide on its level. To consider this – and hopefully to build consensus across the Labour Party – a Low Pay Commission, composed of three employer representatives, three labour representatives and three independents, had been set up after the election. Little of the Commission's thinking had emerged during Jeremy's first months in Number 10, but just before Easter 1998, Ed Balls brought it up during one of their meetings in Café Churchill.

'We believe the Commission is likely to recommend between £3.50 and £3.70 an hour,' Ed told Jeremy, 'which we believe is far too high. At that level the Chancellor thinks it would price younger workers out of jobs, undermining the New Deal.'

Jeremy nodded. The Chancellor's New Deal, which was using a range of measures including training, voluntary work and subsidised employment to reduce unemployment, was by that time well underway. He was also conscious that the Prime Minister shared the Chancellor's cautiousness, partly because the CBI was also nervous. But despite all this, it would still be difficult for Number 10 to overrule the Low Pay Commission, particularly since Margaret Beckett, the Secretary of State for Trade and Industry, had already made it clear she would support its conclusions.

The issue came to a head in a meeting between the Prime Minister, the Chancellor and Beckett a few weeks later. This was always going to be a difficult discussion, but it became explosive after the Chancellor declared that there should be a different minimum wage – a 'development rate' – for 18- to 25-year-olds. Beckett, who was outraged at being bounced into such a major policy change, initially claimed this would be indefensible, but in the end agreed that it might work if it was restricted to those under twenty-three.

This idea was then suggested to the Low Pay Commission, which started talking about setting the development rate at £3.20 alongside a minimum wage of £3.60 per hour. With Margaret Beckett again determined to accept the Commission's recommendation, and the Chancellor still convinced that the development rate was too high, Jeremy was left trying to broker a final agreement with Margaret calling us at home late in the evenings to continue the debate. The situation wasn't helped by the conflicting views held by the Number 10 special advisers with some, like Geoffrey Norris, being pro-business while others, like John Cruddas, being pro-unions – and by a parallel row between the Chancellor and Margaret Beckett over the part-privatisation of the Post Office, which Jeremy was also trying to resolve.

It took many hours of negotiation before they found a compromise, which was to set the development rate at £3.00 per hour. Jeremy later told me he doubted this final battle over 20p per hour had made much difference to youth unemployment but the important thing was that settling the row allowed the government to make its historic announcement on 18 June, introducing a wage floor that has stayed in place ever since.

When Tony Blair conducted his first reshuffle a few weeks later on 27 July 1998, Harriet Harman left the government, partly because of her public rows with Frank Field and partly because the Chancellor held her responsible for leaking details of his working families tax credit ahead of the Budget. In the same reshuffle Field resigned, perhaps sensing his Green Paper was going to be difficult to turn into practical policies. Tony Blair tried to persuade Frank to stay in government and apply his radical thinking to the fight against fraud, but Frank had already decided he would have more influence as a backbencher.

Among other moves, Peter Mandelson, one of the original architects of Blair's New Labour, became Secretary of State for Trade and Industry, Stephen Byers, another Blairite, became Chief Secretary to the Treasury and Nick Brown, a Gordon Brown loyalist, was demoted from Chief Whip to minister of agriculture, fisheries and food. It was an aggressive shoring up of the Prime Minister's position after the difficulties of the first part of the year – but it was only a matter of time, Jeremy told me while we packed our bags for our summer holiday on the west coast of the US, before Gordon took revenge.

Despite this prediction, there was no obvious further souring of relations with the Treasury after Jeremy returned that autumn. However, this didn't mean that the tension had gone away – as the tussle over the creation of the Performance and Innovation Unit (PIU) demonstrated.

Within Number 10, Jeremy had strongly supported the creation of the PIU since it would strengthen Number 10's ability to think about longer-term and cross-departmental issues, a Whitehall weakness that had frustrated him ever since we'd identified it during the Fundamental Expenditure Review. However, while most people agreed, the Chancellor wanted the new unit to be in the Treasury while the Prime Minister wanted it in the Cabinet Office so it wouldn't get caught up in the spending discussions. After an extended sparring match, they agreed a messy compromise – the unit would have offices in the Treasury, but it would report to the Cabinet Office and its steering board would consist of Ed Balls, Ed Miliband, David Miliband and Jeremy. Jeremy also agreed with the Prime Minister that, given his experience of drafting the PSAs, which had by then been published, Suma Chakrabarti should be the unit's first head – something Suma agreed to do despite receiving a visit from Ed Balls, who berated him for his disloyalty in 'switching sides' to go to work for the Prime Minister.

Suma was joined in the PIU by Jonathan Portes, Norman Lamont's old speechwriter, and it was Jonathan who led one of its first projects, which examined the economic impact of migration and concluded, in contrast to public perception, that there was little evidence of British workers being harmed by it. Jeremy later told me that, of all the PIU's early studies, this was the one that most clearly demonstrated the value of having a unit like this in the centre of government that could apply rigorous economic thinking to controversial policy issues.

When the migration report was finished, Suma sent it to the Prime Minister.

'This is excellent: it should be published,' the note on it said when it emerged from Tony Blair's red box the following morning.

David Miliband was alarmed at this – so much so that he put another memo in the Prime Minister's box the following night saying that, while he also agreed with the economic case, the politics were 'difficult'.

'I still think we should publish it,' the reply said the next morning.

Migration: an Economic and Social Analysis was released in September 2000 and it led to a shift in the government's attitude towards migration, including informing the later decision to allow migrants from the new EU member states immediate access to the UK's labour market. However, the Labour government and the ones that followed it remained reluctant to communicate the benefits of immigration to the public, which was one reason, Jeremy believed, why resentment about Britain's membership of the European Union continued to grow over the following years.

Jeremy worked up until Christmas Eve 1998 dealing with a series of issues including Peter Mandelson and Geoffrey Robinson's decisions to resign after a loan between them erupted into a scandal. Back home after Christmas, Jeremy's brother Simon came to admire our newly decorated house with his wife, Ailie, and our three young nieces.

It was, at last, time to relax. After lunch and a few glasses of wine, Jeremy leaned towards the girls. 'We have a monster in our basement,' he said in a low voice.

'Really?'

'Yes. His name is Eric Cantona,' Jeremy said, Eric being Jeremy's longstanding footballing hero. 'And the only way to scare him away is to stand outside his door and shout, "Ooh, Ahh, Cantona".'

The girls tripped along behind Jeremy to the bottom of our stairs.

'Ooh, Ahh, Cantona,' they said, echoing the familiar football ground chant.

Jeremy placed his ear against the basement door. 'I'm not sure he's gone.'

Three pairs of eyes watched Jeremy.

'I'm going down to check,' Jeremy said, before disappearing into the basement.

The girls waited, hopping from foot to foot. There was a yell. The girls screamed, the door burst open and Jeremy reappeared, spitting out tinned anchovies, to howls from the girls and laughter from Simon, Ailie and me.

This, I thought, was potentially our future, and it looked like it would be fun.

9

'When the Levee Breaks': Getting a grip and losing control

February 1999–September 2000

Jeremy became Tony Blair's principal private secretary at the start of February 1999 after John Holmes left Number 10 to become Britain's ambassador to Portugal. This made him the most senior civil servant in Number 10, reporting to Jonathan Powell who continued as chief of staff.

Although this change was in some ways invisible – Jeremy kept the same desk and still attended many of the same meetings – his elevation meant that he began managing both the foreign and domestic private secretaries and became the UK's G7/8 'sherpa' – the official responsible for negotiating agreements in advance of the meetings between the heads of government of the world's most advanced economies. These changes gave Jeremy exposure to some of the international issues he'd enjoyed dealing with at the IMF. However, although he joined a few of the Prime Minister's foreign trips to add an economic perspective and see how that side of the office was performing, Jeremy generally continued to leave foreign issues to the experts.

As principal private secretary, Jeremy was expected to sit behind the Prime Minister during Cabinet and occasionally passed him notes – though Tony Blair's Cabinets rarely lasted long enough for anything unexpected to happen. But the change in his role that he enjoyed most was the serene hour he spent each Wednesday evening sipping tea with Robin Janvrin, the Queen's principal private secretary, in Buckingham Palace. They spent that time mulling over the issues of the day including discussing some of Robin's ideas for how the Palace should change to reflect the lessons it had learnt from its handling of Princess Diana's death.

Jeremy brought in Owen Barder from the Treasury to cover his old economic brief in Number 10 but still remained closely involved in major Treasury events like the March 1999 Budget. This introduced a new 10 per cent starting rate of income tax and cut the basic rate from 23 to 22 per cent – dramatic moves for a Labour government – alongside abolishing the married couples' allowance and replacing it with a guaranteed minimum income for working families and a children's tax credit.

The challenge, however, was that with such a broad brief, it was impossible for Jeremy to go through everything in the level of detail that he had managed in his previous roles. This was probably why he failed to spot in advance the consequences of Tony Blair's pledge in his Beveridge Lecture on 18 March to end child poverty. While Jeremy admired this aspiration, he knew it would be extremely difficult to achieve, not least because the accepted definition of child poverty – whether the child lived in a household with substantially below the UK's median household income – was a moving target. He also worried that chasing this metric would mean not doing things like improving nursery education or recruiting more health visitors, which might be more effective in improving children's life chances.

But there was little opportunity to unpick any of this once ending child poverty, together with helping pensioners, had become the third pillar of New Labour's welfare strategy – alongside encouraging paid work and extending means-tested benefits. It also meant that, whenever Gordon Brown came forward with another measure to help children, like increasing child tax credits, Ed Balls would smile at Jeremy before turning to the Prime Minister and reminding him of his pledge.

While being principal private secretary meant that Jeremy was more stretched, it also meant he could start sorting out Number 10. His first step was to set up a management board made up of the eight or so heads of the Downing Street units, which he used to prioritise the issues. He then – copying an idea that I'd shared with him from McKinsey – created part-time project teams to address each problem, including a Happy People Working Group to improve internal communications and staff events.

The most pressing challenge was space. For many years Downing Street had contained fifty or so staff, but by early 1999, after more people had been brought in to work on media management, policy creation and monitoring functions, there were 177 officials plus 26 special advisers. One team was, therefore, sent to search for unused crannies. They worked their way up the building, finding each floor full of desks for the private secretaries, the press office, the garden room staff and the Policy Unit. In some places they found a few new spaces, but while this helped, space was still tight because Downing Street had been created from a street of residential townhouses and had never been designed to be the centre of the British government. The team, therefore, also proposed some more radical solutions, including moving Number 10 into the QEII Centre near Westminster Abbey to create something akin to the Chancellery in Berlin. This was soon dismissed by the Prime Minister, who liked Downing Street's historic feel, but Tony Blair said he was willing to consider another idea, which was to expand laterally into the Cabinet Office next door.

This is why, a few days later, Jeremy found himself taking Cherie Blair, and more oddly, the Prime Minister's father, on a tour of the finer parts of the Cabinet Office estate. Their first stop was Conference Room A, a grand chamber that still contained George III's red velvet throne and which could, Cherie thought, be turned into an office for the Prime Minister. The Cabinet Secretary's beautiful wood-panelled suite, which they visited next, would then be perfect for the senior private secretaries.

With remarkable timing, Richard Wilson chose that moment to return from a meeting, pausing in his office doorway to peer at Jeremy and his guests.

'We were just taking a look at the historic Cabinet rooms,' Jeremy said, hoping Richard would believe this barely plausible excuse. Without waiting for Richard's reply, and ignoring Cherie, who was winking at him, he then hurried his group back out.

To Jeremy's relief, the idea of lateral expansion was dropped soon after this – mainly because the Cabinet Office was only connected to Downing Street by a single door, a physical limitation that would have been difficult and expensive to change.

'And the truth is, I'm not in any hurry to remove the constraints on the growth of Number 10,' Jeremy told me. 'I believe we're missing capabilities, but I don't think we should become a rival bureaucracy to the Cabinet Office or a sprawling party-political machine.'

In June 1999, after celebrating the glorious moment when Ole Gunnar Solskjaer tucked a ball into the top corner of the net, clinching for Manchester United not only the European Cup but the fabled treble, since they had already won the Premier League and the FA Cup, Jeremy flew out to Cologne for his first G8 leaders' summit. This was held in the sleek steel and glass Museum Ludwig in Cologne, squeezed between the cathedral, the railway station and the Rhine.

The UK was often active in preparing initiatives for these meetings, like the one Jeremy had been negotiating this time on raising global banking standards and increasing transparency. This was agreed at the summit, together with the creation of a Financial Stability Forum to improve the supervision of financial institutions. This forum would, Jeremy told me, address the issues revealed by the 1997 Asian crisis, which had resulted in a series of currency devaluations across the region. The only issue, of course, was whether the next financial crisis would be the same or entirely different.

The summit itself was a mixture of working sessions, lavish meals, and musical and dramatic entertainments. During one of the breaks, Jeremy joined Tony Blair on his hotel balcony overlooking Cologne Cathedral where he was sitting in the sun, chewing over the UK's Jubilee 2000 proposals for reducing third world debt with Bono and Bob Geldof.

'We are pushing as hard as we can, but with so many countries with different agendas, it's like climbing Everest,' the Prime Minister said when Bono and Bob's aspirations began to spiral out of control.

'When you get to Everest,' Bono retorted, 'you don't just look at it, you fucking climb it.'

After the leaders finished negotiating and started tucking into more fine food and wine, the sherpas worked on the G7 Statement, which needed to be issued to the press at the end of the meeting. This celebrated the launch of EMU, which had gone ahead without Britain after the UK had used Norman Lamont's opt-out, welcomed the report on strengthening the international financial system and – after Bono's push – supported faster debt reduction for the poorest countries. And even though finalising the text required Jeremy and the other sherpas to work late into the night, he still came back enthusing about the whole event like someone who'd been on a bizarre but interesting holiday, telling me that he'd found it far less gruelling than the Maastricht Treaty negotiations.

Our real summer vacation that year in Slovenia was a more subdued affair. We walked around Lake Bled, gazing at the church perched on the island in the middle – which surely created logistical issues for its congregation – while discussing our failure to conceive after a year of trying. I feared we never would, though Jeremy tried to reassure me. 'Don't worry, Pearl,' he kept saying – Pearl being by then his pet name for me – 'it's going to be okay.'

Jeremy attempted to distract me from our worries with tales of how he'd tried to keep John Prescott busy after the Deputy Prime Minister had turned up in Number 10 to mind the shop after the Prime Minister went on holiday. This summer residency was always difficult since there was usually little going on in the first weeks of August – at least not much for someone who wanted to show they were running the country. It had, though, provided some entertainment, particularly on the day of the first solar eclipse visible in northern Europe for over seventy years. Shortly before this great event, someone in Number 10 – Jeremy insisted it wasn't him – had sent out an email advising the office that, due to high winds, the eclipse had been brought forward by an hour. Three people took this seriously and turned up early in the garden, much to the amusement of those waiting at the windows.

Jeremy's optimism about our ability to conceive was to prove mistaken. Back in London I was walking down Oxford Street after a work meeting on a damp September afternoon when my mobile rang. The tests he had done, Jeremy told me, had shown we could never have children. I stopped outside Hamleys toy shop to digest this news, staring through my tears at the melting form of a huge teddy bear. That night we shared a cab home and Jeremy said I could leave if I wanted to. Why would I want to stay if we couldn't have children?

'Don't be ridiculous,' I said. 'We'll find a way or accept this is our future. But I'm going to ring the doctor tomorrow.'

'It's pointless.'

'Maybe – but I'm still going to do it.'

The following morning, I rang the Lister Hospital. The diagnosis was clear, the clinic told me, but they had a new form of IVF that might still work. It would be expensive, and our odds weren't great, but there was still hope.

When I discussed this with Jeremy, two things became clear. We couldn't afford the thousands of pounds that IVF would cost. But we also couldn't afford not to try, given our shared desire to start a family. So we signed up for the treatment and began counting down the days to our first attempt in December.

We were distracted from our personal troubles that autumn by our trip with Tony and Cherie Blair to visit the Queen at Balmoral Castle in Scotland. Accompanying the Prime Minister on this annual jaunt was another traditional role for the principal private secretary. For me, though, it meant days of wardrobe panic as I equipped myself with outfits suitable for watching caber tossing at the Braemar Games, attending a royal barbecue of haggis-stuffed pheasants in a bothy on the Balmoral estate, and joining a service in Crathie Kirk on Sunday morning. It meant packing a ridiculously large bag for a single weekend, but that didn't matter because we were sped up to Balmoral from Edinburgh in the Prime Minister's convoy, complete with motorcycle outriders.

After we returned from Scotland, Jeremy became absorbed in the preparations for the November 1999 pre-Budget report. This included many worthy measures but became notorious for only one – the decision to increase the basic state pension in line with inflation. With inflation running at 1.1 per cent, the lowest rate for over thirty years, this meant a rise of only 75p a week.

'Never annoy the pensioners,' Jeremy told me after several days of ever more hysterical outcry. 'Even when their average income has gone from being 30 per cent lower than that of working-age people to being higher and we've given them free TV licences. I'm sure we'll have to do something to gain their forgiveness, but the Prime Minister and Chancellor aren't ready to cave in yet.'

I nodded, but was increasingly focused by then on our impending IVF cycle. It had already become clear that the burden of this process wouldn't be equally shared. For IVF to work it is the woman who needs to take drugs to force her body into a temporary menopause, and then take more to grow follicles, each of which might produce an egg. Jeremy came to the hospital appointments when he had to, or when I insisted that he should, but didn't engage with the medical details and gave the doctor a startled look when he suggested Jeremy might help me administer the injections.

'Do you mind, Pearl?' he asked. 'I can't do that.'

'No,' I said – after all, I knew the man I'd married. 'So long as you're there when I need you.'

In early December the follicles were harvested – yes, that was the word they used – under general anaesthetic.

I came around to find a nurse smiling down at me. 'We collected seventeen eggs,' she said, 'that's excellent. You are so young for this, almost a baby yourself.'

I might have been young, at twenty-nine, but I was also doubled up in so much pain that they gave me morphine, which dropped my blood pressure, low to start with, to the point where I could no longer sit up. It was another day before Jeremy could take me home.

The eggs were fertilised and watched, and three days later the best ones were selected.

'The best ones how?' Jeremy asked when we went back in.

'The ones that have divided,' the nurse said, 'and those that look most regular.'

Two eggs were transferred back, which was a relatively straightfor-ward process, and we waited until my period began three weeks later, a discovery I made on a gloomy day in King's Cross station. I rang Jeremy in tears and dragged myself through several more hours of work meetings trying not to think about the two babies that would never be born. Because they weren't babies, I told myself – only clusters of cells too small to see with the naked eye that might have become our children.

We spent the last night of the millennium with our friends Zoë and Peter, who were also trying to conceive, drinking too much, dancing and wondering if the world would fall apart when the computers tried to change the first digit of the year. The following day, however, dawned sunny and intact so we dragged ourselves out of bed to take my brother, sister-in-law and their young baby around the newly opened Millennium Dome in Greenwich, trying to smile at their complaints about the burdens of parenthood. We would try again at IVF, we'd decided, having surely been unlucky. The question we avoided discussing, though, was how many times we could afford to repeat the process – both financially and physically – and how it would affect us if we failed.

In that first month of the new year, the UK experienced a terrible outbreak of flu, which, when combined with a shortage of beds and staff, meant the papers were full of stories of people waiting for hours to see a doctor or being treated on trolleys in hospital corridors. It was the first time the Prime Minister had faced a crisis on one of his manifesto priorities. This may be why, after two weeks of outcry, he made a bold pledge – to increase the UK's health spending as a percentage of GDP to the EU average by 2006.

'It's an aspiration,' the Treasury briefed while ringing Number 10 to demand to know what was going on.

'It's a commitment,' the Number 10 press office briefed back after a frantic hour spent tracking down the missing page from the transcript of the Prime Minister's interview with David Frost.

It was also a substantial one since moving to the EU average meant increasing spending on the NHS from 6.7 per cent of GDP to 8 per cent at a cost of around £12 billion through to 2006. But though Gordon Brown was reportedly furious, he didn't want to be seen opposing investment in health, so Tony Blair got away with his bounce.

This prime ministerial pledge kick-started a health arms race with the Chancellor, a struggle to become the NHS's saviour that would be fought for several years. Gordon Brown took the next step a couple of months later in his March Budget when he announced a £2 billion increase in NHS spending for the year about to start and a whopping 6.1 per cent per annum increase in real terms in each of the next four years. The day afterwards, the Prime Minister upped the stakes again when he made an unusual statement to the House of Commons in which he said that he would personally develop a ten-year plan for the NHS.

Overall the rest of the March 2000 Budget, which Jeremy worked on with Ed Balls, was a classic New Labour package, designed to satisfy all members of their grand coalition. It included a winter fuel payment for pensioners, calming their fury at the nugatory increase in their pensions, generous reforms to Capital Gains Tax to help entrepreneurs and a rise in tax credits, all balanced by a toughening up of conditionality for out-of-work lone parents and an increase in stamp duty on homes worth more than £250,000.

With the fiscal position stronger than expected and the Budget forecast to be in surplus by £12 billion, the Chancellor also announced that government spending would grow by 2.5 per cent per annum in real terms, in line with the assumed trend rate of growth of the economy through to 2003/4. In other words, Gordon Brown was proposing to 'invest' all the benefits of economic expansion in public services – though much of this was current spending rather than any conventional definition of investment. It was a huge commitment to public services, but – as Jeremy pointed out to me – also meant the country would be banking little during this period of economic sunshine in case the weather deteriorated.

Our home life also continued to be dominated by health issues in the first few months of the new millennium. In early February we tried using the spare embryos that we had frozen after our December IVF cycle. This made the process easier because there was no need to grow, harvest or fertilise new eggs. Instead, as the clinic explained, it was simply a matter of waiting for my cycle to reach the right stage, thawing the embryos and putting them back.

Except that's not what happened.

On the day of the transfer, I was sitting in my office at McKinsey, looking out at the statue of Anteros at Piccadilly Circus, when the phone rang.

'We thawed the embryos,' the nurse said.

'Great,' I said, my face flushing.

'But I'm afraid they've all perished.'

'Perished,' I said. Another strange word. More aggressive than 'died' and less human. To me, they'd died. There was no other word for it.

In March 2000 we tried again, and again we failed. After that I cried so much, I threw up. In the days afterwards, I felt numb, walking around under a permanent, dark cloud. Jeremy tried to reach me, cutting through my moods with humour, his way of coping. But it was never long before the gloom returned.

Jeremy found it easier than I did to distract himself from our personal troubles at work. Having realised in his early foreign trips with the Prime Minister that the UK's international discussions were almost exclusively confined to diplomatic or defence issues, his latest enthusiasm was trying to develop better links on domestic policy with like-minded EU leaders. Tony Blair and Jonathan Powell both supported this, especially after Gerhard Schröder was elected Chancellor in Germany and began talking about building an international network of 'third way' thinking modelled on New Labour's ideology. Jeremy and David Miliband made several visits to France and Germany to discuss this, and later went to Spain where José María Aznar's right-wing government wanted to discuss the new economic challenges and how to build a 'knowledge-based economy', in the jargon of the day.

The high point of this economic diplomacy was the Lisbon EU leaders' summit in March 2000, which Jeremy worked on with Maria João Rodrigues, the Portuguese Prime Minister's sherpa. Ahead of the meeting, they convened groups of sherpas to discuss the issues, cutting out the usual role of the permanent Brussels delegations and the European Commission. The strategy they prepared, with help from Martin Donnelly, the deputy head of the EU Secretariat in the Cabinet Office, Roger Liddle, the passionately

pro-EMU Policy Unit adviser, and Derek Scott, his equally passionate but EMU-sceptic double, aimed to make the EU 'the most
competitive and dynamic knowledge-based economy in the world'.

This Lisbon pledge was a hefty ambition given the dominance,
even then, of the US-based tech firms. And before momentum on
the initiative ebbed away, it led to legislation to liberalise telecoms,
e-commerce and energy across Europe. While it didn't change the
British public's belief that the EU was a sclerotic economic partner,
Jeremy believed it did increase the EU's focus on competitiveness. It
may, therefore, have stopped the French under Lionel Jospin from
moving the single market in a more protectionist direction and
encouraged Schröder's later reforms of the German labour market.

By the time we headed out to Bordeaux at the end of May 2000 for
a long weekend with Zoë and Peter, we were well into our third IVF
attempt and I was flushed and anxious, frustrated by the clinic's
endless postponement of our egg harvest. We drove to Saint-Émilion,
a honey-yellow town of winding streets surrounded by vineyards,
and on our second morning, escaped the heat to visit the underground Grotte de l'Ermitage, carved out of the earth in the twelfth
century to commemorate a hermit.

'The story goes,' our guide said, pointing at a chair fashioned out
of the cave wall, 'that women who sit here will conceive and bear
children.'

I glanced at Zoë, my comrade in this battle against infertility.

'I'm not going to do it,' she whispered. 'I'm going to rely on nature.'

'Well I will,' I said before sitting down briefly on the cool rock and
jumping back up. And when I looked back, I spotted Zoë doing the
same.

After my eggs were harvested and fertilised at the end of May, the
clinic rang in early June to say three had divided and had reached the
eight-cell stage. We transferred all three, no longer worrying about
the risks of a multiple birth. I then rested at home while Jeremy dealt
with the fall out from the Prime Minister's speech at the Women's
Institute, during which Blair had been heckled and booed for sounding too political. I took a blood test at the hospital a few days later
and sent Jeremy a message on his bleeper.

'We mustn't lose hope,' Jeremy said when he rang. 'Maybe it's still too early to tell. And anyway, we can try again.'

'I'm losing hope – I can't keep doing this.'

'We will always have hope, Pearl.'

Perhaps Jeremy was right, but as I watched him packing his bags to go to Portugal to negotiate new bank secrecy laws, I felt jealous of his ability to compartmentalise our grief. I knew he cared, even if he didn't join me in the dark place where I went after each disappointment. But I also knew I couldn't change him, and maybe I didn't want to, because his ability to keep going kept me from falling too far.

By the time Jeremy returned from his meetings, I'd picked myself back up, and in July 2000, we began our fourth IVF cycle while Jeremy helped finalise the Comprehensive Spending Review, provided input into the Prime Minister's ten-year plan for the NHS and amused me with stories of the hunt for a Downing Street mole.

'He or she is sending the press copies of the Prime Minister's Monday morning memos and various internal emails,' he told me. 'Conspiracy theories are raging between the various sub-factions of Number 10.'

The final version of the spending review, published in mid-July 2000, set out the government's three-year plans to build 'opportunity and security for all'. Jeremy was pleased with how he'd managed to shape this on the Prime Minister's behalf, including agreeing that, in addition to the 6.1 per cent increase already announced for the NHS, education would get an average 5.4 per cent annual real increase and the police 3.8 per cent.

The Prime Minister's ten-year plan for the NHS was also completed in July 2000. This comprehensive assessment, endorsed by twenty-five leading NHS voices, laid out a series of new commitments including reducing waiting times in accident and emergency departments to less than four hours. As Tony Blair noted in its Foreword, he'd chaired four to five meetings a week with people from across the NHS to prepare the plan – an enormous time commitment for any prime minister, and one that had been

matched by an equivalent effort from Jeremy and the rest of the
Number 10 team. Of course, many of the ideas weren't new. The
government would appoint thousands more consultants, nurses,
GPs and therapists, build over a hundred new hospitals and create
a tough new inspection regime. More controversially, the NHS
would increase its work with the private sector and patients would
get additional choice over their local doctors. But despite some of
the ideas being recycled, the document still demonstrated the Prime
Minister's intent to lay out a long-term, and hopefully irreversible,
direction for the NHS – even if it was to prove far harder to
implement the plan than it was to spend the additional money
allocated in the spending review.

While most people in Number 10 believed that the Prime
Minister's paper was the knock-out blow in the health arms race,
Jeremy had spotted a little-noticed pledge in the Chancellor's
Budget statement back in March, which talked about commission-
ing 'a long-term assessment of technological, demographic and
medical trends over the next two decades that will affect the Health
Service'.

'We are still planning to do the work – and we expect it will
endorse the existing model of a tax-funded, free at the point of use,
NHS,' Ed Balls told Jeremy over one of their coffees in Café
Churchill. 'And doing a review also means that we don't need to give
the NHS any more money ahead of the next election.'

At least this second part of Ed's explanation was a relief, Jeremy
thought, given the largesse the health system had already received.
And as the months passed, and he heard nothing more about the
assessment, he began to think that the Chancellor, like the Prime
Minister, might have forgotten about it. He was, of course, wrong.

In late July 2000, Jeremy attended his second G8 summit, this time
on Okinawa Island in Japan. Though this remote Pacific destination
sounded glamorous, the three-hour haul from Tokyo in a charter
plane wasn't, and neither was the setting itself, a large concrete hotel
stifling in the tropical heat. The whole event was a disappointment
after the glamour of Jeremy's first summit in Cologne, but riots at
the 1999 ministerial conference of the World Trade Organisation in

Seattle had changed all that, forcing all future international meetings to be held in obscure and isolated locations.

Anticipating hot and humid weather, Jeremy took three short-sleeved shirts with him to Japan, a look few others copied. But even decked out in these, the walks between venues left him damp with sweat and then shivering in the air-conditioned meeting rooms. With no burning crisis for the leaders to get stuck into, the summit passed in an extravaganza of largely unrecognisable, and often jellified, foods. Meanwhile, Jeremy and the other sherpas worked their way through a communiqué covering so many issues that the intended focus on digital inclusion and renewable energy was lost, together with any further meaningful progress on reducing third world debt.

Back home on 10 August, we transferred two more embryos and began another wait. Each moment of every day, no matter how many times I told myself this was likely to result in another wretched disappointment, I was conscious of the possibility I might be pregnant. And it was easy to leap from there to imagining a future – calculating what day our babies would be born and filling in the details of their future lives.

On 24 August I took another pregnancy test. It was too early, but I couldn't wait any longer. I glanced at the result while carrying it through to show Jeremy.

'There doesn't seem to be anything there,' I said, forcing a smile, 'but it doesn't matter because they said I shouldn't take a test before Saturday.' The words were helping me, and I hoped would help him.

Jeremy took the white plastic tube and squinted down at the window. 'Hang on,' he said, 'isn't there a second line?'

I looked again, and sure enough, there was the faintest blush of pink next to the standard red stripe.

'Let's stay calm,' Jeremy said, shaking his head at my grin.

We hurried into the hospital later that morning to take a blood test. Now I had to know, and despite his pretence of calm, so did Jeremy. After a clammy half hour, we had the news – I was pregnant. We hugged on the pavement outside, ignoring the passers-by swerving to avoid us, repeating our news over and over again.

Two days later we headed off in a euphoric mist towards Switzerland on a pre-planned driving holiday listening to 'Yellow' by Coldplay, 'Roseland NYC Live' by Portishead and David Gray's 'Babylon'. The following two weeks were a blur of art museums, waterfalls, rivers and half-timbered buildings as we made our way from Basel to Zurich, Lucerne, Locarno and Bern, including a hair-raising drive in low cloud over the Susten Pass with Jeremy clutching the dashboard and shouting at me to slow down.

At last we were talking again about the future. Perhaps the cloud that had appeared that day I'd stood outside Hamleys was about to lift. Perhaps the sadness that washed over me each time I saw a baby, no matter how much I hated myself for feeling that way, would go away. Jeremy's imaginings were more practical. He wanted to call the baby Stanley, he told me, which I assumed was a joke, though I took the precaution of informing him that it would never, ever, be the name of our child.

'Remember our deal,' I said, referring to an agreement we'd made over dinner in the Red Pepper restaurant near my flat in Maida Vale well before we'd become engaged. We'd been debating surnames that evening in the way you do when you haven't yet admitted that you're going to stay together but know you probably will.

'I want to keep Cook,' I'd said. 'After all, I spent ten years sailing around the world in the Captain's wake.'

'Well,' he said, 'I want to keep Heywood.'

It came down, in the end, to the toss of a coin, which Jeremy lost. And then on the way back to my flat I looked at his face and realised that, for all my feminism, the issue meant far more to him than it did to me. So I compromised. If we ever married, we would all be Heywoods, I told him, but in exchange, I would choose all our children's names.

One morning, sitting by Lake Lucerne, Jeremy gestured towards a patch of water from which the sun reflected back into our eyes.

'That was our wedding day,' he said.

He moved his arm to indicate a section of darker, purplish-blue water interspersed with glints of light.

'And that was our last year.'

I grimaced before watching as he lifted his hand to point towards a stream of warm, golden rays coming over the hills on the far side of the lake.

Jeremy glanced at me and smiled. 'And that is us now.'

10

'Yoshimi Battles the Pink Robots': The fuel crisis

September–November 2000

On our way home through France in early September 2000, we came across a motorway queue near Metz. Jeremy twisted the radio dial until we found an English-language station that identified the cause – a queue of taxi drivers crawling along at a few miles per hour to protest about fuel prices.

'This could never happen in Britain,' Jeremy said, peering out, 'the French government has clearly lost control.'

We stayed in a small hotel across the border in Belgium and made a dash to the Channel Tunnel early the following morning. By that time the radio was reporting that all the entrances had been blocked by truck drivers and fishermen.

'There's another way in that few people know about,' a French friend said when we rang them, 'but it's hard to find.'

'We have to get back to London,' Jeremy said, leaning forward in the passenger seat to glare at the road. 'I'm needed back in the office and your scan is due.' He was stabbing at the map in his lap.

I kept circling the port, occasionally stopping to ask directions. We'd almost given up when I took another turn and came upon a roundabout free of lorries. We shot around it and out the other side to find ourselves on a road leading into the Channel Tunnel car park.

We were still incredulous about our escape when we reached Waterloo station early in the evening of Wednesday 6 September. On our way home, Jeremy glanced through the armload of newspapers he'd bought in the station, which were also shouting about the cost of fuel. 'Your petrol is costing you 80p per litre at the pump,' they said. 'That's a 14p price hike in only 18 months.'

'I feel partly responsible,' Jeremy said, flipping through pages full of pictures of angry motorists and farmers. 'I encouraged Norman Lamont to put in place the fuel duty escalator in 1993 – though I didn't anticipate that, between them, Ken Clarke and Gordon Brown would later double the size of the annual increase.'

This escalator had significantly affected fuel costs – by that point more than half of the price at the pump was due to tax, although the most recent increase had mainly been caused by crude oil prices soaring upwards to hit a ten-year high. But whatever the reason, what mattered was that fuel was more expensive in Britain than anywhere else in the developed world. At least it was for most of us: despite their complaints, the farmers' fuel – red diesel – was still only 24p per litre.

The following day we returned to the hospital. We were hoping to see our baby for the first time, though we'd been warned it would be little more than a speck, possibly with a heartbeat. I lay on the bed while Jeremy stood by my side, holding my hand.

The nurse ran a probe across my stomach and paused. She replaced the instrument on its stand and straightened up. 'I'll be back in a moment,' she said and disappeared out the door.

I looked at Jeremy and he squeezed my hand. The door reopened and the nurse came back in, accompanied by a doctor. She picked up the probe again and they studied the screen.

The doctor turned to face us. 'I'm afraid there's nothing there,' he said.

Nothing there. I moved my hand onto my stomach. For a month, while exploring all those lakes and mountains, I'd thought I'd been carrying one baby, or maybe two. The room spun.

'The pregnancy might be ectopic, or you might have miscarried,' the doctor said. He sounded like he was diagnosing a bad cough. He glanced at the nurse and they backed towards the door. 'We'll let you get dressed,' he said.

This time when we reached the pavement, we both cried, and I don't remember if there were any passers-by. In fact, I don't remember much of the next few hours. My grief came in surges that left me gasping for air like an exhausted swimmer. Each time it eased, I caught my breath and found myself sitting on our kitchen floor, forgetting why I was there before tumbling forward into another chasm.

Jeremy sat by me muttering about it all being okay if we could hold on, but his words, normally comforting, came from a long way away. They reminded me of being shipwrecked as a small child; of being thrown across the cabin when *Wavewalker* was hit by a massive wave in the middle of the Southern Indian Ocean, fracturing my skull when I hit the wall. Several days later we'd stumbled across an island named Île Amsterdam, one of the few dots of land in that barren ocean. And the doctor there, who'd operated multiple times on my head to remove a blood clot on my brain, had kept assuring me it was fine and it would all soon be over.

That had also been a lie.

On the morning of Friday, 8 September, a hundred lorries staged a go-slow protest on the A1, protesters blockaded Texaco's Pembroke refinery in Wales and deliveries from the Buncefield oil depot in Hertfordshire, a key source of London's fuel, were disrupted. But the biggest issue was in Cheshire where a hundred farmers and a few truckers were blockading the Stanlow Shell Oil refinery, a sprawling industrial complex that supplied almost 30 per cent of the UK's fuel.

Jeremy was torn, knowing he needed to go into the office but not wanting to leave me.

'Go in,' I said. 'I'm fine.' It wasn't true, but there was little he could do to help, and he was needed at work.

When Jeremy came home that night he told me the Saudis were proposing to raise their production by 700,000 barrels a day, though this would make little immediate difference to the price being paid by UK motorists. I said we had bigger worries – the hospital had called to say that, following more blood tests, they thought my pregnancy might be ectopic. They wanted me to go back in on Monday for more tests, and in the meantime, I needed to rest.

On Saturday morning, the Chancellor flew to Paris to try to get the other EU finance ministers to put pressure on OPEC, the oil producers' conglomerate, to join the Saudis in producing more oil.

Meanwhile, the protesters continued their blockade and Jeremy and I sat at home discussing the crisis, desperate for distraction. Having never thought about the UK's fuel system before, we were fast becoming experts. The petrol stations held few reserves because they expected supplies to arrive several times each day. This meant the fuel drought that had started in the north-west of England and north London was soon spreading across the country despite the reassuring messages from Number 10.

By Sunday morning, when the Prime Minister disappeared on a pre-arranged trip up to Hull and Hartlepool, the Stanlow refinery was still shut and Kingsbury Oil Terminal in the West Midlands, Britain's largest inland oil terminal, had also been closed. Things were getting out of control, Jeremy told me, poring over the newspapers on our kitchen table, looking at pictures of lines of cars snaking out of petrol stations, harried motorists filling tanks and people hauling jerry cans into the boots of their vehicles.

Jeremy rang Simon Virley, the economic affairs private secretary, who was on duty in Downing Street. 'What's going on?' he asked him.

'I know little more than you do,' Simon said, 'but the Home Office is confident they have the situation under control.'

'Sure,' Jeremy said. He felt uneasy, but like me, he was distracted by the ache in my stomach, which sharpened during the day. Early on Sunday evening, we headed into the Chelsea and Westminster Hospital where I lay on a bed in a ward for hours. At 4 a.m. on Monday morning a doctor came to see us. My pregnancy could still be ectopic, he said, but we could go home because I was stable, at least for the time being.

Jeremy dragged himself back into work later that morning – if I wasn't in danger, he needed to be in Downing Street, particularly with the Prime Minister still away. David North, the home affairs private secretary, greeted him with sobering news. Of the UK's nine oil refineries, virtually no tankers were leaving two – Stanlow and Fawley – and few were leaving another five. There were also ongoing protests at various oil depots including Avonmouth and Kingsbury. Half the nation's petrol stations were closed and most of the rest were rationing supplies. The British Medical Association was worried about doctors getting to work, the British Poultry and Meat Federation was concerned about the welfare of millions of newly hatched chicks and the National Blood Service was on alert.

Jeremy made a list of people to ring, including the police gold commanders who were in charge of responding to each protest, and the leaders of the major oil companies. He really wanted to speak to the people who employed the truck drivers, but no one knew who they were. On a hunch, he rang Lord Sterling, the chair of P&O Ferries.

It was a good guess. 'The Stanlow drivers work for me,' Lord Sterling said. 'We've been trying to explain to them that this is a civil protest, not an industrial dispute. But they're reluctant to cross what they regard as a picket line. The most critical thing now is to get the police to move all the protesters to the other side of the road so they can't intimidate the drivers.'

Jeremy arrived home late on Monday evening to find me resting, but no worse. Back in Downing Street on Tuesday morning he was greeted again by David North this time with his hair askew.

'Did you go home last night?' Jeremy demanded.

'No. I was on the phone until late talking to the gold commanders. They have lots of excuses for why they can't do more – they don't have enough resources, their role is to keep the peace, they're not prepared for this type of event and so on – but they've promised to get more officers out.'

'Good. But what is the Home Office doing? It's madness for Whitehall to expect that a handful of us here can resolve this crisis.'

'Not a lot, as far as I can tell, though they keep assuring me that they have it under control. Oh, and the Prime Minister got back early this morning, so I've given him an update. Thirty-six tankers have left the Purfleet terminal, seventeen have departed Avonmouth and seven have gone from Buncefield.'

'What did he say?'

'"Out of how many?" And when I said, "around two hundred", he said, "what the hell are we going to do now?"'

'Good question.'

Jeremy, Simon, David and Geoffrey Norris, the Prime Minister's industry adviser, kept working the phones all Tuesday morning, calling anyone who might be able to help. They also cleared the Prime Minister's diary. The meeting he was due to have on Europe could wait. Instead he needed to call the leaders of the major oil companies to underline the importance of getting the fuel flowing again. There was also the international angle to consider. The Saudis had said they would pump extra barrels but maybe they could do more. Jeremy added the crown prince of Saudi Arabia and the leaders of other key OPEC countries to the Prime Minister's list.

On Tuesday afternoon the Prime Minister chaired an emergency Cabinet meeting, met the oil company CEOs and spoke to David Omand, the permanent secretary at the Home Office, who again assured him everything was under control. At 5.30 p.m., Blair gave a press conference. By this time, his mood was grim. He was convinced, he'd told Jeremy, and so were Gordon Brown and Alastair Campbell, that this had all blown up because the right-wing press was out to get New Labour. This might explain why he overshot his brief when he got in front of the cameras, saying he hoped, in the next twenty-four hours, to have the situation 'on the way back to normal'.

David North, who was watching the press conference with Jeremy, raised his eyebrows.

'Now I feel like asking him how the hell we're going to do that,' Jeremy said, shaking his head.

Jeremy was right to worry – by the following morning only about 20 per cent of the UK's normal fuel deliveries were taking place, more than 90 per cent of its petrol stations were dry and two hundred trucks were parked in protest along Park Lane. The only good news was that public support for the hauliers and farmers was waning, though so was their support for the Labour Party. One poll even suggested that, for the first time since the election, Labour had slipped behind the Conservatives. And Jeremy's in-tray was full of ministerial squabbles – was it more important to keep the Royal Mail running so letters were delivered or the post offices open so people could collect their benefits?

After a dispiriting meeting with the oil company CEOs, who seemed unable to do anything, Alan Milburn, the health secretary, agreed with the Prime Minister that it was time to make the gravity of the crisis clear to the protesters. 'Those involved in this blockade need to know the very serious effect their actions are having on the NHS,' he told the press. 'Patients are unable to get to hospital. Operations are being cancelled. Drugs, food and medical supplies are now running short. The NHS is increasingly unable to do its job properly.' To ram home the message, NHS staff were encouraged to go out to tell the protesters that they were putting patients' lives at risk, and the NHS announced that it would only be treating emergency cases.

On Wednesday night Jeremy came home late, his eyes red. 'If Alan's statement doesn't make a difference, I don't know what we'll do next,' he told me. 'Half the private office is camped out in Downing Street, we have a continuous crisis meeting going on in the basement of the Cabinet Office, and there's a room full of oil company executives beavering away next door. There's nothing more I can do with the resources I have, it's clear that all the Home Office's reassurances were false, and though it's safe for the tankers to leave the refineries, we can't force them to do so.'

I hugged him, though there was little reassurance I could give. The protest had revealed the vulnerability of the nation's fuel supply and driven the UK close to the edge of a national breakdown.

We slept fitfully but woke to find the world had changed after Brynle Williams, the balding spokesman for the Stanlow protesters, announced they were backing down.

Later that morning Jeremy joined the Prime Minister for a meeting with the CEOs of the major oil companies.

'Most of the protesters have called off their blockades and tanker movements are back up to around 50 per cent of a normal day,' the Prime Minister said, the bags under his eyes clearly visible. He glanced at Ansel Condray, the chair of Esso UK, 'but the protesters returned to Coryton refinery after your price rise.'

'That was a PR disaster,' Ansel said.

The whole thing has been a PR disaster, Jeremy thought.

The Prime Minister looked around the room. 'We need to learn from this. We can't let the fate of the country depend on the actions of a small number of drivers.'

At 4 p.m. on Thursday, Esso announced it was reversing its price increase, and by Friday 15 September, fuel deliveries were back up to almost 90 per cent of normal volumes, though more than half of Britain's petrol stations were still closed.

On Saturday morning, I miscarried. Despite the pain, this at least removed the risk of an ectopic pregnancy. Our relief, though, was temporary because, on Sunday evening, Brenda rang to tell us that Peter, Jeremy's father, had been diagnosed with prostate cancer. It was hard to know what to do with this information, particularly when our world was already so clouded, so we just tried even harder not to think about the future.

In the days following the fuel protest, Jeremy asked Simon Virley and David North to shadow the home secretary's review of the lessons learnt while he worked with the Treasury on fuel options for the pre-Budget report. By the end of September, the Ministry of Defence had agreed to train squaddies to drive fuel tankers and the government had signed a memorandum of understanding with the Association of Chief Police Officers, five of the oil companies and several haulage companies. This committed its members to working together to secure normal supplies of oil during any future protest including through using joint early warning systems, coordinating contingency plans and preventing the intimidation of tanker drivers.

While Jeremy hoped life at home and work would return to something approaching normality after this, fate had a different plan. On 17 October 2000, a train derailed in Hatfield killing four people and injuring over seventy. This was bad enough, but what made it worse was that it came in the wake of a second, even more serious, rail crash a year before when two trains had collided near Ladbroke Grove killing thirty-one people.

It soon became clear that the Hatfield rail crash had been caused by cracks in the track. Gerald Corbett, the CEO of Railtrack – the company responsible for maintaining the rail infrastructure – offered his resignation, but this was rejected by his board, who told him he needed to stay on to help sort things out. This made sense, but Railtrack's response to the crash under Gerald's leadership was to try to minimise any risk of further accidents by imposing hundreds of speed restrictions across the network. Journey times ballooned and reliability and punctuality collapsed. The travelling public initially accepted the need for caution, but dissatisfaction soon mushroomed – safety was important, but so was their need to get to work and back without enduring hours of delay.

Though Railtrack was a private sector company with around 250,000 small shareholders, the government was soon being held to blame for these delays so the Prime Minister asked Andrew Adonis, one of the Policy Unit advisers, and Jeremy to work out how to get the trains moving again. But despite holding a series of meetings with rail experts, they failed to find an answer. Railtrack was being cautious, but it was hard for anyone outside the system to second-guess whether the speed restrictions were necessary.

While Jeremy worried about the railways during the week, during the weekends we visited potential new IVF clinics, having lost faith in the Lister Hospital. At some point we knew we would have to stop trying to conceive, both because of the cost of the treatments and because of their emotional toll, but we hadn't yet reached that point. After visiting several clinics we were faced with a choice. Of the two that had the highest success rates, one could treat us immediately while the other, which had slightly better results, couldn't fit us in until the New Year. I couldn't bear the idea of more waiting, but Jeremy counselled patience. So I rang up the Assisted Reproduction and Gynaecology Clinic on Harley Street and we joined their waiting list.

By late October 2000, Jeremy had given up on trying to find a way to challenge Railtrack's caution and had moved on to worrying about the pre-Budget report. The Chancellor was reluctant to make any concessions in this to the fuel protesters apart from reducing truck excise duty but Jeremy was adamant, on the Prime Minister's behalf, that more was needed. There was a real risk, he told Ed Balls, that if they didn't act, the strikes would start again.

This time Jeremy's input made a difference. In his speech on 8 November 2000, the Chancellor froze fuel duty until April 2002, cut excise duty on ultra-low sulphur diesel, created a fund for scrapping or converting older trucks and increased the tax on foreign lorries using British roads. So there was something for motorists, the environmentalists, the hauliers and even the farmers, since vehicle excise duty on tractors was abolished. The pre-Budget report also included another increase in pensions. The Chancellor had dug the government out of two political holes – though it had cost the taxpayer billions of pounds.

'Fuel protesters, angry pensioners and railway disasters,' I said, 'it seems there's always a crisis in Downing Street.'

Jeremy shrugged. 'It's the nature of the job. But the one thing that I've learnt from the fuel crisis is never again to trust a department when it says it has things under control.'

11

'Anarchy in the UK': Where is Plan B?

November 2000–March 2001

After the pre-Budget report, the Prime Minister called Jeremy and Jonathan Powell into his office. 'I'm going to lose Alastair,' he said, 'so, now more than ever, I need Whitehall to deliver.'

Jeremy nodded. Alastair Campbell had been talking about leaving for some time, though the Prime Minister had somehow managed to delay his decision. But regardless of whether Alastair stayed, it was clear that Number 10 needed to get better at ensuring that the government's manifesto commitments were being delivered. Although the Downing Street team was trying to do this, they only had enough resources to monitor a few of Suma's new PSA targets, mainly those relating to New Labour's five election pledges, including reducing class sizes and cutting NHS waiting lists.

After pondering this issue for a while, Jeremy wrote a note to Jonathan Powell in late November 2000. What they needed, he argued, was a new unit – a Delivery Unit – modelled on the Standards and Effectiveness Unit that Michael Barber was leading in the Department for Education. Michael's unit was making progress by sitting outside the departmental structure and focusing on school literacy and numeracy. If it worked in education, there was no reason why it wouldn't work across Whitehall, particularly if it reported to a new minister, a Chief Secretary to the Cabinet, who would sit alongside the Prime Minister and the Chief Secretary to the Treasury during departmental stocktakes.

'I largely agree with this,' Jonathan wrote back, 'let's return to it in the New Year during our preparations for the second term.'

The other issue on the Prime Minister's mind that autumn, as he started to turn his attention to the 2001 election manifesto, was top-up fees for university students. In 1997, following a cross-party review carried out by university chancellor Sir Ron Dearing, the government had introduced a flat-rate fee of £1,000 per student. It was a start, but in his Sunday evening memos the Prime Minister made it clear that he wanted to go further and allow universities to charge more for their best courses. Given its traditions and language, Blair believed Britain was ideally suited to delivering world-class tertiary education, but without reform its universities would struggle to compete against their US counterparts, which enjoyed a more flexible fee system.

Jeremy also believed university finances needed reforming, both because the existing system was underfunded, and because it represented a subsidy to the middle classes. Since the country gained from having graduates, students shouldn't have to pay the full cost of their education. However, he believed it was fair for them to contribute more, particularly if this was structured as a loan that they only needed to pay back if they went on to earn a decent income. But despite their shared enthusiasm for reforming the funding of higher education, the Prime Minister told Jeremy that he wanted to leave the issue until after the election because many in his party would find it difficult.

'Which is understandable politically,' Jeremy told Andrew Adonis, 'but what I don't understand is why, if the Chancellor can chuck £200 million at disability premiums, and God knows how much at tax credits, he can't afford £500 million for universities? If he could, we might be able to give them the funding they need without having a massive fight over top-up fees.'

Andrew nodded. 'I agree. But when it comes to it, I'm sure we'll have the argument. I can't see Gordon finding the money, and even if he could, both he and the Prime Minister would want to put it into schools.'

* * *

We spent that Christmas in York with Jeremy's parents, relieved that Peter's prostate cancer treatment seemed to be going well. Afterwards, we flew to Malta for a few days away on our own. We had intended to spend time on the island of Gozo exploring its megalithic temples. But when we drove over the hilly ridge on Malta's west coast on New Year's Eve, we were greeted on the far side by blue-black waves that curled over the road. Since it was clear that the Gozo ferry wouldn't be running, we negotiated the last room in the nearby Hotel Dragonara Point, a sprawling concrete resort. We toasted Jeremy's birthday at the New Year's Eve gala dinner there but left before the band started playing to go and look out over the angry sea.

'I think we will have twins this year,' I said, trying to insert confidence into the words that I didn't feel. When Zoë had announced her pregnancy that autumn, my joy for her had been mixed with the hollow realisation that we were now alone in our battle against infertility. And when we'd gone in December to meet our new doctor, Dr Taranissi, I'd started to realise that this was a fight we might never win.

'There are rules,' Dr Taranissi had said, sitting behind an almost bare desk, a blotting pad and prescription book lined up in front of him. 'Appointments have to be when we dictate, which might include weekends, and patients have to undergo a series of preparatory tests and exploratory procedures.'

'Okay,' we said.

'And, if patients fail those tests, they might not be treated.'

Back in Malta, Jeremy smiled at me. 'I hope you're right, Pearl,' he said.

'What else do you predict for this year?' I asked him.

'I think Labour will win the election and I'll return to the Treasury – but I care more about your prediction,' he said. Then he grinned, unable to maintain the sobriety. 'Though I am worried that David Beckham might move to Italy, because that would have a devastating impact on Manchester United.'

* * *

Jeremy returned to Number 10 in January 2001 to find Tony Blair still focused on organisational issues.

'It's not only delivery,' the Prime Minister said, 'it's also how the centre develops long-term policy.'

'The problem is that the role of the Policy Unit has changed,' Jeremy told Jonathan Powell afterwards. 'Under Thatcher and Wilson, it generated new ideas but now it's focused on shadowing the day-to-day work of departments. What the Prime Minister needs is a unit that challenges the status quo and generates innovative policies.'

'Yes. But we also need to get rid of some of the duplication around here,' Jonathan said.

Jeremy nodded – this was certainly true. Across Number 10 and the Cabinet Office, multiple people in different units were interested in the same areas of policy. For example, David North in the private office took notes of the Prime Minister's meetings on health and ensured that the conclusions were sent out to the right people in Whitehall, but Robert Hill in the Policy Unit advised the Prime Minister on health issues. Meanwhile, in the Cabinet Office, Suma Chakrabarti, who was by then heading up the twenty-person Economic and Domestic Policy Secretariat, had health experts in his team. And the Performance and Innovation Unit, which still reported to Suma, often also undertook health-related projects. This duplication was causing confusion and wasted work across Whitehall, with multiple people describing themselves as being the Prime Minister's adviser on the same issue.

'I'm not interested in the mechanics of how the centre operates,' Blair said when they discussed it with him, 'but I do want it fixed, so I think we should get John Birt in to do some radical thinking.'

Jeremy was half expecting this. John, a former BBC director general, had recently done some analysis for the Prime Minister on how to reduce crime. By taking a system-wide view, John had showed that, in contrast to the Home Office's fatalistic view that crime numbers were a consequence of economic conditions, what mattered was what you did with the 100,000 or so repeat offenders who committed around half of all crimes. The Prime Minister had been impressed by John's analysis – but unfortunately the Home

Office, which hadn't been closely involved in his work, had resisted having their worldview dismissed in the space of a PowerPoint presentation, so much of the Birt plan had been left on the drawing board.

Jeremy found John a small office close to the front door of Number 10 and briefed him on his own views about the organisation of the centre. He was keen to keep the Performance and Innovation Unit, he told John, but he thought that many of the Cabinet Office's other units, like the Modernising Public Services Unit and the Centre for Management and Policy Studies, could be outsourced or abolished. And some, like the Regulatory Impact Unit and the Social Exclusion Unit, could be moved into other departments.

'Good,' John said. 'I guess I'd better get started.'

While John started sketching out his thinking, Jeremy turned to a new issue – trying to figure out if the Treasury had started working on the five tests for joining EMU that Gordon Brown had dreamt up before the 1997 election and briefed out to the *Financial Times* from the back of a New York taxi.

When Jeremy had first arrived in Number 10, both Jonathan Powell and Alastair Campbell had warned him that, though New Labour was pro-European overall, the Prime Minister was less positive about joining the euro than was his Chancellor. After all, it was Tony Blair who had insisted in the 1997 manifesto that no decision on EMU would be taken without a referendum and who had written an article in the *Sun* on how much he loved the pound.

But in recent months, having effectively ruled out joining the euro during that Parliament, and having cemented New Labour's economic credibility by making the Bank of England independent, the Chancellor had rarely raised the euro in his bilaterals with the Prime Minister – the only exception being a low-key flurry in February 1999 over the publication of the national changeover plan, which laid out the practicalities of moving from one currency to another.

'The Treasury has no intention of applying the tests any time soon,' Ed Balls said when Jeremy raised the subject during one of their meetings in Café Churchill in early 2001.

Ed had been saying this for months, so Jeremy had anticipated this reply. But back in Number 10, Tony Blair's passionately pro-EU inner circle was running out of patience. For them the political case for joining the euro was getting ever stronger. How could Britain expect to lead in Europe if it remained outside the EU's most important project? It was clear, Tony's team argued, that the Treasury was deliberately running down the clock to make a referendum in the next Parliament impossible.

Jeremy's perspective was somewhat different. For a start, his experience of Black Wednesday made him cautious about the euro. He also agreed with the Treasury that it was essential to undertake a proper economic assessment before any decision was made. But the choice shouldn't be only about the numbers and he agreed with his colleagues that delay was no way to approach an issue of such magnitude.

By early February 2001, with the Treasury still stalling, the Prime Minister decided he'd waited long enough, so in answer to a question from the Leader of the Opposition in the House of Commons, he declared that a decision on the euro would be taken 'within two years'.

The Treasury was furious about this, though there was little they could do once the statement had been made. 'Maybe now at last they will begin work,' Jeremy told me, 'and we can finally make a decision.'

We were distracted soon after this by news of some of our own tests after our IVF clinic told us that we had cleared their hurdles and could start our first treatment. This time, after more weeks of waiting, fourteen eggs were fertilised on Valentine's Day. Five days later when we arrived in the clinic, the embryologist took us down to a darkened basement room.

'Look,' she said, pointing at a screen, 'six of your eggs have divided. The two eight-cell ones are perfect, and the seven-cell one is almost perfect. Aren't they lovely?'

I smiled at Jeremy.

'And how many will you transfer?'

'Two,' I said, squeezing Jeremy's hand.

'That's good,' she said. 'Given your age you have about a 50 per cent chance of getting pregnant here. Many people are tempted to put back three, which means that about 10 per cent end up carrying triplets.'

'Yes,' I said. This rate of triplet pregnancy was far higher than it had been at the Lister Hospital. And I knew that the medical risks that it brought were considerable – both for me and for the babies.

'You need to be prepared to hold your ground,' the embryologist said.

But when Dr Taranissi arrived a few minutes later, he shook his head at our decision. 'Transferring three is wiser given your history,' he said. 'But it really depends how much you want to be pregnant.'

We resisted for a while before we caved. 'Okay, we'll transfer three,' I said, glancing at Jeremy. We both knew we probably shouldn't – but our desperation for children had by then over-whelmed our rationality.

After the transfer, I rested for a week. In our months of trying to conceive I'd made us try various things to increase our odds, including rationing coffee and sugar. Nothing had worked, and Jeremy had particularly hated the reflexology session I'd made him endure, declaring he would never do it again. But the meditation class I'd taken had been helpful. My teacher had advised me to build a safe space inside my head, so I'd imagined a clearing in a pine forest where I sat on a rough-hewn wooden bench, and in my arms, cradled a baby. That was the place I kept going back to during the endless days of waiting to hear if each IVF cycle had been successful.

While I rested, Jeremy coped in his own way by digesting the first draft of John Birt's new PowerPoint deck, 'An Effective Centre'. It wasn't that Jeremy didn't care about our infertility – I knew he did. But he'd grown up in a world where you got through things by not talking about them. In fact we had been going out for several months before Jeremy had revealed that he wasn't one of two children but one of three. He'd told me how he'd lain awake one night when he was five years old listening to his baby sister's shallow gasps before falling back asleep. The following morning, when he'd gone down-stairs, he'd found his father Peter sitting in the lounge. 'Your sister is dead,' Peter had said, 'so go and play quietly with Simon.'

I sometimes wondered whether this culture of not talking about things made it easier or harder for Jeremy to cope with our troubles. In a way it was strange because Jeremy was one of the best listeners I'd ever met. He was also an incisive questioner, probing issues most people would avoid – like the memorable evening when he asked a friend of mine why she pretended to tolerate her open marriage when she clearly hated her partner's other relationships. But somehow Jeremy's ability to make other people open up about their most personal issues sat alongside an equally strong reluctance to share his own feelings.

In any case, the most important thing for me was that Jeremy was there and that we were still talking – even though it was usually about Whitehall.

'John is proposing to merge Number 10 and the Cabinet Office to create a combined department of around 500 rather than 2,100 people,' he told me.

'Really?'

'Yes. And in his grand scheme they would all be housed, together with the Prime Minister, in a modern, open-plan working space within the Cabinet Office, with Downing Street only being used for ceremonial purposes.'

The rest of John's vision was equally radical. Within this new structure, a Forward Strategy Unit would create ten-year strategies for each department, an unheard-of timescale in government, while a Performance and Planning Unit would translate these into three-year implementation plans. These would both report to a new minister – the Chief Secretary to the Cabinet – who would work with the Treasury to make sure Whitehall delivered. The Cabinet Secretary would continue to be the Prime Minister's most senior policy adviser, but a head of the Civil Service would manage Whitehall and the broader public sector and report separately to the Prime Minister.

This plan would, Jeremy said, transform the centre's ability to develop and deliver policy and would accelerate Civil Service reform. But he wasn't at all sure that it would be agreed – after all the Treasury would hate it and it was unlikely to be welcomed by the Cabinet Secretary.

* * *

On Monday 19 February, Jeremy's contemplation of John's plan was interrupted by news of a suspected case of foot and mouth disease in a pig carcass in Essex – the first since 1967. Jeremy wasn't normally interested in agriculture issues. In fact, during one of our rare countryside walks while we'd been dating, he'd suddenly shouted that there was a 'giant rat' in the field we were crossing. When I'd looked in the direction of his trembling finger, I'd laughed. It was, I said, a rabbit – the clue being its bushy tail. But even for a committed townie, the words 'foot and mouth' provoked a chilling memory of the devastation caused by the last outbreak that had taken place while he'd been a schoolboy in Derbyshire.

That evening MAFF, the Ministry of Agriculture, Fisheries and Food, banned livestock movements within five miles of the suspected case and told Downing Street that it was planning to implement the 1967 policy of slaughtering any herd in which the disease was found. Over the following days, the situation spiralled. By Thursday, two more cases had been reported in Essex and there was a suspicious, but unconfirmed, case in Tyne and Wear. Ben Gill, the rosy-cheeked head of the National Farmers' Union, stoked the panic by telling people to avoid visiting the countryside because they might spread the disease and the European Commission announced that it was banning all the UK's animal, milk and meat exports.

'This could be disastrous,' Jeremy told the Prime Minister after Simon Virley produced a bell curve out of an old file showing the progress of the 1967 outbreak. 'And yet again the lead department is insisting that they have it under control.'

On Friday 23 February, after three more cases had been confirmed, the Prime Minister, who was out in Washington, called Nick Brown, the agriculture minister, to demand to know what was going on. It was unfortunate, Jeremy thought, as he listened in to the call, that this was happening on Nick's watch after the Prime Minister had demoted Nick from Chief Whip – but there was little they could do about that.

'We've confirmed that the first case came from a farm in Heddon-on-the-Wall in Northumberland,' Nick said. 'The problem is that it could have been there for two to three weeks, and there were around four hundred animal and vehicle movements in and out of the premises during that period, so the next case could appear almost anywhere. I'm, therefore, going to ban all livestock movements across the country from 5 p.m. today. That should get things under control and, if there are no new outbreaks, we should be able to relax the restrictions after seven days.'

The Prime Minister met John Birt early the following week to go through his planned reorganisation. By this point John's thinking had mellowed a little. It still proposed merging the Cabinet Office and Number 10 but it no longer proposed creating a head of the Civil Service or a Chief Secretary to the Cabinet.

In John's new vision there were four units in the centre. One would manage the Civil Service; another would oversee policy and delivery, bringing together the Policy Unit, the private office, the new Delivery and Forward Strategy Units and the Cabinet Office secretariats; a third would deal with internal and external communications; and a last would manage presentation and politics.

The Prime Minister was enthusiastic about this structure, saying that it would put more emphasis on getting Whitehall to deliver while also creating an attractive role for Alastair Campbell, whom he was still trying to keep.

'I agree – though I think Richard Wilson is still going to object because it blurs the identity of the Cabinet Office,' Jeremy said, 'even though Number 10 is technically already part of it.'

'Maybe you could go through the plan with him?' the Prime Minister asked with a slight smile. 'You talk the same language – I'm sure you can bring him round.'

I laughed when Jeremy told me this, though I was more interested in discussing whether I was pregnant. The following day I gave up trying to guess and bought a pregnancy test. This time, two clear red lines appeared.

I burst into tears and sent Jeremy a message on his beeper.

'Why are you crying?' he asked when he called. 'What's the matter?'

I laughed. 'I'm pregnant.'

Despite our joy at this news, which was soon confirmed by our clinic, this time around it was muted by our fear of another miscarriage. We mustn't get ahead of ourselves, Jeremy kept telling me. His words were wise, though he found it easier to do this than I did – partly because, by then, Number 10 was in full crisis mode after the first case of foot and mouth had been confirmed in Wales, bringing the total across the UK to sixteen.

'I know this is heretical,' David North told Jeremy when they met on Wednesday 28 February, 'but I don't see why we fear this disease so much when it doesn't transmit to humans, the animals who get it often recover, and we can still eat the meat they produce.'

Jeremy shook his head. 'Lots of people seem to be saying the same thing and asking why we're not considering immunisation instead of, or at least alongside, slaughter.'

'I know. But every time I raise the possibility, the department rules it out, and so does the National Farmers' Union, because they say it would damage our exports market.'

'Does the European secretariat agree?'

'They say that immunisation would have an effect on exports because we wouldn't be able to prove we're disease free. But that would only be an issue for about six months – and it doesn't change the fact that vaccinated animals are safe to eat, or that it's more humane.'

'Can you see if you can get a sensible cost-benefit assessment from the department? I'm worried they're dismissing vaccination simply because the industry is opposed.'

On Thursday 1 March Jeremy met Richard Wilson to take him through John Birt's plan. He wrapped the proposals up in as much positive flummery as possible, but at the end of his presentation, Richard still shook his head.

'I'm not prepared to accept any actual or apparent merger of the Cabinet Office and Number 10,' Richard said, 'because it would undermine Cabinet government.'

Jeremy blinked. He'd expected opposition, but he hadn't expected this. 'What do you mean?'

What Richard meant, it emerged, was that, since – at least in Richard's view – the Prime Minister had virtually no executive powers, with these instead being vested in his secretaries of state or other ministers, the split of accountabilities between Downing Street and the Cabinet Office made sense. Downing Street helped the Prime Minister deal with party issues and connected him to Whitehall, while the Cabinet Office was where collective government came together.

'But each prime minister will want to govern in their own way,' Jeremy said. 'It should be possible for us to evolve how we work while maintaining the checks and balances we need.'

Jeremy came home that evening shaking his head. 'I have a battle going on with MAFF, which won't consider immunisation despite the countryside being littered with burning corpses. And I have a Prime Minister determined to transform Downing Street who is on a collision course with a Cabinet Secretary who is determined to stop him from becoming too powerful.'

'What will you do?'

'Help Tony Blair fight the first and negotiate a compromise on the second. Wish me luck.'

On Friday morning Jeremy, Andrew Adonis, Jonathan Powell and John Birt met the Prime Minister. After summarising his discussion with Richard Wilson the night before, Jeremy paused. 'I don't think there's any point in having a full-frontal row about this, particularly not with everything else going on. In fact, I think we can achieve much of what you need without merging Number 10 and the Cabinet Office.'

Blair raised his eyebrows. 'What would the alternative look like?'

'Well, if we combined the private office and Policy Unit within Number 10, we would remove some duplication,' Jeremy said. 'And we could live with the Cabinet secretariats remaining in the Cabinet Office if they were willing to take more direction from us. We could also allow Richard to manage the new Delivery and Forward Strategy Units – the important thing is to get them set up. Our original model would have been neater, but this still reduces duplication and gives us more resource focused on strategy and delivery.'

When, after a weekend of reflection, this proposal was put to Richard Wilson in a meeting on Monday morning, he accepted it. He even said he was happy for both the Delivery Unit and the Forward Strategy Unit to sit within Number 10. At the end of their discussion, the Prime Minister smiled, and Jeremy exhaled. It wasn't a perfect outcome, but it was a workable compromise.

Although one battle had been resolved, the foot and mouth crisis was still spiralling out of control. When David North came to see Jeremy later that morning, he said that 127 cases of the disease had been confirmed. It was time, Jeremy advised the Prime Minister, to instruct the department to consider immunisation – a message that, when it was later delivered to Nick Brown, earned Jeremy a glare from the agriculture secretary.

The number of cases continued to mount over the following days. By Thursday 15 March, there were 240.

'I need you to talk to Richard Wilson,' the Prime Minister told Jeremy after another difficult meeting with the department. 'The Civil Service needs to focus on foot and mouth until we get this crisis under control.'

A few days later, Richard convened his first COBR meeting on foot and mouth – so called because, like the ones that had taken place during the fuel crisis, they were held in the Cabinet Office's Briefing Room. He also agreed with David King, the government's chief scientific adviser, that they should assemble a team of leading epidemiologists to provide advice on how to handle the disease.

'We need to cull all animals within three kilometres of each case in under forty-eight hours,' King told Jeremy. 'Time is of the essence. There's no point in identifying animals and then not culling them, which is what we're doing now. That's why this outbreak has got out of control.'

'I talked to this guy Dave King, who reminds me of Dr Strangelove, this afternoon,' Jeremy told me when he got home, 'and in a few lucid sentences, he made it clear what we need to do to get a grip on foot and mouth.'

'What are you going to change?'

'I've advised the Prime Minister to bring in the army to help us get on top of the logistics of the cull. I'm also going to get the data sorted – it turns out that the department's database can only be operated by one person and doesn't include a lot of critical information like how long it takes from when a suspected case is reported to the disease being confirmed. If we can fix those things, I'll feel calmer – but I still think we need a Plan B.'

12

'Never Going Back Again': Changing the Centre

March–June 2001

By Friday 23 March the army was engaged, the backlog of animals to be culled was diminishing, and Jeremy was trying to calculate the cost of the foot and mouth crisis.

'What I don't understand is why the Treasury isn't more engaged,' he told David North. 'They often don't even bother sending someone to COBR.'

The Treasury's apparent indifference was indeed odd since, when they assembled the figures, Jeremy and David discovered that the cost of tackling foot and mouth was approaching £1 billion. The cost had soared because there was no time to haggle over the value of an animal when it had to be slaughtered – and those values were increasing as the number of animals likely to be left alive at the end of the crisis dwindled. Farmers were also being compensated for healthy animals that had to be killed because of the government's movement restrictions and the rates for those were so attractive that the Rural Payments Agency had been overwhelmed by applications. And of course, the government was also spending millions on haulage, digging burial pits, employing vets, cleaning and disinfecting.

When Jeremy met the Prime Minister early the following week, he updated him on the costs and pressed him again to consider vaccination.

'I will,' the Prime Minister said, 'but the more urgent issue is whether I should postpone the election.'

Jeremy paused. Tony Blair was right – with the papers still full of pictures of burning carcasses, and with half the countryside closed,

3 May wasn't an ideal date for the local elections, let alone a general election. But after an hour-long meeting with the Chancellor that afternoon, the Prime Minister was still undecided, with most of his advisers counselling against a delay since Labour was well ahead in the polls and it would suggest the government had lost control.

'What do you think?' the Prime Minister asked Jeremy.

This was, Jeremy knew, a political choice, not a matter of policy. 'It is your decision,' he said, 'but we still have a lot to do to fix this crisis.'

Another week passed. By this point, the Prime Minister was chairing the COBR meetings and vaccination was gaining increased support, including from the Family Farm Alliance, which argued that the government should put the rural economy and the protection of the UK's cattle, pig and sheep herds above the value of the export market. But each time the issue was raised, MAFF and the National Farmers' Union again dismissed it – the disease was, they said, about to peak so the priority had to be to get the cull done.

No decision had been taken on vaccination by the time Jeremy left for the G8 sherpa meeting in Sicily on 29 March 2001. However, the Prime Minister was by then on the verge of postponing the election, which he did on 2 April having seen the results of Philip Gould's focus groups in Shropshire.

While Jeremy was away, our twelve-week pregnancy scan became due, so I went back into the clinic to have another gel-laden sensor run over my stomach.

'Hold on a moment,' the nurse said a few minutes into our consultation. She put the scanner down, and as I watched the door close behind her, I tried to shut out of my mind the memory of a similar moment six months previously.

The nurse returned, as her predecessor had done, accompanied by a man in a white coat.

'What is it?' I asked.

The nurse's eyes darted around to meet mine, the probe back in her hand. She glanced at her companion. 'We can see blood inside the embryo's stomach,' she said, pointing towards the screen where, in the baby's tiny tummy, white speckles floated like stars.

I watched the baby's arms and legs waving at me. 'What does that mean?' I asked, my words emerging like an extended wheeze.

'It could mean nothing,' she said, giving me a tight smile, 'or it could be serious. I'm afraid you'll need to come back in three days' time when our expert scanner will be here.'

Seventy-two hours later, I was back outside the clinic, walking up and down on the pavement next to its black metal railings while I talked to Jeremy who was still in Italy.

'It's going to be okay,' he said like he always did. 'But ring me the moment you can. I'm stuck out here in an airless room discussing a communiqué on HIV, malaria and TB and I can't concentrate.'

I walked into the clinic and lay down. Minutes passed while I listened to my heart pumping, replaying in my mind all the horrible things I'd learnt from the internet about what this symptom could mean. The next few minutes could be life changing, and for once I resented the fact that Jeremy wasn't there.

A new doctor came in, picked up the probe and moved it over my stomach.

'This is absolutely fine,' he said to the nurse, 'can't you see that?'

They kept talking while I lay on the bed, tears rolling down my cheeks. 'Hello baby, you're okay,' I whispered.

'I knew Stanley would be all right,' Jeremy said when I called him afterwards.

I smiled. 'He won't be called Stanley. Remember our deal.'

By the time Jeremy returned from Italy at the end of March, 950 cases of foot and mouth had been reported in the UK and the department had asked the EU Standing Veterinary Committee for contingent permission to vaccinate.

'It's now clear that the economic impact of culling on tourism is far greater than the losses caused by a year or so of reduced exports if we vaccinate,' David told Jeremy.

'We should have known this weeks ago.'

'I know. And my relations with the department are now so poor that the last time I went over to join one of their meetings, they threw me out.'

Over the next few days, work accelerated across Whitehall to try to work out whether vaccination was still feasible. The answer that came back was that they were too late – there were only 500,000 doses of vaccine in the UK so another 4.5 million would have to be ordered from Europe. Getting these would take a week, another week would pass while they were administered, and the vaccine wouldn't start to work until four days after that. In those two and a half weeks, the spread of the disease could be extensive.

Despite this, on 10 April, by which time more than 1,200 cases had been reported, David King and the government's chief veterinary officer, Jim Scudamore, both began to support vaccination, though Nick Brown and the National Farmers' Union remained opposed. But by this point, Jeremy had given up. When the crisis was over, they would work out why it had been impossible to persuade the department to create a Plan B, but for now they just had to get the cull done and eradicate the disease.

While the various agriculture factions continued to squabble, Jeremy turned his attention to his next issue – the government's escalating row with Ken Livingstone, the popular left-wing first Mayor of London, over the public–private partnership for London Underground. This partnership had been put together in March 1998 with one objective in mind – getting the Tube, and the estimated £7 billion of investment that it required over the following fifteen years, off the government's balance sheet without privatising it, something that Labour had ruled out in its manifesto. The solution that the Treasury and the Department of the Environment, Transport and the Regions had devised separated the trains from the track. Three private sector consortia would maintain the track, handing it over each morning to London Underground so they could run the trains. In theory, the better the consortia did their job, the lower the penalties they would receive when trains didn't run, and the higher their returns would be. It looked like a win-win.

The reality was, of course, far more complex. Detailed contracts had to be put in place to allocate penalties, but such a legalistic approach made it difficult to run a railway in real time. And London Underground needed some influence over the maintenance schedules for the track, but if it had too much, there was a risk that the whole convoluted structure would be classified as still being within the public sector.

Outside the Treasury and the department, the partnership had few admirers. But opposition to it was subdued – after all, everyone wanted to see more investment in the Tube, parts of which, Jeremy often argued using our local Clapham South station as an example, looked like they hadn't seen a lick of paint for decades. But this uneasy truce was broken after Ken Livingstone appointed Bob Kiley, an ex-CIA agent and head of New York's Metropolitan Transport Authority, as London's first Transport Commissioner. The public–private partnership was fatally flawed, Bob declared, and investment in the track should instead be paid for by a £3.8 billion bond secured against future ticket sales.

In March 2001, the Prime Minister decided to act. He'd never shown any interest in the Tube before, but his political antennae were twitching, partly because the criticisms about the public–private partnership bore an uncanny similarity to the concerns about Railtrack, and partly because he had a secret, grudging respect for Ken Livingstone – a view not shared by Gordon Brown. 'Ken and Bob Kiley may have a point,' Blair told Jeremy, 'so can you go and talk to Bob to see if we can find a compromise?'

This request made Jeremy feel nauseous. While the Prime Minister's faith in his ability to sort things out was flattering, this was a horrendously complex deal, laid out in thousands of pages of legal text. 'I think I should take a Treasury official with me,' he said.

But the Prime Minister shook his head. 'No. It's better if you go alone – all the Treasury will do is defend the current arrangement.'

So, Jeremy headed out for several meetings in Bob's grand, rent-free Regency townhouse in Belgravia. Since he was happy to ignore Bob's mildly patronising tone, these sessions were amicable enough. They even identified a few areas where the partnership could be simplified. But for all the polite chat, the discussions ultimately went nowhere since it was clear Bob wanted the scheme scrapped not tweaked.

In the middle of all this, Jeremy and I joined a friend's birthday dinner at the St. John restaurant in Smithfield. I sat down next to Shriti Vadera, one of the Chancellor's special advisers and a key architect of the Tube deal, and glanced across the table to see Jeremy tipping his head towards the door. When I smiled back, his twitches became more frenetic. I sighed and put down my glass.

'Whatever you do,' Jeremy said when we met outside the door, 'you mustn't mention my meetings with Bob Kiley. The Treasury will go nuts if they think I'm trying to unravel their work of beauty.'

I laughed. 'Of course, I won't.'

On 17 May 2001, for the first time since the start of the foot and mouth outbreak, a whole day passed with no new cases being reported. As the crisis receded, Whitehall turned its attention to helping the regions most affected by the disease and the Prime Minister and his political advisers focused on the election, which had been rescheduled for 7 June.

On a rainy Wednesday morning in mid-May, Jeremy left everyone working on their various issues while he went to meet Michael Barber in Café Churchill. It was time at last to shape the Delivery Unit.

'The Prime Minister and Richard Wilson are both signed up to it,' he told Michael after describing his thinking, 'and I'm going to try to warm up the Treasury while the Chancellor and Ed Balls are out on the campaign trail.'

'I'm sure the unit will make a difference,' Michael said, nodding.

Jeremy sipped his coffee. 'The Prime Minister and Jonathan are talking about heading it up with someone from the private sector, but would you consider doing it?'

'Maybe – though I was thinking of applying to be the Director of Schools.'

'You should still apply for that because this might not happen. But whatever you decide, I'd be grateful if you could do a paper for me on how a Delivery Unit might work.'

A few days after Michael agreed to do this, Jeremy had a similar conversation with Andrew Turnbull, the permanent secretary to the Treasury. Andrew was, however, far less enthusiastic. He was worried, he said, that the unit would cut across the Treasury's responsibility for holding departments to account.

Jeremy rang Michael Barber afterwards. 'I tried to moderate Andrew's view, including by pointing out that the unit will only focus on a few PSA targets,' he said, 'but I don't think he's convinced. However, if it has the Cabinet Secretary's support, there's still a good chance of it going ahead, so it would help if you could take Richard through your thinking.'

'Sure,' Michael said – and this tactic worked, with Richard coming to see Jeremy afterwards to say he still supported the idea of a Delivery Unit and that Michael Barber had promised to work up, with remarkable speed, a paper on how it might operate.

With the thinking on the Delivery Unit progressing, Jeremy turned his attention to the rest of his pre-election thinking. As part of his preparation for the Labour win that the polls were suggesting, his red folders included a draft Queen's Speech that laid out the new government's legislative programme based on their manifesto. He was also preparing, at the Prime Minister's request, thinking on several possible machinery of government changes. These included merging MAFF, which had become too close to its industry, with the Department of the Environment, Transport and the Regions and a small part of the Home Office. The new department emerging from this mash-up would be called the Department for the Environment and Rural Affairs, with both farming and food eradicated from its name.

While he prepared his briefing folders, Jeremy was also monitoring the parties' pronouncements on the campaign trail. These included Tony Blair's speech in Gravesend, Kent in late May in which he declared that he would set aside his first-term mantra of reforming the public sector by changing 'standards not structures'. In his second term he would instead set three goals: achieving high minimum standards in every public service, building public services around the consumer and devolving greater responsibility and authority to local leaders.

Jeremy was delighted by this shift in emphasis since he shared the Prime Minister's view that, in many cases, structural change would be needed to make the UK's public services world class. This was, he told me, an agenda he was keen to help make happen.

13

'The Times They Are A-Changin'': Civil servants must have ideas

June–September 2001

On 7 June 2001, Tony Blair was re-elected with a majority of 167, one that was only slightly reduced from his original majority of 179. 'It has been a remarkable and historic victory for my party,' he said on the steps of Number 10, 'but I'm in no doubt at all as to what it means. It is a mandate for reform and for investment in the future and it is also very clearly an instruction to deliver.'

A few days after the election, Jonathan Powell put the latest version of John Birt's *An Effective Centre* back into the Prime Minister's box, but for several days Blair was so focused on persuading Anji Hunter and Alastair Campbell to stay on that Jeremy began to wonder whether their much-debated reorganisation would ever happen. In the meantime, however, they announced their machinery of government changes – although, after complaints from the National Farmers' Union, they agreed to include food in the title of the new environment department, making it the Department for the Environment, Food and Rural Affairs, or Defra.

A week later, on Thursday 14 June, the Prime Minister at last agreed the new structure for the centre of government. Some of the changes that this required, like combining the Private Office and Policy Unit to form a Policy Directorate that Jeremy would lead with Andrew Adonis as his deputy, were relatively straightforward to put in place over the following few days. It was also simple to implement the only remnant of the plan to merge the Cabinet Office and Number 10, which involved making David Manning, the Prime

Minister's foreign policy adviser, also the head of the Defence and Overseas Secretariat in the Cabinet Office and Stephen Wall, the Prime Minister's Europe adviser, also the head of the European Secretariat. Geoff Mulgan was, meanwhile, appointed to lead the new Forward Strategy Unit and found offices for it in the back of Downing Street.

The birth of the Delivery Unit was far more difficult. Michael Barber, who'd agreed in the end to lead it, established with the Prime Minister the subset of PSA goals that it would pursue across health, education, crime and transport. But despite Jeremy's careful positioning and Richard Wilson's support, the Treasury remained so unhappy about its creation that the Chancellor refused even to let Michael circulate details of the new unit's objectives around Whitehall.

The final piece of the reorganisation jigsaw was the creation of a new team focused on public sector reform. This was also controversial because, although Richard Wilson was responsible for public sector reform, the Prime Minister had somehow forgotten to mention it to him in their first bilateral after the election.

'Can you talk to Richard?' Blair asked Jeremy. 'I'm sure he won't mind.'

'Okay,' Jeremy said, though he was certain the Prime Minister knew how difficult the conversation would be.

After pondering this issue for a while, Jeremy set up a meeting with Richard to discuss public sector reform and invited the proposed head of the new unit, Wendy Thomson, a Canadian public sector reformer, to join this. In the meeting they then recreated the idea of the new unit, which, when Richard Wilson proposed it to the Prime Minister, was enthusiastically agreed.

The press reaction to all this restructuring was mixed. The *Financial Times*, for example, muttered about Blair's 'Napoleonic' tendencies. However, it also quoted a 'Labour insider' who believed, as Jeremy did, that it 'wasn't possible to run a modern democracy' without the Prime Minister being 'properly briefed and able to lead strategy and monitor delivery'.

* * *

While Jeremy was pleased with the organisational changes in Downing Street, and happy that things were also calm at home – I was four months pregnant and no longer feeling nauseous – he told me he was still worried about the difficult relationship between the Chancellor and the Prime Minister. There were endless arguments between them but relations hit a new low in July 2001 during a ferocious bilateral in which they argued about why the government's case against Bob Kiley wasn't being made and who should be making it.*

'They've got off on the wrong foot ever since the election,' Jeremy told me. 'Unless this gets better, it's going to be harder to get things done in the Prime Minister's second term than it was in his first.'

Jeremy had this in mind when, towards the end of July, he joined Blair and the rest of the Number 10 team in the wood-panelled drawing room at Chequers to discuss the agenda for the new Parliament. At the Prime Minister's request, he summarised the state of the economy and its likely impact on the 2002 spending review. The situation was deteriorating, Jeremy said, because manufacturing output was falling, probably due to the gloomier global economic outlook. This, in turn, was likely to impact GDP and would constrain the UK's ability to increase public spending – particularly since the measures already agreed, like the Chancellor's tax credits, were eating up an ever larger slice of the available pie. In the future they would face tough choices about where to invest.

After Jeremy's update, Michael Barber took the floor to describe more welcome news – the Delivery Unit had agreed baseline data for each of its PSA targets and was beginning to understand what was blocking delivery. This then led into a debate about the Prime Minister's objectives for public sector reform and the three principles he'd described in his Gravesend speech before the election.

As he listened to this, Jeremy found himself again getting excited about Tony Blair's reform agenda. But he also realised that there was

* The fight over the public–private partnership for the Tube had been trundling on since Jeremy's failed intervention back in April and would continue for several more years before one of the private sector consortia maintaining the tracks collapsed and the other was taken over by London Underground.

something missing from the Prime Minister's list of principles – something that, from an economist's perspective, could be more effective than anything else in raising standards.

'I think we're missing a fourth principle,' he said after a while. 'What if we add in choice? We've already seen how allowing parents to have a choice of school impacts education standards and we're expecting school vouchers to have a similar effect.'

This idea divided the room. Alastair Campbell and Fiona Millar – one of the other special advisers and Alastair's partner – argued that, for most people, choice was meaningless and Sally Morgan, the director of government relations, thought it might not resonate with the broader Labour Party. But everyone else, including the Prime Minister and Andrew Adonis, was intrigued, so they agreed to discuss it again in the autumn.

Shortly after their meeting in Chequers, most of Number 10, including the Prime Minister, dispersed to various exotic holiday destinations. We were the exception because, after spotting an irregularity in the blood flow through our baby's umbilical cord, our doctor had grounded us in the UK. So, we instead spent the summer ambling around ruined castles and abbeys in Wales while debating whether Jeremy should leave the Civil Service to go and work for BEA Systems, a software company in Silicon Valley. But while Jeremy was finding his sixteen-hour days in Number 10 exhausting, and was grateful to Michael Levy, Tony Blair's close friend and the special envoy to the Middle East, who had found this opportunity for him, he told me he didn't want to be beholden to anyone for getting him a job.

In early September, the Number 10 team brought their tans back to Chequers for another debate about choice, this time informed by a paper from the Forward Strategy Unit. Again, Jeremy argued in favour, pointing out how helpful it would be for working parents with small children – a category he hoped he was about to join – to be able to choose a GP surgery with opening hours that suited them. And this time, most people agreed. The more controversial point was then whether, alongside choice, the government should push for greater 'contestability' – by which they meant making it easier for organisations outside the public sector, including profit-making private companies, to provide public services.

This second discussion went on for some time, but in the end, the Prime Minister was clear. 'I've listened to the debate,' he said, 'and I'm in favour of both choice and contestability.'

Ironically for Jeremy, who also supported contestability, back in Downing Street he was still worrying about Railtrack, a company that had come to symbolise private sector failure. After imposing speed restrictions across the rail network, Railtrack had seen both its popularity with its customers and its financial performance deteriorate, and in May 2001 had reported a loss of £500 million. Within Number 10, Andrew Adonis was leading the thinking on what could be done, working closely with the Department for Transport and with Shriti Vadera, the Chancellor's special adviser, who mixed technical brilliance and creativity with a deep impatience with lesser mortals.

Though Railtrack was privately owned, the government couldn't let it collapse because, without its vital public service, the country would literally grind to a halt. By July, Jeremy was clear that the best option – if it turned out that Railtrack could not continue – was for it to become a not-for-profit trust. Ideally, someone would buy Railtrack, but given the political nature of its role, and the fact that it knew little about the infrastructure it maintained, no one was interested. And Terry Burns told Jeremy that a not-for-profit trust was working well in the case of Dŵr Cymru (Welsh Water), which he was chairing – though that was a far smaller business.

Andrew Adonis agreed that a trust was a possibility – he even told the Prime Minister that it could be a classic 'third way' solution. But his preferred solution was to nationalise Railtrack.

Jeremy shook his head when they discussed this. 'Nationalisation led to years of under-investment in the railways,' he said. 'A not-for-profit trust would remove the profit motive from what is a monopoly public service and the bond markets will help enforce market discipline.'

'I don't like either option because I'm not keen to take Railtrack out of the private sector,' Tony Blair said. But he didn't rule out the possibility of creating a trust, so through the autumn of 2001 the Department for Transport worked through the legal and financial consequences of putting one in place, closely monitored by Andrew and Shriti.

The other issue again in Andrew and Jeremy's in-trays that autumn was reforming the funding of higher education. Despite his efforts to avoid taking a decision on this before the election, the Prime Minister had felt forced to rule out top-up fees in the manifesto. The problem, therefore, was how to implement them without breaking that commitment. One way to do this would be to label top-up fees as taxes – after all, they resembled a tax in that they were paid for a period after graduation rather than being paid up front. The Chancellor, however, resisted this labelling. Although he agreed that graduates should bear some of the cost of their degrees, he believed a fixed fee would put off students from working-class backgrounds. Instead, he wanted to put in place a 'true' graduate tax that students would begin paying when they began work, with higher earners paying more for the whole of their careers.

Andrew Adonis and Jeremy spent hours with the Treasury and the Department for Education working through different versions of top-up fees and graduate taxes. Jeremy, however, was clear from early on that a fixed fee was preferable to a graduate tax. Leaving aside the fairness of taxing graduates more heavily than non-graduates who were earning the same amount, including those with inherited wealth, a tax would only begin generating money after people graduated. It, therefore, wouldn't help universities in the short term and would increase borrowing – something the Treasury would normally reject out of hand. He was also concerned that the amount people would pay would bear no relationship to the quality of their degrees, so it wouldn't drive up standards by creating competition as the Prime Minister intended. And a 2 or 3 per cent increase in income tax would mean people at the upper end of the earnings distribution paying more to go to university in England than they would if they attended Harvard or Yale.

After months of negotiation, they reached an impasse. Ed Balls told Jeremy the Chancellor wasn't willing to accept top-up fees and

Jeremy told Ed that, if the Chancellor still wanted a graduate tax, the Treasury would have to come up with a different version of it. And there they left the discussion, though they knew it was only a question of time before it would have to be resolved.

All in all, although Jeremy was delighted that the Prime Minister had embraced choice and contestability as ways to accelerate public sector reform, the autumn of 2001 had been frustrating. Despite his attempts to resolve the various domestic policy rows swirling around the government, Railtrack remained on the brink of collapse, top-up fees were stuck, Bob Kiley and Ken Livingstone were still trying to take the government to court over the public–private partnership for the Tube and there was no sign of the Treasury doing any work on the Chancellor's five tests for joining EMU. Meanwhile, my tolerance for Jeremy's working hours was waning as my stomach grew and I began to worry about how we would cope when, in addition to us both working, we were also caring for a baby.

Then something happened that made all of this feel irrelevant.

14

'The Rising':
Nothing will ever be the same

September 2001–January 2002

On Tuesday 11 September 2001, Jeremy got back to his desk from lunch at the Institute of Contemporary Arts to find Sky News showing footage of the twin towers in New York. One tower had a cavernous hole in its side, out of which spurted streams of fierce, black smoke.

'A plane has crashed into the World Trade Center,' the presenter said.

Jeremy picked up the phone. 'Are you watching this?' he asked Richard Wilson's private secretary.

'Yes, it's horrific.'

'Where's Richard?'

'He's having lunch with Wendy Thomson at the Gran Paradiso. He's not due back for a while, but I'll see if I can track him down.'

Jeremy replaced the handset and looked back at the screen. A second plane was approaching the towers. It hit. Jeremy looked away.

The door into the Prime Minister's office burst open and Jonathan Powell appeared. 'Is it true there are two planes?'

'Yes,' Jeremy said, shaking his head. He picked up his phone again.

'I'm sorry,' the girl at the other end of the line said, 'but the civil contingencies team is in Easingwold doing a team-building exercise.'

Both of the towers were collapsing. People were jumping out of windows, arms outspread. The world was falling apart, and no one was around to help.

When the phone rang on Jonathan's desk, Jeremy refocused, Jonathan was waving to indicate that Jeremy should pick up his handset.

It was Tony Blair calling from Brighton where he was due to talk to the TUC. 'I've cancelled my speech. I'm just going to say a few words before coming back up to London,' he said.

'Good,' Jeremy said, 'we need you here.'

'Are you sure there aren't any planes flying towards Downing Street?' the Prime Minister asked.

Jeremy hadn't considered this. His hands felt clammy. No one had issued any warnings, though it was possible the people who operated the UK's air defence systems were also having a day out. 'I'll find someone who can tell us,' he said.

While the Number 10 switchboard tried to locate President Bush so the Prime Minister could talk to him on his way back up to London, Jeremy spoke to Richard Wilson, who was by then in his car.

'No one seems to know whether Downing Street might be targeted but the White House has been evacuated,' Jeremy said. 'Do you think we should do the same?'

The line was silent for a moment. 'Where would you evacuate to?' Richard asked.

'I don't know.'

'In that case stay where you are. I'm coming back in to set up a COBR meeting.'

'Okay.'

On the other side of the room, Jonathan was listening in to the Prime Minister's conversations with various world leaders including Jacques Chirac, Gerhard Schröder and Vladimir Putin, though not President Bush, who was on Air Force One. While Jonathan did that, Jeremy watched the TV. The scale of the destruction was hard to comprehend. Thousands of people had been killed and nothing seemed safe anymore.

When the Prime Minister arrived back in Downing Street a while later, Jeremy and Jonathan joined his briefing with Stephen Lander, the head of MI5, and John Scarlett, the chair of the Joint Intelligence Committee, before going to Richard's COBR meeting, which was crowded with intelligence and defence experts. They started by considering what else could be done to protect the country, London and Downing Street. The answer was not much – apart from closing the UK's small airports, stopping commercial flights over the centre of London and confirming who had the right to decide to shoot down a plane if it looked like it was heading for a UK target. After that they pondered the Americans' likely reaction to the attack, though this was mainly surmise since, although they had the views of the British embassy in Washington, no one had yet managed to talk to the US administration. They finished with a briefing on Al-Qaeda and the Taliban. Jeremy knew little about these exotically titled groups, and judging by the knotted faces in the room, he suspected he wasn't the only one.

That night, Tony Blair made a statement from the pillared room on the first floor of Downing Street, his words capturing the emotion of the day, making it into something more: 'This is not a battle between the United States of America and terrorism, but between the free and democratic world and terrorism. We, therefore, here in Britain stand shoulder to shoulder with our American friends in this hour of tragedy, and we, like them, will not rest until this evil is driven from our world.'

In the week after 9/11 there were so many meetings at so many different levels that Jeremy feared the critical would be drowned out by the urgent. The Prime Minister worried about handling the Americans while Richard concentrated on the legality of the government's decision to close the privately owned City Airport and how long the airspace over London should remain shut. The Number 10 foreign policy team rallied support for a new UN Security Council resolution and pressed other countries to ratify the UN convention on terrorism, and the security experts put together the available evidence on the attack, including the extent of Osama bin Laden's culpability.

Jeremy, meanwhile, focused on the policy consequences of 9/11 including trying to figure out with the Treasury and the Bank of England how to disrupt terrorists' funding and working with the Home Office on how the asylum rules could be changed to make it possible to deport suspected terrorists without breaching the European Convention on Human Rights. He couldn't do anything to bring back the lives lost on 9/11, but it would be unforgivable if he missed this opportunity, while barriers to change in Whitehall had been lowered, to make the country safer.

That moment when the Prime Minister had asked whether more planes were flying towards Downing Street was also preying on Jeremy's mind – a worry reinforced a few days later when an envelope full of fake anthrax arrived in the post room. He, therefore, asked Simon Virley to review their vulnerabilities, and as one result of this, the Forward Strategy Unit was booted out of the building to find a new home in Admiralty Arch.

As part of his review, Simon took the Prime Minister and Cherie Blair through Downing Street's evacuation plans, so they knew where they should go in any future emergency.

'Cherie wasn't amused by the prospect of being cooped up in a suite of airless rooms,' Simon told Jeremy when he returned, 'and the pictures of golf courses on the walls and the plastic plants didn't help.'

'At least she's invited,' Jeremy said, remembering a conversation we'd had the night before, where he'd told me that I wasn't on the list. Which made the whole thing rather pointless, he'd added, at least for him.

It was soon clear that one of the consequences of 9/11 was that the Prime Minister would need to spend far more time on foreign affairs – a point Blair brought up with Jeremy and Andrew Adonis when they went to meet him in his flat above Number 11 one evening in late September. While he was doing that, the Prime Minister wanted them to keep pushing forward his domestic policy priorities.

I nodded when Jeremy told me this, and said it was fine if he was busy at work until my due date. The pregnancy was going well, with none of the potential complications having come to pass. My main guilt was my reluctance to watch the news, as I was finding it difficult to cope with other mothers' grief when we were at last on the verge of having a child of our own.

It was lucky I was comfortable with Jeremy's working hours because, in addition to Jeremy's other priorities, a report from Credit Suisse First Boston in late September showed that, if the government didn't inject £4 billion into Railtrack within weeks, it was likely to go bankrupt. With few options left, the Prime Minister reluctantly accepted that they should convert the company into a not-for-profit trust.

On Friday 5 September, Stephen Byers, the Secretary of State for Transport, went to tell John Robinson, Railtrack's chair, that his company was about to disappear. Days of drama followed. On Sunday, the company went into administration, and on Monday a row exploded when people realised that the government had said nothing about compensating Railtrack's shareholders.

The issue of compensation had, of course, been discussed within government – it just hadn't been resolved. The Chancellor and Shriti Vadera were insisting that shareholders should receive nothing, while Stephen Byers, Andrew Adonis and Jeremy thought there was little sense in outraging shareholders who would then do whatever they could to block Railtrack's conversion into a trust.

With Railtrack's directors threatening to serve the government with an injunction, the Prime Minister decided that he was also unhappy about clawing back everything possible. After all, as his economic adviser Derek Scott pointed out, without investors there would be no new railways. Following considerable negotiation, it was, therefore, agreed that shareholders would receive the residual value in the company, though not the benefit of any new money from taxpayers.

By this time Jeremy had begun joining me at our weekly antenatal classes. He was, I knew, excited about our imminent parenthood. In fact, Jeremy had originally been more anxious than I'd been about starting to create a family and I'd recently filmed a video of him talking about his expectations of fatherhood – though these mainly centred around his hope that his firstborn son would take on some of his already short list of household chores.

But while the pregnancy dominated my life, for Jeremy it was something he fought to include, almost always turning up late for our classes, sitting on the teacher's doorstep to finish off calls about Railtrack, the Autumn Statement or even asylum, after David Blunkett, the home secretary, decided he wanted to spend £500 million building a network of fifty accommodation centres to house claimants after the numbers had reached record levels the previous year.

'Gordon was so furious about the cost of the home secretary's proposal, which hadn't been agreed with the Treasury in advance, that he turned up in person for the Prime Minister's meeting on it,' Jeremy told me one evening while we watched our teacher demonstrate how to change a nappy.

'So, what will happen next?'

'The usual. We didn't reach an agreement, so the Prime Minister has asked me to go through the Home Office's plans.'

I smiled at this, but before we could continue, Jeremy was called forward and handed a plastic doll with its bare bottom covered in Marmite.

He held it at arm's length. 'What on earth do I do with this?' he hissed at me.

'No questions,' the teacher said, while I grinned, 'I want to see how you cope on your own.'

'Okay,' Jeremy said. But while the other partners got to work on their dolls, opening packets of wipes and dabbing at plastic cheeks, Jeremy stood motionless in the middle of the room. After a few minutes, he strode into the kitchen, turned on the cold tap and shoved the doll bottom-first underneath.

The rest of the class crowded in behind him, laughing, while the instructor looked stern. 'That is not the ideal method,' she said.

Jeremy kept working while my belly kept growing. By the time David Blunkett reviewed his revised proposal with the Prime Minister on 17 October, I was thirty-five weeks pregnant and trying to construct an IKEA baby changing table on my own, having discovered that Jeremy's inability to think in three dimensions or to use a screwdriver rendered him virtually useless as an assistant.

This time the asylum debate was about whether the government should build two or six accommodation centres over the next two years. Again there was a massive row, with the Prime Minister and David Blunkett on one side and the Chancellor on the other.

After this Jeremy chaired a series of official-level meetings in which they wrestled their way to a compromise. This allowed David Blunkett to announce on 29 October that four trial accommodation centres would be built, together with more removal centres to speed up the deportation of failed applicants. A smart card for asylum seekers would also be introduced to improve identification and cut down on illegal working. These measures helped address some of the concerns about asylum, but perhaps in retrospect the government should have accepted something closer to David Blunkett's original proposal, given the role that the public's resentment about immigration would later play in Britain's decisions about its place in the world.

Early one Sunday morning in November, I went into labour. After going into hospital for a check-up, we spent hours at home watching the movie *Proof of Life* in short segments between contractions, with Jeremy taking detailed – if somewhat irrelevant – notes of the times when they occurred.

This is not the place to recount our birth story. I know we were lucky, at least during this stage of becoming parents. Although there was significant pain and some fear, after we went back into hospital that evening, the pain was soon under control and there were no complications. The last few minutes while we waited for our consultant to turn up to supervise the delivery were magical. I no longer felt the contractions, Jeremy was sipping a glass of wine from the bottle that he'd snuck into my hospital bag, and on the TV above us, the White Stripes were playing a set on Jools Holland. Afterwards, when we'd become three – Jeremy, me and Jonathan, or Jonny for short – we stayed overnight in the hospital, with Jonny tucked up in a clear plastic cot while Jeremy and I shared a single bed next to him, too happy to sleep.

Jeremy returned to Number 10 after a week at home on paternity leave to find Andrew Adonis in the middle of the traditional fight with the Treasury over the November pre-Budget report.

'Tony wants a tax credit for in-work training and a £1 billion injection into the NHS to help clear waiting lists. Neither should be contentious,' Andrew said, 'but both certainly are.'

Andrew was right – in fact the negotiations were so difficult that they only concluded late on 25 November, the evening before the report was published. The most significant part of the report, at least in Jeremy's view, was the announcement of the interim conclusions of the Wanless Review. This long-term assessment of the health service was the one that the Chancellor had mentioned back in his March 2000 Budget Statement and the latest move in the health one-upmanship that the Prime Minister had kicked off at the start of the millennium.

Jeremy had been worried about this assessment ever since it had been proposed, and his concern had increased after he'd heard that Derek Wanless, a former banker with no known healthcare views or expertise, had been appointed to lead it. The interim conclusions in the pre-Budget report reinforced his anxiety – in fact they were so similar to Gordon Brown's views that some suspected Derek was being ventriloquised by Ed Balls. Healthcare in Britain was inferior to what was available in comparable countries, it would take two decades of investment to repair the damage and alternative models for financing the NHS were likely to be less fair or would offer worse value for money.

After the pre-Budget report, the Treasury fell silent again on the NHS. But by then Jeremy knew it was only a matter of time until the Chancellor revealed his full plans – particularly since, through various verbal contortions and non-answers in the run-up to the election, he'd kept alive the possibility of increasing NHS funding by raising National Insurance contributions, something Tony Blair had set his face against since becoming Labour leader. There was little Jeremy could do to change this – though he did start thinking through some of the health reforms that the Prime Minister might want to demand in exchange.

At home, I was finding Jeremy no better at caring for a real baby than his performance in our antenatal classes had suggested. But he was clearly delighted by our little family because he often came home early to cuddle Jonny on his lap while he made calls or read papers, and never tired of discussing baby trivia with me, like Jonny's early smiles, which we were both convinced were not wind.

Many of Jeremy's discussions at that time were about Northern Ireland. Although this was a topic he knew little about and, therefore, usually left to the experts, the Prime Minister had asked him to help the Northern Ireland Executive negotiate an agreement with the Treasury that would allow them to convert sites like the Maze Prison into community facilities. As usual, however, this Treasury discussion wasn't straightforward – this time because Northern Ireland also wanted to be given permission to borrow, a power the Treasury was refusing to relinquish.

By December 2001, Jonny was a month old and definitely smiling and Jeremy's Northern Ireland work was well on the way to becoming the Reinvestment and Reform Initiative, which was agreed in May 2002. This was also when Jeremy told me that, at long last, the Treasury had begun the preliminary and technical work on the euro that it needed to do before it started thinking about the five tests.

When I laughed at this, Jeremy grinned. 'Yes, I know it sounds ridiculous, but you wouldn't believe the excitement this has caused in Number 10.'

'Do you think we might join the euro?'

Jeremy shook his head. 'Many of my Number 10 colleagues do, but I don't think we'll pass the tests. It's also notable that, though he keeps telling people he's keen, the Prime Minister didn't make any further commitments on the euro in the manifesto, and even before 9/11, he wasn't raising the possibility of joining in his bilaterals with the Chancellor.'

The other issue on Jeremy's mind at the end of 2001 was Richard Wilson's planned retirement the following summer. Despite the occasional tense moments between the Cabinet Office and Downing Street – something Jeremy was later to experience for himself – Richard had much to be proud of from his tenure as Cabinet Secretary, including the role he'd played in the foot and mouth crisis and after 9/11. But now it was time for Richard to move on, and what this created, Jonathan Powell argued, was an opportunity to implement John Birt's plan of bringing in a senior private sector leader to lead and reform the Civil Service while the Cabinet Secretary focused on managing the Cabinet and Cabinet secretariats. The Prime Minister was enthusiastic about splitting the Cabinet Secretary's responsibilities in this way, but Jeremy wasn't surprised when a note laying out Richard's objections arrived in time for Blair's Christmas box. It seemed, Jeremy told me, that one final battle was going to take place before Richard's departure, and he had no idea this time who would win.

After spending most of his Christmas break entertaining Jonny, Jeremy returned to Number 10 to find the Prime Minister more excited about Andrew Adonis's Christmas memo on choice and contestability, which included ideas like rolling out choice for elective surgery nationally from the end of 2005, than he was about this looming fight with Richard Wilson.

'I want all of it,' the Prime Minister told Andrew. 'But I also need my ministers to understand my ambition for public sector reform.'

'We could use a Cabinet committee to do that,' Jeremy said, somewhat mischievously.

The Prime Minister eyed Jeremy. 'I don't want any more committees.'

Though this was a 'no', it was less definitive than Jeremy had expected given Blair's well-known dislike of formal structures. 'It's how Margaret Thatcher ensured her ministers knew what she wanted,' he said, 'and perhaps we could make it a group rather than a committee?'

The Prime Minister sighed. 'Okay. If that's what it will take.'

This was, for a change, a piece of news that Richard Wilson welcomed. Over the next few days, he set up the Public Services Reform Group, which included the Chancellor together with various ministers sympathetic to the Prime Minister's thinking like Charles Clarke, David Blunkett and Stephen Byers.

'It was useful,' the Prime Minister said with a degree of surprise after the group's first discussion on 31 January. So, after that it met regularly to discuss some of Tony Blair's favourite topics including reducing the bureaucracy in public services and delegating power to frontline service providers. Which showed, Jeremy told me, that if it was helpful, then even the most bureaucracy-allergic Prime Minister could be tempted to use the system.

On Friday 18 January 2002, the Number 10 team gathered to agree their objectives for the April 2002 Budget and the July spending review. They called this an away day despite the fact that they didn't go far – only to the Cabinet Room – though Tony Blair turned up in jeans to mark the occasion. But despite the casual attire, it was a difficult discussion. The Policy Unit had worked up a long list of policy priorities based on the 2001 manifesto and insisted that all of them were essential. However, others like Derek Scott were far more cautious because, as Jeremy had warned six months earlier, the economy was weakening. Manufacturing output was falling at its steepest rate for a decade although consumer spending was keeping the UK out of recession.

The debate went on for some time with Derek arguing that spending shouldn't increase by more than 2.2 per cent – the expected growth rate of the economy – while virtually everyone else, Jeremy included despite some qualms, argued that more than this would be needed to deliver the Prime Minister's reform agenda.

At the end of a long day, which culminated in Jeremy performing a series of back-of-the-envelope calculations to work out the implications of the different numbers being put forward, the Prime Minister sighed. 'I think we will need significant increases for the NHS, education and defence,' he said, 'and I'm willing to see taxes rise to fund them. But only if they come with real reform.'

This was a substantial shift in the Prime Minister's position. But, Jeremy reflected as he threw away his scribbled numbers, while it was good for Tony Blair to be clear about what he wanted, getting the Chancellor to share that view was likely to be an entirely different matter.

15

'Do I Wanna Know?':
The euro professor

January–September 2002

On 23 January 2002, almost a year after the Prime Minister had promised that a decision on the euro would be taken within two years, Jeremy and Stephen Wall met Ed Balls and Gus O'Donnell, who was by then the Treasury's managing director in charge of international and macroeconomics, to demand to know what work was being done.

By this time the Treasury's comments about the euro in articles and briefings were becoming increasingly negative. In contrast, even if he also had qualms, Tony Blair was still telling his inner circle that he was prepared to be bold if the economics were right. 'There is,' he declared in one of their meetings, 'no point in being Prime Minister if you don't take risks to do the right thing.'

'The Prime Minister wants to see the preliminary and technical work on the euro,' Jeremy told Ed and Gus. 'He thinks he's waited long enough.'

'Okay,' Gus said, 'but it will take time to go through our seventeen studies and the changeover plan. Why don't we set up a series of seminars to do that?'

Jeremy tried to avoid rolling his eyes. 'That's fine,' he said, 'but this can't take too long – the Prime Minister wants to make a decision by the end of the year so that, if the answer is "yes", it will still be possible to hold a referendum in June 2003.'

The first of these seminars was scheduled for Tuesday 19 February. At 4 p.m. on the Friday beforehand, Kevin, the Treasury's messenger, arrived in Downing Street and placed a sealed brown envelope into Jeremy's hands with all the reverence of transferring a Ming vase. After he left, Jeremy ripped the envelope open, slid out the Treasury's first euro study and set to work. He had to understand the details of the argument and write a briefing note on it for the Prime Minister before the Friday night box deadline – a cut-off he'd imposed himself to allow the Number 10 staff to get home at a reasonable hour after the rest of Whitehall dumped its week's work into their in-trays. The paper was technical, and picking it apart based on a quick skim read late on a Friday was ridiculous. Nevertheless, the Prime Minister's requirement was clear – he wanted Jeremy to provide him with arguments that he could use to rebut the Treasury's most anti-euro conclusions.

On Tuesday morning, the Chancellor, Ed Balls and Gus O'Donnell lined up along one side of the Cabinet table facing the Prime Minister, Jeremy, Jonathan Powell and Stephen Wall. At the far end of the room, Dave Ramsden, the Treasury's head of EMU policy, delivered a ninety-minute seminar. While Dave went through the study's detailed economics, Stephen fidgeted, Jonathan sat glassy-eyed and the Prime Minister's attention came and went. This performance was repeated sixteen times over the following weeks as they ploughed their way through various scintillating topics such as equilibrium exchange rates, the macroeconomic balance approach and the Wren-Lewis estimate.

'This is all very well, Professor, but do we pass the tests?' the Prime Minister asked at the end of each of these lectures. But Dave's reply was always the same – he couldn't give any view until all the technical and preliminary work had been completed.

We were planning to go to Cyprus at the end of March to visit our old flatmate, Philip Barton, who by then had become the deputy high commissioner there. It was a good moment for a break – there was time to spare before the mid-April Budget and the euro seminars were progressing in a stately fashion. But after the Queen Mother died, and the Prime Minister was accused of pushing to make his role in her lying in state more substantive by meeting her coffin when it arrived in Westminster Hall, Jeremy had to stay behind. I tried to be sympathetic about this – after all, the row wasn't Jeremy's fault. But my tolerance was tested during the five hours I spent attempting to calm a screaming baby on his first flight while trying to ignore the evil stares from the other passengers.

Later that week, after tempers eased, Jeremy flew out to join me. Once reunited, we savoured our few days away, but were back in London in time to catch the final act in the long-running saga of finding Richard Wilson's successor. After discussing the issue with the Prime Minister earlier in the year, Richard thought he had seen off the idea of splitting his role and agreed that his replacement would come from within the Civil Service. He'd, therefore, shared this good news with his colleagues and set up a panel to consider candidates.

Unfortunately, the understanding within Number 10 was rather different. While Jonathan had also given up on the idea of dividing the Cabinet Secretary's role, he'd become enthused about the idea of appointing an outsider with Civil Service experience to do the whole job. Maybe by doing this, he'd argued, they could still get a reformer. The potential candidate who kept coming up when this was discussed was Michael Bichard who, prior to his retirement, had worked in local government and been permanent secretary at the Department for Education. But in early March, when Richard discovered that Michael was being considered, and that Jonathan Powell had appointed head-hunters to propose other external names, he demanded a meeting with the Prime Minister.

'Richard was incandescent,' Tony Blair told Jeremy afterwards, shaking his head. 'He told me that what I was proposing was a breach of faith. So I think we'll have to limit ourselves to his internal suggestions. But I've said I want each of them to submit a personal statement about their plans for Civil Service reform.'

After accepting this olive branch, Richard continued his process, informing the Prime Minister on 8 March that he'd interviewed four outstanding candidates and thought that David Omand, an expert in intelligence and security issues, and David Normington, the permanent secretary from Education, were particularly strong because they both had delivery experience.

'What do you think?' the Prime Minister asked Jeremy and Andrew Adonis after Richard left.

'I don't think you should rule out Andrew Turnbull,' Jeremy said. 'He comes from the Treasury, so his background is in policy rather than delivery. But he's pragmatic and he made it clear in his statement that he is open to reform.'

'He's also clever, and knows how to deal with a crisis,' Andrew Adonis said.

'Okay, I'll talk to them all.'

Jeremy spent most of early April deep in the Budget end-game negotiations. He still believed that more spending was needed to deliver the Prime Minister's objectives for public sector reform, but he was becoming increasingly concerned about the overall size of the package. Although debt relative to GDP was falling, the economy was fragile and only time would tell whether the government had built in enough contingency to deal with the unforeseen. However, although Jeremy raised this concern, there was little he could do to change the direction of the Budget, or the significant increase in NHS spending that he was expecting the Chancellor to announce alongside the final Wanless report.

By this point, given the state of relations with the Treasury, Ed Balls wasn't sharing any of the Budget documents, so Jeremy had no idea what Wanless was recommending. But given his interim conclusions, Jeremy had a good idea of where Derek was heading – and he knew how worried the Prime Minister was about middle Britain's response to more taxes being funnelled into health in the absence of any real reform. This, therefore, spurred on the work he'd started with the Number 10 Policy Unit and Alan Milburn's team in the Department of Health to create a package of Blairite health changes that could go alongside the Chancellor's expected announcement.

The Budget on 17 April played out as Jeremy had anticipated. The government would increase public spending by £4 billion in 2003/04, and NHS funding would increase by a breathtaking 48 per cent in real terms by 2007/08, backed up by the Wanless report, which called for a 'very substantial' increase in health spending. The day afterwards, Alan Milburn announced his new set of NHS reforms. These aimed to reduce the maximum waiting time for hospital operations from fifteen months to three by 2008 through the deployment of – among other things – new financial incentives for hospitals, greater choice for patients over where and when they were treated, and penalties for local councils that failed to provide alternatives for people stuck in beds they no longer needed.

Jeremy was relieved that they'd managed to get these health proposals agreed – though he knew, of course, that the NHS would find it far easier to spend the Chancellor's money than to implement the Prime Minister's reforms. He was also disappointed that the Wanless report hadn't spent more time thinking about social care – the means-tested care that took place within the community. Resolving how this should be funded was a long-neglected issue and one that, with an aging population, was becoming increasingly critical. Jeremy was determined to address this, although sadly, despite multiple attempts to do so during his career, he never managed to do so.

Shortly before the Budget, the Prime Minister told Jeremy that, after meeting all the candidates, he'd decided Andrew Turnbull should be the next Cabinet Secretary. Alongside Andrew he also wanted to appoint someone to work on propriety issues. This role had originally been suggested by the Committee on Standards in Public Life, an advisory body to government, and Tony Blair hoped that, by creating it, he would give Andrew more time to work on public sector reform. But while Jeremy thought it was a reasonable proposal, both Richard Wilson and Andrew Turnbull opposed it because they felt it would diminish the Cabinet Secretary's role. This meant yet another negotiation, at the end of which it was decided that, rather than appointing an adviser on propriety, Hayden Philips, the permanent secretary at the Lord Chancellor's Department, would help Andrew with another part of his role, overseeing the honours system. And with that agreed, the identity of the new Cabinet Secretary was at last announced on Friday 19 April.

In May 2002 I went back to work part time. Jeremy had encouraged me to do this, assuring me that it was the right thing to do despite the temptation to stay at home with Jonny. Our new nanny, Maggie, swept in and was already busy clearing out what she referred to as our 'horrific' collection of Babygros, many of which I'd sawn off at the ankles to accommodate Jonny's long legs.

While I began juggling motherhood and work, Jeremy became engrossed in another issue – street crime. This had been increasing for some time, both because more people were carrying around expensive mobile phones and because, in the aftermath of 9/11, the police were focused on countering domestic terrorism. But addressing it became a priority after Iain Duncan Smith, the Leader of the Opposition, claimed in Parliament that criminals on Britain's streets 'only need to walk' from the scene of a crime, and the Prime Minister responded by declaring he was confident the problem would be brought under control 'by the end of September'.

The shock that this Prime Ministerial declaration created within Whitehall was deliberate. Tony Blair knew that the Metropolitan Police's Safer Streets initiative was already beginning to make a difference and he wanted to build on that. He also believed – as did Jeremy – that it was easier to crash through departmental boundaries and get the system thinking creatively in a crisis, even one that was self-imposed.

Jeremy tried to calm this outrage while setting up a series of COBR meetings to work on the Prime Minister's pledge. In these they worked their way along the 'pathway' to offending, starting in childhood, well before crime was contemplated, and going through to rehabilitation and reintegration into the community. At each step, the Prime Minister wanted to know what might make a difference. Diversionary activities, like football or summer camps, would help keep children off the streets and prevent them from being apprenticed as criminals. Bringing police into the roughest schools might also help. And if this failed, and a crime was committed, detection rates would be increased if the police drove victims around to see if they could spot the perpetrators.

In Queen Anne's Gate, John Gieve, the permanent secretary at the Home Office, brought together officials from different departments and representatives from the police and the Delivery Unit to work on street crime – an innovative approach at the time. Blair was right – creating a crisis did make a difference. By September 2002, street crime had reduced by 15 per cent in the ten worst areas, though the team in the Home Office continued working for several years afterwards to cement the gains.

Jeremy came home excited about this progress and boasting of the 30 per cent reduction in street crime that had been reported in our borough of Lambeth. In fact, he was so enthused about the role that the Delivery Unit had played in achieving these improvements that he told me he thought they could also help tackle the rampant opium trade in Afghanistan, where the UK was playing a part in NATO-led operations – though, sadly, no one else seemed keen to take up this suggestion.

For the Prime Minister, like Jeremy, the work on street crime proved the value of the Delivery Unit. They also both remained convinced of the value of the other changes that had been made to the centre of government, which was one of the reasons why, in mid-July, Tony Blair broke years of tradition to discuss these in person with a select committee in the House of Commons.

Given Blair's way of working, Jeremy told me, his role as Prime Minister extended well beyond the constitutional job of managing the Cabinet that Richard Wilson had highlighted to include dealing with senior appointments, machinery of government changes, the Budget and major economic decisions, foreign and defence policy and public sector reform. And the need for more resources in Number 10 became even clearer when this breadth of interests was combined with the Prime Minister's desire to oversee the delivery of his manifesto commitments, manage major crises and feed an always-on news machine.

The publication in July of the long-awaited *Lessons to Be Learned* report on the foot and mouth crisis reinforced Jeremy's view that the centre of government had needed to change. The report criticised the lack of any contingency plans to carry out vaccinations and the delay in bringing in the army. It also revealed that, while the Ministry of Agriculture, Fisheries and Food had been assuring Number 10 that it was sufficiently resourced, it had simultaneously been asking its counterparts in Australia, Canada, the USA and other EU member states for help.

But while Jeremy supported the restructuring, he still didn't believe Downing Street should expand exponentially. What mattered, he told me, was the quality of the staff and their relationship with the Prime Minister, and this provided a natural cap on its size. Despite the expansion of Number 10, even after five years of a Labour government, Tony Blair's closest advisers were still those who had come into Downing Street with him, including Alastair Campbell, Anji Hunter, Peter Mandelson, Jonathan Powell, Sally Morgan and Philip Gould. Jeremy sat in the next tier down from this group, alongside people like Andrew Adonis and Peter Hyman, the chief speechwriter. They saw the Prime Minister off and on throughout the day, but weren't the first people he turned to when he wanted banter and downtime. This didn't worry Jeremy. Although those informal sessions were an important part of Blair's day, he had more than enough to do to listen to his boss strumming away on his guitar or doing – admittedly rather good – impressions of John Prescott or Gordon Brown.

Jeremy was still, at this time, occasionally talking about leaving Downing Street to find a new challenge. He was torn, however, because he was still excited about the things he could achieve in his existing role, like the additional funding he'd managed to secure in the July spending review to tackle street crime, support universities and reduce the numbers of asylum seekers. The government had also just started the first trial of using choice to drive public sector reform, during which heart patients in London would be allowed to switch NHS hospitals or go private if they had more than a six-month wait for their operation.

In addition to the satisfaction Jeremy gained from helping the Prime Minister to develop policy or accelerating its implementation there were also times when his job enabled him to be a bystander in a moment of history. One example of this had happened in mid-April when the Queen and the Duke of Edinburgh visited Number 10 to have dinner with all five living prime ministers – Jim Callaghan, John Major, Edward Heath, Margaret Thatcher and Tony Blair.

Over drinks, Mrs Thatcher had kept Jeremy entertained with a monologue about how worn the carpets were in Downing Street and how the colours in the Green Room didn't coordinate. She almost fainted when she went into her old study and found it had been turned into a spartan meeting room, and was only distracted from her march downstairs to inspect the Prime Minister's new office by the arrival of the Queen, who looked appropriately regal and said how lovely it was not to have to be introduced to anyone.

The Queen had dinner with her prime ministers in the small dining room in Downing Street – an event that went well despite Blair's pre-match nerves – while Jeremy ate his with Alastair Campbell, Fiona Millar and Robin Janvrin in the room outside. Afterwards, when they regrouped for drinks, Jeremy watched Ted Heath chatting to Jim Callaghan and Prince Philip talking to Tony Blair. He'd worked for three of these prime ministers – Blair directly and John Major and Margaret Thatcher indirectly. But that evening, he wasn't thinking of all their many policy initiatives. Instead, he was conscious of the historic significance of the people gathered in that room – and of his own belief in the enduring institutions and traditions of the British state.

16

'Thunder Road':
A rare memo

September–November 2002

By the autumn of 2002, well before Jeremy could share his desire for a new challenge with Andrew Turnbull, he found himself embroiled in another row that pitted the Prime Minister against the Chancellor.

Back in June, Alan Milburn – who was by then a fully paid-up and intellectually self-confident Blairite outrider – had told the Prime Minister in one of their Public Services Reform Group meetings that he wanted to change the legal structure of NHS hospitals to allow them to govern themselves with more freedom from the National Health Service. These foundation trusts would, Alan said, mirror elements of the school academies movement and self-governing universities.

While the idea of giving higher-performing hospitals more freedom had been around for a while – indeed Jeremy and Ed Balls had debated it before the 2002 Budget – the Chancellor was unamused by this suggestion. Giving foundation trusts more freedom to borrow would be impossible, he told Alan, because it would breach the Treasury's rules.

The next round of this fight began in August 2002 when Alan Milburn, who had been equally offended by the Chancellor's decision to commission the Wanless report without consulting him, wrote an article in *The Times* that put his thinking in a wider context. In this, Alan again rehearsed the arguments for using choice and contestability to transform public services, citing the results of the heart treatments trial – in which, much to Jeremy's delight, half the eligible patients had switched hospital when given the chance to do so, even if this meant travelling long distances. Alan then contrasted the views of the 'transformers' in government who believed in this agenda with the approach of 'consolidators' who wanted to expand public services simply by spending more.

Technical discussions on foundation trusts between the Treasury and the Department of Health continued after this article appeared. But when it became clear to the Treasury that the political side of Number 10 supported Alan's proposals, the issue escalated into a major fight. Gordon Brown and Ed Balls, who had been enraged by being labelled consolidators, saw the trusts as the start of a march towards privatisation – even though, despite being classified as private bodies in some versions of the Milburn model, there was never any intention of selling them. The Chancellor was also reluctant to give them the freedom to set pay and continued to argue that they shouldn't have unfettered access to loans.

Although Jeremy was sympathetic to some of these Treasury concerns, he was personally relaxed about who provided public services so long as they were of high quality and free at the point of use. In any case, he saw this row as much as a symptom of the deteriorating relationship between the Prime Minister and the Chancellor as a cause of it. When Jeremy had first arrived in Number 10, Tony Blair and Gordon Brown had been meeting two or three times a week. But by this time serious discussions rarely took place more than once a week and Jeremy and Ed were negotiating many issues on their principals' behalf in Café Churchill.

Foundation trusts also neatly illustrated the policy fault line between the Prime Minister and Chancellor. While ostensibly worried about controlling borrowing, the Chancellor was primarily concerned about not upsetting his Labour supporters by starting down a road that might expose public services to market forces. Blair, on the other hand, having abandoned his mantra of 'standards, not structures', was happy to look at any reform, however unpopular, if it would improve public services. He also believed that progress depended on allowing frontline leaders to innovate and expand, if necessary, through competing for business. So, if foundation trusts continued to treat patients free at the point of use, and in line with the NHS's clinical priorities, the more freedom they had the better. And, of course, the Prime Minister was also conscious of the signal he would be sending to Whitehall if he gave way on an issue that so clearly represented his thinking on public sector reform.

Jeremy was at a permanent secretaries' offsite in Sunningdale in September 2002 when he was dragged out to take a call from Andrew Adonis. 'Gordon Brown has just circulated a 44-page critique of Alan Milburn's proposals around Cabinet,' Andrew told Jeremy.

'Really?' Jeremy asked, because normally Gordon and Ed went to extraordinary lengths to avoid writing notes, with the few that existed being collectors' items. And it was unheard of to distribute something so controversial without talking to the Prime Minister first.

After Andrew's call, Jeremy consulted Tony Blair and Andrew Turnbull before ringing the Number 10 duty clerk to instruct him to retrieve and destroy every copy of the Chancellor's memo. He then spent the following week ricocheting back and forth between the Department of Health and the Treasury attempting to close the policy divide between them while ignoring the politics raging around him – which wasn't easy when some of the Number 10 special advisers saw the Chancellor's memo as a declaration of war.

After a few days, it looked like a compromise might be possible, but it took two difficult meetings between the Prime Minister, the Chancellor, Alan Milburn and John Prescott to get it agreed. Only Jeremy and Andrew Turnbull were allowed to attend these discussions, which left Ed Balls stewing in the Treasury. At one point, Ed even resorted to calling Jeremy over for an 'urgent discussion' in his office to try to keep him out as well – which worked until the Prime Minister paged Jeremy and told him to come back.

At the end of all of this, Gordon won the battle, keeping control over borrowing, but he lost the war, since it was agreed that foundation trusts would become independent entities no longer owned or run by the NHS. Jeremy was then able to step back from the next phase of the fight, which took place in Parliament. Many bitter arguments later, and after sixty Labour MPs, including many Brown allies, tried to block the changes, the legislation establishing foundation trusts was approved – though only with the support of Scots and Welsh Labour MPs to whom the proposals didn't apply.

'Of course, this whole row has only been about policy,' Jeremy told me. 'Although,' he added with a slight smile, 'Alan is also seen as a potential successor to Tony Blair.'

In August 2002 we flew to Crete for a short break, much of which we spent spooning mashed prunes into Jonny's mouth since he was refusing to eat his normal baby concoctions and we were worried he might starve. Jonny was far more relaxed than his inexperienced parents, and rather than showing any sign of wasting away, spent most of our holiday seeking out the nearest set of steep stone steps to fling himself down.

After we returned to London, Jeremy went to see Andrew Turnbull to talk about his future. He told Andrew he was ready to run a department, though he would be happy to start by leading a small one. Or, if that wasn't possible, maybe he could manage the Economic and Domestic Secretariat while continuing to be the Prime Minister's principal private secretary?

'Andrew said "no" to all my suggestions,' Jeremy told me when he got home. 'He believes that, at forty-one, I'm too young to become a permanent secretary and allowing me to manage one of the secretariats would be yet another infringement of the Cabinet Office's turf. So it's time to consider other options.'

'Like what?'

'Well, John Studzinski tells me he's about to move from Morgan Stanley to HSBC. He wants me to join him there so we can build their investment banking business together.'

Studzinski – 'Studs' to his friends – was clearly serious because, a few days later, Jeremy was invited for lunch by the chair of HSBC, John Bond, who offered him a two-year secondment. Jeremy was tempted, but when he proposed this to Andrew Turnbull, Andrew again shook his head. It would be impossible, Andrew said, for Jeremy to move until a decision had been taken on the euro and any consequences of that decision had been worked through. In the meantime, though he wasn't prepared to promote Jeremy or give him any new responsibilities, he would give him a £6,000 pay rise.

Jeremy came home frustrated by this outcome. He'd made himself valuable by creating the only relationship between Number 10 and the Treasury that was still functioning, he told me, but in doing so he'd trapped himself in Whitehall.

Andrew was, however, right that there was plenty of work for Jeremy to do. By this point Downing Street was increasingly focused on Iraq, which after agreeing to halt its biological and nuclear weapons programme in 1992, had been resisting visits by the UN's weapons inspectors. When the Prime Minister returned from his summer break, he told his team he thought he'd persuaded President Bush not to launch an attack before agreeing another UN resolution that would give Iraq a final opportunity to let these inspections go ahead. And on the euro, he again said that he was convinced, subject to the economics, of the case for joining since it would allow the UK to strengthen its relationships with France and Germany.

There was much nodding on the sofa at these messages – though Jeremy knew, and suspected the Prime Minister did too, that at least on the euro, the economics were unlikely to support the UK joining. But whatever his personal views, the Prime Minister was determined to keep his options open and again urged Jeremy to find out what the Treasury was doing.

The Prime Minister was also showing no sign of slowing down on public sector reform. His party conference speech that autumn emphasised the importance of treating citizens as individuals who should be able to choose their public services. 'We are at our best when we are boldest,' the Prime Minister declared, and he concluded by exhorting his colleagues not to abandon their modernisation journey.

Not long after this, however, Estelle Morris, the Secretary of State for Education, decided to abandon her own journey, telling the Prime Minister she was resigning because she didn't feel up to the job. After considering and rejecting the idea of moving Alan Milburn from Health to replace Estelle, the Prime Minister instead appointed Charles Clarke, the Labour Party chair. This put a strong loyalist in charge of the debate over tuition fees – although, much to the Prime Minister's frustration, Charles made it clear that his mind wasn't made up, and over the next four weeks, reconsidered multiple ways of increasing university funding, including through creating an endowment tax. This was admirable, though it meant Jeremy and Andrew Adonis – or 'Zoffis' as Charles dubbed them, a shorthand for 'Tony's Office' – had to trawl yet again through arguments they thought they'd long put behind them.

On 12 November 2002 we celebrated Jonny's first birthday, which he marked by making short dashes across our bedroom floor, toppling over each time after only a few steps. Jeremy took a rare afternoon off to join the party in our local church hall, though he disappeared from this periodically to join calls about the revelations being made by Paul Burrell, a former royal butler, about Princess Diana.

The Burrell crisis was a transitory one, at least for Downing Street. However, a far bigger issue was the continuing deterioration of the Prime Minister's relationship with his Chancellor. In addition to its previous fault lines, this was also being tested by thinking the Treasury was developing about the 'limits to markets', which many saw as a direct challenge to the Prime Minister's choice and contestability agenda.

That autumn also saw a worsening in one of the Prime Minister's other relationships, this one with the Lord Chancellor, Derry Irvine. Jeremy felt partly responsible for this since one of the flashpoints happened in mid-November 2002 after he encouraged the Prime Minister to press Derry to make more use of the asset seizure powers recently introduced in the Proceeds of Crime Act. Jeremy had urged this because he believed, both from his work on financial crime in the Treasury and his efforts after 9/11, that the UK could be far more proactive in uncovering the money flows supporting criminal gangs, including those driving the surge in street crime. However, when the Prime Minister raised it, Derry refused to discuss the idea and instead continued telling the Prime Minister about the Judicial Studies Board's improved training.

After attempting to shift the conversation a couple of times, the Prime Minister snapped. 'Go and look at this please, Derry,' he said.

Jeremy glanced at Sally Morgan, who raised her eyebrows. They had never heard the Prime Minister speak sharply to the Lord Chancellor before and it was worrying, not least because Derry was central to the Prime Minister's political narrative of tackling crime. It was hard enough delivering the manifesto commitments with the Prime Minister and Chancellor not getting on – if Tony Blair's other political relationships also fell away, it would become impossible.

17

'Friction':
Students and asylum seekers

November 2002–January 2003

On Monday 18 November 2002, Jeremy met Gus O'Donnell, who was by then permanent secretary to the Treasury, to tell him again that the Prime Minister wanted to get a decision made on the euro.

'I understand,' Gus said, 'and I've no idea what the Chancellor's view is, but I think there are two possible answers. The first is "yes" and the second is "not quite, but we should look again next year".'

It was clear to Jeremy from Gus's tone, and from the suggestions he went on to share for how 'not quite' could be presented, that this was the more likely option.

'Politically "not quite" is a "no",' Jonathan Powell said when Jeremy brought this news back to Number 10. 'If we say, "not quite", Schröder and the rest of them will give up on us, the markets will mark sterling down, and Gordon will push the decision off until after the next election. His aim isn't to have a year's delay but for Tony to be out of power by the time we join.'

'You may be right,' Jeremy said, although he still thought 'not quite' was likely to be the correct economic assessment. The UK's economic cycle was out of sync with the EU's for a number of reasons, including the fact that its house prices were far more sensitive to changes in interest rates because most homeowners had variable-rate mortgages. Unless these issues could be addressed, it was hard to see how the UK would avoid problems if it joined the euro. But this was Jeremy's personal opinion, and since the Prime Minister might take a different view, he had several more meetings with Gus to go through possible 'automatic stabilisers' that might offset fluctuations in the economy and, therefore, make it easier for the UK to adopt the euro.

We made our New Year's Eve predictions at the end of 2002 in Brussels, with Jeremy telling me he thought Tony Blair would still be Prime Minister in a year's time but that he was pessimistic about Gordon Brown remaining Chancellor given how unwilling he was to share his thinking on the euro. He also thought we would have a second baby – a girl called Juliette in 2004 – while I predicted a boy called Peter in 2003.

'Wouldn't that be wonderful?' he said, and we both smiled – though after the trauma we had gone through trying to conceive Jonny, we were taking nothing for granted.

The Prime Minister may have made a similar prediction about his Chancellor over his New Year's break, because that January he began talking about sacking Gordon Brown. At home, however, our other predictions looked more doubtful after we only produced six embryos from our first IVF cycle of the year. But we did the transfer anyway, this time with only two.

While we waited for news, Jeremy was distracted at work by the final battle over student fees. The Prime Minister had made his position on this issue clear again when Jeremy and Andrew Adonis met him in early January to discuss Andrew's Christmas note, in which Andrew had again described ways to increase choice and contestability, particularly in health and education.

'I want all of it,' Blair said, 'and I also don't want to compromise on student fees. Reforming universities' finances is vital for our prosperity.'

Jeremy still agreed with this, though he knew many of the Number 10 political advisers thought it was crazy for the Prime Minister to try to challenge mainstream Labour Party thinking on this issue while he was also trying to deal with the possibility of a war in Iraq. But regardless of his other priorities, Jeremy believed that Blair was right to keep pursuing reform because, at least in his view, to have a viable premiership, all prime ministers needed a plan to improve key public services.

Charles Clarke had, by this time, joined the fees camp, partly thanks to the efforts of Robert Hill, who'd moved from Downing Street to become his special adviser. But the Chancellor was continuing to advocate a 'pure' graduate tax. With the mid-January publication date for the White Paper on Higher Education fast approaching, everyone knew that the two sides were going to have to thrash it out – and that it was likely to be a gruesome battle.

The starting pistol for this fight was at last fired in one of the final discussions about the White Paper in the domestic affairs Cabinet committee.

'Nothing has been resolved,' Andrew Adonis said, bursting into the Prime Minister's office after the meeting.

'What do you mean?' the Prime Minister asked.

'GB launched a full-throated attack on tuition fees, saying that universities are not in financial crisis and fees would be too expensive.'

'Did he address any of our issues with a graduate tax?' Jeremy asked.

'No, but he sounded compelling, so people started falling in behind him. It was almost a complete disaster, but Charles rescued the discussion, taking on Gordon's points one by one and saying he would circulate a paper to summarise his arguments.'

For once a Cabinet committee had been helpful, Jeremy thought, though Charles's paper would be critical to secure their position. After a scramble to get this ready, it was circulated to the committee members that Sunday evening. For a moment, Number 10 relaxed. And then, on Monday morning, the Treasury shot out a bumper 22-page riposte.

'But,' Andrew Adonis pointed out when they met the Prime Minister to discuss this, 'Gordon still hasn't articulated a credible version of the graduate tax.'

Tony Blair shook his head. 'Indeed. He keeps attacking our proposal while keeping his ideas vague.'

Jeremy joined multiple official-level meetings over the following few days, but despite their efforts, they couldn't find a compromise that would work for both the Chancellor and the Prime Minister. Meanwhile, the print deadline for the White Paper came and went.

But by 22 January, the Prime Minister had won the battle – from September 2006, universities would be able to charge variable fees of up to £3,000. Students could take out loans to pay these, which they would only be required to start paying back after they were earning at least £15,000 a year. However, in a last-minute compromise with the Treasury, although the sums outstanding would be adjusted for inflation, no interest would be charged on them. Alongside these changes, which would increase universities' funding per student by about 30 per cent, a new access regulator would agree how they should attract more students from poor backgrounds and those students would again start receiving maintenance grants.

It was, Jeremy believed, a fair set of reforms. The *Economist* agreed, writing on 23 January that student fees could be 'the best thing that has happened to British universities for decades'. But many disagreed, with the proposals triggering a wave of opposition from Labour MPs and students. The suspicion in Number 10 was that, as on foundation trusts, the Chancellor was making it clear that he was opposed, a view that became entrenched when Nick Brown, a known Gordon Brown supporter, emerged as the leader of the Labour rebels. Despite this, after another painful year, student fees were approved in the House of Commons by a wafer-thin majority – though only after Nick decided to vote with the government and to encourage other defectors to do the same. And even though the Chancellor hated student fees, Jeremy told me that, given the logic of the reforms and the amount of pain that it had taken to put them in place, he would be surprised if Gordon Brown reversed the policy even if he became Prime Minister – a prediction that turned out to be correct.

By February 2003, I was again ready to do a pregnancy test, and this time, the second red line was clear. Two weeks later we were back in the clinic for our scan.

'Excellent,' the doctor said. 'Two egg sacs – do you see?'

I studied the screen. Inside the sacs I could see tiny, pulsating lights – the heartbeats of two babies.

Jeremy was on the other side of the room clutching Jonny, who was trying to get down to explore the examination room.

'Everything looks fine,' the doctor said, replacing the sensor. 'I'll need to see you again in four weeks' time.'

'Okay,' I said, sitting up and starting to wipe the jelly off my stomach.

'I have a question,' Jeremy said, still struggling with Jonny. The doctor and I looked around.

'Yes?' the doctor asked.

'Are we expecting twins?'

Back in the office, while most people focused on finalising the draft United Nations resolution that would give Saddam Hussein a final opportunity to disarm, Jeremy digested this surprising news about my pregnancy while worrying about the Treasury's snail-like progress on the euro assessment and the end game on foundation trusts. Unexpectedly, asylum joined this list.

Actually, it wasn't that unexpected. After the record number of asylum seekers in 2000 had prompted the construction of David Blunkett's asylum centres and the closing of the Sangatte refugee camp near the French end of the Channel Tunnel, the numbers had dropped slightly in 2001. However, before anyone could relax, it was predicted that the numbers would rise by more than 20 per cent in 2002. The Home Office remained confident that their measures would get things under control. But after the *Sun* claimed the UK had become a 'doormat for the world to wipe its feet on', the Prime Minister decided that more focus was needed. Therefore, on 8 February, he announced that the number of asylum seekers would be halved by September.

'What on earth is going on?' David Blunkett's private secretary asked when he rang Jeremy. 'You must know we've no plan in place to get the numbers down by that amount.'

'That may be the case – but we have to do something,' Jeremy said. 'The anger about asylum is growing, people are being left in limbo with their cases undecided, and when they lose their applications, it seems to be impossible to send them back to their home countries.'

In the days after the Prime Minister's pledge, Jeremy put back in place many of the measures they'd used to address street crime including setting up a series of COBR discussions that Tony Blair made time to lead in between his meetings on Iraq. Again they worked their way through the process, this time beginning with what attracted people to the UK and finishing with how decisions were made about who could stay, and how failed applicants were repatriated.

'Let's take the case of someone who flushes their papers down the toilet on the plane,' Jeremy would ask. 'How long would it be before their case was heard? Where would they be held until it was? Would they get legal aid? And what would happen to their children?'

The Delivery Unit worked with the Home Office to prepare the briefings for these discussions. As part of this, Michael Barber even spent a night by the Channel Tunnel watching immigration officials catching illegal immigrants coming in on goods trains. 'The fence around the yard in Calais is no more effective than the one around the tennis court in Islington,' he reported when he returned – an analogy beautifully targeted for the Prime Minister to catch.

What the COBR meetings revealed was that, while the Home Office was right to say the UK couldn't affect underlying asylum trends, it could – even within the constraints of the European Convention on Human Rights – make Britain less attractive. This could be done, for example, by making it an offence to enter the UK without a valid passport unless there was a reasonable excuse for doing so, or by saying that asylum seekers from safe countries like Jamaica could only appeal their deportation after they had left the UK.

Once again, grabbing Whitehall's attention worked: by 2003 the number of asylum cases was down to under 50,000, 41 per cent lower than in 2002. And what this asylum effort had again demonstrated, Jeremy told me, was the power of 'open policy making' – connecting policy officials in Whitehall with people who knew what was happening in the real world – in this case the immigration officers who were dealing with asylum applications every day.

18

'I Don't Feel Like Dancin'': Concluding the EMU debate

January–June 2003

At the end of January 2003, Jeremy rang Ed Balls. This time he was close to losing his temper. 'We're running out of time,' he said. 'I need to see the draft papers on the five tests now. The Treasury can't run the clock down on the euro decision this way. It's outrageous, as you must know.'

What Ed and Jeremy both also knew, though few others did, was that the Prime Minister had already told the Chancellor that he wanted to publish the final euro assessment on Budget Day, Wednesday 9 April. Despite Ed's protest that this forced the decision into the Treasury's busiest time of the year, the Prime Minister had refused to budge. Publishing early maximised the time for conditions to change so a referendum remained possible before the general election. It also meant that a 'not quite' decision could be announced alongside a set of Budget measures that could help the UK pass the five tests the next time around.

'Okay,' Ed said, 'let me see if Gordon is happy to let Dave Ramsden take the Prime Minister through our preliminary work. When we've done that, we can start reviewing the results of the five tests.'

Jeremy's exasperated tone – which he reserved for special occasions – this time had an effect. More EMU seminars were scheduled to go through the preliminary work, running through February and the first half of March. When they reached the last of these, after many more hours of presentations, the Prime Minister sighed. 'Thank you,' he said, 'but now we need to see the results of the five tests.'

'That will be the subject of our next set of seminars,' Gus O'Donnell said.

Jeremy glanced at Jonathan, who raised his eyebrows. The Treasury's view on the euro was already pretty clear, so there seemed little point in drawing out this extraordinary assessment. It was also personally frustrating for Jeremy given Andrew Turnbull's refusal to let him move until a decision had been taken – if the Treasury didn't hurry up, he was likely to have three children at home by the time he was allowed to start a new role.

On 17 March 2003, the UK and the US gave up trying to agree a second resolution authorising force against Iraq. Instead, President George Bush said that, unless Saddam Hussein and his sons left the country within forty-eight hours, they would face war. Three days later, after they failed to do this, the UK gained the backing of the House of Commons to join the US in invading Iraq.

Inside Number 10 almost all the Prime Minister's time was absorbed by this descent into war. But with only a week to go until the Budget, the big issue still being discussed in the 'inner non-war circle' – Andrew Adonis's title for the small group focused on domestic policy issues that he and Jeremy were leading – was the euro.

On Tuesday 1 April 2003, the main players gathered again in the Cabinet Room to hear the conclusion of the Treasury's five tests. It was, Jeremy thought, as he laid out his pad and pens, almost impossible to believe that they were about to reach the dénouement of this process. But they did – though only after fifty-five slides of preamble. The UK had passed the financial services test, Dave Ramsden said, but it had failed the one on convergence and the other three, on flexibility, investment and employment, were near misses. A clear and unambiguous case for UK membership had not been made.

A moment of silence followed before the Prime Minister spoke. 'I can't believe this is unequivocal,' he said. 'I will need to discuss the conclusions with Gordon.'

When Jeremy walked back into his office after the meeting his phone was ringing.

It was the Number 10 private office. 'Kevin has brought over the Treasury's final euro assessment,' Owen Barder said.

With his father Peter, 1962.   A rare moment behind the wheel, 1963.

With father Peter, mother Brenda and younger brother Simon, 1970.

As a student at Ralph Butterfield Primary School, Haxby *c.*1968.

Giving instructions on the cricket field at Bootham, 1977.

Glossop, 1966.

With friends in France, 1986.

Posing in France, 1986.

Looking cool, 1983.

In the Financial
Secretary's office, 1986.

At home, 1985.

With Norman Lamont, 1992.

In the Chancellor's Office, 1992.

Working for David Mellor, 1991.

With Norman Lamont in the Chancellor's private office, 1992.

With me on holiday in
Hungary, 1995.

Our wedding day, 1997.

Admiring our new garden, 1997.

Outside Number 10, 1999.

'What? How can it be final when this is the first time we've seen it?'

'Well, that's the message from the Treasury. They seem anxious to get it signed off.'

Jeremy sighed and went back to speak to the Prime Minister before ringing Ed Balls. 'The Prime Minister won't accept that he's received the final version,' he told Ed. 'As far as he's concerned, this is a draft. We need to go through it in detail and, if necessary, change the wording to get it right.'

'None of it is up for negotiation,' Ed said. 'This is the Treasury's official view. The only text we can change is Gordon's parliamentary statement.'

'I disagree. This isn't just an economic decision – it's also a political one.'

On the other side of the office, Jonathan Powell was shaking his head.

'It's not only Tony who's furious,' Jonathan said after Jeremy replaced his handset. 'Multiple Cabinet members have been telling me that this shouldn't only be Gordon's decision.'

Jeremy nodded – Jonathan was right, of course, though everyone knew that this issue could only be resolved by two people.

When the Chancellor came over for his bilateral with the Prime Minister the following day, the conversation exploded, and Jeremy and Ed were ordered to leave the room. After Gordon left, glowering, Jeremy stuck his head around the door.

'How did it go?'

'Not now.'

Another bilateral took place the next day, though this time Jeremy and Ed were called back in before it concluded to be told they needed to work together to create an agreed text.

'The decision is made,' the Prime Minister told Jeremy afterwards, 'but I need you to work on what we say because I don't want to lose the possibility of returning to this issue again before the end of the Parliament.'

Jeremy wasn't surprised that the Prime Minister had conceded on the euro. Even if Tony Blair still believed in its economic and polit- ical benefits, as Jeremy thought he did, it would be impossible for him to win the public's support for it without his Chancellor's backing.

'We don't have long,' Ed said after Jeremy arrived in the Treasury the following evening to find him sitting at the table in his office flanked by Treasury officials. 'Everything is ready to go at the printers – we just need the final text.'

'It will take as long as it takes,' Jeremy said, pleased he'd taken the precaution of having already had dinner.

After that, they began negotiating the 300-page euro assessment line by line. In some places, Jeremy inserted phrases like 'despite the risks and costs from delaying the benefits of joining' to make the text more balanced. In others, he brought forward favourable paragraphs, like a section on the trade benefits of the euro. He also argued for some parts to be deleted, for example the proposed narrow range of 'safe' exchange rates that the pound had to achieve against the euro before it could join.

After they finished editing at half past midnight, Kevin brought a fresh copy of the assessment over to Downing Street at 7 a.m. on Friday morning. Jeremy and Jonathan read it through before taking it into the den.

The Prime Minister glanced through it. 'It's better,' he said, 'but it's still far too negative.'

There was a long pause.

'Are you sure we can announce this now anyway?' Jonathan asked. 'The Americans are closing in on Baghdad and I'm not sure we should mix the euro decision up with that.'

The Prime Minister nodded. 'You're right,' he said. 'I think we should postpone.'

Jeremy couldn't resist a slight smile. The Treasury had run the euro assessment down to the wire and had then tried to bounce them into agreeing the text. If the timetable moved, there would be far more opportunity to change the presentation of the decision.

'Tell me you're kidding,' Ed said when Jeremy rang him. 'Dave is already at the printers. We'll have to redo everything.'

'I'm afraid I'm not joking. You should never take the Prime Minister for granted,' Jeremy said. 'I guess you'd better let Dave know.'

Ed was right that delaying the euro decision meant that much of the analysis had to be updated in the following weeks because it was time-sensitive. But as Jeremy had anticipated, the delay did give him more time to work with the Treasury on the text and to press for other measures to reinforce the sense that the answer was 'not yet' rather than 'not ever'. These included changing the definition of the inflation target from the Retail Price Index to the Consumer Price Index, which excluded mortgages, to bring it in line with the measure used in the EU, and commissioning studies from outside experts on topics like how to increase the number of fixed-rate mortgages in the UK. The pause also meant they had time to circulate the 1,982-page euro analysis and the final assessment to the rest of the Cabinet.

'Has it been worth it?' I asked Jeremy when he crawled home in early June and told me the work was done. By this time, I was three months pregnant with twins but looked closer to six and was beginning to waddle.

'Maybe,' he said. 'The tests are at least being presented in a more positive way with one passed, two failed and two that would be met if the others were. The Chancellor will also state that being a part of a successful single currency would benefit Britain.'

Jeremy thought that, after the euro decision was announced on 9 June, that would be the end of it, at least for a while. But he was wrong, because many in Number 10 were keen to keep the euro dream alive. A new ministerial group chaired by Tony Blair was set up to oversee the government's pro-Europe campaign strategy and preparations for the UK's entry into the single currency, while the Cabinet Office started work on a referendum bill. But despite this enthusiasm, it was clear by early July that the press and voters didn't share Downing Street's enthusiasm, and that most companies had put their currency conversion programmes on hold. And in the end, with the mismatch between the UK and the eurozone economies remaining stark and the government consumed by the aftermath of the Iraq war, the second assessment was never carried out. Even so, it was not until 2010 that another Chancellor at last stood down the final remaining member of the euro preparation team in the Treasury.

19

'Take Me Out':
Time for a change

June 2003–January 2004

There was no time for Jeremy to pause after the euro statement, and even less for him to raise with Andrew Turnbull the long-delayed decision about his next role, because immediately afterwards he was consumed by the final preparations for a Cabinet reshuffle. When this took place three days later on 12 June 2003, it became one of the most controversial in years.

The main piece of thinking that lay behind this reshuffle was sound, at least in Jeremy's view. For many years constitutional experts had been highlighting the anomalous position of the Lord Chancellor, who combined three roles – being a senior member of the government, being the head of the 'independent' judiciary and being the Speaker of the House of Lords. However, the Prime Minister had decided to let it be since he knew Derry Irvine would fight any change.

Despite some early media stumbles, including comparing himself to Cardinal Wolsey, as Lord Chancellor Derry had made a significant contribution to the Prime Minister's first term. He had helped shape the constitutional reform agenda and negotiated the most fundamental reform of the House of Lords for almost a century. However, his row with Tony Blair the previous November had been only the latest in a series of disputes, which all stemmed from the Prime Minister's belief that Derry was overprotective of a system that cared more about suspects' rights than justice for victims. This became particularly clear, the Prime Minister felt, when they debated issues such as sentencing policy, where Blair was often pushing for longer prison sentences in the face of judicial resistance.

This tension had become public in January 2003 when Derry had suggested in an interview on *Today* that people would be happy for burglars to stay out of jail even if they committed a second offence. The media pounced on this statement, contrasting Derry's words with the Prime Minister's determination to be tough on crime. Derry then made the situation worse by accepting a £22,000 pay increase and enhanced pension rights for himself despite the Prime Minister's opposition.

When the Prime Minister launched his reshuffle on 12 June, it was revealed that Derry Irvine would step down as Lord Chancellor and Charlie Falconer, another brilliant lawyer and Tony's old Wandsworth housemate, would become the Secretary of State for Constitutional Affairs. The Prime Minister also announced some changes to this retitled role, based on thinking that Jeremy, Andrew Adonis and others had been doing. In future, the new secretary of state wouldn't oversee the appointment of judges, which would instead be done by a judicial appointments commission, someone else would become the Speaker of the House of Lords and a new Supreme Court, composed of the existing law lords, would replace the House of Lords as the country's final court of appeal.

Jeremy expected that this long-overdue set of reforms would be welcomed by all but the most die-hard traditionalists. But the need to keep them secret before the announcement because they were bound up with Derry's move meant that important stakeholders, like the Lord Chief Justice and the Leader of the House of Lords, were caught unawares. Not unreasonably, this led to criticism and allowed the Conservatives to suggest the government had put the proposals together on the fly. In particular, opposition to the reforms focused on the abolition of the 1,400-year-old title of Lord Chancellor. When closer inspection revealed that this would also require complex primary legislation, Jeremy advised the Prime Minister to keep the title while retaining the rest of the changes, most of which were generally thought to be sensible.

If this had been the only issue, the reshuffle might have been manageable. But the day was also complicated by Alan Milburn's decision to resign as Health Secretary, citing the difficulty of combining family life in north-east England with being a Cabinet minister in London, a decision he'd only shared with the Prime Minister a few days previously. Alan's departure left a gap in the Cabinet line-up on reshuffle day because it wasn't easy to find a Blairite replacement. Several hours passed while the Prime Minister considered his options and the press dissected the announcements already made, reading dark motives into Alan's departure, particularly since his bitter relationship with Gordon Brown was well known.

When the Prime Minister alighted on the ever-reliable John Reid, Leader of the House of Commons, the Downing Street team exhaled. But even then, things weren't straightforward since John thought that, as a Scottish MP, he couldn't oversee the NHS since it didn't operate in Scotland. Luckily though, on further reflection, he decided that he could make it work.

The final element of the reshuffle involved combining the roles of the Secretaries of State for Scotland and Wales with other Cabinet positions, since these roles had few functions remaining after many of their powers had been devolved to the regions in 1998. In future, Alistair Darling, the Secretary of State for Transport and a Scottish MP, would speak on Scottish issues in Parliament and Peter Hain, the new Leader of the House of Commons and a Welsh MP, would do the same for Wales. When they did this they would be supported by civil servants in the new Department for Constitutional Affairs – a fact that initially created more confusion in the minds of waiting journalists who thought this meant Charlie Falconer had been given the roles.

All in all, it had been a ragged day – even though Jeremy remained convinced of the logic of the constitutional reforms. And although the Scottish and Welsh roles were later reseparated, the changes to the Lord Chancellor's role were retained, so others clearly shared his view.

In July 2003, I stopped work after my doctor told me that, seven months pregnant with twins and barely able to walk, I had to rest. My world shrank to the scope of our living room, where I lay on the sofa reading books or chatting to Jonny and our nanny Maggie.

In the evenings when he got home, I quizzed Jeremy about his plans to change jobs since I was desperate to have some certainty before the twins were born. However, I stopped after he told me he was finding it hard to focus on anything other than the Hutton inquiry.

This inquiry had its origins in a BBC *Today* programme back in May that had accused Downing Street of 'sexing up' the dossier published before the decision to go to war with Iraq. This dossier described the available intelligence on Iraq's defences and the BBC alleged that Number 10 had amended it to include the claim that, with only forty-five minutes' notice, Saddam Hussein could launch weapons of mass destruction. The government denied this and Alastair Campbell had made a rare appearance before the Foreign Affairs Select Committee to demand an apology.

A few weeks later, on 3 July 2003, Geoff Hoon, the Secretary of State for Defence, told Jonathan Powell that one of his officials believed he might have been a source for the BBC's story. After some agonising, Number 10 decided that they had to make this fact public, particularly because both the Foreign Affairs Committee and the Intelligence and Security Committee in the House of Commons were already investigating issues relating to Iraq. When Dr Kelly's identity was then revealed by the press, the story darkened. He was interrogated by both committees after which he left his house for a walk and didn't return.

When Jeremy was told of Dr Kelly's death on the morning of 18 July 2003, he felt sick. Dr Kelly might have breached the rules in speaking to the press, but that should never have led to this. He picked up the phone. The Prime Minister needed to know this news because, as well as being a personal tragedy, it also had the potential to unleash another surge of fury about Iraq from which Tony Blair might not recover.

It took a while for the switchboard to get through to the Prime Minister who, having just addressed both houses of Congress in the US, was on a plane heading for Japan. When he came on the line, Jeremy took a deep breath. 'My advice,' he said after sharing the news, 'is that we should set up an independent inquiry led by a judge to get to the bottom of what happened. If we don't put everything we can into the open, conspiracy theories will haunt you for years.'

After the Prime Minister agreed with this, Charlie Falconer was dispatched to find a judge who might be available at short notice and came back with Lord Hutton, the former Lord Chief Justice for Northern Ireland.

Within Number 10 Jeremy set up a small team, led by Clare Sumner, one of the private secretaries, to assist the inquiry. Over the following weeks, Clare and her team handed over mountains of papers, including thousands of internal emails and transcripts of Alastair Campbell's diaries, the existence of which Alastair had only just revealed. Although Clare led this work, Jeremy was always conscious of it, telling me that it felt like a veil of sadness had settled on Number 10 from the day on which they'd heard the news of Dr Kelly's death.

When the Hutton Report was published six months later in January 2004, it cleared Jeremy's Number 10 colleagues of any wrongdoing – and didn't mention Jeremy at all since he hadn't been involved in any of the key meetings or decisions. The BBC was, however, criticised, and in the aftermath, both its chair and its director general resigned. None of this, of course, changed the fact of Dr Kelly's suicide, or anyone's view about whether the decision to go to war with Iraq had been justified, but at least the issue had been thoroughly examined.

I was in the final few weeks of my pregnancy when Jeremy at last began to talk again about leaving Number 10.

He was still incredibly busy at work, he told me, not least because John Birt had just started looking again at the organisation of the centre of government. This project was a lot more radical than its code name, Project Teddy Bear, suggested because John's new idea was to split the Treasury into two parts – a Ministry of Finance overseeing macroeconomic issues, taxation and financial services and an Office of the Budget and Delivery that would manage departmental spending from inside the Cabinet Office.

While Jeremy could see benefits in these changes, he knew that, at least in part, their purpose was to reduce the Chancellor's power.

Since relations with the Treasury still showed no sign of improving, many Number 10 advisers felt the Prime Minister needed to act, and this was one way of doing it.

'But even though all this work is interesting, I still think it's time for me to leave,' he told me.

'Why now, after waiting so long?' I asked, trying to keep my exasperation out of my voice.

Jeremy smiled. 'I've been in Number 10 for six years so it's time for me to try something new. I also can't believe any other job would be more stressful. I might even be able to spend more time at home with you after the babies arrive.'

While I didn't believe this last point, I decided not to make a fuss. While I knew I could probably convince Jeremy to stay in Downing Street, not least because he was far more risk averse than I was, his need for a fresh challenge had been obvious for some time. So, instead, I reclined on my sofa and listened with interest to the reports he gave me of his conversations with his head-hunter, Martin 'Stretch' Armstrong – so called because of his height. Martin's advice was clear – given Jeremy's Treasury background and economics training, they should start their search with the investment banks.

That summer passed in a haze of listening to 'Twinkle, Twinkle, Little Star' on repeat at Jonny's insistence while trying to survive a London heatwave that forced me to abandon our bedroom in favour of sleeping in our bath. By the start of September, I was enormous and counting down the days until the twins' arrival, while in Number 10 the Prime Minister was coming to terms with Alastair Campbell's long-delayed departure. In the future, David Hill would cover Alastair's political functions while Godric Smith and Tom Kelly would take on the Civil Service aspects.

Jeremy's focus, alongside going to his first job interviews, was on the annual spending review in which he was championing more investment for research and development. This time the negotiations were almost all taking place in Café Churchill because, though no one thought that Jeremy and Ed's bilaterals were the best way to align the Prime Minister's and the Chancellor's views on something so significant, there was often no other way.

In the early hours of one morning in late September, I started having contractions.

'We need a taxi,' I told Jeremy, shaking him awake.

'I don't think you're in labour,' Jeremy said, his eyes still shut, 'go back to sleep.'

'You know about many things,' I said, shoving him again, 'but you know nothing at all about this.'

After Maggie arrived to look after Jonny, I gave birth four hours later to a baby girl, Elizabeth, and a boy, Peter. This time things moved too quickly for the doctors to sort out any pain relief, so my labour was excruciatingly painful. But Jeremy was there throughout, apart from when he made an irritating, though brief, disappearance to buy a bagel and a copy of the *Financial Times* on Praed Street. Afterwards, I looked across the room and saw two cribs – and only then fully registered the reality of what had just happened.

The following weeks were a blur of nappies, snatched sleep and feeding babies. The exhaustion I'd felt with Jonny was incomparable to the sleep deprivation that resulted from caring for twins. I was on autopilot, doing things with only a small part of my brain functioning. Sometimes, in desperation, I threw out all the rules – like on the morning when Maggie arrived to find two-year-old Jonny sitting alone in the living room watching *Postman Pat* on television. She searched the house for several minutes in an increasing state of panic before looking out the back window to see me in my pyjamas, wheeling the double buggy in circles around the garden.

Jeremy, though also bleary-eyed, was still working. The Labour Party conference in early October had made public the gulf between the Chancellor, who argued that the party should be truly Labour, and the Prime Minister, who remained committed to reforming public services, saying he wanted to go further, faster. For a while this gave Project Teddy Bear renewed momentum, although to make the overall scheme more palatable to the Chancellor, the team was proposing by this time to move some of the Department of Trade and Industry's functions, including competition policy, into the Treasury. But, in the end, the Prime Minister decided to back away from the changes and instead met Gordon Brown in John Prescott's flat in Admiralty House to discuss how to patch up their relationship.

'What did they agree?' Jeremy asked when Peter Mandelson told him this.

'Well, Gordon thinks they agreed that, if he supports Tony on domestic policy, then Tony will step down before the next election.'

'What does the Prime Minister think they agreed?'

'It's unclear.'

By this point, Jeremy had two job offers himself – one from Lazard and the other from UBS. He was on the verge of deciding between them when he received a call in late November from Amelia Fawcett, a senior executive at Morgan Stanley.

Jeremy knew Amelia from when she'd come to talk to him in the past about the competitiveness of the City, but this time she wanted to talk about something different.

'I gather you're thinking of moving,' Amelia said, 'but you can't make a decision before talking to us.'

'Amelia, I'm too far down the road to add in new options. I don't want to mess anyone around.'

'I really want you to talk to our UK chair, Simon Robey, before you decide.'

Jeremy sighed and tried again. 'It doesn't make sense.'

'Just do it. There's no commitment.'

After Stretch said that he should at least talk to Morgan Stanley to see what they were offering, Simon Robey came in to see Jeremy in Number 10. By this time, Jeremy had done his homework. Before Amelia's call, he'd known relatively little about Morgan Stanley because it hadn't played a significant role in the UK's privatisation programme. But on any measure it was one of the world's leading investment banks.

'I would love you to help me build Morgan Stanley's business in the UK,' Simon said. 'You can sit in the office next to mine, you'll be on the UK steering committee and I'll help you navigate the transition to banking.'

Jeremy met several more Morgan Stanley managing directors over the following days, who seemed similarly enthusiastic about him joining, and after Terry Burns told him that, if he wanted time out of the Civil Service, he couldn't do better than Simon, Jeremy was persuaded. This was, he told me, the start of a new career.

'Really?' I asked.

'Yes. I want to give it every chance of being a long-term move.'

I smiled. 'Okay. But I don't think we should allow ourselves to adjust to your new salary.'

Jeremy left Number 10 on Christmas Eve 2003. Following the three months of unpaid leave required by the Cabinet Office, he would start work at Morgan Stanley at the beginning of March. Before Jeremy left, Tony Blair gave him a letter:

> I am, of course, in a complete state of denial about your departure. For that reason, I have been singularly lacking in expressions of regret. But take it that the regret is too great to articulate and it's a backhanded compliment that I haven't found my voice properly to thank you. The truth is, as you know, you have been the mainstay of my operation these past years, carrying an enormous part of the burden and doing so with extraordinary skill, wisdom and good nature. And I have had need of all three! In particular, you have helped me to grasp at least the beginnings of real, radical reform.

Jeremy was also proud of the part he'd been able to play in helping Tony Blair reform public services. Even when he hadn't had the support of his own party, the Prime Minister had kept pursuing this, and by doing so, had improved many people's lives. A huge amount of Blair's second term had been absorbed by the dispute over whether the Iraq war was justified and by feuds with his Chancellor over marginal issues like the borrowing powers for foundation trusts. And yet more had been spent on plans for restructuring Number 10 that had led to relatively little. But Jeremy was still pleased with what they had achieved – and I was sure, even then, that he was likely to go back in the future to see if he could do more.

20

'Lose Yourself':
A new world

January 2004–June 2007

I went to view a house one morning in January 2004. It was guarded at the front by a hedge and four large lime trees, and when I pushed Lizzie and Peter's pram through a small gap in the vegetation, a blackened brick façade loomed down.

The estate agent fumbled with the key and ushered me in. Unlike our terraced house on Klea Avenue, which was crammed full of toys, the large rooms here, with their high ceilings and tall sash windows, had space to breathe. Even the garden felt generous – who cared if it was overrun or if its farthest quarter was occupied by a garage covered with ivy? And after we closed the front door at the end of the visit, I looked up and saw a ring of bricks embellished with flowers.

'It's beautiful,' I told Jeremy that evening.

Jeremy visited the house with my parents a few days later.

'It reminds me of Miss Havisham,' he said. 'And the mortgage would be daunting, even with my new salary. It also requires a ton of work.'

I smiled. 'There's room there for our family to grow.'

By 1 March 2004, the day Jeremy began his new job, we'd moved into our new house and I was trying to decide how quickly we could afford to replace the avocado-coloured bathrooms while simultaneously attempting to stop the twins from pulling over boxes in their excitement to explore their new world.

Each morning, Jeremy escaped the mess at home to catch the Docklands Light Railway to Canary Wharf and luxuriate behind his new desk. After years in private office, spending his days ricocheting between meetings and ploughing through an overflowing in-tray, he'd arrived in a place where there were few papers or emails. He could invite anyone he liked to breakfast or lunch in Morgan Stanley's plush dining rooms and sit at his desk admiring the view out across the skyscrapers.

Jeremy was, however, finding that he had limited time to explore these luxuries because Simon Robey had been true to his word and was inviting Jeremy to all his meetings, no matter how sensitive. And when he wasn't attending those, Jeremy was spending hours learning the obscure facts he needed to pass his Financial Services Authority exams, including the opening and closing times of every stock exchange around the world.

Although Jeremy was enjoying his new world, he was finding the transition challenging, not least because, for the first time in his career, he was able to add little to the discussions he was joining. It was a few weeks before this changed, but eventually it did after Simon pulled Jeremy into Morgan Stanley's pitch to work for the technology company QinetiQ, a former government defence research agency. Jeremy knew little about defence technologies, but he understood how government thought, which was handy since the Ministry of Defence retained a golden share in the company. Unexpectedly, Morgan Stanley won the mandate, which was a cause for celebration since QinetiQ was a new client and they might be asked to help float it on the Stock Exchange.

'See, this is going to work,' Simon told Jeremy.

This was reassuring, though Jeremy still doubted his ability to transform himself into a banker. He also knew that QinetiQ wasn't enough – he needed to get his name attached to bigger deals that were generating significant revenue. Simon's support bought him time to do this, but Morgan Stanley would never accept him as one of their own unless he did.

Jeremy's next client call came from the Shaw Group in Louisiana, which wanted to buy Westinghouse, a company that designed and maintained civil nuclear reactors. After the usual firm-wide conflict call to see if any of Morgan Stanley's existing clients were also tempted by Westinghouse, it was agreed that Jeremy could serve the

Shaw Group, though most of his colleagues doubted that this little-known American company would succeed in its ambition. Fortunately for Jeremy, in this case most people turned out to be wrong because, after many twists and turns, the Shaw Group teamed up with Toshiba to win the Westinghouse auction. Along the way, Jeremy made several visits to Louisiana and Japan and joined multiple late-night phone calls with Morgan Stanley product experts, bankers, lawyers and advisers. When the deal closed, he was exhilarated.

But it wasn't all wins. On several occasions Jeremy worked hard to develop a client, offering them analysis, new ideas, sector intelligence and innovative financial products, only to be rejected when the moment came for Morgan Stanley to be hired to do paid work. His first major loss occurred when Morgan Stanley wasn't selected to advise on the sale of part of the government's interest in British Energy. This hit Jeremy hard because he'd thrown himself into developing the relationship, and the numerous calls that followed as senior Morgan Stanley colleagues tried to establish who or what was to blame, only made him feel worse. Jeremy could see why clients liked to allocate work in this way since it meant they heard ideas from multiple teams of bankers. But he found it hard to accept the short-termism of companies who then ignored all the effort that went into building those relationships and went with whichever bank did the best pitch on the day.

In late March 2004 we paused for a moment of celebration when Jeremy was made a Companion of the Order of the Bath in recognition of his work with Tony Blair. I said – only partly in jest – that this meant Jeremy should take over bathing our babies, but he resisted, saying he was too tired. But so was I, despite Maggie's help. And when the roof of our new house began to leak, and I realised there was no way we could afford to replace it, I added to our workload by employing a roofer to help me do it myself.

John Burrows, who arrived the day the scaffolding went up in July, was small and wiry and looked like he hadn't washed for a week, which was probably because he hadn't. When he clambered out of our upstairs bathroom window and hoisted himself onto our roof, I followed him up, thankful for my years of practice growing up on *Wavewalker*.

'Good,' John said, looking about. 'We should be able to get this done in about a month. Now, how about a glass of cider?'

That morning set the pattern for John's residency. Evenings spent drinking us under the table were followed by mornings wobbling around on the roof emitting whiffs of fermented apple, while I passed him slates and savoured being perched up on the pitched timbers. By August 2004, the roof was complete, I'd cancelled the cider order and Jeremy was telling me he was settled in at Morgan Stanley. I was also back at work part time – though only after Jeremy had again intervened to encourage me to go back. 'You'll be happier long term, and so will the kids,' he'd told me, 'and despite the challenges, it won't feel anywhere near as daunting once you've started.'

We spent that summer in a cottage in Cornwall. While we were there, the twins began to walk, clutching the furniture and Jeremy told me about John Birt and Andrew Turnbull's preparations for Tony Blair's third term.

'They rang to ask my advice on their new plan to restructure Downing Street and the Cabinet Office and their priorities for public sector reform. The Prime Minister thinks he's running out of time so he wants to hit the ground running after the election. I told them I'm outside government now, but they still seem determined to get my views.'

In John Birt's occasional calls to Jeremy over the following weeks, he described his progress on the new version of Project Teddy Bear that he was preparing with Andrew Turnbull. This time they were proposing to break the Treasury into three parts: a macroeconomics department that would generate forecasts and set overall spending limits, an Office of Management and Budget that would allocate money to departments and the Treasury's productivity and growth teams that would move into the Department of Trade and Industry.

'Is the Chancellor aware of this plan?' Jeremy asked John.

'No, they aren't speaking again. But unless Tony does this, he'll always be trying to move forward with the handbrake on.'

In December 2004, and again in the spring of 2005, Jeremy was invited to join the Prime Minister and his team to discuss their preparations for a third term. Each time he did, he encouraged Blair to go further on public sector reform, for example by pursuing academy schools, allowing more private provision in the NHS and reforming lone parent benefits to encourage parents to go back to work from when the youngest child reached eleven rather than sixteen.

We spent the end of 2004 in Lanzarote, enjoying a few days of warm weather. Jeremy had been right that I would find a way of coping once I was back at work, but it had still been an exhausting year, particularly because Maggie had been unwell for some of it. But somehow we'd made it through, and over dinner on New Year's Eve, we again made our predictions – Jeremy's enthusiasm for this ritual never having been dampened by his previous failures. This time he thought Gordon Brown would become Prime Minister, Camilla Parker Bowles would marry the Prince of Wales, Manchester United would win the European Champions League and the UK would succeed in its bid to host the 2012 Olympics – all of which, of course, eventually came true, although not all in 2005.

On 5 May 2005 Tony Blair was re-elected with a significantly reduced majority of sixty-six. Teddy Bear was, however, never implemented, because by the time the polls opened, the Prime Minister had made up with the Chancellor, buying him an ice-cream on the campaign trail in Kent. The only part of the proposal that did survive was the idea of transforming the Department of Trade and Industry into the Productivity (P), Energy (En), Industry (I) and Science (S) Department – which seemed like a win until its Secretary of State, Alan Johnson, objected to what the name spelt out.

A fair amount of plotting had also been going on at Morgan Stanley during this period. Back in 1997, when the bank had merged with Dean Witter, an American stock brokerage, Phil Purcell had become CEO, kicking out his predecessor, John Mack. But by 2004, many bankers were frustrated by the decline in the bank's stock price, Phil's aversion to risk and his remote leadership style.

The events that then unfolded showed that bankers can be just as aggressive as politicians in deposing their leaders. One dark night in January 2005, eight disgruntled Morgan Stanley bankers gathered in a New York apartment to agree that Phil had to go. They wrote to their board demanding Phil's resignation and made the letter public after he retaliated by sacking those who opposed him. More letters were published, and by the end of June 2005, Phil was out and Mack was back.

Mack's return, perhaps even more surprisingly, changed Jeremy's role. 'Mack has made Franck Petitgas the head of Europe,' Simon told Jeremy shortly after the coup, 'and Franck wants you and Brian Magnus to co-head the UK investment bank.'

'Really?' Jeremy said, half expecting Simon to add, 'only joking' – after all, unlike Brian, he wasn't a banker.

But odd though it was, it worked. Brian and Jeremy created the bank's first coverage map for the UK, clarifying who should own the relationship with each client. Jeremy then negotiated this with the individual bankers concerned and spent time searching out people in neglected corners of the bank who might be interesting to British clients.

'But I'm not going to stay here long term,' Jeremy told Simon when they met in the spring of 2006. By this time Jeremy was leading multiple projects for Morgan Stanley, including a plan he was preparing with Barbara Judge, the chair of the Atomic Energy Authority, to buy up other decommissioning businesses to make the UK a world leader in this space.

'Why not?'

'I enjoy the work but I'll never have enough technical expertise to be a banker.'

Simon shook his head. 'Yes you will. My skills and yours are all about persuading senior people to do what they need to do. And it's clear you can be commercial. The rest you can build over time.'

Jeremy smiled at this, but he knew that his heart was still in the Civil Service. When London had suffered a series of horrific suicide bombings killing fifty-two people the year before, his first reaction had been to reach out to Whitehall to see what he could do. And though he was now reading the business section of the *Financial Times*, usurping our long-established division of the newspaper, he still read the front section first.

* * *

Jeremy was approached several times in 2005 and 2006 about returning to Whitehall, with Tessa Jowell, the Secretary of State for Culture,
Media and Sport, mounting a particularly enthusiastic campaign to
persuade him to become her permanent secretary.

In June 2006, Alastair Campbell – almost the only person left who
still had a decent relationship with both Tony Blair and Gordon
Brown – met Jeremy for lunch in Frederick's café in Islington.
Alastair had just brokered the Prime Minister's announcement that
he wouldn't serve a full third term and thought Jeremy should
consider going back.

'But why do you think I should when you won't yourself?' Jeremy
asked.

Alastair smiled. 'Because, in reality, they've never actually let me
leave.'

But while tempted by these offers, Jeremy didn't take them up
because he was still enjoying Morgan Stanley. He was also conscious
that his banking colleagues had taken a risk in hiring him and he
didn't want to let them down – and of course, his salary was also nice
to have.

In early September 2006, the Prime Minister at last clarified the
exact timing of his own departure, though only after another row,
which began after he gave an interview to *The Times* in which he
refused to commit to a date or a time to leave office. It then took the
forced resignation of a defence minister, Tom Watson, and the loss
of seven parliamentary private secretaries, for Blair to change his
mind and say he would step down within a year.

With this deadline set, Gordon Brown seemed certain he would
take over, while Tony was determined to make full use of his remaining months. In addition to announcing a new slew of city academies
and renewing the Trident nuclear submarines, the Prime Minister
also wanted to reform the pension system. In 2002, long before
Jeremy had left Number 10, the collapse of several private sector
pension schemes had convinced Tony that the system needed
modernising and Adair Turner from Merrill Lynch had been asked
to think through what needed to be done.

The launch of this review had resulted in yet another row with the
Treasury, which had wanted to exclude public sector pensions from

Adair's thinking, fearful of expensive reform. This was understandable, but as Jeremy advised the Prime Minister, was also unworkable, since it made no sense to review only half of the pensions system. A fierce battle ensued in which Jeremy and Ed Balls were, as usual, on the front line. This was only settled hours before the Pensions Green Paper was presented to Parliament, which meant that the review's terms of reference – including the cryptic requirement for it to look at 'other saving' – had to be shoved into a blank space at the end of Chapter 2.

Three years later, in November 2005, Jeremy sat in his Canary Wharf office reading Adair's final report, *A New Pensions Settlement for the Twenty-First Century*. The content of this had made his fight with Ed Balls worthwhile because, with the help of a group of outside advisers, supported by a strong Civil Service secretariat, Adair had addressed a set of issues that the government had dodged for years. And, ironically, the extended timeline demanded by the Treasury, which had wanted the report to come out after the election, and perhaps under a new prime minister, had allowed Adair to build support for his conclusions across businesses, unions and political parties.

The report proposed, among other things, that the state pension should be more generous as well as being less reliant on means-testing because this discouraged people from saving. It also recommended automatically enrolling employees who didn't have a work-based pension into an approved low-cost pension scheme. This measure would later become the poster child for 'nudge' policy interventions – small changes that could significantly alter how people behaved – which Jeremy would go on to champion in many different areas. In his final months in office, Tony Blair backed these reforms, publishing a pensions White Paper that was later turned into legislation. As a result, by 2018, more than nine million people had been auto-enrolled into work-based pension schemes.

In mid-January 2007, Jeremy attended the Anglo-French Colloque, an event that brought together senior business and government leaders from both sides of the Channel within the gilded Palace of Versailles. Between talks, Ed Balls, who was by then City minister in the Treasury, came to find Jeremy. 'I'm spending most of my time working on the transition,' Ed said, 'and if that happens, Gordon is keen to see you return to Number 10 or the Cabinet Office.'

Jeremy paused. 'If he's serious, I'll think about it,' he said, because – in contrast to his previous conversations about returning to Whitehall – he knew that, if he was called back by a new prime minister, who had the opportunity to make change happen, he would find it impossible to resist.

By that time back in Morgan Stanley, debt-fuelled buyouts, at ever racier debt-to-earnings ratios, seemed to be happening everywhere, and many of Jeremy's colleagues were keen for the bank to take on more risk and to push securitisation techniques into ever more exotic areas. There were warning signs – with some kind of sixth sense, Franck Petitgas distributed copies of *The Black Swan* by Nassim Nicholas Taleb within the bank and to his clients – but in the countdown to what looked set to be a bumper 2007 bonus season, most people were in no mood to read about the impact of rare and unpredictable outlier events or to link Nassim's thesis to warnings from economists about the housing and credit bubble in the US.

Jeremy also didn't pick up on these signals, partly because he was still focused on Whitehall. After their meeting in Versailles, he'd had several further conversations with Ed about going back into government.

'Gordon wants a smaller, less political and weaker Number 10,' Ed had told Jeremy, 'with a stronger Cabinet Office and more decisions taken in Cabinet or by formal Cabinet committees. The Cabinet Office will be led by three senior people and Gordon wants one of them to be you.'

'I'm tempted,' Jeremy had said, 'but I need to talk to Suzanne.'

I wasn't surprised when Jeremy raised this with me because I'd continued to believe that, one day, he would return to Whitehall. And despite the huge salary cut that would come with his move, and the likely longer working hours, I had no intention of standing in his way – not when I could hear the excitement in his voice. 'The reason why we both work, is to allow us to make these choices,' I said. 'But isn't it astonishing that Gordon Brown is asking you to do this when you worked for Tony Blair for so long?'

Jeremy laughed. 'You won't be the only person saying that. The Treasury will be shocked. But there was never an issue between Gordon and me – I always respected him and I think he respected me. Anyway, Gus assures me that Gordon doesn't hold a grudge.'

On 16 May 2007 Gordon Brown secured the backing of enough MPs to become the leader of the Labour Party without a contest – the first time this had happened since 1932. Not long afterwards, Jeremy went to meet the Chancellor in his bare-walled waiting room in the Treasury. After a brief exchange of pleasantries, Gordon handed Jeremy a scrap of paper on which about twenty phrases, like 'constitutional reform', 'border police' and 'new homes', were written in thick black ink.

'This is my plan for the first twenty days – your job would be to put flesh on each of these announcements,' Gordon said.

Jeremy looked at the paper. The list was little more than a series of half-formed ideas. But when he looked back at the Chancellor, they both smiled. After that, they spent a while discussing each item, which confirmed both Gordon's seriousness and the huge amount of work needed to make any of his proposals happen.

'Okay, I'll do it,' Jeremy said.

With this decision made, Jeremy sold his Morgan Stanley shares and attended a farewell dinner with the bank's European board and senior leadership. They asked him to say a few words, so, after thanking them for the trust they'd placed in him, he said that, though he had no knowledge of the government's thinking, heavier banking regulation was probably coming and many of the perks they received, including attractive tax rates for those not domiciled in the UK, were likely to disappear. His colleagues looked shocked at this, but it was Jeremy's honest view. However, like everyone else, he had no idea of the scale of the crisis that was about to hit the global financial system.

21

'Born This Way':
Taking charge of domestic policy

June–September 2007

When Gordon Brown became Prime Minister on Wednesday 27 June 2007, he said he wanted a clean start. But he arrived in Number 10 under the long shadow of the Iraq war, and as the head of a party that had been in power for over a decade and which was still riven by divisions between the Brownites and Blairites.

While Tony Blair made his farewell remarks in the House of Commons and walked out of the chamber to unexpected applause, Jeremy and most of the Brown team were in Gus O'Donnell's office in 70 Whitehall, getting ready to make their way through the link door into Number 10. In the end, the long-discussed transition had been smooth. But for Jeremy those final minutes were full of conflicting emotions. After three and a half years of making his way in the cut-throat world of investment banking, he was back in Whitehall. And though he'd relished the challenge of sparring with the Brown team over the previous decade, and was keen to get stuck into Gordon's agenda, he still felt considerable loyalty to Tony Blair.

Later that morning, after helping clap Gordon Brown into Number 10, Jeremy went to meet Gus and the other two of the 'three amigos' who were taking charge of the Cabinet Office – Jon Cunliffe from the Treasury who would cover European and international finance issues and Simon McDonald from the Foreign Office who would oversee foreign and defence policy.

'Together the three of you will have a view on everything,' Gus said. 'We've never tried to do this before, so it's up to you to make it work.'

'Making it work' could have been difficult given the amigos' overlapping job titles, but Jeremy and Jon had already discussed how to split their roles over pizzas on Tottenham Court Road. Jon wanted to include trade and climate change issues in his brief and would also be the G7 sherpa, the Prime Minister's European adviser and the head of the European Secretariat in the Cabinet Office, turning it into the European and Global Affairs Secretariat. Merging European and international finance issues like this made sense, Jon argued, since the Prime Minister saw Europe as only one of many international forums that could be used to get initiatives progressed.

Jeremy had agreed with this. 'That's fine,' he'd said, 'and I'll do everything else that isn't international.' Which was, he felt, more than enough to be getting on with.

After Gus's meeting, Jeremy went to find his temporary office, which was tucked into a corner of the Cabinet Office, sandwiched between Downing Street and Whitehall. There wasn't much in it – just a couple of standard-issue cream metal desks and a bookshelf. But on one shelf there was a mahogany brown bust of Gandhi.

Jeremy carried the bust over to his desk and sat down, propping the Prime Minister's list under Gandhi's chin. The most urgent item was constitutional reform. After all the criticisms levelled at Tony Blair about his informal style and his tendency to spin stories in the media, Gordon Brown wanted to increase trust in government. To do so, he was proposing to publish almost immediately a series of changes to limit prime ministerial power. The draft Green Paper describing these, which Gordon had prepared while he was still Chancellor, suggested giving up rights in twelve areas, including the power to declare war, to ratify international treaties, to request the dissolution of Parliament, to choose bishops and to control the Civil Service.

This last point was, of course, particularly interesting to Jeremy. Legislation to enshrine the core principles of the Civil Service, including its impartiality, had first been advocated as part of the Northcote-Trevelyan reforms of 1854. Now, at last, it was going to happen. But even if Jeremy applauded some of the Green Paper's intent, the draft had been written in secret by a team of Treasury officials more used to controlling departmental spending than reforming the constitution. He was, therefore, not surprised when Gus's private secretary, Ciaran Martin, appeared in his office early that afternoon.

'Have you read the paper on constitutional reform?' Ciaran demanded.

'I'm going through it,' Jeremy said, indicating the document.

'Gus is particularly worried about the proposal to change the laws of succession.'

Jeremy nodded. The rules governing succession to the crown, which insisted that older girls had to give way to younger boys, had long required reform. But changing them was complex for all sorts of reasons, not least because each of the sixteen countries affected, from Canada to tiny Tuvalu in the Pacific Ocean, would need to make the change at the same time. And, of course, it could potentially trigger a far broader discussion about the monarchy.

Ciaran flipped through the draft Green Paper and indicated a page. These subtleties had clearly been lost on the Treasury fast streamers.

Issue: Male primogentor (sic)

Recommendation: we should end the archaic practice whereby an older girl gives way in the line of succession to a younger boy.

Timing: should be an early win, but you may want to consult Buckingham Palace.

Jeremy smiled. 'Consulting the Palace seems a minimum requirement. Leave it with me.'

After Ciaran left, Jeremy called his old friend Suma Chakrabarti, now permanent secretary at the newly formed Ministry of Justice. 'Suma,' he said, 'we have an issue.'

Over the following few days, while Suma coordinated amendments to the Green Paper, Jeremy negotiated some of the trickier passages and encouraged departments to be radical even when long-held principles were being challenged. Sometimes a face-saving compromise was all that was required. The Church of England, for example, wanted the Prime Minister to remain involved in appointing bishops but was happy with the suggestion that, in future, this would simply mean passing on a single name to the Queen.

The Prime Minister's first Cabinet meeting discussed still-warm copies of *The Governance of Britain* Green Paper. Although a few people said it lacked coherence, it received broad approval in a long tour de table, unfamiliar to those accustomed to the brevity of the Blair Cabinets. Some ministers were doubtless perplexed as to why Gordon had chosen to give this dry set of issues such prominence but there was no doubting the scale of the Prime Minister's ambition, or the message he was trying to send.

With governance settled, at least for the moment, Jeremy returned to the list under Gandhi's chin. He was developing a methodology for tackling Gordon's priorities. From his time in private office he usually knew who to ring in Whitehall, and often beyond, on each issue and would bring them together in meetings so they could figure out what needed to change. And when they managed to reach agreement, he would sum up their conclusions in a way that left no one in any doubt about the next steps.

What was less clear was how to get the Prime Minister to endorse any policy changes that emerged from these working sessions unless they were required to form part of a speech or interview. This is what happened, for example, when the *Scottish Sun* demanded an interview on ending the residual legal discriminations against Catholics, including the bar on the heir to the throne marrying a 'Papist'. An agitated discussion in the Prime Minister's office followed during which Jeremy helped Ciaran Martin, who was incongruously clad in the red swimming shorts he'd worn to run into the office, explain how this could be changed and why it would take time.

But without such a trigger, getting policy approval was difficult because, unlike most of his predecessors, Gordon Brown was unwilling to take decisions by gathering the relevant people in his office, hearing their views and giving his opinion. Each prime minister works in his or her own way, so this in itself wasn't a problem. But because no one had found an alternative method, Whitehall had become backlogged.

This logjam soon began creating disquiet. Some blamed Tom Scholar, Gordon Brown's chief of staff, but observing Tom at close quarters, his wiry frame hunched over another pile of submissions, Jeremy thought this was unfair. The Prime Minister had convinced Tom to come back from Washington to head up his private office because he knew he was effective and they worked well together. Tom's appointment was also symbolic. After a decade during which the newly created title of chief of staff had been held by a special adviser, the Prime Minister had given it to a civil servant. To underline the point, shortly after his appointment, Tom had signed a letter rescinding the orders in council that Robin Butler had put in place to allow special advisers to manage civil servants. This was a good thing, at least in Jeremy's view. Although formalising special advisers' management rights had been done with the intent of curbing their power, based on his own experience, Jeremy felt that the orders had inadvertently decreased the status of senior civil servants.

But while Tom's appointment had been made with good intent, Tom found it harder than Jonathan Powell had done to pick up the phone to negotiate issues with senior ministers. This might have been fine if Ed Balls or Ed Miliband, Gordon's political lieutenants, had stepped in to fill the gap. But Ed Balls had by then become Secretary of State for Children, Schools and Families, and while Ed Miliband was closer to hand as a minister in the Cabinet Office, he was no longer part of the Prime Minister's day-to-day team.

To be fair, many of Jeremy's policy decisions probably felt second order to the Prime Minister, who was managing a series of domestic crises. These included an unexploded car bomb that had been found outside of the Tiger Tiger nightclub on Haymarket in London two days after he took office; a burning jeep that crashed into Glasgow airport at the end of June; floods that threatened GCHQ in Cheltenham, Gloucester prison and Waltham power station in July; and a new case of foot and mouth disease in August.

While Jeremy's Cabinet Office role meant he wasn't pulled into the government's response to these crises, the Prime Minister did ask for his help on the 2007 spending review. The trickiest part of this was the defence and intelligence budget, where the Prime Minister wanted more savings found so that he could confirm the purchase of the two aircraft carriers that had been proposed in the 1998 Strategic Defence Review.

Jeremy addressed this challenge in his usual way – gathering the relevant Treasury and Ministry of Defence officials together and asking them questions while putting forward possibilities sourced from his network of contacts. He rarely imposed solutions in these discussions, believing this would only result in temporary compliance. Instead, he tried to get the different sides to stop framing elegant descriptions of the problem – something Whitehall loved doing – and start coming up with practical solutions.

This method took many hours of patient debate, but it was often effective – in this case, it allowed enough savings to be squeezed out of the defence budget to enable a delighted Des Browne, the defence secretary, to confirm the carriers after years of Treasury-led scepticism under Gordon's rule.

After this was settled, Jeremy left Number 10 to its crisis management while he worked on the draft Queen's Speech. This was normally published in November, but as one of the Prime Minister's constitutional changes, he'd pulled it forward to early July to allow time for consultation, and some believed, to pave the way for an early election.

While giving people time to comment on the Queen's Speech was admirable in principle, finalising Gordon Brown's legislative programme in days rather than months required a massive acceleration of work led by the Economic and Domestic Affairs Secretariat in the Cabinet Office. However, they managed to get it done, which meant that the Prime Minister was able to set out his stall, including an ambition to build three million new homes by 2020, to speed up the development of the largest infrastructure projects and to introduce new requirements for all young people to be in education or training until the age of eighteen. As they moved into July, Jeremy was then able to get the Prime Minister's approval for some more domestic policy proposals including a consultation on how to tackle drug use, additional funding for sport in schools, a new crime strategy and the invitation of bids to establish eco-towns. Gordon Brown also agreed thinking Gus had been leading on creating a unified border police force, bringing together officials from the Border and Immigration Agency, Revenue and Customs and UKVisas.

But though this probably all seemed productive to Whitehall, it was still taking Jeremy a huge amount of effort to get each policy negotiated at official level and then agreed by the Prime Minister. This meant he was working long hours, coming home exhausted and emailing late into the night. Since I'd just become a partner at McKinsey and was also working hard, we were barely seeing each other. During the week we would eat a late, snatched dinner together while attempting to catch up on each other's news, and at weekends we took it in turns to look after the children or to take naps.

We knew this wasn't ideal, but we were too tired to worry about it – we just needed to get through each week, while juggling all the different things we needed to do. And I was reassured by the fact that, when we did get time together – like when Jeremy joined me that August for a trip to Turkey with McKinsey's other newly elected partners – we reverted to our normal relationship. We largely ignored my work colleagues, many of whom seemed intent on convincing Jeremy to hire them, and instead spent our time exchanging stories and laughing.

Jeremy hoped that appointing more GOATs, the nickname given to the non-political experts Gordon Brown wanted to bring into his 'Government Of All the Talents', would help to reduce his workload. These included Ara Darzi, a leading surgeon, who became a minister in the Department for Health and began a review of the National Health Service. The only problem was, to mix metaphors, some GOATs ruffled feathers across Whitehall that Jeremy had to smooth back down.

Jeremy was, by this stage, also starting to worry about how he would ensure the Prime Minister's initiatives were implemented once he'd found a way to get them decided. He knew one way of doing this – the Delivery Unit – but while he'd been away in Morgan Stanley, this had been absorbed into the Treasury and had lost its bite, its colour-coded reports lying ignored in Number 10's in-trays.

'To bring the unit back to life I'm going to need more access to ministers and senior officials,' its new head, Ray Shostak, told Jeremy when they met to discuss the issue.

Jeremy chewed his pen. A large part of the Delivery Unit's previous success had been due to the Prime Minister's patronage, but he doubted Gordon Brown would be willing to play a similar role. 'I'll talk to Nick Macpherson,' Jeremy said. 'The answer may be for you to report to both of us. I'll also find you an office in Downing Street and perhaps we can get the Prime Minister to send a letter out around Whitehall congratulating you on your appointment.'

Given that Nick was by then permanent secretary at the Treasury, this plan represented Jeremy's nuanced judgement of what everyone would accept. And once agreed, while it didn't restore the Delivery Unit to its former glory, it did at least reinvigorate it.

Jeremy also spent time in the run-up to the summer of 2007 with the units that reported to him in the Cabinet Office, trying to make sure they were focused on the government's priorities. While he did this, he also tried to spot any interesting policies they were incubating. One of these, which he found in the Office of the Third Sector, was the concept of social impact investing. This idea, which Jeremy was to come back to several times in his career, involved encouraging investors to put money into social programmes in exchange for modest returns. By doing so, it provided those programmes with more capital and it forced public sector providers to be transparent about the outcomes they achieved.

After Jeremy invited a group of City figures into Number 10 to discuss this idea, Ronald Cohen, a venture capitalist, launched the first social impact bond with Peterborough prison. This raised £5 million from social investors, which was used to reduce reoffending by 9 per cent compared to a national control group, triggering repayment of the original investment and a 3 per cent return. This was the start of a productive partnership since Jeremy and Ronnie later went on to do other things together, including setting up a Reclaim Fund to use some of the money that had been lying untouched for years inside banks and building societies to benefit social enterprises.

* * *

In August 2007 we escaped to Sardinia for our first family holiday since Jeremy's return to government. We sank ourselves into our vacation, building our days around mornings on the beach and long, lazy lunches. But one afternoon Jeremy was woken from the nap he was taking in solidarity with the twins – unrelated to the limitless wine available at lunch – by a phone call. It was Shriti Vadera, by then a minister in the Department for International Development, who wanted to discuss reports that Northern Rock, a Newcastle-based bank, was facing difficulties.

'Northern Rock's balance sheet is packed with mortgages that are worth less than the houses against which they're secured,' Shriti said, 'and no one in the Treasury or the Bank seems engaged.'

It helped that Shriti had a banking background, Jeremy thought – though he was also familiar with Northern Rock from his Morgan Stanley days, where it was often used to illustrate how a small player could build a UK mortgage book without the deposit base the large incumbents enjoyed. After being established in the 1960s, Northern Rock had eaten up over fifty competitors in the north of England, quintupling the size of its balance sheet between 1998 and 2007.

The calls continued after we returned to the UK and drove up to Whitby with Jeremy's parents to spend a few days on the trail of Captain Cook. Peter was frailer by then, though his prostate cancer was still under control. So we ambled at Peter's pace while I herded scuttling children and Jeremy kept disappearing into discussions on the faltering banking system.

By this point the vulnerability of Northern Rock's model was becoming clear. Because only 20 per cent of its loans were covered by retail deposits and mortgage payments, most of its cash requirements came from short-term borrowing. When BNP Paribas, a prominent French bank, had frozen $2.2 billion of its funds early in August, citing worries about the US sub-prime mortgage sector, the markets had taken fright and Northern Rock's foundations had begun to crumble.

Jeremy returned to the office at the end of August keen to make more progress on the Prime Minister's domestic policy priorities. Since these didn't include Northern Rock, which the Number 10 private office was handling directly with the Treasury, he was unaware of the efforts that were being made to ensure that its mounting, but apparently unique, problems didn't spill over into a loss of confidence in other banks. Jeremy was, therefore, as shocked as the rest of Britain when the decision to give Northern Rock emergency financial support was leaked to the BBC on Thursday 13 September in time for their evening news broadcast.

'This does not mean that the bank is in danger of going bust. There is no reason for people with Northern Rock savings accounts to panic,' said the BBC's reporter, Robert Peston.

'Disastrous,' Jeremy said, shaking his head at our TV. 'Of course, people will panic when they hear that. This is going to be like the fuel crisis. Who on earth has leaked this?' He picked up his phone. 'I need to find out what's going on. There aren't many of us around who lived through the aftermath of BCCI, when we had to look after several of the smaller banks.'

I nodded at this – Jeremy had been working for Norman Lamont in 1991 when the Bank of Credit and Commerce International had collapsed after a massive fraud created a $14 billion hole in its balance sheet. On a much smaller scale, that had also caused significant disruption to the banking system that the Treasury had stepped in to address. 'Well, don't forget you're supposed to be Mr Domestic Policy now,' I said. 'You don't want to get sucked into the day-to-day crises like you used to do when you were in private office.'

'No, I don't,' Jeremy said, tapping away.

At 7 a.m. on Friday morning, the Chancellor confirmed the emergency financial support for Northern Rock, adding, in an unusual statement of confidence, that the bank was solvent and had a good-quality loan book. This impressed Jeremy's City contacts, but unfortunately, didn't have the same impact on Northern Rock's customers, who were queuing up at cashpoints to withdraw their savings. 'I'm going to put my money under my mattress,' they told the reporters who shoved microphones under their noses, 'or down the road in a safer bank.'

It was extraordinary footage. There hadn't been a run on a UK retail bank for well over a century, but scenes were now being broadcast across the globe that made us look like a banana republic. Since most of Northern Rock's cash came from the financial markets rather than from the money in its customers' savings accounts, in theory this panic mattered less than in bank runs of the past – but traders are no more immune to television footage than anyone else.

The rest of Jeremy's day disappeared into meetings and phone calls with the Chancellor, key Treasury officials and Mervyn King, the governor of the Bank of England.

'If we don't do enough to support the banks, we may need to get troops on the streets to keep people calm,' someone observed, only half joking, during one of these discussions.

At this Mervyn King shook his neatly combed grey hair. 'If we do any more than act as a lender of last resort, we will create moral hazard,' he said. 'The banks need to take responsibility for their actions. We shouldn't reward them for choosing the wrong business model.'

Jeremy frowned. While Mervyn had a point, these weren't usual times – and if the governor remained obstinate about refusing to help, there was a danger that the whole banking system could disintegrate.

The cashpoint queues were undiminished by Sunday morning when Shriti rang Jeremy again. 'Lloyds TSB says they're prepared to buy Northern Rock if the Bank will provide them with liquidity for two years.'

'Great.'

'It would be, but Mervyn says he isn't willing to guarantee funds to Lloyds when they aren't in trouble.'

Jeremy sighed. 'Given that he's also said something similar to the Treasury Select Committee, he's going to be hard to shift.'

'If he refuses to help, Northern Rock could collapse.'

'I know. Have we made any progress on putting in place a savings guarantee? This is like Black Wednesday – people need to see actions as well as words.'

'Alistair is reluctant to do that because he wants to link it to a sale of Northern Rock …'

By Monday 17 September around £2 billion had been withdrawn from Northern Rock, presumably to be stowed under the nation's mattresses. After Lloyds decided against purchasing Northern Rock and the bank's share price tumbled, it became clear that the government had to act – after all if Northern Rock collapsed, it could take several other former building societies like Alliance & Leicester and Bradford & Bingley down with it. With almost no options left, that afternoon the Chancellor decided to put in place a savings guarantee even in the absence of a sale. This took Northern Rock out of intensive care, at least temporarily, and the cashpoint queues began to shrink.

'But all we've done,' Jeremy told Tom Scholar, 'is to stop a weak bank from falling over. It doesn't change the fact that Northern Rock may be full of bad assets or that it is reliant on short-term debt.'

Tom agreed with this assessment – and so did the Chancellor, who gave John Kingman, the Treasury's managing director in charge of public services and growth, the job of trying to find someone else who might be willing to buy Northern Rock. If this failed, the only other feasible option was nationalisation – but no one wanted that, not least since it would undermine New Labour's credentials for economic competence that Gordon Brown and Tony Blair had taken a decade to build.

22

'Pressure Drop':
Foothills of a crisis

September 2007–January 2008

Despite these banking troubles, in the autumn of 2007, Gordon Brown was still getting good press, thanks both to his deft handling of the summer's crises and the symbolism of being invited to a meeting with President Bush at Camp David. With Labour ahead in the polls, speculation, therefore, mounted that, having become Prime Minister without having to fight for his party's leadership, he would call an early election.

While the special advisers in Number 10 debated this, Jeremy kept plugging away on the Prime Minister's domestic policies. It wasn't his job to advise on elections, but it was his job to find ways to make it easier for people to access psychological therapy, a Labour manifesto commitment, which he did with the help of Professor Richard Layard, one of his old tutors at the London School of Economics.

But each time Jeremy solved one policy issue, another was waiting. One of these that autumn was trying to work out how to get Whitehall moving on climate change. In March 2007, one of Tony Blair's final decisions as Prime Minister had been to support the ambitious targets for reducing greenhouse gas emissions being proposed by the European Council, which included increasing the percentage of total energy coming from renewables to 20 per cent by 2020. In doing this he had gone against his Whitehall briefing – including from the Treasury under Gordon Brown. When Gordon became Prime Minister, Whitehall had maintained its view that the targets were impossible to achieve, but Gordon had reversed his position and insisted they should be maintained.

Jeremy called a meeting with officials from Defra, which was responsible for climate change policy, and the Department for Business, Enterprise and Regulatory Reform (BERR), which oversaw the energy companies, to work out how the Prime Minister's ambition could be delivered. But what this revealed, rather than the beginnings of a plan, was that drastic action was needed if any progress was to be made because the two departments were struggling even to understand each other's perspective. So with the help of the Policy Unit, Jeremy proposed merging parts of both to create a new department, the Department of Energy and Climate Change. After being agreed by Gordon Brown, this was announced alongside the autumn 2008 reshuffle and Ed Miliband was appointed as its first secretary of state, keen to make his mark.

Jeremy generally avoided recommending machinery of government like this because creating a new department was expensive and caused huge disruption. But in this case it signalled the government's commitment to tackling climate change and enabled progress to be made on a series of difficult issues like defining the carbon capture and storage requirements to be imposed on new coal-fired power stations. Some of the actions that the government needed to take to meet its climate change targets, like declaring that all new homes should be net zero carbon by 2030, were also highly unpopular, so after being convinced by the new department that they were necessary, Jeremy championed them within and outside Whitehall.

The trickiest policy issue on Jeremy's desk that autumn, however, wasn't climate change, or indeed any of the Prime Minister's other policies that were still sitting on the list propped under Gandhi's chin. Instead it was prisoners, or more specifically the fact that the prison estate was so full of inmates that court and police cells were often being used to provide additional capacity. To try to address this, Gordon Brown had been authorising the early release of around a thousand of the least dangerous prisoners each month since taking office, though that hadn't been enough to fix the problem.

This crisis had been building for some time, seeded by years of underinvestment in prisons, combined with persistent optimism about the size of the prison population. But rather than shrinking, the prison population was growing. The introduction of the Sexual Offences Act in 2003, which had defined several new crimes, combined with Tony Blair's narrative about being tough on crime, and the nation's panic about social disorder, had encouraged judges to get tougher rather than more lenient, causing the prison population to surge from around 45,000 in 1990 to over 80,000 in 2008.

At the Prime Minister's request, Jeremy and Matt Cavanagh, the Home Affairs, Defence and National Security special adviser, worked with Suma Chakrabarti to try to find more prison capacity. They trawled through every plausible option, for example creating prison ships or building huge 'Titan' prisons, renting unused prison cells in Romania or circling ex-RAF bases in Norfolk with razor wire and staffing them with retired Gurkhas. Inevitably, despite ministers' desire not to appear soft on crime, they also looked at sentencing policy, though they knew that anything requiring legislation wouldn't provide any immediate relief. This included working with Lord Carter, who was finalising his independent review of prisons, to create a sentencing framework based on learnings from the US – an encroachment on their independence that was fiercely resisted by the judiciary.

Based on all of this, Jeremy, Matt and Suma created a plan that, at least in the medium term, would improve the balance between the flow of offenders into the prison estate and its capacity to house them. But even with this agreed, the tension between the views of ministers and those of the judiciary, combined with the historic underinvestment in prisons, meant that the issue of prison capacity would continue to haunt Whitehall for years to come.

Jeremy was often in Downing Street that autumn for meetings on climate change, prisons and various other topics. He rarely saw the special advisers, however, since they were busy preparing for a possible election including by drafting a manifesto, and in the case of Spencer Livermore, the director of political strategy, developing a 'not Flash, just Gordon' campaign with Saatchi & Saatchi. Indeed, it seemed the only person in Number 10 who wasn't talking about the possibility of an election was the Prime Minister. Instead, when

Jeremy saw him, Gordon Brown was focused on the consequences of a potential military crackdown in Burma after its government triggered widespread protests by removing fuel subsidies.

Election frenzy built during the Labour Party conference that September, but by the end of it, the Prime Minister still hadn't decided whether to go to the polls. Then in his speech to the Conservative Party conference four days later, George Osborne, the shadow Chancellor, changed the game by pledging to more than triple the threshold for inheritance tax to £1 million. This would be paid for by the levy on wealthy foreign residents that Jeremy had warned his Morgan Stanley colleagues might be coming. It was a good line – 'only millionaires will pay death duties' – and it drew an exuberant response from the right-wing newspapers.

The government's press coverage then worsened after the Prime Minister flew to Basra before the end of the Conservative conference to announce the withdrawal of a thousand British troops by Christmas, in what some saw as a cynical attempt to steal back the limelight. After seeing the latest polling results on his return from Iraq, the Prime Minister decided that the game was up. On Saturday 6 October 2007, he recorded an interview in which he said he wouldn't be calling an election because he wanted more time to explain his 'vision'.

'Bottler Brown', the *Observer* screamed when it landed on our doorstep that Sunday morning. Jeremy spread it out on our kitchen table and shook his head. Even if the Prime Minister had not intended to be misleading, he'd taken too long to make up his mind, and the media's view of him, once so positive, had been shattered.

While the political side of the office licked their wounds and blamed each other for the election that never was, I succumbed to the outbreak of bird flu that was spreading across the UK. I'd boarded a train to go to Cambridge feeling normal, but by the time I'd disembarked an hour later, had barely been able to stand. During my week quarantined at home, I made the children keep their distance, but Jeremy still came in to sit at the end of the bed and chat to me each evening. Both of us were gloomy. We'd been hoping to escape for a few days during the election campaign but instead I was ill, and

Jeremy was working harder than ever to try to get things done despite the fraying tempers in Number 10.

The mood in Downing Street worsened a few days later when HM Revenue and Customs lost a set of disks containing the personal details of virtually every child in the UK – which even the Metropolitan Police, who were sent into the department armed with crowbars, failed to find. But while this was arguably out of Number 10's control, other missteps felt more avoidable. These included the Prime Minister's trip in mid-December to sign the Lisbon Treaty – a controversial document because it strengthened various European powers – during which, due to unresolved diary conflicts, he arrived just as the celebratory lunch for the other twenty-six leaders was ending.

After he returned to Whitehall, Gordon Brown called Jeremy in. 'I need to restructure Number 10,' he said, 'and I want you to become my chief of staff.'

'But I'm now a permanent secretary,' Jeremy said, his heart sinking. 'It was one of my conditions for coming back into government. And in any event, what would Tom and Olly do if I did that?'

This was a fair point since Tom was still the Prime Minister's chief of staff and Olly Robbins was his principal private secretary. However, Gordon Brown was clear he needed Jeremy to sort out Downing Street, and while Jeremy was equally certain that he didn't want to repeat a role he'd played for Tony Blair, in the end, they agreed a compromise. From January, Jeremy would become permanent secretary to Number 10, a new position, and would do his best to sort things out.

After consulting Gus O'Donnell, who welcomed the idea because it meant that Jeremy would also continue to advise the Prime Minister on domestic policy, the move was settled. Jeremy appointed James Bowler, Alistair Darling's principal private secretary, to replace Olly Robbins, who was due to move on, and agreed with Gordon that, to avoid duplicating roles, he wouldn't replace Tom Scholar when Tom returned to the Treasury in late January.

After that, we assumed everything was settled – at least we did until we were interrupted in the middle of decorating our Christmas tree by a call from Ed Balls. 'The Prime Minister has changed his mind,' Ed told Jeremy. 'He wants to make Stephen Carter his chief of staff.'

It turned out that Stephen, the CEO of a public relations company, had been recommended to the Prime Minister by his chair, Alan Parker. It must have been a strong recommendation because, following his conversation with Alan, the Prime Minister had become convinced that Stephen would make a difference, even though he'd never met him.

Jeremy called the Prime Minister while walking down to Clapham Junction to finish off his Christmas shopping. 'I don't mind if Stephen comes in,' he said, 'but if he does, I think I should stay in the Cabinet Office because I'm enjoying the role there.'

'No,' Gordon Brown said. 'I need both you and Stephen. You'll be a brilliant double act – bringing together the Civil Service and the politics.'

They went around the issue several times, but by the time Jeremy had to sign off because Lizzie was tugging his arm to go into a shop, it was clear the Prime Minister wasn't going to change his mind. So, while Jeremy didn't commit to the new arrangement, he did agree to talk to Stephen.

This was why, two days after Christmas, Stephen appeared on our doorstep and went to perch with Jeremy on the sofa in our playroom among piles of newly unwrapped Duplo.

'We need to discuss how we will split our roles,' Stephen said, studying Jeremy through his spectacles. 'The important thing will be to demonstrate that we're working closely together.'

'How did it go?' I asked Jeremy afterwards.

'It's going to be messy,' he said. 'I could turn the Prime Minister down, but he needs help getting Whitehall to work and I know I can do that. However, I do need to clarify what my and Stephen's responsibilities will be. That's what I told Ciaran Martin when I rang him this morning, searching for Gus.'

'What did Ciaran say?'

'He laughed and said he thought it was very unlikely that I would be marginalised.'

23

'Somewhere Only We Know': Back in Number 10

January–June 2008

On New Year's Day 2008, the Prime Minister made a speech describing his domestic policy agenda, and a few days later, he shared some of the early thinking on increased screening and preventative vaccines that was coming out of Ara Darzi's healthcare review.

Jeremy arrived back in Whitehall keen to work with the Delivery Unit to turn these ideas into action. That afternoon he moved, together with Gandhi, into the small, nondescript office on the left-hand side of the Cabinet Room in Number 10 where he'd been interviewed by Tony Blair over a decade before. Gavin Kelly, the Prime Minister's deputy chief of staff, took the other desk in that office, while Stephen Carter moved with his secretary into the next room along.

Jeremy was fiddling with his first ever government-issued BlackBerry – something he'd been agitating for ever since returning from Morgan Stanley – when Gavin called him over.

'What should I do about this?' Gavin asked, pointing to an email from Gordon Brown on his screen. 'THANKS,' it said. Attached to it was an email from Stephen commenting on the competence of each member of the Number 10 political team.

'What's that?'

'I don't think Stephen realises that every email Gordon sends gets copied to all the senior members of the private office,' Gavin said. 'It's one of the things we've been doing to keep track of what's going on.'

Jeremy shook his head. 'As his loyal deputy, I think you need to warn Stephen before any further mayhem ensues.'

After Gavin disappeared, Jeremy returned to his BlackBerry. Stephen's email had made his job of rallying the political team more difficult, but there was little Jeremy could do about that. Far more urgent was the financial crisis, which was dominating his in-box. Having spent much of his Christmas holiday reading around the subject, Gordon Brown had concluded that the main reason why the banks weren't lending to each other was because no one knew how bad anyone else's assets were. And by the time he flew to Davos at the end of January 2008, the series of US banks reporting big losses on their sub-prime lending had increased his concern about this.

As usual, Jeremy didn't join the Prime Minister in Davos because he generally found that going on foreign trips was an inefficient use of time. In any case, he was keen to use this opportunity to start sorting out Number 10. His first step was to work with Sue Nye, the director of government relations, on the backlog of diary issues so they were ready to negotiate time from the Prime Minister when he returned, knowing how much Gordon hated his day being clogged up with meetings. But a tour around the office with James Bowler, during which they opened cupboards to find them full of unanswered letters and unread policy submissions, made it clear how much more needed to be done.

'The Prime Minister doesn't seem to understand what's required to make Number 10 work,' people kept telling Jeremy. 'He doesn't like traditional policy meetings. He prefers to ask several people close to him to work on the issues on his mind, and while they do that, he develops his thinking through amending draft articles and speeches.'

Jeremy disagreed with this – it was up to them to make Number 10 work for the Prime Minister rather than the other way around. When Gordon returned Jeremy, therefore, tried a new approach. He instructed the private office to feed the Prime Minister memos and emails about policy proposals relevant to whatever he was writing, or to insert ideas directly into his drafts. If something became embedded, they should assume the Prime Minister had agreed it and let Whitehall know the decision. And in extremis, there was also Gordon's preparation for Prime Minister's Questions, during which

James Bowler could suggest possible challenges from David Cameron, who had by then become the Leader of the Opposition, that could only be resolved by taking a policy decision.

These techniques were clearly less efficient than receiving written comments on carefully crafted submissions. Nor could they work if someone needed to resolve an urgent agricultural policy question while the Prime Minister was drafting a speech on monetary policy. But they were often effective, so the backlog of unanswered questions began to decrease and Whitehall relaxed a little.

Jeremy was still meeting the Treasury regularly during this period to discuss the sale of Northern Rock, which was borrowing more and more each day to stay afloat. The prospect of finding a buyer was, however, looking remote. Only Virgin Group, J.C. Flowers and a Northern Rock-led restructuring plan were still in play and they all wanted the taxpayer to take on some or all of the bank's bad debts and for the Bank of England to provide liquidity. The buyers were also worried that the EU might later decide that the government's support breached state aid rules and demand they paid it back – even if that pushed Northern Rock into bankruptcy.

These meetings soon fell into a familiar pattern, with the Treasury team maintaining that Northern Rock had to be nationalised while the Number 10 team tried to keep other options alive, given the Prime Minister's hostility to the N-word. To be fair, no one wanted nationalisation since it would make it difficult to get taxpayers' money back from the bank, at least in the short term, and it could make the government responsible for every decision Northern Rock made, from refusing a loan to a small business to repossessing a family home. But for Gordon, an architect of New Labour, it would be particularly painful.

Despite this, by late January, Jeremy was advising the Prime Minister that nationalisation was likely to be the best option. While not ideal, this would at least stop Northern Rock going bust and mean the taxpayer would benefit if the bank was turned around. In early February, the Treasury and Number 10 teams crowded into the Cabinet Room to take a decision that, by then, felt inevitable. Northern Rock would be nationalised and the widely respected Ron

Sandler, who'd previously turned around Lloyds of London, would become its executive chair.

After the decision was announced on Sunday 17 February, the legislation to make it happen was rushed through both Houses of Parliament in three days, much to the delight of left-leaning Labour MPs who'd waited their whole careers to nationalise the banking sector. The Act also gave the government the ability to carve out bad debts or nationalise part or all of other banks – provisions that Jeremy supported, since a queue of other troubled financial institutions was already beginning to form.

'We will not back nationalisation,' George Osborne declared when the government's plans were announced. 'We will not help Gordon Brown take this country back to the 1970s.'

But by this point the Prime Minister was convinced that nationalisation was the right answer, so this barb had little impact. In any case, Number 10's attention had already moved on to Alistair Darling's first Budget, which would be presented against a backdrop of rising food and oil prices.

Final Budget preparations are always chaotic, but this time they were particularly so. Alistair Darling's appointment as Chancellor had felt like a safe choice – after all he had a history of stepping successfully into troubled briefs, including replacing Harriet Harman as social security secretary and taking on the transport portfolio during Railtrack's collapse. But Alistair was less mild-mannered than he appeared, which may be why his speechwriter crumbled under the pressure of aligning his views with those of the official Treasury. And when Jeremy rang Dan Rosenfield, Alistair's principal private secretary, with the Prime Minister's final input on the speech, this was the last straw – Dan slammed the phone down on Jeremy and disappeared for several hours to work on a new version himself.

Despite this drama, the Budget on 12 March 2008 was a modest affair. Its centrepiece was another increase in child benefit and child tax credits to lift more children out of poverty, paid for in part by an increase in alcohol duties. Growth was expected to slow given the disruption in the global financial markets and the rise in commodity prices but the Treasury was still forecasting public sector debt to peak at 39.8 per cent of GDP, just below the 40 per cent ceiling set in the government's fiscal rules.

With nothing much in the Budget to set pulses racing, the press instead focused on the abolition of the 10 per cent tax band that Gordon Brown had announced in his final Budget as Chancellor the previous year. Abolishing this had been politically helpful because Gordon had used the proceeds to reduce the basic rate of income tax, repositioning himself away from his high tax, high spend caricature. At the time it also had gone largely unnoticed – except by Frank Field, by then a backbench MP, who'd spent months writing articles about how lower earners would lose far more than they would gain. But a year later, with only a few days left before the band was due to disappear, the media and many of Frank's fellow MPs were at last listening.

'No one will lose out,' the Prime Minister insisted when Jeremy raised the matter with him. 'We made sure of that through the package of measures we announced last year, particularly the changes to tax credits.'

'I don't think this is going to go away, Prime Minister,' Jeremy said, 'and the Treasury is now saying that some people will be disadvantaged. In any case, people find it hard to sum up changes in that way – they just look at the impact of removing the 10p tax band in isolation.'

Gordon Brown eyed Jeremy. 'You know Frank Field, don't you?'

'Yes, from when he was minister for welfare. Your predecessor asked me to try to knock his extraordinary welfare reform paper into shape.'

'Well, can you talk to him?'

'Without the Treasury?' Jeremy asked, trying to imagine how Gordon would have reacted to such a move when he'd been Chancellor.

'Yes, of course.'

So Jeremy invited Frank into Number 10. Their discussion was cordial – after their welfare experience, they'd also worked together while Jeremy had been at Morgan Stanley on a project to incentivise indigenous Brazilians to maintain the Amazon rainforest – but Frank was in no mood to compromise.

'Whatever Gordon says, there are losers,' Frank said, his pale eyes steely, 'and they're the least able to afford it.'

After Frank left, Jeremy tried to talk to the Prime Minister again. But by this time the US investment bank Bear Stearns was collapsing, and Gordon had refocused on the banking crisis. The Prime Minister was still convinced that, unless the banks became more transparent about the risks on their balance sheets, more of them would follow Bear Stearns over the cliff. He was also worried that, because of this risk, the banks were reducing their lending to the 'real economy', including to people needing mortgages or small businesses requiring loans.

Jeremy shared the Prime Minister's alarm, particularly after two of his City contacts, David Soanes and Simon Warshaw from UBS, told him in late February that the UK's mortgage market was seizing up, exacerbated by Northern Rock's shrinking mortgage book. However, he also worried that the row over the abolition of the 10 per cent tax band couldn't be ignored for long. He was right about this – on 31 March, two weeks after Bear Stearns collapsed, the tax issue exploded during one of the Prime Minister's meetings with the Parliamentary Labour Party.

Gavin Kelly returned to Downing Street shaking his head. 'It was terrible,' he told Jeremy. 'They're calling it a justice deficit – the bankers do well while poor people get hit. Gordon kept insisting that there were no losers, but I don't think anyone believed him. People were catcalling and heckling.'

'Someone should have gripped this earlier,' the Prime Minister said when Jeremy went in to see him. 'It was bound to be an issue, especially with Frank leading the campaign.'

Gordon Brown was right – Jeremy did feel guilty about not forcing this issue, even given the difficulty of trying to get the Prime Minister to focus on something he thought he'd already sorted out. Despite his annoyance, Gordon wasn't yet ready to change his position on the 10 per cent tax band, but this time Jeremy decided to get ahead of the issue, so he asked the Treasury to begin working up compensation options.

* * *

While the Treasury began its thinking, Jeremy went back to worrying about the banking crisis. When the CEOs of the major banks came in for a breakfast meeting with the Prime Minister later that week, they were still arguing that they didn't need to be more transparent about their assets or to add more capital to their balance sheets – they just wanted more liquidity. It was clear, Jeremy felt, as did the Prime Minister, that the crisis wouldn't be addressed until the banks faced up to their issues. However, Gordon Brown was still minded to do something on liquidity because, even if it wasn't the only problem, a contraction in credit could tip the market into recession.

Jeremy worked on this new liquidity measure with the Treasury and the Bank of England while the Prime Minister flew to New York and Washington to hold more discussions on the global financial system. The Special Liquidity Scheme, which came out of this thinking and was announced on 21 April, allowed banks to swap illiquid assets like mortgages for UK Treasury bills.

With uncanny timing, 21 April was also the day when Frank Field lodged an amendment to the Finance Bill to prevent the 10 per cent tax band being abolished until measures had been introduced to compensate the losers. This was signed by thirty-nine backbench MPs – enough to remove Labour's majority and halt the progress of Alistair Darling's Budget through Parliament, an almost unheard-of breach of protocol.

'I need you to find a solution,' the Prime Minister told Jeremy and Gavin after he emerged from a fraught meeting with Frank.

Jeremy promised he would, though he knew by then that there were no easy solutions – they could either introduce a highly complex, means-tested compensation payment or, at far greater expense, they could raise the personal allowance. After some debate, he recommended the second option because it was far simpler. On 23 April 2008, the Prime Minister then announced his intention to do a U-turn. This saw off the threat to the Finance Bill but allowed David Cameron to crow about Gordon Brown's 'weakness' and 'dithering'. It also left voters unimpressed – as they demonstrated a week later when Labour came third in the local elections and Boris Johnson, a Conservative, succeeded Labour's Ken Livingstone as London mayor.

The Prime Minister may have been slow in addressing the 10 per cent tax band issue, but Jeremy was increasingly certain that he was right on the banks. Despite the introduction of the Special Liquidity Scheme, there was little sign of any increased lending to the real economy. And despite denying that they needed more capital, most of the banks were soon trying to raise funds in the market. Royal Bank of Scotland (RBS) plunged in first, launching a £12 billion rights issue on 22 April 2008. It was joined by HBOS on 29 April with a £4 billion issue and then Bradford & Bingley on 14 May, which was looking for £300 million. Collectively this was the biggest rights issue in British history and, if successful, would at last allow the banks to come clean about the losses sitting on their balance sheets.

While the banks tried to raise capital, Gordon Brown started worrying about another issue – the oil price. At $135 a barrel, this threatened, together with the credit crunch, to trap the economy in a pincer movement. He, therefore, began sending Jeremy obscure global news cuttings on the issue, demanding to know what Downing Street was doing about it.

Jeremy knew little about the oil market – indeed no one in Whitehall did. But after a few days of this bombardment, he decided he had to act. So he picked up the phone to call Martin Donnelly in the Foreign Office, because he knew from experience that Martin could turn his mind to anything.

'But I know nothing about oil prices,' Martin said.

Jeremy paused. Maybe this was a task too far even for Martin. 'Well, neither do the Treasury, the Foreign Office or indeed the Business, Innovation and Skills Department,' he said. 'But I'm sure you'll figure it out.'

After this morale-boosting speech, Martin spent several weeks talking to the major oil producers, ambassadors from the relevant embassies, academics and the International Energy Authority. Meanwhile, the pressure to address the oil price was building with riot police deployed in Malaysia after it reduced its fuel subsidies, fuel-related strikes taking place in India and ports being blockaded in South Korea. Based on this research, Martin put together a proposed set of actions including getting better data on the oil supply by counting the number of tankers in the straits of Hormuz and trying to convince countries like the United Arab Emirates and Qatar to partner with UK firms to invest in renewable energy.

After the Prime Minister shared this thinking with the deputy oil minister of Saudi Arabia, he was invited to go to Jeddah in June 2008 to address a meeting between the oil states and the major oil consumers. The result of this was a promise to step up production and improve the way the oil market operated – which in turn helped dampen renewed anger about petrol prices in the UK, where lorry drivers had been conducting a go-slow on the M6.

All in all, the work had been a success, Jeremy thought, despite Whitehall's collective lack of knowledge – though, of course, the oil price was about to be dampened by something else entirely.

24

'What If':
Are we turning into Zimbabwe?

June–September 2008

At the start of June 2008, Shriti came to tell Jeremy that Bradford & Bingley had issued a profit warning, their shares were down by a third and their underwriters were trying to walk away from their rights issue. This was a big problem – if Bradford & Bingley's rights issue failed, the bank would be in significant trouble – so Jeremy and Shriti rang both Citi and UBS to try to convince them to stay in the process.

In normal times, intervening in this way would have been a huge deal, but by then it was only one of a plethora of issues that Jeremy, Shriti and the rest of the Number 10 team were managing. And each day that passed, their list of problems was growing as food prices rose, the mortgage market seized up, house repossessions soared and the Bank of England continued to resist any substantial reduction in interest rates.

At home I was barely seeing Jeremy. Most nights he came home late, exhausted and monosyllabic, eating a rapid dinner before grabbing a few hours' sleep and returning to the office. And in those moments when he was present, he was usually typing out messages on his BlackBerry or talking on his phone. It was going to get better, he assured me. We just had to get through this crisis.

Jeremy was walking towards the door of Number 10 after one of his meetings with Shriti a few days after the Bradford & Bingley crisis when James Bowler intercepted him.

'The Prime Minister wants to speak to you,' James said.

'I've been talking to Alistair,' Gordon said when Jeremy walked into his office. 'We need to do something on food and fuel for the next G8.'

'We've been developing ideas for that, but I'll have to go through them with you later. I'm going out for lunch.'

The Prime Minister frowned. Lunch out was an unusual treat. 'Who with?'

'With Peter Mandelson,' Jeremy said since he had arranged to catch Peter, who was by then the European Commissioner for Trade, during one of his rare trips back to London.

Gordon Brown raised his eyebrows. 'I was due to see Peter tomorrow. Why don't I join you?' He raised his voice. 'Sue, I need to change my diary. I'm going out with Jeremy.'

The Prime Minister's diary secretary appeared at the door. 'You can't,' Sue Nye said. 'We won't be able to rearrange your meetings in time.'

'What?' Gordon turned back to Jeremy. 'Well, tell Peter I want to see him after your lunch.'

So Jeremy went alone to meet Peter, telling him over a fillet of sea bass in the Royal Festival Hall about the state of the government and how Number 10 was working. In exchange, Peter told him that, after bumping into Gordon at the Commission earlier in the year, the frost between them – which had first formed after Peter had supported Tony Blair for the leadership of the Labour Party – had thawed and the Prime Minister seemed keen to continue the conversation.

After dropping Peter off in Number 10, Jeremy returned to worrying about the banks. His initial relief about the rights issues had been dented by the Bradford & Bingley hiccup and now HBOS was also struggling, with its shares worth less than the price of its rights issue. The market thought HBOS might be carrying more bad debts on its balance sheet than was already known, Jeremy's City contacts told him when he reached out for a front-line view. This increased his unease – and his disquiet felt justified when, three weeks later on 21 July, HBOS revealed that it had sold only 8 per cent of its rights issue and its share price dropped by 6 per cent. It was also becoming clear that HBOS wasn't alone in its troubles since RBS's share price was below its rights price and there had been so little interest in Barclays' issue that the Qataris had taken most of it.

When the Prime Minister decided to take a two-week break in Southwold with his family at the end of July, he asked Jeremy to join him there to discuss what they should do next. Jeremy, therefore, left Harriet Harman, the deputy leader of the Labour Party, issuing instructions from the Cabinet Room, to arrive at Shadingfield Hall, a small cream-coloured Georgian pile in the Suffolk countryside. Inside he found the Prime Minister and Shriti sitting among piles of books.

'I'm reading everything I can about Japan,' the Prime Minister said, 'and it's clear that their failure to write off enough of their banks' loans is what pushed them into a decade of economic stagnation. We don't want the same thing to happen here.' He shifted Anthony Badger's book on Franklin Roosevelt's first 100 days to one side and picked up a large volume beneath it. 'I want you both to read this,' he said, passing it to Shriti.

'What is it?' Shriti asked, opening the cover.

'Ben Bernanke's *Essays on the Great Depression*. He argues that, to avoid Japan's experience, you need to put credit into the economy.'

Shriti flipped through the pages, nodding. But when Gordon walked away to talk to his wife Sarah, she turned to Jeremy. 'We're going to turn into fucking Zimbabwe if we do this,' she hissed.

Jeremy grimaced. 'I think it's time to get Tom properly involved.'

Shriti nodded – Tom Scholar, who by then was leading the Treasury's International and Finance Directorate, was already joining many of Jeremy and Shriti's conversations, but this hadn't been officially sanctioned by the Treasury.

'Prime Minister,' Jeremy said when Gordon returned, 'can we ask Tom to help us work up this thinking?'

'Okay. But don't let the Treasury slow us down. And I also need you to do some work on other ways to stimulate the economy. We're getting nothing from them on that.'

Despite the crisis, we also got away to Nottingham that summer for a few days with Jeremy's parents before heading out to Sardinia, keen to recreate the easy summer we'd spent there the year before. But this time, despite the beach and the lazy lunches, Jeremy's BlackBerry was always close at hand. Some days were quiet but others, like the one on which David Miliband, the Foreign Secretary, wrote an opinion piece in the *Guardian* that was seen by many as the start of a coup against the Prime Minister, certainly weren't.

Jeremy was back in the office for the next *Guardian* broadside, this one issued by the Chancellor from his Isle of Lewis croft. Britain was facing the worst economic downturn in sixty years, Alistair Darling declared, and it would be more profound and longer lasting than people thought.

'What on earth does Alistair think he's doing?' the Prime Minister said, prodding the newspaper, when Jeremy went in to see him. 'He needs to tell people he's been misquoted. Doesn't he realise his job is to sound confident, so he doesn't frighten everyone? And why talk like that when we don't yet have a solution?'

Jeremy shrugged and shook his head – these were impossible questions to answer.

'And we also need to sort out Stephen Carter.'

'Yes,' Jeremy said, glad to move on, though this topic also wasn't easy to resolve. Despite his early misgivings, Jeremy hadn't had any issues with Stephen, but Stephen's relationship with the political team in Number 10 still wasn't working. For months, articles had been appearing in the press criticising everything from Stephen's pay to his supposed bias towards the Blairites, the cost of his secretary and his Liberal student politics. And Stephen, or his supporters, had been fighting back with their own stories, including a particularly incendiary one in *PR Week* that had put Stephen at the centre of a Number 10 organogram. It was clear things had to change – it just wasn't clear how.

At the start of September 2008, Lizzie and Peter started primary school, joining Jonny in dinky navy blue and red outfits clutching plastic folders. Jeremy, meanwhile, was continuing to work with Shriti and Tom on measures to address the banking crisis and stimulate the economy.

The urgency of this thinking increased on 10 September when Lehman Brothers, a 158-year-old US institution, creaked, posting a three-month loss of $3.9 billion from its huge book of sub-prime mortgages. The market again marked down Lehman's shares, which by this point were worth only 10 per cent of their value at the start of the year. The other banks watched Lehman sway and demanded huge amounts of collateral to back up its debts. All of this again ratcheted up the unease in Downing Street – though it still wasn't clear to Jeremy, or it seemed to anyone else, what they should do.

On Saturday 13 September, Dan Rosenfield rang Jeremy. 'Sorry about the background noise. I'm calling from Hampstead Heath. Hank Paulson has just told the Chancellor that he wants Barclays to buy Lehmans.'

'Really?' A call from the US Treasury Secretary was rare and the request was extraordinary. 'On what terms? And what happened to Bank of America? I thought the US wanted them to buy Lehmans?'

'We don't know,' Dan said, 'but if Bank of America is walking away, there must be something wrong. I'm sure it would be helpful if someone bought Lehmans. But the Chancellor doesn't want to do anything that would make Barclays more fragile.'

'I agree,' Jeremy said, 'although Bob Diamond as their CEO might disagree – after all, it would give Barclays a substantial equities business and a presence on Wall Street. Keep me in touch and I'll brief the Prime Minister and Shriti.'

On Sunday afternoon, Dan rang again. 'You were right – Bob does want to pursue the deal, but we still don't think it's a good idea. Hank says Barclays would have to take on Lehman's $60 billion of losses, and he expects the Bank of England to guarantee liquidity. We would also need to suspend the Companies Act so that Barclays shareholders wouldn't get a vote. And he wants a decision before the markets reopen tomorrow.'

'That's an extraordinary set of requests. How worried does Hank sound?'

'To be honest, he just sounds knackered. I'm not sure he's expecting us to do this. He's not forced any of his own banks to step in so that tells its own story.'

While the US's position was unclear, there was no doubting the UK's view – no one outside Barclays thought it was wise for them to buy Lehman's assets.

After relaying this decision back to Hank on Sunday evening, Alistair came into Number 10 on Monday morning to meet the Prime Minister, Shriti and some of the Number 10 advisers in the small wood-panelled dining room on the first floor. They were supposed to be discussing the pre-Budget report over breakfast but instead, after the news of Lehman Brothers' bankruptcy became public, they worried about HBOS, whose shares had slumped by 34 per cent. The market was losing faith in HBOS's ability to keep funding its operations, the Chancellor said, and short sellers were exacerbating the crisis.

This time – much to Jeremy's relief – the Prime Minister was immediately willing to discuss the possibility of nationalisation. The issue was whether, if they nationalised HBOS, they could afford to nationalise the other banks who might also need it, including RBS, which had a balance sheet similar in size to the German economy.

'It is, though, possible that Lloyds might want to buy HBOS,' Alistair said.

'Yes,' Shriti said. 'I've spoken to them about it. Their concern is whether a deal would be referred to the Office of Fair Trading. They say that would be the kiss of death because it would put them in limbo for months.'

'If the right answer is for Lloyds to buy HBOS, then we might need to accelerate the process,' the Prime Minister said. 'These aren't normal times. Let's get the Financial Services Authority and the Bank to give us a view.'

When the markets opened on Tuesday 16 September, HBOS's shares halved in value again. While the UK tried to clear the way for a Lloyds deal, over in the US, Hank Paulson spent the day bailing out AIG, the world's largest insurer, at the cost of $85 billion. By Wednesday, the UK team had a plan – in the absence of any other white knights, and given HBOS's acute situation, they had decided to amend competition law so that concerns about financial stability could be taken into account when assessing takeovers. Barclays had also been busy, since it announced on the same day that it would buy a chunk of Lehman's remaining business, including most of its US investment banking and capital markets operations, for $1.75 billion.

When the HBOS takeover became public on the morning of Thursday 18 September, the reaction was muted, the main story being whether Gordon Brown had given Victor Blank, the chair of Lloyds, the go-ahead at a cocktail party that they'd both attended on Monday evening. But Jeremy was relieved. They'd taken one more patient out of intensive care although many others were still lined up at the door.

In the US, Hank Paulson clearly had the same worry because, after rescuing AIG, he started putting together a more comprehensive response to the crisis – the Troubled Asset Relief Program (TARP) – which would be able to purchase up to $700 billion of bad assets from the banks.

'TARP looks superficially market-friendly because it will enable them to buy assets rather than to nationalise banks,' Jeremy told the Prime Minister when the details of Hank's programme emerged, 'but it would cost us 1 per cent of GDP to do the same here.'

'We don't need TARP,' the Prime Minister said. 'It's impossible to value bad assets in this market and anyway it transfers all the risk to the government – we don't want to take on those assets unless we absolutely have to. We need a comprehensive solution, but I'm still convinced the best approach is to put capital into the banks rather than to take their bad assets out.'

Jeremy agreed with the Prime Minister – putting capital in would be far better. What was less clear, however, was how that should be done.

25

'The Wall Street Shuffle': Rescuing the banks: Part 1

September–October 2008

By the time the Prime Minister headed up to the Labour Party conference in Manchester on Saturday 20 September 2008, the change in him was clear. He'd grasped the crisis with both hands, spending every moment he could reading about it, debating it and worrying about it, and each time Jeremy heard him say what needed to be done, the more powerful his words became.

Jeremy asked James Bowler to go with the Prime Minister to Manchester, just as he'd once done with Norman Lamont – though this time it was because the world's financial system was crumbling, rather than to nail a spending review. This was a good decision because it meant that, while Gordon was in the final throes of drafting his conference speech, James was able to relay messages to him about Goldman Sachs, which by then was also faltering.

Despite the weakening banking system and continuing rumours of a leadership coup against him, the Labour Party conference went well. When the hall quietened on 23 September, Sarah Brown made a surprise appearance, giving a short address and introducing 'my husband, the leader of your party, your Prime Minister, Gordon Brown'. This generated a thrilled ovation and a perfect moment for Gordon Brown to take the podium. Once the room quietened, he spoke about the financial crisis but was also contrite about the mistakes he'd made. Five words resonated within the hall and beyond – it was, he said, 'no time for a novice'.

In fact, the only sour note from Manchester was the increased clamour for Damian McBride, the Prime Minister's head of political communications, to be sacked. Damian already had a reputation for briefing the press about individuals behind their backs, but after Harriet Harman, the deputy leader, stepped out onto her hotel balcony during the conference to overhear him complaining about her to a journalist on his phone, she declared that he had gone too far and had to go.

'He's bad news. He's damaging your reputation,' Jeremy said when the Prime Minister asked his opinion. But despite similar views from others, the Prime Minister was determined to keep Damian. He did, however, bring in two new political spokesmen, Michael Dugher and John Woodcock, and ask Damian to take a more back-stage role.

From Manchester, the Prime Minister flew to New York to join a United Nations meeting on the Millennium Development Goals. Gordon's determination to do something about global poverty was, in Jeremy's view, one of his most admirable qualities since there were few votes to be gained in reducing third world debt or ensuring African children were fed. What was harder to comprehend was how that coexisted with his tolerance of people like Damian McBride.

'It's the worst possible week to talk about development,' Shriti said when she called from New York, 'though Gordon gave a brilliant speech this afternoon.'

'Are you making any progress on the idea of a G20 leaders' meeting?' Jeremy asked. The idea of convening the G20 at leaders' rather than finance ministers' level had been suggested by the Canadian prime minister in the aftermath of the 1997 Asian crisis. It hadn't happened then, but now the UK team thought it would be the best way of finding a global solution to the financial crisis. In the past, the G8 would have been enough, but with Asia's growth, they needed a broader group – and it was, of course, also helpful that the UK was about to take on the G20 presidency.

'I think we are,' Shriti said before going on to tell Jeremy how, after Tom Fletcher, the government's foreign and defence policy adviser, had ambushed various heads of government in the UN's corridors, the Prime Minister had managed to convince many of them that a G20 leaders' meeting was a good idea. The exception was Nicolas Sarkozy of France, who wanted a meeting of 13 global leaders at Ground Zero, the site of the 9/11 terror attacks. The Prime Minister had, therefore, decided to divert his plane to Washington the following day to try to get President Bush onside.

'Really? Will the President see you?'

Shriti laughed. 'We hope so. And Gordon is also keen to read the thinking you've been doing on recapitalisation, so could you send him something to review during our flight back to London?'

The following day Shriti called again, this time from inside the White House. The meeting with President Bush had gone well, she reported, and he seemed to be warming to the idea of a G20.

Jeremy's news was more sobering – the Chancellor needed an urgent conversation with the Prime Minister because Bradford & Bingley was on the verge of collapse.

'They've already borrowed more than £3 billion from the Bank of England, and their shares have plunged by around 90 per cent over the last year,' Alistair Darling said when this began. 'There's no obvious buyer, so I think we'll have to take it over. And we don't have much time because, if people start withdrawing their money, it could collapse.'

'Okay, let's get on with it,' Gordon said after testing the different options.

After the call ended, Jeremy reconnected with Shriti. 'Have you got my note on bank recapitalisation?' he asked her.

She laughed. 'I'm standing in the boardroom opposite the Oval Office surrounded by sheets of fax paper. The arguments seem clear.'

'Yes. The Bank of England thinks we could need to put in up to £85 billion of capital. I think that's too high – they're assuming all the losses are realised within a year and they're including Bradford & Bingley and HSBC. But it gives us a ballpark figure.'

'I agree. I'll go through it with Gordon.'

Shriti's third call came from Heathrow the following morning.

'We spent the whole of the flight back discussing recapitalisation,' she said, 'with Gordon covering reams of paper in black felt tip pen. He's decided to go ahead.'

Jeremy took a deep breath. 'He's going to do it alone?'

'Yes. We can't wait for Bush to realise TARP is wrong.'

This was the boldest decision Jeremy had ever known a prime minister to take. 'Okay,' he said, 'but it's not going to be easy to get the banks to agree to what is effectively part-nationalisation.'

'Well if they don't participate, they're saying they're solvent and, therefore, they shouldn't need access to the Special Liquidity Scheme. But they might not have a choice. If they opt out, the market may trade down their shares until the point where they're forced to accept capital.'

On Monday 29 September 2008, Alistair Darling announced that the government would take Bradford & Bingley's £50 billion loan portfolio onto its books and would sell the rest to the Spanish banking giant Santander, which was keen to become a bigger player in the UK retail banking market. This meant that at least part of Bradford & Bingley survived, and its branches were able to reopen, though it was impossible to avoid significant job losses. Meanwhile, over in the US, Congress rejected TARP, and the Dow Jones index fell by 778 points, the largest one-day drop in its history. The FTSE plunged with it, with RBS losing a fifth of its value.

'A cold in the US creates flu here,' Jeremy told Shriti, 'and it shows why we need to act. The Bank says recapitalisation will take three months, but Rothschilds' advice is that we should do it over a single weekend to minimise uncertainty.'

'Rothschilds are right.'

'I agree. Can you and Tom finalise your thinking while I try to get the Treasury on board? I'll also need your help with the governor because he's insisting on coming in here for daily meetings.'

'Into Number 10 rather than into the Treasury?'

'Yes. He'll see Gordon for half an hour and then you or I will need to spend time with him.'

Shriti shook her head before glancing at her papers. 'I'm worried about how we make sure that this new capital is translated into more lending. I've talked to a few people, and to make that happen, I think we will need to offer guarantees for senior unsecured debt between the banks.'

After discussing this with Shriti for a while, Jeremy was also convinced that something like this would be needed. If the Prime Minister agreed, this meant there would be three parts to the government's banking intervention – liquidity to ensure the banks didn't run out of money, recapitalisation to strengthen their balance sheets and a credit guarantee scheme to make them more willing to lend to each other.

On Tuesday 30 September 2008, we woke to news of a new problem – the Irish government had announced that it would guarantee the liabilities of its six largest lenders and all the deposits sitting within them.

Jeremy disappeared out our front door with his phone already clamped to his ear. That left me dealing with the children while ringing my office to let them know – yet again – that I would be in late. It was irritating, but I was keeping my temper. After all, the potential consequences of the Irish statement were huge. It wasn't only the scale of the debt they were underwriting, which could bankrupt Ireland, but also the impact on the rest of the global banking system if people started flinging their savings into this new safe haven. It, therefore, wasn't surprising when, a few days later, the UK decided to raise protection for savers in UK banks from £35,000 to £50,000 and Greece, Italy and the US made similar pledges.

It was becoming increasingly clear by this point that more resources were needed in Number 10 to handle the multiplying threads of the crisis so, after talking to the Prime Minister, Jeremy rang Peter Mandelson. 'The Prime Minister wants to see you to discuss the reshuffle,' he told Peter. 'He wants you to do something big.'

'In what way big?' Peter said, his voice slightly raised.

'That's something you'll have to discuss with the Prime Minister.'

'If he's planning to get rid of someone by promising them my job here in Brussels, he should know I'd be furious.'

'It's not that. We'll talk again.'

Shriti was also looking for help when she came to see Jeremy that afternoon. 'I've worked up the credit guarantee scheme,' she said, 'but I need to test it with some of the banks.'

'You can't do that. The Prime Minister doesn't want us sharing any of this thinking outside of Whitehall.'

'Standard Chartered should be okay – they won't be affected by it. All I want to do is to bounce a few policy ideas off them and a few others.'

Shriti had a point, Jeremy thought. After all, he'd always believed in the importance of open policy making, particularly on highly technical measures. So, the following evening, when Shriti put on her coat and the Prime Minister demanded to know where she was going, Jeremy stepped in.

'It's best that you don't know,' he said, while Shriti glided out.

Later that evening, Shriti came to find Jeremy in his office. 'It was a useful meeting,' she said. 'Standard Chartered, UBS and a few others gave us some of their thinking on recapitalisation. The first part of their paper set out their conditions around the government taking equity, which Tom and I ignored, but the second half contained thinking on the size of the intervention required and on loan guarantees, which was surprisingly useful.'

Jeremy was still working on the recapitalisation plan with Shriti and Tom when Sue Nye came to find him on Thursday 2 October. 'Peter Mandelson has had a meeting with the Prime Minister,' Sue said, 'but he's still not convinced. So, Gordon wants you to talk to him.'

'I don't know if I should do it,' Peter said when Jeremy went upstairs to find him contemplating a plate of leftover sandwiches and a browning banana in the small dining room.

Jeremy took a deep breath. 'You have to do it,' he said. 'The Prime Minister needs you. Gavin does a brilliant job. But the Stephen Carter experiment hasn't worked so we're lacking a senior political figure in Number 10. Plus, there's also the day job. I think we're already in a recession whatever the figures say. The need to maintain confidence and develop a proper industrial strategy has never been greater.'

'I know. I know. But how can I be sure it will work with Gordon after a decade or more of bad blood?'

'Peter! Your country needs you!'

While Peter went away to ponder this, Jeremy went to talk to the Prime Minister about another issue. 'I've pulled together some ideas to try to stimulate growth, but we need more,' he said before taking him through his thinking.

Gordon Brown frowned. 'The economy is bound to weaken given the lack of credit and the impact on confidence so we are going to require a lot more than this. What we need is an economic council.'

This was, Jeremy thought, a good idea – after all, there was a limit to what he could dream up in Number 10 and negotiate with the Treasury. 'Maybe we should use COBR again but keep it at Cabinet minister level?' he said, getting more excited as he spoke. 'So, including people like Peter Mandelson, Ed Balls and Margaret Beckett. I imagine the Treasury will be sensitive so we should probably make Alistair Darling deputy chair.'

After the Prime Minister agreed, Jeremy rang Gus.

'The Treasury will hate it,' Gus said.

'I know. But we can protect their position on tax and macro. And this is a crisis. That's why it should be in COBR.'

'Really? They'll like it even less.'

Jeremy laughed. 'Can we get some of those funky financial news displays projected onto the screens down there?'

Gus sighed. 'I'll see what my office can rustle up.'

A little later that afternoon, Peter rang to say that he'd decided to come back into government. His appointment as Secretary of State for Business, Enterprise and Regulatory Reform, therefore, became the eye-catching announcement in the reshuffle the following day. Less noticed was Shriti's appointment as a parliamentary secretary in the Cabinet Office, which she was going to do in addition to her role in the Business Department to bring her closer to Number 10. This had been a compromise – the Prime Minister had wanted to appoint Shriti to the Treasury, but Alistair had resisted, wanting to be able to brief the Prime Minister directly rather than having it done through intermediaries.

The other significant moves in the reshuffle, at least from Jeremy's perspective, were Stephen Carter's departure from Downing Street to get a peerage and become minister for communications, technology and broadcasting and the appointment of Paul Myners as City minister in the Treasury.

Jeremy knew Paul, an independent-minded ex-City fund manager, from their time together on the Tate art galleries' finance committee while Jeremy had been at Morgan Stanley. After Paul's appointment, Jeremy and Shriti gathered around the small circular table in Jeremy's office to take him through their thinking on recapitalisation.

'You look pale,' Shriti told Paul at the end of their presentation.

'That's because I've just realised that I'm responsible for implementing this massive scheme,' Paul said. 'I had no idea of the scale of what you were proposing – or that you were going to do it so soon.'

The final details of the banking package, which by that time involved a capital injection of between £50 billion and £75 billion, were worked on over the weekend of 4 and 5 October. After the Prime Minister returned on Saturday from a trip to Paris – where he'd used a summit convened by Nicolas Sarkozy to try to convince other leaders, including Angela Merkel and Jean-Claude Juncker, to take similar action – this culminated in a meeting on Sunday evening in the Cabinet Room with officials and special advisers from Number 10, the Treasury, the Financial Services Authority and the Bank.

By this time it was very clear how fragile HBOS and RBS were.

Despite Lloyds' intention to buy it, HBOS was still finding it difficult to access funding, its credit rating was dropping, and its retail and corporate customers were withdrawing tens of billions of pounds from their accounts. It was looking increasingly likely that it would collapse before Lloyds could take it over and, if it did, the impact would dwarf the earlier risks from Northern Rock.

Meanwhile, the balance sheet of RBS, one of the world's largest banks, was stretched to the limit after it had gone on a spending spree that had culminated in the purchase of its Dutch rival, ABN AMRO, for $100 billion in April 2007. With the market concerned about how much capital the bank had and the quality of its assets, there was a real risk that its peers might stop lending to it. And, while it would be bad if HBOS collapsed, the impact of RBS collapsing was almost unimaginable. Given its size, if it did, it was likely to take the whole of the UK's financial system with it, and possibly most of the rest of the world's.

Despite this looming Armageddon, Jeremy was still worried that the Treasury would resist a rescue plan for the banks that they hadn't been fully involved in developing. But the main issue the Chancellor raised when they gathered in the Cabinet Room that Sunday night was whether it was legal to force the banks to take the government's money. And, if it was, should all the banks be compelled to participate or only those in the direst straits?

After confirming the legality of the package, and the desirability of including everyone, they digested the implications of the shadow Chancellor's television interview that morning.

'I was staggered by how much George knew,' Alistair said. 'He even mentioned the possibility of recapitalising the banks, though he must have known he was playing with fire.'

Everyone looked at the governor. 'I met George on Friday,' Mervyn King said, 'but the Chancellor knew about that meeting.'

Shriti rolled her eyes. 'It means we don't have much time.'

'Let's try to get our announcement out on Tuesday,' the Chancellor said, and the Prime Minister nodded.

'This is a theoretical conversation,' Shriti said. 'We can't do anything until we're ready.'

A duty clerk walked up to Jeremy. 'You have a call,' he said in a low voice.

'Now?'

'Yes. It's Peter Mandelson. He says it's urgent.'

Jeremy followed the clerk into the private office. 'He's probably got questions about his new role,' Jeremy said, picking up the handset.

Peter's voice was weak. 'I'm dying.'

'What?'

'I'm in Dennis Stevenson's house. I keeled over during dinner and I've been repeatedly sick ever since. I need to go to hospital. If I was in Brussels, I'd go to the Commission doctor – so do I go to A&E and wait in front of everyone else or should I go private?'

Jeremy was trying to process the fact that the Secretary of State for Business was in the chair of HBOS's house while the government was finalising a major banking intervention. But he decided to focus on the more immediate question. 'I don't think it's wise to go private,' he said.

'It's urgent. You don't understand.'

'Wait there, Peter. I'll get the Prime Minister.'

Jeremy made his way back into the Cabinet Room. 'We've finished here now, haven't we, Prime Minister?'

Gordon shook his head. 'I don't think we have.'

Jeremy frowned at him. 'Prime Minister, I need you.'

'Peter, under no circumstances can you see a private doctor,' the Prime Minister said when he picked up the phone.

'I know you're dealing with the banks but I'm in pain here,' Peter said.

'Don't be ridiculous,' the Prime Minister said, 'I'll get the minister of health to come and see you.'

'I need a doctor, Gordon, not a bloody minister.'

'Ara Darzi *is* a doctor, Peter. He'll come and find you.'

By 9 a.m. on Monday 6 October 2008, the FTSE was in freefall, on its way to its biggest crash since Black Wednesday.

While it fell, multiple teams worked through the final details of the banking package. A political team including Harriet Harman, Ed Balls and David Miliband was in Number 10, Shriti and Paul Myners were holed up in the Treasury with advisers from UBS and J.P. Morgan Cazenove, Jon Cunliffe and Tom Fletcher were talking to their EU counterparts and the Prime Minister was writing and rewriting his statement. Jeremy, meanwhile, was checking in on each of them, trying to coordinate the different strands. It felt like everyone was lashing down the last few loose timbers before a storm was due to hit while not knowing what the next few hours would bring.

The first meeting of the new National Economic Council at 11 a.m. was crowded. The Prime Minister had created the Council because he believed there was a real risk, in the middle of all this activity, that the real economy would be overlooked. It was already clear that it was going to be popular in Whitehall. Even Peter Mandelson was there, high on morphine, after Ara had snuck him up in the laundry lift at the back of St Mary's Hospital to get a small kidney stone diagnosed.

Back at his desk after the meeting, Jeremy sent out a swarm of follow-up emails. Every so often, while pausing to sip his coffee, his eyes wandered up to Sky News, which was broadcasting footage of lurid red stock market numbers and people withdrawing their savings from cash machines. If the recapitalisation plan didn't work, there was a real risk that multiple banks and building societies would fall, causing economic chaos and untold personal misery. He shook his head and went back to work.

By the end of Monday, it felt like they were close to finalising their intervention. Jeremy was certain they were doing the right thing, but the bank CEOs, when they were called back into the Treasury to meet the Chancellor, were still resisting recapitalisation. Jeremy's face was gaunt when he came home. He didn't tell me the government's plans, but he did tell me he feared the financial system was close to collapse. We woke the following morning to worse news – the *Today* programme was leading with a story about how RBS, Barclays and Lloyds had been into the Treasury the previous evening to beg the Chancellor for capital.

This scoop was the latest in a series by the journalist Robert Peston, though no one seemed able to find his source. It was also incorrect, though that didn't stop the banks' shares crashing when the jittery markets opened. RBS was particularly badly hit – its shares fell by 39 per cent, wiping £10 billion off its value, and trading in its shares was suspended twice. The banking system was on the brink of breaking down, and if people found they couldn't get their money out and were unable to buy food or medicines, there was a real risk of anarchy. The government might even need to put the army on the streets to keep the peace.

Jeremy's phone rang. It was Dan Rosenfield. 'I've just dragged the Chancellor out of his meeting in Luxembourg to take an urgent call from Tom McKillop,' Dan said.

'What did Tom want?' Jeremy asked – though he knew that, if the chair of RBS was demanding to talk to the Chancellor, it wasn't good news.

'He says that RBS is haemorrhaging money.'

'How long does he think they can last?'

There was a pause. 'A couple of hours without help. But the Chancellor is going to ask the Bank to give them enough liquidity to keep them afloat until the markets close.'

At 7.30 p.m. on Tuesday evening, the Chancellor called the bank CEOs back into the Treasury. They couldn't wait any longer – the recapitalisation programme had to be announced before the markets reopened the following morning. After that, the Financial Services Authority would determine how much capital each bank needed and, if they couldn't raise it in the market, they would have to accept it from the government in exchange for equity.

'How did the banks respond?' Jeremy asked when Dan Rosenfield rang after the meeting.

'They looked pale and didn't say much. But Fred Goodwin is still resisting recapitalisation.'

Fred Goodwin – nicknamed 'Fred the Shred' for his aggressive cost-cutting – was the CEO of RBS and the man who'd led it on the acquisition spree that had brought it close to collapse.

'I know,' Dan said when Jeremy expressed his astonishment. 'Fred's view is that admitting that the banks need so much capital will destabilise the market. But the Chancellor told Fred and the other CEOs that there's no other plan – and if this doesn't work then God help the lot of them.'

It had been a long day – in addition to their other problems, that afternoon, the Icelandic government had taken control of Landsbanki, their second largest bank. Somehow, the world had believed for years that Iceland – a country with the population of a mid-sized British city – could operate three major banks. And if those collapsed, they would take with them hundreds of millions of pounds of British savings, including a large amount belonging to local councils.

This new problem called for an extraordinary solution – in this case, the Chancellor proposed that the UK should use its anti-terrorism legislation to freeze UK assets in Iceland's banks. Jeremy had gasped when the suggestion was made. To use such powers against another country would have been unthinkable only a few weeks previously. But if the global banking system was crumbling, British savers needed protection. And though dramatic, this decision was a sideshow compared to the intervention package they were planning to announce the following day.

26

'Union City Blue':
Rescuing the banks: Part 2

October 2008

At 5.30 a.m. on Wednesday 8 October 2008, Jeremy joined a bleary-eyed meeting in Number 11 with the Prime Minister, the Chancellor and the core Number 10 and Treasury teams to finalise their banking intervention.

'We've no idea how this will play out,' the Prime Minister said. 'We don't know how the markets will react or even if our numbers are right. But we have no choice.'

After the meeting the Prime Minister started calling other leaders to share an outline of his package with them.

'Gordon told me that he might have to resign tonight if this goes wrong,' Shriti told Jeremy as they walked back to their offices. 'He's told Sarah to be ready to leave Number 10.'

Jeremy also felt queasy. 'I doubt he'll be resigning. But he is taking a massive political risk. The question is whether people understand that this is about supporting jobs in the real economy, not just bailing out the banks.'

A little while later, Jeremy went back to see how the Prime Minister's calls were going. 'They're going well,' Tom Fletcher told him. 'In fact, most of the leaders are saying they might do something similar. Even Angela Merkel.'

'Good.'

'The only issue is that, because this is so last minute, I'm doing the translating myself – and I'm not sure I got the French right for "naked short selling". That may be why President Sarkozy has invited the Prime Minister to come to Paris to meet the eurozone leaders this weekend to explain his plans in more detail.'

Jeremy laughed. 'Well, whatever the reason, the invitation is extraordinary, since we aren't even in the eurozone.'

Just after dawn broke at 7 a.m., the Treasury made its announcement. The government would inject £25 billion into the banks and make another £25 billion available if required. It would also put aside £250 billion to guarantee interbank loans and the Bank of England would increase the size of the Special Liquidity Scheme to £200 billion.

Not long afterwards, Jeremy and the rest of the Number 10 team gathered in the state dining room to watch the Prime Minister and Chancellor face the press. Jeremy felt high on exhaustion, euphoria and nervousness. This intervention was vital, but they needed the Prime Minister to nail the message that went with it. And despite his nerves, that is what Gordon Brown proceeded to do, leaving the cynical press corps at least partially convinced.

In contrast to the journalists, Jeremy had no doubt that the package was needed. The sums involved were dizzying, but to save the financial system, the government needed to make a game-changing intervention. And, if the banks became stronger, the liquidity would be paid back, the guarantees wouldn't be called in, and the shares would be sold at a profit.

Before getting there, though, they had to determine how much of this new capital each bank should take. The markets underlined the need for speed – after a jump following the Treasury's statement, the FTSE fell again, slicing another 40 per cent off the value of RBS and HBOS.

Later that afternoon, Shriti rang Jeremy to tell him that Fred Goodwin had called her. 'He told me not to fall off my chair,' she said, 'which was actually unlikely since I was lying on the sofa in my office at the time trying to get some sleep.'

Jeremy smiled. 'I know the feeling.'

'He said that, despite his previous statements about not needing capital, he now thought he would need five to ten billion. I told him my only surprise was that his number was so low.'

Jeremy was more interested in whether Fred knew that his time at RBS was coming to an end. 'Did he mention the Prime Minister's comment this morning about not supporting bank management that has failed?' he asked Shriti.

'No,' said Shriti. 'Maybe he thought it didn't apply to him or would happen over months.'

'Maybe,' Jeremy said – though if that was the case, Fred was in for a shock. The public wouldn't understand it if the government made so much money available to the banks that had created this mess, but no one lost their job.

Over the next couple of days, the Prime Minister continued calling other leaders to explain the intervention package, the Treasury and Number 10 prepared for their negotiations with the banks and the FTSE continued to drop, wiping another £90 billion off the value of Britain's biggest companies.

Shriti, meanwhile, told Jeremy she'd burst into tears in Gordon's flat after telling him she thought she would be blamed if the plan failed.

Jeremy shook his head. 'What did Gordon say?'

'He handed me a glass of wine and said Alistair already blames me. Apparently, Alistair told Gordon that, if it all goes wrong, he knows who to sack. But Gordon said I wasn't to worry because it's going to work.'

On Friday morning, the Treasury began discussing with the banks how much capital they should each receive. By this time Jeremy was worried that their intervention might be too late. People were withdrawing money from their accounts at such an extraordinary rate that there was a real chance that RBS and HBOS wouldn't last the weekend. Despite this, some of the banks were still refusing to accept the jeopardy they were in – perhaps because their leaders were at last grasping the consequences of the crisis for their own roles.

'Barclays are being particularly difficult,' Dan Rosenfield told Jeremy when he rang with another update. 'They say that, if they need extra capital, they can find private sources in the Middle East. And Lloyds say they need support to acquire HBOS, but they don't want any capital themselves, particularly if Barclays is also walking away.'

Jeremy shook his head. The banks didn't seem to understand that, if they refused help, they would be incredibly vulnerable when the markets reopened. At least, though, Dan had some progress to report on leadership changes with Stephen Hester being lined up to take over from Fred at RBS – though the Treasury was in the midst of a difficult negotiation over the scale of Fred's redundancy package.

Jeremy came home on Friday evening with his shoulders drooping. 'Our financial system is on the verge of collapse,' he said, 'and we're trying to implement a rescue plan that's never been tried before.'

'Will it be enough?' I asked.

'I don't know,' he said, though he wouldn't be drawn into a discussion about it. That night he barely slept, and neither did I.

Saturday 11 October dissolved into a series of phone calls, in between which I tried to tempt Jeremy with food and coffee. John Varley, the chief executive of Barclays, was still resisting any capital injection and suggested that he might buy RBS, an idea that was swiftly dismissed. Meanwhile, Shriti was furious after Yvette Cooper, the Chief Secretary, shut her out of the negotiations with the banks on the Chancellor's instructions.

Then on Sunday Jeremy disappeared on a rare foreign trip, joining Gordon Brown for his guest appearance at the eurozone meeting in Paris. In an opulent chamber in the Elysée Palace, the Prime Minister told his fellow leaders that the crisis wasn't confined to the US or Britain – the European banks were even more heavily leveraged than their US counterparts. He explained his plan, and emphasised the need for the EU to act together.

Gordon Brown's audience listened to him in silence, many taking notes. Jeremy had never seen a British prime minister treated with such respect by his fellow EU leaders.

'I support the UK plan,' Silvio Berlusconi said when Gordon finished, a view echoed by others.

'You should reconsider joining the euro, and staying for the rest of the meeting,' Nicolas Sarkozy said, coming up to shake Gordon's hand before they left.

On their way back to the plane, the Prime Minister rang President Bush. When he put the phone down, he was smiling. 'Bush has decided to use some of the TARP funds for bank recapitalisation,' he said.

Jeremy laughed. 'The world is following you, Prime Minister, but don't let it go to your head. By the way, did you see your approval rating has gone up by nineteen points over the last month? If you carry on like this, you'll be in positive territory by Christmas.'

At 4.30 a.m. on Monday 13 October 2008, Jeremy slogged back into work, exhausted but determined, leaving me once again waiting for Maggie back at home. The UK was showing the rest of the world how to address the crisis, he'd told me the night before, and others were beginning to listen. More of the management issues had also been resolved, with Tom McKillop joining Fred Goodwin in leaving RBS and Andy Hornby and Dennis Stevenson agreeing to step down from HBOS after its merger with Lloyds.

Shriti was frowning when Jeremy sat down beside her in Downing Street.

'I've had a hell of a morning,' she said in an undertone.

'Already? It's only 6 a.m.'

'Yes.' Shriti glanced at the Chancellor, who was talking to the Prime Minister. 'I got here at four to find Alistair staring at the final recapitalisation numbers for each of the banks. He said that, because they meant that the government would become RBS's largest share-holder, he couldn't agree them without talking to Gordon. I said that Gordon already knew the numbers – after all we've broadly known for several days where they would settle – so perhaps we could wait until he joined us at six.'

'What did Alistair say?'

'He kept insisting I should go and get Gordon. So I went up to the flat, but I didn't know where Gordon and Sarah's room was and couldn't find the light switch. I stumbled around in the dark until I fell over John's tricycle, almost killing myself, at which point Gordon emerged in his pyjamas.'

Jeremy tried not to smile. 'Well, he's here now.'

By 6.25 a.m. all the numbers had been agreed by both the Prime Minister and Chancellor and they were ready to make their announcement. In the biggest banking nationalisation in British history, the government would spend £37 billion to buy 58 per cent of RBS, which would indeed make it the largest shareholder of the world's largest bank, and 43 per cent of the merger of Lloyds and HBOS. These part-nationalisations came with a series of conditions including suspending dividends to shareholders, maintaining lending to homeowners and small businesses, linking senior pay to long-term value creation and cancelling directors' cash bonuses for that year.

Gordon Brown's intervention at the eurozone meeting also seemed to have borne fruit because, on the same day, deposit guarantees across Europe were increased and France, Italy and Germany announced recapitalisation funds. By the time the London stock market closed, it was up almost 10 per cent. And after the US announced that it would use TARP for its own recapitalisation programme, the Dow Jones industrial index closed up 11 per cent, its largest increase in percentage terms for fifteen years.

'This isn't the end of the crisis by any means,' Jeremy told me when he got home, 'but I think the wound has been cauterised and bound.'

27

'Running Up That Hill':
Averting recession

October–December 2008

In the days after announcing its rescue package, the Treasury focused on setting up UK Financial Institutions Ltd, the organisation that would manage the government's burgeoning banking investments at arm's length from Whitehall, while the Prime Minister, Jeremy and Shriti worried about how to head off the looming recession.

The Prime Minister worked on this issue in his new 'war room' in 12 Downing Street. This large, wood-panelled conference room, which had housed the Number 10 press office during Tony Blair's second term, and more recently the whips' office, was reached by a narrow corridor running through Number 11. Its layout was inspired by Michael Bloomberg's office in New York, with a horseshoe-shaped table dominating the space, surrounded by nine or ten chairs. The Prime Minister sat at a desk positioned across the far end of this, like an iron filing stuck to a magnet.

'The idea,' Gordon had explained, 'is to break down organisational silos.'

'Great,' Jeremy had said even though he hated the idea of working in an open-plan space through which people were endlessly coming and going. But he made the best of it, claiming the seat at the end of the left leg of the horseshoe – which was coincidentally on the Prime Minister's blind side since he'd lost the sight in his left eye in a rugby accident as a young man – while also keeping his old office next to the Cabinet Room in Number 10 to use whenever Gordon was away.

The Prime Minister arrived early in the war room each morning to begin work. After eating a fried breakfast and dumping the dirty plate on Jeremy's desk, he spent most of the rest of each day making phone calls or bashing out text on his computer, the large black capitals on his screen that he used to aid his eyesight visible to anyone passing by. WE ARE FIGHTING THIS GLOBAL FINANCIAL RECESSION EVERY WAY WE KNOW. GETTING THE BANKS STARTED AGAIN …

Informal discussions took place in the horseshoe, but for more formal discussions the Prime Minister could retreat into the small office next to the war room, which contained an old walnut dining table and four chairs. He would take a seat in there, dragging papers out of his loose leather bag and spreading them across the table while everyone else followed him in, pulling in extra chairs from outside.

One of the things they discussed in those meetings was the mood in the City. Jeremy was still getting regular updates from his contacts and their news wasn't good. Despite the banking intervention, the cost of interbank lending, the LIBOR rate, wasn't coming down. Since LIBOR determined the rates paid by most other borrowers, including homeowners with floating-rate mortgages, this was worrying. Even more concerning were rumours that Barclays was paying above LIBOR to get its funding. After discussing this with the Prime Minister, Jeremy emailed Paul Tucker, the markets director at the Bank of England, to ask if he understood what was going on and Paul emailed back to assure Jeremy that the Bank was monitoring the situation.*

Despite these signals, Jeremy and the Prime Minister's other advisers knew they had to give the new measures time to take effect before they could consider making additional interventions. In any case, most of the rest of October and early November 2008 was taken up by preparations for the first G20 leaders' meeting on 15 November in Washington. When this meeting had been called a month previ-

---

* This email exchange, which took place on 22 October, has been simplified here. It was later to become public after it emerged that, following a later concerned call from Paul Tucker to Barclays, Barclays reduced its LIBOR submissions, misconduct for which it was later fined. Jeremy was, however, unaware at the time of Paul's call to Barclays or Barclays' subsequent actions.

ously, it had been intended to address a financial crisis, but with little sign of stock markets strengthening even after billions had been injected into the banking system, it was clear they were facing a more pervasive global emergency.

At President Bush's request, the UK had taken the lead in agreeing the agenda for the Washington meeting, preparing the papers for it and building alignment between participants. The Prime Minister wanted to use it to give the world's economy a Keynesian kick-start. But when the delegates assembled, it became clear this would be impossible, particularly given Germany's fear of high inflation. Nevertheless, the leaders declared their determination to work together to restore global growth – and they also agreed to meet again before the end of April in London.

Even if the G20 had been reluctant to agree a global stimulus, the Prime Minister, who was by this time reading Paul Krugman's *The Return of Depression Economics*, still wanted to offer something to help the real economy in the pre-Budget report in November. And his determination to do this increased when, despite a cut in interest rates to 3 per cent on 6 November 2008, GDP again declined in the third quarter.

After going through a list of proposed measures drawn up by Jonathan Portes, who was by then the chief economist in the Cabinet Office, Jeremy recommended a temporary cut in VAT from 17.5 per cent to 15 per cent. This could be implemented in time for the Christmas rush, he argued, and would particularly help low-income families. The Prime Minister agreed, saying he wanted it to be the centrepiece of the pre-Budget report, and luckily, since the Treasury had already been briefed, so did the Chancellor.

The details of how this cut would work were, however, far harder to settle. The first issue was whether to have a short-term reduction, as favoured by the Treasury, or something longer lasting, which the Prime Minister preferred. Several tough meetings later they compromised on thirteen months, by which time they hoped the economy would be in a self-sustaining recovery. Even more difficult was agreeing what the new rate should be at the end of the thirteen months. The Treasury argued for 20 per cent, saying this would help the UK's fiscal credibility and increase the impact of the reduction. But the Prime Minister, who was concerned about stalling growth in the economy, wanted it to return to its original level, with the remaining funds needed to balance the budget coming from an increase in National Insurance.

With two days left before the report was published, this argument was still raging and Jeremy's phone calls with Nick Macpherson were becoming increasingly frayed. 'The Prime Minister knows that raising National Insurance could be seen as a tax on work,' Jeremy told Nick, 'but better that, in his book, than increasing VAT, which he sees as a tax on poverty.'

In the end the Prime Minister won this battle. VAT would be restored to 17.5 per cent after the temporary reduction and National Insurance would be increased by 0.5 per cent from April 2011. The pre-Budget report also introduced a new 45 per cent rate of income tax for those earning over £150,000 a year. Although redistributive, this new rate flew in the face of New Labour's philosophy of encouraging aspiration, so it was made more palatable by also being post-dated to 2011.

In addition to these changes, the Chancellor's speech on 24 November also contained a broader package of stimulus measures that Jeremy and others had helped prepare. These included bringing forward £3 billion of capital spending, setting up a small business finance scheme and making more help available to people struggling with their mortgage payments. Although significant at £20 billion, these accounted for only around 0.1 per cent of GDP because, with the economy contracting, the government couldn't afford to spend any more.

But nothing could conceal the most shocking revelation in the pre-Budget report – the increase in the expected deficit for 2009/10 from the £43 billion forecast in March to £118 billion. Unsurprisingly, the Opposition leapt on this figure, not least because, only a few days before, they'd abandoned their pledge to match Labour's spending commitments. The economic gap between the parties had become a gulf, setting the stage for the 2010 election battle.

* * *

After the pre-Budget report, Jeremy's work quietened down a little and our life returned to a more normal pattern in which we alternated who left the house first in the mornings and who would be home for bath time. We even managed a visit to Chequers, where our children played Lego with John and Fraser Brown. It had been a good time to go, Jeremy told me on our way home, because the Prime Minister's conference speech had gone well, and he'd silenced many of the critics in his party. In fact, many people felt he'd had a good financial crisis despite the impact on the deficit – he'd even won a by-election.

Back in the office towards the end of December, the Treasury's paper on quantitative easing (QE) – the policy described in the essays that Gordon Brown had given Jeremy and Shriti in Southwold – at last arrived. *To Zero and Beyond: How Monetary Policy can Tackle Deflation* explained how QE might work in the UK – the Bank of England would buy gilts from the market in exchange for cash that should lower the cost of borrowing and support new lending or investment. Though simple, this was radical, and no one knew what its impact would be.

'I know all this,' Gordon said, throwing the document into the bin by his desk. 'Now can you get them to work out how to do it?'

Jeremy glanced at Shriti.

'It looks like we'll need to start all over again with the Treasury,' she said, 'and perhaps we should also find a more confidential place for that paper.'

There was, after that, only one event left for Jeremy to attend before heading home for Christmas – the office party. That year the organising team had gone to town, transforming the state dining room, Sir John Soane's architectural masterpiece, by rolling up the carpet and installing disco lights and a sound system at one end of the room. Jeremy hit the floor early, keen at least for one evening to shed the stresses of the year, rolling up his sleeves and getting into the music. The rest of the office followed suit, and the dancing continued into the early hours of the morning, long after Jeremy left.

28

'Up All Night':
Flying to Israel

December 2008–January 2009

We flew to Lanzarote after Christmas 2008, this time with Jeremy's Hertford College friend, Jeremy Clarke, and his partner Railton. For several days we were undisturbed, settling into our usual holiday routines, until one night while watching our children dancing, Jeremy's phone buzzed. After ignoring it for a minute, focusing on the action up on the stage, he told me he was going to check if the call was urgent and disappeared outside.

'We need to get the Treasury to be more activist and creative,' the Prime Minister said, 'they don't seem to realise we're in the worst economic crisis of the century.'

'Okay.'

'So I'm thinking of putting Gus in charge of both the Cabinet Office and the Treasury and making Nick Macpherson Cabinet Secretary.'

Jeremy blinked. 'Nick and Gus are unlikely to support that structure because it would be a complete muddle,' he said, conscious that Gordon could probably hear the pop music blaring out behind him. 'If you're not happy with the policies we have, then why don't we push the National Economic Council harder to develop new thinking? If that doesn't work, then we can look at more drastic options.'

By the time Jeremy returned to the office in January, the Prime Minister had stopped talking about organisational changes but he was still worrying about the economy. The Bank of England had announced another half-point reduction in the interest rate on 8

January, taking it down to 1.5 per cent – the lowest in its 315-year history – but Gordon believed more needed to be done to help the economy. He, therefore, took Jeremy's advice and started accelerating the thinking in the National Economic Council.

Jeremy made his way down to the basement in the Cabinet Office for each of the Council's meetings, pausing to hand in both his BlackBerrys before stepping into the windowless COBR room. His seat was at the end of the table next to Gus O'Donnell and the Prime Minister, with the Chancellor and Nick Macpherson placed on the Prime Minister's other side. This seating plan was designed to quell any suspicion – perish the thought – that the Council was stealing the management of economic policy from the Treasury, though Nick generally still assumed an air of disengagement from the whole business.

In contrast to Nick, most people still thought the Council was one of the hottest tickets in Whitehall, so the room was full of ministers, special advisers and officials jostling for seats close to the Prime Minister. On the agenda would be a presentation from a minister on how their department could support the economy. And despite the Treasury's scepticism, the pressure that Gordon Brown was putting on ministers to come up with concrete propositions, and his insistence on follow-up actions, was soon generating momentum. This was aided by the intensity of being in a bunker – and, of course, the realisation of the scale of the crisis.

Outside the Council, Jeremy was still spending time on other issues like supporting the negotiations on airport expansion between Geoff Hoon, the Secretary of State for Transport, and Ed Miliband.

To Jeremy at least, the economic case for additional runway capacity had been clear ever since Alistair Darling had produced a White Paper on the issue back in 2003. If more capacity wasn't built then, in addition to making life worse for passengers, there was a risk that international businesses would be encouraged to relocate abroad. But getting to a decision on this issue meant squaring these considerations with the government's commitment to reducing carbon dioxide emissions. In the end, this tension was addressed by initially capping the extra runway capacity at 125,000 aircraft movements a year, rather than the 222,000 originally planned, and by allowing only the greenest aeroplanes to use the new slots. The government also pledged to limit the UK's aviation emissions to below 2005 levels by 2050. At the time Jeremy felt that this appropriately balanced the environmental and economic impacts of a new runway – though this was, of course, later to be re-evaluated.

When, on 15 January 2009, Geoff Hoon announced the decision to build a new runway at Heathrow, he also promised to create a new high-speed rail line from London to Manchester. Andrew Adonis, the new Minister of State for Transport, had managed with Jeremy's help to get this second proposal agreed. He had, though, only succeeded because Alistair Darling thought it would never happen. 'Not even if you drove the train yourself,' as he told Andrew in one meeting.

On the day of the announcement, this proposal to build a new high-speed rail line wasn't controversial, although it would become so later. However, the Heathrow decision certainly was for many Labour MPs, voters in west London and, above all, environmentalists.

'So, what happens now?' I asked Jeremy at the end of January after the government narrowly survived a vote on airport expansion in the House of Commons, in which twenty-eight Labour MPs had rebelled.

'Not much,' he said, 'unless Gordon wins the next election. But I'll keep making the economic case for airport expansion whenever I can.'

After official figures confirmed on 23 January 2009 that the economy was in recession for the first time since 1991, the Prime Minister's fear that the UK might copy Japan and fall into a decade of stagnation began to feel prescient. While the National Economic Council was still churning out ideas – including, for example, a car scrappage scheme that would neatly help both the environment and the struggling motor industry – it was increasingly clear that such micro policy interventions would never be enough on their own to turn around the economy. Jeremy and his colleagues knew that the fiscal injection they'd announced in November's pre-Budget report should be starting to strengthen the economy, but there was a risk that, if they waited to see if it was enough, they risked doing too little too late. The Prime Minister, therefore, started talking about introducing a new package of stimulus measures, this time including QE, which the Bank of England had agreed to implement so long as the government indemnified it for any losses.

In mid-January, when the Prime Minister flew to Egypt for a summit on Gaza, Jeremy tagged along so that he could finalise their thinking on these additional measures on the way. When the meeting concluded, the UK team ran for their plane, which was waiting on the tarmac in Sharm El Sheikh with its engine running. There was no time to waste because their next stop was Jerusalem where Benjamin Netanyahu, the Israeli prime minister, was offering only one bilateral, to be claimed by the leader who arrived first. The UK team thought they had a good head start, but as they approached their plane, they looked back to see the French delegation behind them on the runway.

'We need to get to Israel before the French,' the UK team told their pilots as they scrambled aboard. By coincidence the Prime Minister's jet was a French charter plane, flown by French crew. But the captain still grinned when he heard this, revved up his engines and left his compatriots in his wake.

After Gordon Brown successfully stole the Netanyahu bilateral, they finalised the new intervention package during their flight home and announced it on 19 January 2009. An asset protection scheme would increase the banks' willingness to lend by allowing them to insure against losses on their balance sheets and the Bank of England would spend up to £50 billion on QE. The government would also increase its shareholding in RBS to nearly 70 per cent and extend the credit guarantee scheme.

The market reaction to these new measures was, however, disappointing, partly because, on the same day, RBS announced it was writing off between £7 billion and £8 billion of assets, causing its share price to drop by 67 per cent. But Jeremy was again convinced that the measures were needed and that their approach was right. For example, an essential feature of how they'd designed the asset protection scheme was that they were leaving bad assets on the banks' balance sheets so that, in contrast to the US's approach, the banks would remain in charge of funding and managing them. This approach had less impact on the government's accounts and was legally and operationally simpler. Though, of course, Jeremy added when he told me this, the government didn't rule out taking on bad assets when it had to – indeed it was already the not-so-proud owner of Bradford & Bingley's loan book.

'So, do you get a pause now?' I asked, conscious of the hollows under Jeremy's eyes.

He laughed. 'Not until the London G20 is over. While Shriti and I have been finalising this package with the Prime Minister and the Treasury, preparations for that have been gathering pace. Given the state of the world economy, it's likely to be the most important international meeting in decades.'

29

'Take It to the Limit':
An unconventional negotiation

January–April 2009

From the moment it had been scheduled, it had been clear that shepherding a large and unwieldy group of countries to a meaningful conclusion at the London G20 would be one of the most complex policy and logistical challenges Whitehall had ever faced.

On the policy side, the Prime Minister's intent was clear – he wanted to bring international leaders together to do something to support the world economy. But it wasn't clear what that something was. And Barack Obama's recent election in the US didn't help, since his backing was essential to agreeing strong policy conclusions or institutional changes and no one knew what he thought.

Preparing for the summit was made more complicated by the Prime Minister's tendency – driven by his desire to get multiple clever brains working on his priority issues – to allocate overlapping roles to different people. Jeremy tried to impose some discipline on this. After all, having been a G7 sherpa himself, he knew Jon Cunliffe had to have lead responsibility at official level for drafting the communiqué and advising the Prime Minister on what was negotiable. But maintaining order wasn't straightforward. At one point, for example, Mark Malloch Brown, the Minister of State for Africa, Asia and the United Nations, started calling himself the G20 sherpa, which made Jon threaten to quit and leave them all to it. At the Prime Minister's request, Jeremy stepped in, refocused Mark on his brief, and the work continued.

This overcrowding wasn't confined to the core organising team. The summit was the biggest game in town, and everyone wanted to be part of it. Gus O'Donnell was chairing a regular meeting of permanent secretaries to discuss the preparations and various ministers were trying to use the G20 to unblock long-stuck issues in their own portfolios. Harriet Harman, for instance, wanted the communiqué to include a reference to women and Ed Miliband was lobbying for climate change to be mentioned.

As the meeting approached, the Prime Minister spent hours talking to fellow leaders about what they were willing to agree. The fact that the final ambition for the summit hadn't been resolved made this difficult, but what made it worse was that it also wasn't clear who was going to be invited. The UK knew, of course, who they wanted to attend, but for obscure reasons, certain key countries weren't part of the G20. With the meeting only weeks away, there was no time to resolve these historic anomalies, so instead the team started thinking up various ad hoc wheezes that could be used to adjust the list of attendees.

The Dutch and Spanish, who both had large banking systems, clearly needed seats. They had been squeezed into the Washington G20 after the French had agreed to give them the two extra spaces they'd been allocated because they held the EU presidency. The EU flag had then been hung in front of one corner of the negotiating table and the Dutch and Spanish had taken their places. However, this harmony hadn't lasted long. When a family crisis caused the Dutch prime minister to dash home, the Dutch state secretary for finance, a mere official, claimed his seat. At this point, Christine Lagarde, the French finance minister who'd been forced to sacrifice her place, had become annoyed and dragged her sherpa chair back up to the main negotiating table. This had led to an unseemly scuffle and left the EU corner looking chaotic, particularly because Christine's seat was far lower than those of the other delegates.

Jon Cunliffe was determined to avoid such amateur-hour scenes at the London G20. So this time they named the Dutch and Spanish leaders as 'EU advisers' and gave them two of the four EU presidency and European Commission chairs. That solved one issue, but it still left the Swedes, the next holders of the European Council presidency, shut out. Since there was no easy way to resolve this, the team decided simply to issue the Swedish prime minister with an interpreter's badge.

But these were only the European issues. Another problem was how to exclude Colonel Gaddafi, the highly divisive chair of the African Union. Here the excuse was that, since this was an economic rather than a political forum, it was more appropriate to invite the head of the New Economic Partnership for Africa's Development. Since this issue also sat firmly within Mark Malloch Brown's portfolio, he was then given the unenviable job of trying to stop Gaddafi carrying out his threat to put his tent up in Hyde Park during the meeting.

Diplomatic issues aside, Jeremy's real worry was how to make the summit more than a one-day traffic nightmare for Londoners culminating in a bland communiqué. The world needed action, and as had been the case at critical moments in the past, this meeting was the best chance for the UK to get its international partners to act. Jeremy just hoped that, with the IMF warning that for the first time in sixty years global activity might contract in 2009, this time the UK would be persuasive. Domestically they were doing what they could, including through starting QE – which Jeremy believed, both then and looking back, was the turning point in the fight against a depression. But important though this was, restoring confidence in the global financial system would require coordinated global action.

Over the weeks, two policy ambitions for the G20 had begun to come into focus. The first was ensuring that the world's financial institutions – the IMF, the World Bank and so on – had enough firepower to deal with the crisis and the second was getting the world's richest countries to work together to stimulate demand in the global economy, including through domestic fiscal interventions.

On the first matter, the challenge was to make the firepower so big and immediate that it would shock the world into regaining confidence in the financial system. Firepower would come from multiple sources. Although an IMF quota increase wasn't possible, since that would require Congressional approval, the US was happy for countries to supplement the IMF's resources through bilateral borrowing agreements. The Japanese stepped forward, offering $100 billion, and Norway, Canada, Switzerland and various EU countries followed their lead. In total, this gave the IMF an additional $250 billion, to which it added a further $250 billion of special drawing rights, its own currency.

Late one night, Shriti listed all the agreed firepower in a table, totalling it at the bottom: $840 billion. Underneath this she added some question marks before leaving copies of it on Jeremy and Gordon's desks.

'The Prime Minister rang me,' Jon Cunliffe said when he arrived in Downing Street the following morning for a meeting with Jeremy and Shriti. 'He says that, given we are so close, he wants to make this a £1 trillion summit. How the hell am I supposed to find another $160 billion?'

'I'm sure you'll find a way,' Shriti said.

'You have to be kidding me,' Jon said, picking up his papers and walking out.

Jeremy watched him go – Jon was brilliant, but not surprisingly, he hated being micro-managed, second-guessed, and above all, given impossible objectives.

While they were making progress on firepower, however, the second ambition for the summit, agreeing a set of coordinated national interventions to stimulate growth, was proving more difficult, particularly with the Americans who were focused on their domestic agenda following Obama's inauguration and the Germans given their horror of high inflation.

In the week before the summit the Prime Minister, therefore, chartered a plane and flew to Brussels, New York, Brasilia, São Paulo and Santiago to persuade other leaders of the need for intervention, landing back in London two days before the meeting. The trip had gone well, an exhausted-looking Tom Fletcher told Jeremy – though the comment by Lula, the president of Brazil, that this was a crisis caused by 'white people with blue eyes', while underlining the resentment felt by poorer countries about the crisis, hadn't helped.

Jeremy and Shriti spent much of the final evening before the London G20 perched on the red-padded fender surrounding the fireplace in the entrance hall of Number 10. With the wording of the communiqué still not resolved, this enabled them to pounce on each of the leaders as they arrived for dinner with the Prime Minister. Even better, the leaders were arriving on their own since their sherpas were being entertained at a separate dinner hosted by Jon Cunliffe on the other side of town.

By the time the cavalcades containing the G20 leaders began drawing up outside the sprawling ExCeL Exhibition Centre in east London the following morning, this fender diplomacy meant that most of the communiqué was agreed, although Angela Merkel was still refusing to agree the text on national fiscal interventions.

Jeremy – who like the rest of the UK team was operating on almost no sleep – arrived early at the centre so that he could check out the meeting room. The G20 team had set this up in their usual way, with delegates seated around a circular table so large it was hard to make out anyone on the far side. Jeremy knew from his time in Washington what this layout would produce – a series of formal speeches with little opportunity for leaders to roll up their sleeves and talk through the issues.

'But the place where the leaders are having lunch is better,' Jeremy told Gordon Brown when they discussed it, 'because it is relatively small.'

After the meeting began, the Prime Minister, therefore, informed the delegations that, sadly, they would have to break into different groups to have their lunch, with the leaders eating on their own. This caused muttering in the finance minister and sherpa ranks, but there was little they could do. And to no one's great surprise, after a long round of formulaic statements, the meeting adjourned early.

When the Prime Minister got up to take the other leaders into their private dining room, Jeremy, Shriti and Tom Fletcher followed along behind to make sure no one got lost. After everyone was inside, Jeremy shut the door, posting some Number 10 staff outside and Tom on the inside, and telling them not to let anyone out or in.

Inside the room, Gordon took his seat, pushed his plate to one side, and began taking the other leaders through the communiqué, a thick black pen in his hand. He made swift work of the first few paragraphs, partly because everyone was getting settled and some people were attempting to eat. But the pace slowed when they reached the controversial issue of the IMF's gold. Gordon wanted the IMF to sell some of its holdings to generate funds to help the poorest countries – something Jeremy supported since he'd never understood why the IMF needed to hoard so much gold.

To Jeremy's surprise, however, with only a few small amendments, the gold sale was agreed. Gordon then ploughed on, writing amended pieces of text on scraps of paper that were sent out of the room to be typed up, past Tom who was still guarding the door. While the Prime Minister did this and waiters scurried around attempting to serve the delegates, Jeremy's attention was caught by Cristina Fernández de Kirchner, the Argentinian president, who was getting up. She walked around to where Tom was standing and pushed him against the wall.

Jeremy went over to see what was going on, but by the time he got there, Cristina was making her way back to her seat.

'She was demanding that I should let her sherpa in,' Tom said. 'But it's okay, she seems to have calmed down.'

Jeremy walked back to stand near the Prime Minister's chair. In front of him, Shriti was sitting in the only spare seat munching a bread roll that she had presumably scrounged from beside a leader's plate.

'I need to sit down,' Jeremy said.

'Well you can't. I'm wearing heels.'

'Well take them off – we're doing the fiscal section now so it's my turn.'

'Let's move on and assume that's agreed,' the Prime Minister said, ticking off another paragraph.

After displacing Shriti, Jeremy leaned back in his seat. This wasn't the normal way to run an international meeting, but maybe it was the only way to agree such a huge intervention. And having got through the issue of IMF gold, and even more remarkably, the text on domestic fiscal interventions, they were making good progress. While there might be quibbling over the details, and some suspicion that Gordon was trying to pull a fast one, no one wanted to walk out and take the blame for blocking progress.

Or maybe someone did because, moments later, Jeremy saw President Sarkozy reaching forward to adjust his microphone. 'I will only agree to this communiqué if you endorse the OECD's list of tax havens,' he said. 'Tax havens – and the failed system of Anglo-Saxon capitalism – are one of the prime causes of this crisis.'

Jeremy glanced over at Shriti who raised her eyebrows. If Sarkozy decided to dig in on this point, they were in trouble.

The Prime Minister looked up, his marker pen poised.

President Hu Jintao shook his head and said something in Chinese. 'Tax is not a G20 issue,' the interpreter said.

At this a row erupted, with people leaning in to join the debate. The Chinese thought the French were attacking Macau and Hong Kong and wanted no mention of tax havens, while others supported President Sarkozy's plea to have the OECD's list included in the communiqué.

The remains of lunch shrivelled on plates.

The Prime Minister turned to President Obama who was sat next to him, the seating being alphabetical by country. 'Could you see if you can find a solution on tax havens?' he asked.

After Obama nodded, Shriti jumped into action. 'Obama will need someone who can speak English, Chinese and French,' she told Jeremy before running over to the interpreter booths that ringed the room.

Jeremy followed President Obama across to where Presidents Sarkozy and Hu Jintao were standing.

'So, how are we going to work this out?' President Obama asked with a smile.

Over the next few minutes, through a slowly translated dialogue, Obama began to make progress. It seemed that everyone could live with the OECD's list of havens being included in the communiqué, so long as Macau and Hong Kong were somehow excluded.

'Great,' President Obama said to Sarkozy and Hu Jintao, and after shaking hands, the three leaders made their way back to their seats.

Jeremy watched President Obama go. 'He couldn't have been more gracious,' he told Shriti.

On the other side of the room, the Prime Minister was also wrapping up and the banished sherpas were beginning to make their way into the room. 'I think we are all agreed then,' Gordon said with a nod before standing up. It seemed the meeting was over.

'How long will it take to get the final version of the communiqué?' Jeremy asked Paul Rankin from the European and Global Issues Secretariat when he spotted him standing by the door clutching a sheaf of Gordon Brown's black ink amendments. 'The press conference is due to start in forty-five minutes.'

'I have literally no idea,' Paul said shaking his head. He turned around and headed out of the room, back towards the plenary hall, with the rest of the UK delegation in close pursuit. When he arrived, Paul knelt on the floor and began laying out sheets of paper around him. Everyone gathered around, pointing out different sections.

'Will you all shut up?' Paul asked.

After that they hushed while Paul arranged the pieces of the communiqué, scribbling linking words, reordering sections and cutting out duplications. Jeremy watched him, glancing at his watch. The press conference was due to start in thirty minutes.

Jon came in. 'I've talked to Ángel Gurría at the OECD,' he told Jeremy. 'It wasn't an easy discussion – after all, he wasn't even invited to the meeting. But I think that, if we can get the Prime Minister to talk to him, he'll let us note their list of tax havens. He's even agreed to insert a footnote saying that the list excludes China's special administrative regions.'

'Brilliant,' Jeremy said.

'We need to get this typed up,' Paul said, shuffling his papers back together.

Jeremy glanced at his watch. 'We have fifteen minutes left.'

'Well, it will take as long as it takes, particularly because all the working photocopiers are on the other side of the building,' Paul said.

Ten minutes later, Tom Fletcher appeared. 'Jeremy. What's going on? Gordon's demanding to get going.'

'We can't start yet,' Jeremy said, trying to exude calm. 'The final communiqué is still being prepared.'

'Well, we need to hurry up – Sarkozy just tried to steal our thunder by holding his own press conference.'

Jeremy blinked. 'That's outrageous.'

'It's okay,' Tom said with a smile. 'I pulled the plug on his room.'

With moments to go before the start of the press conference, one of the garden room staff arrived in the press briefing room, panting and holding still-warm copies of the communiqué. The Prime Minister then stood up in front of a bank of flashing cameras to announce his $1 trillion global rescue plan. 'This is the day the world came together to fight back against the global recession,' he said, 'not with words but with a plan for global recovery and for reform.'

After the Prime Minister finished speaking, various other leaders made their own statements. President Obama said the summit had agreed measures that were 'bolder and more rapid than any international response that we've seen to a financial crisis in memory', while Nicolas Sarkozy declared that agreement on a new regulatory regime and crackdown on tax havens showed 'a page has been turned' on an era of post-war 'Anglo-Saxon' capitalism.

The summit was the culmination of months of work and a masterful, though unconventional, negotiation on the day. And the communiqué, which Jeremy flicked through while people rushed around trying to find Stephen Harper, the Canadian prime minister, who'd disappeared just ahead of the family photo, had something in it for everyone. It even recognised the need to build a 'fair and family-friendly labour market for both women and men' and to create an 'inclusive, green and sustainable' recovery.

When the Prime Minister walked back into the war room in Downing Street later that day, he was met by a standing ovation. James Bowler produced bottles of champagne and everyone clustered around.

'The London G20 will be the crowning achievement of Gordon Brown's premiership,' Jeremy told Shriti who was standing beside him at the back of the room, her eyes red. 'I've never seen anyone do what he did today, and I doubt I ever will again.'

By the end of the day, the FTSE 100 was up 4.3 per cent, passing 4,000 points for the first time in six weeks, while the S&P 500 closed 2.9 per cent higher. The world had agreed how to address the immediate financial crisis and to put in place controls to prevent similar crises in the future. And in contrast to the IMF's warning ahead of the summit, in the three months afterwards, the world economy grew by 4.5 per cent.

30

'Heroes':
Afghanistan

April–June 2009

A prime minister never has the luxury of focusing on a single issue, even when they are trying to save the global economy. During Gordon Brown's bilateral with President Obama before the G20 summit, in addition to discussing the $1 trillion stimulus package and the need for domestic action, Obama also made it clear that he wanted the UK to send more troops to Afghanistan.

Gordon had come into Number 10 unconvinced of the case for doing this. The UK had first sent troops to Afghanistan in 2001, and after working with other NATO forces to secure the downfall of the brutal Taliban regime, 1,700 British soldiers had remained in the peacekeeping force. By 2006 the Taliban were regrouping, and Tony Blair had sent out an additional 3,300 troops. Their focus, John Reid, the defence secretary at the time had said, would be on helping the Afghan people reconstruct their economy and democracy and he would be perfectly happy for the UK to leave 'without firing one shot'.

This sentiment, though laudable, turned out to be wildly optimistic. By September 2008, the UK's force in Afghanistan had grown to around 8,300 and the Taliban's adoption of improvised explosive devices (IEDs) meant that the number of deaths and life-changing injuries was escalating. Despite this, the UK military – led by Jock Stirrup, the chief of defence staff, and Richard Dannatt, the chief of the general staff – was keen to increase the UK's presence so that it could clear and occupy more territory. Various proposals were put forward, with the most ambitious advocating an increase to 9,800 troops.

Jeremy wasn't an expert on military affairs, and generally left such issues to Simon McDonald, the foreign policy adviser. But in his role as the Prime Minister's permanent secretary, he was interested in the financial consequences of military decisions and he tried to ensure Gordon Brown heard a diversity of views. He also sympathised with the question the Prime Minister kept asking – was the war worth the human and other costs? There was no doubt that Afghanistan was a breeding ground for terrorists. It was also the source of the opium used to produce about 90 per cent of the world's heroin, which in turn was being used to fund the Taliban. But addressing such matters came at a huge price.

The issue of whether the UK would send more troops had taken a long time to resolve, not least because Obama's review of the war, which he'd commissioned soon after coming into office, had dragged on for months. The UK had largely been excluded from this thinking, which meant that they'd only found out that it had concluded when Tom Fletcher received an email from his US counterpart, Mark Lippert, the day before the G20 summit. The US had decided to deploy a further 40,000 troops to Afghanistan, Mark told Tom, and they wanted the UK to contribute another 1,000.

'Mark says our service chiefs have been encouraging the US to make this ask,' Tom told the Prime Minister when they met to brief him ahead of his bilateral with the President.

'What?' the Prime Minister asked with a scowl.

Jeremy also frowned – it was outrageous for the UK's military leaders to encourage another country to put pressure on the Prime Minister. But on this topic, he also knew that Gordon Brown felt trapped, both because having a strong UK defence was part of New Labour's philosophy and because he was less engaged in the detail of defence matters than he was on other issues.

'I'm only going to approve an increase in troops,' Gordon concluded at the end of a tetchy debate, 'if it's accompanied by a plan to improve the training of Afghan forces and if I get a written undertaking from the chiefs of staff that troops will only be sent out if they are fully equipped.'

Despite this tension, the bilateral between the Prime Minister and Obama before the G20 went well, Tom told Jeremy afterwards – though neither of them had eaten their heavy Scottish breakfast, briefed out to the press as *Barack O'Banger*. The President had been softer in his request for troops than expected and the Prime Minister, having signalled in advance that two battalions were out of the question, said he would reflect on what could be done and later agreed a temporary increase of 700 troops.

After the G20, the Prime Minister headed up to Scotland to enjoy a well-earned Easter break. We followed his example, loading up our car with children and bags and driving to East Anglia. I was hoping for a peaceful long weekend after weeks of frenzy, but the respite only lasted until Saturday morning when Jeremy's phone rang while we were standing outside Framlingham Castle.

'Bad news,' Michael Ellam, Downing Street's head of communications, said.

Jeremy sighed. 'What?'

'Some of Damian McBride's emails have leaked.'

'What do they say?'

It wasn't good. Damian had been sending emails from his Number 10 account to another Labour Party adviser. In these he had discussed circulating false rumours about Conservative MPs being gay, having sexually transmitted diseases or spouses with mental health problems. Long before the term had been invented, this was a plan to disseminate fake news on a grand scale.

'Damian has lost the plot. He'll have to go,' Jeremy said. 'Have you talked to the Prime Minister?'

'Yes,' Mike said, 'but he didn't sound ready to act. You know how dependent he is on Damian.'

'Okay. Let me talk to him.'

'Come on Jeremy,' I said, 'the kids are going mad.'

'Sure. Mini crisis. Give me fifteen minutes and I'll catch you up,' Jeremy said, putting on his most apologetic face.

So, I took the children to get dressed up as knights and a princess in a castle tower while Jeremy, and just about everyone else, including Alastair Campbell, advised the Prime Minister that Damian had to go. By early evening, Damian had resigned, saying he apologised for the inappropriate and juvenile content of his emails and was appalled they'd reached the public domain. The calls then continued through the weekend as Jeremy, Peter Mandelson and Gavin Kelly tried to persuade Gordon Brown that he also had to apologise for Damian's actions. The Prime Minister refused to do this because he said it would be humiliating, but they all knew it was only a question of time. In this case it was three days. At the awayday Cabinet meeting in Glasgow on Thursday, Gordon was caught by the press.

'I take full responsibility for what happened,' he said. 'That's why the person responsible went immediately.'

With this apology made, little more could be done. But the affair left a taint it was hard to shake off. What was frustrating, Jeremy told me, was that, despite his talent, they'd all known Damian was an accident waiting to happen. And for this to explode so soon after the triumph of the G20 was particularly painful. It was like Gordon was playing snakes and ladders with a particularly bitter rival, and within a few steps of victory, had landed on the head of an enormous snake.

As a result of these various distractions, discussions with the Treasury on the April 2009 Budget began late. The economy had contracted by an extraordinary 1.9 per cent in the first quarter, and despite the confidence boost from the G20, the Treasury's forward forecast was still gloomy.

The main issue to resolve soon became how pessimistic that forecast should be. The Chancellor defended the Treasury's figures, while the Prime Minister argued that, if such negative projections were published, they would dampen consumer and business confidence and become a self-fulfilling prophecy. This came to a head in a particularly heated discussion four days before the Budget in which the Prime Minister accused the Chancellor of having been taken over by the Treasury.

'Why,' he demanded, 'are you not more focused on stimulating growth given the UK's precarious economic position?'

Jeremy looked at Ed Balls who, much to the Chancellor's irritation, was joining many of these discussions despite still being

Secretary of State for Children, Schools and Families. Ed nodded while Alistair Darling glared at his papers.

Jeremy knew, of course, that the Chancellor also wanted to stimulate growth. But Alistair believed any 'pro-growth' plan had to be balanced by credible medium-term spending and borrowing numbers. Otherwise, markets would punish the UK with higher interest rates, ultimately costing taxpayers more. Jeremy had some sympathy with this, but by this stage, he was just desperate to get a decision – brinkmanship was no way to determine the government's fiscal strategy.

Peter Mandelson, who'd arrived late for the meeting, was standing in the doorway watching their discussion. 'I think everyone should calm down,' he said.

For some reason, this moment of Peter magic worked. The conversation restarted, this time in a more agreeable way, and they reached a brokered truce – a cautious short-term economic view giving way to sunnier uplands. They would aim to halve the cyclically-adjusted deficit over four years partly by reducing public spending. However, there was no hiding the severity of the downturn. Even after Gordon Brown's intervention, the economy was still forecast to shrink by 3.5 per cent in 2009 with borrowing for 2009/10 rising to 12.4 per cent of GDP. In all his years in government, Jeremy had never seen numbers like this.

The rest of the Budget was no easier to settle. On the spending side, although the Prime Minister was willing to say that public spending should be reduced, he wanted to focus the political narrative on the Labour Party's continued willingness to invest in public services. He, therefore, didn't want to specify where savings might come from or to conduct a detailed spending review.

The taxation choices were also difficult. The Treasury again proposed raising VAT above its original level once the temporary reduction expired, arguing that, alongside this, they could make other changes to help the poorest. But this was again blocked by the Prime Minister. Apart from anything else, the issue of VAT was totemic for Gordon Brown because, fifteen years previously, he had made a name for himself by attacking Norman Lamont's decision to put VAT on gas and power. It was one of the peculiarities of being a civil servant that Jeremy had helped Norman develop that policy and was now helping the Prime Minister oppose something very similar.

But while Gordon wasn't budging on VAT, he did agree to bring forward by a year the introduction of the new top rate of income tax, and to raise it by a further 5 per cent to 50 per cent, even though this was yet another affront to New Labour's political positioning. The Budget also included various stimulus measures developed by the National Economic Council. But despite this progress, the final Budget discussions still deteriorated, with the Prime Minister throwing all the Treasury officials out of the room. This left Dan Rosenfield trying to advise the Chancellor on the entire Budget, with Jeremy helping him as much as he could as they clawed their way through to a set of final decisions.

The press reaction to the Budget that emerged from this tortuous process on 22 April 2009 was ghastly. There was outrage about the increase in income tax – 'Red all over: Chancellor reads last rites over New Labour', *The Times* shouted – combined with horror about the borrowing figures and the lack of a detailed plan for bringing the numbers back into balance. With no sign of the pressure easing, the first Cabinet meeting in May descended into a row about whether to announce specific departmental cuts. James Purnell, the work and pensions secretary, argued that doing so was essential – if the government didn't make clear the source of its savings, people would assume massive tax rises were coming.

This debate felt intractable because the Prime Minister remained determined to differentiate himself from the Conservatives, even though the government's figures assumed similar levels of spending reductions. But since this was a piece of political positioning, particularly in the run-up to an election, Jeremy kept out of the argument and instead turned his attention to another issue that was threatening to grab the headlines: the right of Gurkha veterans to settle in the UK.

Historically, retired Gurkhas – Nepalese soldiers who'd served in the British Army – hadn't been given permanent residency in the UK. Tony Blair had, however, decreed, somewhat arbitrarily, that Gurkhas who'd retired after 1997 could receive this. After the High

Court threw out the process originally put forward for implementing this decision, it had fallen to Gordon Brown to come up with a new solution. His first proposal was to allow Gurkhas to settle if they met one of five criteria including length of service or gallantry. But campaigners, led by the popular actress Joanna Lumley, who'd been born in India and whose father had served with the Gurkhas during the Second World War, felt this was unacceptable. They argued that all Gurkha veterans should be allowed to remain if they wished to do so.

'The Home Office says it would cost £1.4 billion to let all Gurkhas settle,' Simon King, the home affairs private secretary, told Jeremy.

'That's ridiculous,' Jeremy said, 'how do they get to that figure?'

'Well, as well as assuming all 36,000 former Gurkhas will uproot their families to come and live in Britain, it also includes everything from their housing benefits to their health and education costs. And it excludes any tax that Gurkhas or their dependants might pay.'

Jeremy shook his head. 'I know the Home Office hates letting anyone in, but I'm worried about this one. Let's start by challenging those figures.'

A few days later, Jeremy picked up the phone to find the Number 10 switchboard wanting to put Joanna Lumley through to him.

'I'm getting nowhere with the Ministry of Defence,' Joanna said in a velvety voice, 'so can I come and see you?'

Jeremy had no choice but to say yes to this – which meant that Joanna materialised in Jeremy's office the following day trailing silk scarves and looking incongruously glamorous.

'You have to understand that Gordon and I are on your side,' Jeremy said after extricating himself from her embrace.

Joanna smiled at this but was in no mood to negotiate. Anything other than full settlement rights for the Gurkhas was unacceptable, she argued, and it was hard not to be convinced by the simplicity of her plea.

After his meeting with Joanna, Jeremy spoke to the Prime Minister. This time he tried harder than he had with the 10p tax band, knowing the danger of postponing such decisions. It was, he advised, time to concede. But the Prime Minister was again reluctant to do this, torn between his desire to support the Gurkhas and his concern about the cost, which though it had reduced, was still significant. In any case, his mind was on other things – this time Afghanistan and the aftermath of the financial crisis. But in another parallel with the tax debacle, the timing of Gordon Brown's U-turn on the Gurkhas was again taken out of his hands, this time by an Opposition day motion that the Liberal Democrats called in late April.

Gordon Brown's position during Prime Minister's Questions on the morning of this debate was unchanged. 'We have got to balance our responsibilities to those who have served our country with the finance that we need to be able to meet these obligations,' he told the House.

The discussion that followed lasted several stormy hours. When the vote was called, twenty-seven Labour MPs marched into the Opposition voting lobby to defeat the government. The resulting cheer inside the chamber was echoed by the crowd of Gurkhas gathered outside of Parliament with Joanna Lumley.

When Gordon returned to Number 10, he called Jeremy and Simon into his office. 'Okay. We'll have to concede,' he said.

Gordon Brown announced his change of mind on 21 May – in future, he said, all Gurkha veterans would be allowed to come to Britain. He then invited Joanna Lumley and a retinue of former Gurkhas to come into Downing Street to celebrate.

'You are a brave man who has made today a brave decision on behalf of the bravest of the brave,' Joanna said. 'A great injustice has been righted. The Gurkhas are coming home.'

The Prime Minister smiled.

'*Ayo Gurkhali*,' Joanna cried, and the famous battle call was taken up by the Gurkhas surrounding her in the garden of Number 10.

Amid the hubbub, one Gurkha came up to the Prime Minister and offered him a scarf.

'I'm not wearing that,' Gordon said in an undertone to Jeremy, eyeing the pale-yellow cloth, which all the Gurkhas were wearing.

'You're worse than my seven-year-old son who refused to wear a sticker at Legoland last weekend,' Jeremy said with a laugh. 'Just put it on, Gordon!'

* * *

Jeremy hoped that the Gurkhas' battle cry would signal a turn in the government's fortunes. Surely after Damian McBride and the grim reception to the Budget, it was time for the Prime Minister to get the credit he deserved for stabilising the banks? Buoyed by this hope, Jeremy started to talk about taking a long weekend away, or maybe even a week in Wales with the children. But despite the sunshine and the garden party, worse was yet to come.

Like many crises, this next one had been building for some time, and might have been manageable if it hadn't been ignored. But instead, a series of delays turned a parliamentary scandal into a crisis that deeply damaged the public's perception of politicians. This story began back in early 2005, when two freedom of information requests were submitted to the House of Commons demanding details of the expense claims of fourteen MPs and ex-MPs. The suspicion was that the claims were high because, ever since Margaret Thatcher's time, MPs' pay had been tightly controlled.

For three years the House of Commons had resisted releasing this information until, in 2008, the High Court ruled that it had no choice. The Members Estimate Committee then started scanning in receipts and loading them onto electronic disks, but in February 2009, before their work was complete, the details of the home secretary's expenses leaked. These revealed that Jacqui Smith had designated her sister's home in London as her 'main home', allowing her to claim £116,000 of 'second home' expenses on the house in Redditch where she actually lived with her husband and children.

At this point the Prime Minister decided, rather belatedly, to act. In April 2009 he wrote to Christopher Kelly, chair of the Committee on Standards in Public Life, proposing a simplified expenses system, backing this up with a YouTube interview in which he explained the proposals, while unfortunately smiling at all the wrong moments. Despite this presentational glitch, Jeremy thought the Prime Minister's proposals were sensible. But since they'd been produced with little consultation, they weren't supported by either Christopher Kelly or the opposition parties.

After this, the expense scandal exploded. The next onslaught began with an article in the *Daily Telegraph* on 8 May that implied – incorrectly – that the Prime Minister had abused the expenses system by paying his brother for their shared cleaner. Jeremy couldn't get directly involved in handling this since it was parliamentary rather than governmental, but he did urge Gavin Kelly to get the facts clear and communicate them out to the press as quickly as he could. However, by this time the story had too much momentum to be stopped. After its revelation of the Prime Minister's expenses, the *Daily Telegraph* went on to reveal a host of other expense claims, including those made by John Prescott for the cost of fitting mock Tudor beams in his house, Sir Peter Viggers for his duck house and David Cameron for removing wisteria from the walls of his constituency cottage.

The timing could hardly have been worse. Coming hard on the heels of the financial crisis, which had been presided over by sharp-suited bankers who retained their bonuses, the sight of this other privileged, though less well paid, group abusing its position reinforced the public's growing alienation from the British establishment. And unfortunately for Gordon Brown, he was the man at the helm.

Though Jeremy and Gus largely avoided becoming involved in this highly political issue, when the Prime Minister asked for their help in devising a new way to regulate MPs' expenses, they agreed to step in. They appointed James Bowler to lead this thinking, working with an official seconded from the House of Commons. James's proposed solution – the Independent Parliamentary Standards Authority (IPSA) – was discussed with the leaders of both opposition parties before being announced on 20 May and rushed through to become law on 21 July. In the future, IPSA would oversee MPs' expenses claims – although past claims continued to stoke outrage for several more months, claiming several more political scalps along the way.

With the expenses scandal still dominating headlines, the European and local elections on 4 June 2009 were always going to be difficult. But for the government, the results were far worse than anyone expected.

Two days before the polls opened, Jacqui Smith, the popular families minister, Beverley Hughes, and the Brown loyalist, Tom Watson, all resigned following allegations about their misuse of expenses, some trivial compared to what had been revealed about others. The following day, the *Guardian*, for long the only broadsheet newspaper still supporting Gordon, turned against him. In a searing editorial the paper stated that 'any assessment must recognise the strength of Mr Brown's response to the financial implosion … But flaws in his character that drove his party close to revolt last summer now dominate again. He is not obviously able to lead.'

On the same day, the Secretary of State for Local Government, Hazel Blears, demanded a meeting with Gordon Brown, cutting into his precious preparation time for Prime Minister's Questions to declare that she was also resigning because of expenses. To the media's delight she dressed up for the occasion, the brooch on her jacket bearing the words 'Rocking the Boat'.

When Jeremy arrived home on election day, he told me that the political team in Number 10 was braced for a catastrophic set of results. In fact, he'd seldom seen a government in such disarray and with so little support – but despite everything, there was no sign the Prime Minister wanted to throw in the towel or that his critics could muster the killer blow.

'However, Gordon Brown might trigger the implosion himself if he goes ahead with the reshuffle he shared with me earlier this evening. He wants to appoint Ed Balls as Chancellor,' Jeremy said.

'He's seriously planning that?'

'Yes. Although, after all they've been through, I think it's tough on Alistair.'

I agreed with this. From everything Jeremy had told me, Alistair Darling's steadiness was a useful foil to the Prime Minister's occasional impetuosity. But Gordon was increasingly turning to Ed Balls for macro policy and fiscal advice and Jeremy worried that this created an unsustainable dynamic at the heart of the government.

We were still discussing this when the phone rang shortly before the polls closed at 10 p.m.

'James Purnell has resigned,' Mike Ellam said. 'He says Gordon is making a Tory government more, not less, likely.'

'Oh, God. Anybody else? I'd better come back in,' Jeremy said, glancing at me.

'Sure,' I said.

Jeremy walked into the war room half an hour later to find it full of ministers and special advisers walking around with mobile phones clamped to their ears.

'We're ringing Cabinet ministers to see if they're backing James Purnell and, if not, whether they'll put out statements supporting Gordon,' Gavin Kelly said.

The person everyone wanted to talk to was David Miliband because, if such a heavyweight minister resigned, the Prime Minister probably wouldn't survive. The sweaty minutes stretched on before there was a shout from Peter Mandelson – 'He's secure,' Peter said. 'I tracked him down at a dinner with Ed Miliband and Will Hutton. But I've heard rumours that Charlie Falconer is involved in this, or maybe Charles Clarke.'

Jeremy left the political team scrambling and went to find the Prime Minister in his snug. Up on the magnetic whiteboard, Alistair Darling's name was back in the Treasury column.

Gordon Brown looked at Jeremy. 'It's the wrong time to do it,' he said, 'halfway through an economic crisis.'

Jeremy didn't comment – this was a decision for the Prime Minister to make, based on a complex mix of personal, political and media management factors. But he was glad Gordon had reversed his view because, even if David Miliband was secure, adding the loss of a Chancellor to all the other recent ministerial resignations, ran a real risk of collapsing the government.

In the aftermath of the Labour Party's worst local election results for nearly a century and similarly awful European results, the Prime Minister announced a more moderate reshuffle. The most eye-catching change, alongside the announcement of the National Economic Council, was the proliferation of Peter Mandelson's titles. Initially Peter was going to become Deputy Prime Minister, but after Harriet Harman objected, pointing out that she was the deputy leader of the Labour Party, he'd instead become First Secretary of State and Lord President of the Council.

Jeremy had argued against the latter title. 'Jan Royall needs to stay as Lord President,' he'd told Peter and the Prime Minister, 'because, if she's only leader of the Lords, she won't get a full Secretary of State's salary.'

'But Lord President of the Council is the title I really want,' Peter said, 'because it's the one my grandfather once held.'

Jeremy turned to Sue Gray, the guardian of propriety issues in the Cabinet Office. 'Can we find a different role for Jan?'

'I'm working on it,' Sue said, flicking through the Bradshaw Tables, which sets out the limits to the number of salaries payable, based on the Ministerial and other Salaries Act.

It wasn't straightforward, but in the end, Sue found a solution – Jan would become Chancellor of the Duchy of Lancaster, which would enable her to collect the spare salary released by abolishing John Denham's role as Secretary of State for Innovation, Universities and Skills.

While Peter's new titles gave the press some fun, particularly since no one doubted who the Prime Minister's deputy was anyway, the rest of the reshuffle, which contained few other excitements, was criticised for being timid and reflecting the Prime Minister's lack of authority.

'But we're hoping it has removed all the ministers tainted by the expenses scandal,' Jeremy told me when he got home. 'And Andrew Adonis has been promoted from Minister of State to Secretary of State for Transport, which should make it easier for the Prime Minister to get at least some of his domestic policy ideas implemented.'

31

'Let England Shake': Building Britain's Future

June 2009–February 2010

In the aftermath of the local elections on 29 June 2009, the government published a 125-page document called *Building Britain's Future*.

'What we need,' Peter Mandelson had told Jeremy when they'd begun working on this earlier that year, 'is a clear narrative to take Gordon through to the general election.'

Jeremy had agreed with this – there had to be more to Gordon Brown's premiership than dealing with the banking crisis, and as the country pulled out of recession, people would want to know his views on issues like the future of the NHS and schools. So, while the G20 reached its crescendo and the expenses scandal seethed, Jeremy, Peter, Nick Pearce, the head of the Policy Unit, and Gavin Kelly had plugged away on drafts of *Building Britain's Future*.

Preparing this thinking had been complicated because the work wasn't being done alongside a spending review, so there was no new money to allocate. And though the Prime Minister supported the thinking, he'd had little time to work on it. Therefore, the document, which became the most substantive domestic policy statement of the Brown administration, had instead emerged from a long series of official-level meetings through which Jeremy and the rest of the team had nudged Whitehall's thinking forward.

The core theme of *Building Britain's Future* was constitutional reform, the issue that had dominated the start of Gordon's premiership. The Prime Minister had always been determined to find a coherent intellectual underpinning for the United Kingdom as a strong, modern union. But after his first blaze of activity, other issues – combined with his nervousness about implementing more radical reforms, such as creating a British bill of rights – had stalled progress.

The widespread view that Parliament had failed to maintain its legitimacy during the expenses scandal gave the Prime Minister the excuse he needed to return to a subject that most of his political colleagues probably regarded as a sideshow – restoring public trust in politicians and the country's institutions and systems, while giving citizens more control over their lives and the services they relied on and paid for. To do this, the paper described a slew of new measures including reforming the House of Lords, reducing the time taken to release official documents from thirty to twenty years, creating a written constitution, devolving and decentralising power away from Whitehall, changing the voting system and getting young people more engaged in politics.

The section on public sector reform was even more novel. Throughout Gordon Brown's long Chancellorship, apart from the 'limits of markets' speech that he'd made at the height of his argument with the Prime Minister about foundation trusts and top-up fees, he'd mainly confined himself to supporting Tony Blair's top-down, target-led approach. The philosophy outlined in *Building Britain's Future* was, therefore, the first real attempt to codify his views. And while it didn't embrace the full package of Blairite principles, and it certainly used different language, its focus on putting citizens in the driving seat again made it possible to consider a broader range of public service providers. It also brought attention back to the lever that Jeremy had always championed – consumer choice.

Following pressure from Number 10 – most notably on a reluctant Department for Children, Schools and Families where Ed Balls had a different agenda – the document also contained policy initiatives designed to demonstrate this philosophy. These included a guarantee that, if children fell behind at school, they would get one-to-one tuition to help them catch up, and 'enforceable rights' for NHS patients such as access to a cancer specialist within two weeks and free NHS health checks for those aged forty to seventy-four.

Despite the enormous effort that had gone into it, *Building Britain's Future* received mixed reviews when it was published. This was partly because it was overshadowed by James Purnell's resignation, but also because it came late in the Parliament, and as David Cameron pointed out, because most of its proposals were uncosted. But Jeremy was still pleased with what they had been able to put together – and determined that the best of its thinking shouldn't be forgotten, whatever the outcome of the election.

By July 2009, Afghanistan was again dominating headlines after Operation Panther's Claw in mid-June resulted in hundreds of British soldiers being flown into a Taliban stronghold to secure canal and river crossings. Although the military reported that this operation had gone well, it was followed by a surge in British casualties, including a horrific tally of eight deaths during a single day in July.

With the press, and particularly the *Sun*, vilifying the Prime Minister for sending British troops into the field with the wrong equipment, including vehicles poorly equipped to resist IEDs, Gordon Brown called Jeremy in. 'I need you to find out what's going on,' he said. 'Why are we losing so many people? Are our troops being sent without the right equipment? And if they are, what can we do about it?'

Jeremy consulted Nick Catsaras, the assistant Foreign and Defence Affairs private secretary, and Matt Cavanagh. They both said they were worried that there wasn't enough of the right equipment in the field – though they also pointed out that it was the military who decided what kit to send with the troops, and who were keen to meet requests from NATO or the US for further reinforcements.

This may have been true, but it didn't help the Prime Minister or change the facts of bereaved families or soldiers sent home with life-changing injuries. So Jeremy called in the relevant officials from the Ministry of Defence, the Treasury and the Foreign Office, armed himself with a strong, black coffee and started asking questions.

'Can we get more helicopters?'

'We've asked Westland, but it will take months.'

'Why will it take months? Do I need to call the CEO of Westland?'

'That's our usual procurement timeline.'

'If we can fix that, do we have enough pilots?'

'No.'

'How do we get more pilots? Can we shorten their training? Or the time they take off between tours? How do these timings benchmark against what the French do? Or the Israelis? I want numbers and detail, not just "this is how we do it".'

Matt and Nick had been right. British troops had been sent to Afghanistan geared up to fight a conventional war rather than an insurgency. The department had also sold the previous generation of IED-resistant armoured vehicles after the Balkans and their orders for new equipment had been too limited and were taking too long to be delivered.

The good news, however, was that the correct orders were by that stage mainly in place. The bad news was that, even after the kit's arrival, it would take a long time to get it out into the field. For vehicles, this usually took two years; for helicopters, four or more. This was frustrating, but what really puzzled Jeremy was why the Ministry of Defence couldn't make better use of the equipment it already had in service.

'Why,' he asked the department, 'does a quarter of the kit have to be in training, a quarter in light maintenance and a quarter in deep maintenance? Is the hold-up deep maintenance or light maintenance? Why are so many delays caused by a lack of spare parts? And why do we need to train whole brigades together rather than in individual battle groups?'

Jeremy found Nick Houghton, the vice-chief of the defence staff, invaluable in these discussions. The self-effacing vice-chief was effective at chairing meetings and moved with ease across the forces. After a while, Nick even agreed to let a Delivery Unit team come inside the Ministry of Defence's massive concrete headquarters to help figure out the fastest way to get equipment into theatre and keep it there. With the help of Richard Stokes, a pragmatic submarine captain, the team was soon churning out data-heavy charts and Jeremy calmed down – the issue was being gripped.

* * *

The newspapers spent the rest of the spring of 2009 speculating about whether Gordon Brown would resign, although the *Guardian* was also muttering about phone hacking. The other dispute occupying the front pages was whether the independent inquiry set up to learn the lessons from the Iraq war should be held in public or private. The Prime Minister thought that Gus O'Donnell had agreed with the Conservatives that it should be held in private and led by a privy councillor, like the Franks inquiry into the Falklands War. But if this agreement existed, it unravelled on 15 July when Gordon announced this approach in the House of Commons and David Cameron objected to it. Unless the inquiry was held in public, David said, people would think the process was fixed.

The Prime Minister returned to Number 10 enraged both by this Conservative 'betrayal' and by the fact that he'd been left this time bomb by his predecessor. However, Jeremy's advice was that, despite his fury, Gordon should concede. An open inquiry would create a press circus, but it was the best way to put the issues to rest. And once he calmed down, the Prime Minister agreed, although he insisted on giving John Chilcot, the chair of the inquiry, the final choice on how the inquiry should be run – which gave the press another opportunity to criticise Gordon Brown.

In August 2009 we left all this behind us to go on a short Mediterranean cruise that we had booked when we thought Jeremy's parents might be able to join us. Sadly, though, by then Peter was too ill to travel. Back in England, we headed for rural Lincolnshire where, in a bid to convince Jeremy that the outdoor life could be fun, I'd reserved a week's stay in a large canvas tent complete with a wood-burning stove.

This camping plan, though well intended, went badly wrong. For a start, Jeremy was ill with what was later diagnosed as colitis, a chronic digestive disease, which is hardly ideal in a tent. In between suffering from that, and playing Monopoly by candlelight with Jonny, Jeremy spent hours on the phone to the Prime Minister, who was still worrying about getting equipment out to Afghanistan and fretting about his press coverage. He made these calls from the only place where there was a mobile signal – standing outside our tent in the drizzle while Lizzie and Peter chased chickens around him in the mud.

At the end of August the Prime Minister went out to Helmand Province to visit the UK's troops, announcing while he was there that another 270 armoured vehicles would be delivered by Christmas. With this equipment issue at least partly resolved, and with the Prime Minister on his way to New York to attend a UN Security Council summit on nuclear non-proliferation, Jeremy turned with some enthusiasm to the neglected papers in his in-tray on issues like schools, prisons and the health service. Unfortunately, it wasn't long before his peace was disturbed by a call from Nick Catsaras in the Number 10 private office.

'Simon McDonald has just called from the cockpit of the Prime Minister's 747,' Nick said. 'He says that the Prime Minister has briefed the press that we might only need to order three new nuclear submarines rather than four. I think we need to put a process around this decision.'

'We certainly do,' Jeremy said, appalled at the thought of policy on such a significant issue being made up on the hoof. He put his phone down and waited for the outrage to roll in from across Whitehall – which it soon did, particularly from the First Sea Lord, who threatened to resign.

'Don't worry,' Jeremy reassured each caller, 'we'll have a meeting, and there will be a proper discussion. I'm sure the Prime Minister's words have been over-interpreted.'

A few days later, in a somewhat calmer mood, the relevant military and civilian officials gathered in Number 10.

'The Prime Minister would like us to consider this issue properly now it has been raised,' Jeremy said. To shuffling around the table, he started probing. 'Why do we need a continuous at-sea deterrence? Do we know it works? And, if we need it, could we maintain it with fewer than four submarines by better managing their deployment and maintenance?'

Asking such questions was like poking a large, angry and heavily uniformed bull with a red-hot poker, but once the military began talking, Jeremy could unpack the issues. However, this time his interrogation didn't change Whitehall's advice – the government should still plan to buy four new nuclear submarines, while keeping the matter under review ahead of a final decision in 2012.

In the aftermath of this furore, Jeremy and Nick were invited up to Faslane in Scotland to inspect a nuclear submarine. They were taken by launch out to the open sea where the shiny, curved hull of HMS *Vanguard* lurked in the grey ocean, a white skull and crossbones painted on its side.

'The skull shows they've made a kill,' Nick told Jeremy. 'Though this one probably just represents their accidental collision with the French in the Atlantic Ocean in February.'

Once aboard, Jeremy and Nick were shown around the cramped interior, where the crew could be confined for up to three months. They were given a debrief of the events leading up to an active conflict and watched a drill to launch the missiles. At the end of their tour, the captain showed Jeremy the trigger for the nuclear deterrent, which was fashioned from a Colt pistol.

'It's not connected,' he said, 'so try pulling it.'

Jeremy put his finger through the cold metal loop and squeezed. Even though he knew it wasn't real, this was still hard to do, and it was even harder to block out thoughts of the devastation that would be unleashed if it were.

'I think the navy won that one,' Nick said on their way back to shore.

'Yes,' Jeremy said. 'No one wants to mess with our nuclear submarines. But impressive though they are, we still need to keep asking why it takes four of them to ensure one can always be at sea.'

Jeremy would come back to the issue of the UK's nuclear deterrent once more, over three years later in June 2013 when the Coalition government undertook its Trident Alternatives Review. This was, at least in Jeremy's view, a pointless exercise since by then they'd already confirmed the order for the four new submarines. But it did give him another chance to probe the effectiveness of the vessels, the likelihood they would ever be used and the possibility of using alternatives like cruise missiles. His conclusion, however, was unchanged – the alternatives were untested, and in any case the value of the submarines came down to how important people believed it was for the UK to have a weapon that could inflict a level of damage on an aggressor that dwarfed the benefit they would derive from an attack. And that was impossible to calculate.

In late September 2009 the Prime Minister returned from the G20 meeting in Pittsburgh where, despite flagging momentum, the assembled leaders had agreed more actions to stimulate global growth.

'There's still so much to do,' Gordon Brown told Jeremy before going on to explain his plan to create a global banking constitution to set standards on things like banking leverage ratios and liquidity. However, this ambition sat alongside more immediate grievances including the stories in the press of President Obama turning down Gordon's requests for a meeting and worries about whether to join the proposed televised debates with his rivals before the election. The Prime Minister's mood then worsened after the *Sun* decided to switch its support to the Tories despite the powerful speech that he'd given at the Labour Party conference in which he'd listed Labour's achievements since 1997.

When the Prime Minister raised these issues, Jeremy's role was to listen, offer sympathy, provide occasional advice on non-political topics and help his colleagues weather Gordon's mood. There was little more he could do, even if he often agreed with the complaints.

Worse was, however, to come. In early October, about a week after the Labour conference, Sue Nye called Jeremy to one side. 'Gordon went to bed last night without taking his contact lenses out, and this morning he can barely see,' she said. 'We're going to get him up to Moorfields Eye Hospital.'

'Oh no,' Jeremy said, shaking his head. Since Gordon was already blind in one eye, if his other one was failing, he risked losing his sight altogether. 'How is he?'

'He's worried but okay.'

After Sue left, Jeremy tried to distract himself by focusing on something tractable – what the constitutional implications would be if the Prime Minister needed to have an operation under general anaesthetic. But to his relief, by the time Gordon reached Moorfields on 9 October, the sight in his good eye was returning so Jeremy was able to lock his thinking on this away in his desk, where it nestled alongside a select few other secret documents, and didn't need to take up Peter Mandelson's kind offer to chair Cabinet on the Prime Minister's behalf.

Gordon Brown's recovery was, however, the only piece of good news around. Labour was trailing the Conservatives in the polls, the Tories were campaigning ever more stridently on the need for public spending cuts, and in an extraordinary breach of confidentiality, General Dannatt told the press that the Prime Minister had turned down the military's request to send 2,000 more troops to Afghanistan.

Things became even more toxic when, despite knowing about the Prime Minister's poor eyesight, the *Sun* decided to report his misspelling of a surname on a letter to the mother of a soldier killed in Afghanistan. 'Bloody shameful', their headline cried on 9 November.

This was, Jeremy told me, an example of British journalism at its worst. However, even if the *Sun* had been cruel, he still blamed himself for the mistake. He, therefore, tightened the system for proofreading everything the Prime Minister signed, while Gordon started composing more personal, handwritten missives, each one taking its toll.

While Jeremy couldn't change the *Sun*'s ethics, he could give Gordon Brown more positive things to talk about. So, though the ink was barely dry on *Building Britain's Future*, soon after this he proposed that they could start some new thinking on how technology could be used to take costs out of government.

'If we can get this finished in time for the pre-Budget report, it is one area where the Prime Minister might be prepared to announce cuts,' Jeremy told Martin Donnelly, whom he'd yet again dragged in to lead the work.

Martin nodded. They both knew it would be difficult to implement anything if Gordon didn't win the election. But staking out a new agenda was still exciting, even if most of Whitehall, including the Treasury, regarded it as displacement activity.

While Martin's new *Smarter Government* team, which included various external experts like Tim Berners-Lee, the inventor of the World Wide Web, and Nigel Shadbolt, a professor of artificial intelligence, started work, Jeremy turned his attention to the rest of the pre-Budget report. By this time, the Treasury's economic forecasts, which Jeremy reviewed with Dave Ramsden, were far less controversial because they showed modest growth through to 2010 before accelerating from 2011. After six quarters of negative growth, the stimulus measures in the previous November's pre-Budget report at last seemed to be moderating the effect of the financial crisis.

Once the forecast was settled, Peter Mandelson tried to ensure that, this time, the politicians were aligned on the political narrative of the report. Meanwhile, Jeremy set up working breakfasts at official level with the Treasury, hoping that large helpings of Number 10's canteen food would help them reach agreement on how to allocate the spending reductions from the April 2009 Budget.

Their intent was good, but Peter and Jeremy both failed.

At political level, Peter's failure became clear when Alistair Darling again started pressing for an increase in VAT. The Prime Minister blocked this, and instead insisted on another 0.5 per cent jump in National Insurance from April 2011. To protect those earning less, this would be accompanied by an increase in the point at which people began paying this tax.

The Prime Minister and Chancellor were, however, agreed on one measure – a one-off 50 per cent levy on bankers' bonuses, to raise £550 million. The Treasury worried that this might drive City rainmakers out of London, but Jeremy felt this was unlikely. In any case, banker compensation had grown out of all proportion to pay in other industries. As the Bank of England had pointed out, if the bankers had paid themselves 10 per cent less in compensation between 2000 and 2007, they would have had enough capital to get themselves through the crisis without taxpayers having to offer up to £50 billion to keep them afloat.

On the spending side, things were also difficult. The Chancellor was determined to set out how the government would meet its Budget target of cutting the cyclically adjusted deficit from 6.7 per cent in 2009/10 to 3.2 per cent in 2013/14. Jeremy and Peter Mandelson agreed – arguing that, alongside its next set of stimulus measures, the government needed to show it was serious about tackling the deficit, particularly if there were signs of recovery.

But the Prime Minister remained opposed to this, as did Ed Balls and most of the Number 10 political team. 'You're not going to turn me into Philip Snowden,' Gordon exclaimed during one of their discussions – a reference to the Labour Chancellor who, during the Great Depression, resisted calls to increase government spending to help people get back into work.

But it wasn't only a question of convincing the Prime Minister – it was also the challenge of finding credible spending reductions when the Chancellor had committed to protecting public spending on health, education, policing and overseas development. Jeremy's official-level meetings had made little progress on this, though he was hopeful that the *Smarter Government* team would make a contribution. By this stage the team was recommending a series of measures that they believed could release over £12 billion a year. These included reducing the size of the senior Civil Service by 10 per cent, merging or abolishing many of the government's 120 arm's-length bodies, accelerating the move to digitalised public services and making swathes of public data available to the public.

When the team came to Cabinet to present this thinking, their advisers also joined the discussion to add a little glamour to the event.

'So, what did you think of Tim Berners-Lee?' Gordon Brown asked his ministerial colleagues after they left.

'It was like meeting the man who invented the wheel,' Jack Straw said.

'Well, what was that like, Jack?' David Miliband asked with a grin, generating a ripple of laughter.

But despite its radicalism, the *Smarter Government* proposals alone were never going to be enough to deliver the Chancellor's deficit target. Jeremy, therefore, asked the Policy Unit to help him create an Excel model of the UK's finances and used this to inform his negotiations with Nick Macpherson on the allocation of additional reductions – while doing his best to ignore the bust of Philip Snowden that had mysteriously appeared in Nick's waiting room.

These discussions meant that, when the Prime Minister at last accepted a narrative on cuts a few days before the pre-Budget report, Jeremy and Nick had at least identified some potential savings.

However, perhaps because of the Prime Minister's continuing lack of enthusiasm, several of the critical spending ministers were still refusing to reduce their budgets early in the morning of 9 December – the day the report was due to be presented. This left Jeremy holed up on our sofa, drinking coffee while he tried to get the most recalcitrant to budge. It made him wonder, he told me when I came downstairs to see how he was getting on, whether Ed Balls and Yvette Cooper, who was by then Secretary of State for Work and Pensions, were taking his calls while sitting in different rooms of the townhouse they shared in Stoke Newington.

Overall, the 2009 pre-Budget report had been one of the most difficult that Jeremy had ever had to help settle. And unfortunately, all the last-minute wrangling showed in the report's incoherent narrative, which the press mocked, though they loved the levy on bankers' bonuses. This also meant that most of the economic good news in the report was missed, like the fact that redundancies, house repossessions and bankruptcies were running at about half the rate of the previous two recessions. It was impossible to know how much difference the National Economic Council had made to these figures but Jeremy believed that its policies had enabled, albeit at a cost, thousands of families to stay in their own homes.

Despite the traumas of the pre-Budget report, Labour's position in the polls strengthened slightly at the end of 2009. This didn't, though, stop two ex-Cabinet ministers, Patricia Hewitt and Geoff Hoon, attempting another coup, this time by calling for a secret ballot on Gordon Brown's leadership. This was seen off by the political team in Number 10 who hit the phones again, despite prolonged silence from several senior Cabinet members.

After this, the mood in Downing Street lifted. Jeremy was excited about the progress he was making with Ian Watmore, permanent secretary at the Department for Innovation, Universities and Skills, in securing land behind St Pancras railway station for the new Francis Crick Institute, which would be the biggest biomedical laboratory in Europe. Jeremy and Ian also convinced the Treasury to return to the Laboratory of Molecular Biology some of the dividends from the sale of its cancer-curing drugs so that they could construct their own new building. The special advisers were, meanwhile, telling Jeremy that they were making progress on the manifesto and felt they'd turned the heat onto the Tories. The economic data from the last quarter of 2009 was also positive since it showed that Britain had, by a breath, returned to growth. And even the blanket of heavy snow across the UK helped, after Jeremy was able, by cross-examining the Department for Transport, to spirit up enough of the right type of salt from Spain to grit the roads.

With the May 2010 deadline for calling an election fast approaching, in February Gordon Brown announced the next steps on some of the constitutional changes foreshadowed in *Building Britain's Future*. These included inserting clauses into Jack Straw's Constitutional Reform and Governance Bill that would enable a referendum to be held on the voting system and drafting a new bill on House of Lords reform.

The press reaction to these reforms was again mixed. Many saw them as an attempt by Labour to differentiate itself from the Conservatives while getting closer to the Liberal Democrats, their potential coalition partners. The actions also came too late to make a difference – the new referendum clauses ended up being dropped by the Chief Whip in the two-day wash-up period between 6 April 2010, when Gordon Brown called the election, and the prorogation of Parliament, and the House of Lords Reform Bill was never introduced. However, in its last few breaths, Parliament did approve the remainder of the Constitutional Reform and Governance Bill, enshrining many of the constitutional changes that Gordon Brown had laid out back at the start of his premiership in July 2007.

32

'Everybody's Changing':
Preparing for an election

January–May 2010

With the possibility of only the second government transition since 1979 looking increasingly likely, in mid-January 2010, Gus O'Donnell held a meeting in his office in 70 Whitehall to role-play different election outcomes.

Jeremy took his seat for this next to Edward Young, the Queen's deputy private secretary, who was representing his boss, Christopher Geidt, the head of the Queen's private office. Together with Gus and Jeremy, Christopher formed the third leg of the so-called Golden Triangle, the glamorous-sounding structure that was responsible for resolving an unclear election result and recommending the next prime minister to the Queen. It was odd, Jeremy had told me, and sobering, to know that at one particular and rare moment in public life, he might have to help make this judgement. His aim, which Gus and Christopher shared, was to avoid having to do so if they possibly could and instead to leave the decisions to the elected politicians.

Alex Allan, the chair of the Joint Intelligence Committee, who was helping Gus prepare for the election, explained the role-play. Gareth Davies, head of the Strategy Unit in Number 10, would be Nick Clegg, the leader of the Liberal Democrats, Robin Fellgett, the deputy head of the Economic and Domestic Secretariat, would be Gordon Brown, and Edward Troup, the managing director of the Budget, Tax and Welfare in the Treasury, would be David Cameron. They would work through six different election outcomes, and for each one, would discuss how the parties might act, the constitutional implications and the role of the Civil Service.

After this introduction, Alex handed around the first scenario and they began work. They cleared away this and the following two scenarios, in each of which it was obvious who would become prime minister, relatively quickly. When they paused for coffee, Jeremy checked in with Alastair Campbell, who'd been pulled back into Number 10 to work on the election campaign and was supervising Gordon Brown's rehearsal for his first leaders' debate. The day was going well, Alastair reported, and the Prime Minister was in a good mood.

Back in Gus's office, Alex handed around the papers for scenario four, in which the Conservatives were the largest party but were thirty-one seats short of a majority. Jeremy read the brief. This was the first scenario in which two outcomes were possible – Gordon Brown could remain as Prime Minister if the Liberal Democrats and a few others supported him, or David Cameron could take over if the Liberal Democrats sided with him.

They began the role-play.

'This is going to take a long time,' someone said after a while to nodding around the table. It was already apparent that, while a coalition between Labour and the Lib Dems was difficult given the numbers, a coalition between the Conservatives and the Lib Dems also wouldn't work unless the Conservatives agreed to the Liberal Democrats' referendum on the voting system and the Liberal Democrats agreed to the Conservatives' deficit reduction plan.

What was clear, however, was that Gareth (as Nick Clegg) was spending far more time talking to the Conservatives than he was to Labour. This left Robin (as Gordon Brown) sitting on his own and starting to talk about resigning – after all why should he stick around while Gareth sorted out a deal with the Conservatives? Jeremy glanced at Gus. They were trapped between a Prime Minister who wanted to resign and a potential coalition that wasn't ready to appoint his successor. And though they spent some time going around the different options, no one could see a way out.

'But what would help,' Gus told Jeremy when they pondered this after the session, 'is if we could at least get all the existing precedents in the same place.' In the following days Gus, therefore, agreed with the Prime Minister that he should create a Cabinet manual setting out the main laws, rules and conventions affecting the conduct and operation of government. This wouldn't change the existing rules and practices, so it wouldn't solve scenario four, but it would bring the existing conventions together. Given that few civil servants had seen more than one government transition, this was important. It was also an opportunity for Gus to see if his interpretations were shared by the UK's leading constitutional experts, in the hope that, if the moment came, they would support the Golden Triangle's recommendations.

The next issue was how to get the most critical parts of this document onto the public record before the election. The answer, Gus decided, after debating it with Jeremy, was to ask the Prime Minister for permission to send the chapter on elections and government formation, together with an outline of the others, to the House of Commons Justice Committee. Gus then took advantage of his appearance in front of the committee in late February 2010 to put on the record his view on one of the most important issues: that it was the responsibility of the incumbent prime minister not to resign until it was clear who the next prime minister would be. Jeremy shared this view, as did most of the constitutional experts, one of whom described it as a 'national duty'. It was, however, to prove far less clearcut when applied in the real world than any of them anticipated.

The pre-election Budget on Wednesday 24 March 2010 was more straightforward to prepare than many of its predecessors because, by then, the politicians were mainly focused on aligning it with their manifesto. The final version included a phased increase in fuel duties together with a number of pre-election sweeteners including increased child tax credits for families with toddlers, more generous winter fuel payments for pensioners and a two-year stamp duty holiday for most first-time house buyers, paid for by an increase in the stamp duty on the sale of homes worth more than £1 million.

In addition, the Chancellor at last revealed which departments would shoulder the £11 billion of savings that he'd promised in his 2009 pre-Budget report. While Jeremy would have been happier if a comprehensive spending review had been used to identify the source of these savings, the Chancellor did at least suggest some cost-cutting themes including improving government procurement, making better use of estates and reducing IT costs.

At the end of March, Gus came to see Jeremy. 'If there are coalition negotiations after the election,' he said, 'I'd like you to be the liaison between the Civil Service and the Labour Party. I considered asking James Bowler to do it, but that won't work – after all, Gordon would still be Prime Minister and will expect you to continue to be his lead adviser.'

Jeremy frowned. He wanted to support the Prime Minister, but he also knew how easy it was for civil servants to be labelled as political – after all, hadn't he been told before the April 1992 election that, because of his close relationship with Norman Lamont, he would probably have to leave the Chancellor's office if Labour won? 'I'll do it if you really want me to,' he told Gus, 'but I'm worried it will affect what I can do after the election if Labour doesn't win.'

Gus smiled. 'Don't worry. I'll make it clear that I asked you to play this role.'

When Gordon Brown announced the dissolution of Parliament on Tuesday 6 April 2010 ahead of an election on 6 May, it was hard to tell what the public would decide. After thirteen years of a Labour government, and with most of the press against him, Gordon faced an uphill struggle despite having addressed the financial crisis. The Conservatives, meanwhile, had the benefit of being headed by a fresh, young leader in David Cameron and were running a campaign that combined introducing an austerity programme to address the deficit with the aspiration of creating a 'Big Society' in which local communities were empowered to help themselves.

It was not Jeremy's role, however, to influence the public's choice. So, four days later, when the Civil Service went into purdah – the period during which officials were precluded from announcing new initiatives – we retreated to Worcestershire. While we were there, Jeremy told me about his pre-election contacts with the Conservatives, which had included a dinner with George Osborne, the shadow

Chancellor, in George's house in Notting Hill. They'd been joined for this by Matt Hancock and Ed Llewellyn, George's and David Cameron's chiefs of staff, the latter of whom Jeremy had met in Hong Kong back in 1993. Their conversation had focused on the economy, Jeremy said, and afterwards George had rung Gus to say that he probably wanted Jeremy to take over from Nick Macpherson as the Treasury's permanent secretary.

'Why do they want to replace Nick?'

'I'm not sure. Maybe George wants some fresh thinking.'

'Would you do it?'

'It's the job I've always wanted to do. I love the Treasury, for all its faults. So, if Nick is happy to move, I'd do it. But I've learnt not to take half promises like this too seriously. The Conservatives need to win the election first and these early views often change. In fact, it's the second job offer I've had. Francis Maude, the shadow minister for the Cabinet Office, has also asked if I will run the new efficiency group he's planning to set up in the Cabinet Office. That could also be interesting given our *Smarter Government* work.'

We saw the first of the televised debates between the party leaders while we were still in Worcestershire. It was the first election where these had featured, and watching Nick Clegg answering Alastair Stewart's questions with confidence, positioning himself as a valid alternative to the two traditional parties, it was clear they had the potential to change the dynamic of the campaign.

Jeremy glanced at Jonny, who was sitting between us on the bed, staring at the screen, before looking back at me. 'We could have a hung Parliament, you know,' he said. 'Nick Clegg's performance tonight makes that possible.'

By the time we returned to London, Jonny, Lizzie and Peter were all engaged in the election, though they each had different election posters stuck up on their bedroom doors. The closeness of the battle was also reflected in Whitehall where this time the red, blue and yellow folders of Civil Service briefing notes were all bulging.

A few days before the election, Jeremy met Ed Llewellyn and Kate Fall, Ed's deputy, in the Park Plaza hotel by Westminster Bridge. 'They've been thinking about how they would run Number 10,' he told me that evening. 'They want to make Downing Street smaller by reducing the number of special advisers, slimming down the Policy Unit and abolishing the Delivery and Strategy Units.'

'But I thought the Delivery and Strategy Units were effective?'

'I told them that. I also said I've always found it helpful to have special advisers in government – they provide political advice that Civil Service can't give. And though some behave badly, that's the exception in my experience, and those who do rarely last. But the Conservatives are determined to reduce bureaucracy and cost. The centre will be cut back, and Ed says that ministers will be left to run their own departments so long as they implement the manifesto commitments and play ball with Francis's new efficiency group.'

I nodded.

'Oh, and we discussed one other issue. David Cameron wants his office to be in the White Room upstairs.'

'Not that argument again.'

Jeremy grinned. 'I haven't tried to talk them out of it yet.'

33

'Everybody Hurts':
Coalition negotiations

May 2010

The BBC exit poll at 10 p.m. on Thursday 6 May 2010 predicted a hung Parliament with the Conservatives nineteen seats short of a majority. Though they had the most MPs, the Conservatives had done far worse than they'd expected, while Labour had done better. And though his campaign lustre had gained him votes, Nick Clegg had still lost several seats.

By the time our phone rang at six a.m., Jeremy had implemented his usual election night strategy, waking at two in the morning to watch the results on playback. Having caught up on the night's events, he was watching the live commentary with me, Jonny and the twins strewn in various states of wakefulness along the sofa beside him. By then we also knew that the exit poll had been accurate – this was scenario four.

Jeremy picked up the handset to find Gavin Kelly on the line. 'Gordon is still Prime Minister, so I'm going back into Downing Street,' Gavin said.

'Okay,' Jeremy said. 'I'll see you there.'

'What do you think it will be like?' I asked while he began to get ready.

Jeremy frowned. 'Difficult. Gavin's right. Gordon Brown is still Prime Minister, at least for now, so I need to make sure he gets the support he needs. And though the focus will be on the Conservatives and Lib Dems because they can more easily form a government, Gordon also has a chance of staying in power if he manages to get the help of the Liberal Democrats and some of the smaller parties.'

Jeremy arrived in the war room shortly after seven to find Gordon Brown making his way through a plate of bacon at his desk. Most of the Labour special advisers were also there, bleary-eyed from the campaign. It was hard to tell he thought, looking at them, whether this was a band of die-hard optimists ready to fight to the last to keep their man in power or a team of stoics, here to give Gordon Brown one last send-off. However, when Andrew Adonis bounced in grinning broadly, it was clear which group he was in.

Andrew's arrival also seemed to wake everyone else up. Gavin Kelly looked across at Jeremy and gestured towards his computer. 'After being forced to come in through the back door, we found that we'd been shut out of the Number 10 system, which means we can't get hold of any papers or print anything,' he said.

'I'll sort it out,' Jeremy said, trying not to smile at Gavin's indignation. 'We had to disable your accounts after you resigned to take part in the election campaign.'

'Good,' Gavin said before huddling with Andrew and the Prime Minister to debate the election results and discuss the offer they might make to the Liberal Democrats.

After asking Sue Gray to look into Gavin's plea, Jeremy left them deliberating while he headed over to the Cabinet Office to join Gus's first meeting with the officials supporting the coalition negotiations.

'The Prime Minister has approved Gus's statement on how we'll operate during this period,' Jeremy told the group once they were settled.

'It will go out at 10.30 a.m,' Gus said, 'and will remind people that the government needs to stay in office until it's clear someone else can command a –'

A siren wailed. Everyone groaned.

'It's the weekly fire alarm test,' Gus said.

'The emergency is over,' a disembodied voice said.

'Somehow, I don't think it is,' Gus said, and everyone laughed.

After the howls ceased, Gus summarised the party support arrangements. Edward Troup was leading with the Conservatives,

Chris Wormald, the head of the Economic and Domestic Secretariat, was doing the same with the Liberal Democrats and Jeremy was providing the link with Labour. 'But you mustn't talk directly to each other,' Gus said, 'because that might breach confidentiality.'

'The Conservatives say they don't need any support at this stage,' Edward said.

'Same here,' Chris said.

Gus looked at Jeremy. 'What about Gordon?'

'It's not clear yet. But it's already obvious how uncomfortable it's going to be to be sitting alongside the Labour team in Downing Street while they try to negotiate with the Liberal Democrats.'

Jeremy got back to the war room to find the Prime Minister still talking to Andrew Adonis.

'I've told Danny Alexander you are ready to start discussions,' Andrew said, Danny being Nick Clegg's chief of staff. 'The Lib Dems should want to talk – after all, they don't want austerity any more than we do.'

'Can I brief you on the eurozone crisis, Prime Minister?' Jeremy asked when Gordon finished his conversation with Andrew. 'We may be asked to help bail-out Greece.'

Gordon nodded, switching with ease back into his role of Prime Minister. Greece was in serious trouble – having joined the euro in 2001, it was struggling under a mountain of debt. The austerity programme launched by its new socialist government to address this had sparked riots and its borrowing costs had soared as investors ran away. Now the Commission was intending to step in, but the fund they wanted to use covered all EU member states, which meant the UK would be expected to contribute despite being outside the eurozone.

Jeremy's explanation of the latest developments in this saga was, however, interrupted by Alastair Campbell's arrival alongside a crumpled-looking Peter Mandelson.

'Well, home from home,' Alastair declared. He glanced at Andrew Adonis and narrowed his eyes. 'And all at the beck and call of your pesky Liberals.'

Various people looked up and smiled at this reference to Andrew

Adonis's past political allegiance. A few were working on laptops, propped in front of the Number 10 computer monitors.

'We're still waiting to get access to the system,' Gavin said, gesturing at the dark screens.

Jeremy rang Sue Gray again. 'Where have we got to on reopening the IT accounts for the Number 10 special advisers?' he asked her. 'Gordon Brown is still Prime Minister, so he's entitled to political advice.'

'We can't give them access because they no longer work for the government,' Sue said, 'and we can't reappoint them because we don't know who the prime minister will be.'

'We're tying ourselves in a bureaucratic knot. We need to find a way to do this.'

There was a pause. 'Okay. What if we give them guest access?'

'Great.'

'Paddy Ashdown and David Laws have cancelled the meetings I'd set up with them this morning,' Andrew Adonis was telling the Prime Minister when Jeremy put down the phone. He sounded, Jeremy thought, remarkably cheerful despite this rebuff by two senior Liberal Democrats.

Up above them, Sky News switched to a close-up of Nick Clegg, the ticker underneath revealing his intention to talk to the Conservatives. This was followed by the news that David Cameron would make a statement at 2.30 p.m. on his plans to form a 'strong and stable' government.

Voices filled the room. 'Cameron is going to try to copy Alex Salmond,' someone said in a reference to Salmond's success in claiming power in Scotland in 2007 without having won a majority.

'I need to make a statement offering to talk to the Liberals before Cameron does,' the Prime Minister said.

It was, Jeremy thought, time to call Gus.

'If Gordon wants to make a statement about the party talks, then he can't do it from inside Number 10,' Gus told Jeremy.

This view, when Jeremy relayed it back to the Prime Minister's team, wasn't well received. But over the following hour, Jeremy negotiated a compromise – if Gordon wanted to speak as party leader rather than as Prime Minister, then he could use a plain lectern on Downing Street since that was technically a public thoroughfare.

With this clear, the political team drafted Gordon's statement, which Jeremy reviewed to check it correctly described the Queen's role and reflected what Gordon could say as party leader. He then had time to consider its message – Gordon was willing to give the Conservatives and Liberal Democrats as much time as they wanted for their discussions. And, if those came to nothing, he was also prepared to talk to Nick Clegg.

A short while after Gordon's statement, David Cameron appeared on Sky News. Behind him, a large sash window framed a view of St James's Park. 'I want,' David said, 'to make a big, open and comprehensive offer to the Liberal Democrats.'

This time there were gasps in the war room.

'It's an error,' Gordon said shaking his head. 'Cameron has underestimated his strength.'

But Jeremy remembered scenario four. They hadn't managed to find a way through that because they'd assumed the Conservatives wouldn't compromise on policy. And now, with the game barely started, David Cameron had already signalled that he was prepared to move.

At half past five, the Prime Minister rang Nick Clegg. After congratulating him on his campaign, he offered to share some thinking on their overlapping priorities. At the end of what sounded like a cordial conversation, Gordon paused. 'There's something else I want to talk to you about,' he said, 'but we should do that face to face.'

After this call, Andrew and Gavin went into a huddle to discuss what David Cameron's 'big, open and comprehensive offer' meant for their chances of wooing the Liberal Democrats. Others were debating in low voices what the 'something else' was that Gordon Brown wanted to discuss with Nick Clegg, though Jeremy thought that was clear. The Prime Minister was on the phone again. There was, Jeremy concluded, nothing more he could do, so he headed home.

* * *

The Prime Minister was hammering away on his keyboard again when Jeremy walked back into the war room on Saturday morning.

Gavin Kelly caught Jeremy's eye. 'Gordon's furious about the *Sun*'s headline.'

Jeremy wasn't surprised. The *Sun*'s accusation that Gordon Brown was 'squatting' in Number 10 was unfair because, as Jeremy and Gus had been advising him since the election, he had an obligation to stay until it was clear who would be the next Prime Minister.

'I want to put out another statement,' Gordon said, looking up. 'I'm going to set a deadline for the coalition discussions. If there's no decision by Tuesday, I'm going to resign.'

Jeremy found a quiet desk and rang Gus again. It was becoming clear that the constitutional niceties that they had clarified before the election were all very well, but they didn't recognise the human cost of asking a Prime Minister to stay in position when he had little chance of being reappointed. Gus, however, wasn't changing his view – until the Conservatives and Lib Dems had agreed a deal, Gordon had a duty to stay on.

The mood in the war room remained grim through the rest of Saturday and wasn't helped by the VE Day celebrations which took place outside on Whitehall. These marked sixty-five years since the end of the Second World War and should have been a moment of thanksgiving. But watching the TV coverage from the war room, Jeremy was conscious of the Prime Minister's discomfort when he was forced, despite his poor eyesight, to shuffle forward in line with David Cameron and Nick Clegg to lay his wreath, rather than being allowed the usual courtesy as Prime Minister of laying his first.

Thankfully, the atmosphere felt lighter when Jeremy returned to Downing Street on Sunday morning. The Prime Minister had escaped to Scotland overnight and Andrew Adonis told Jeremy that Labour's first official-level meeting with the Liberal Democrats the night before had gone well. They'd talked about speeding ahead with a referendum on the voting system, Andrew said, which was something the Tories were unlikely to offer.

'That sounds like progress,' Jeremy said.

'I hope so,' Andrew said. 'In fact, Gordon is going to meet Nick Clegg at four to continue the discussion. Can you sort out a location?'

'Sure,' Jeremy said – although, with Whitehall packed with reporters, this wouldn't be easy. But after a lengthy call with Gus to review the options, he proposed the permanent under-secretary's room in the Foreign Office, since this was both discreet and relatively easy to reach.

By this time, however, having heard Gavin's more downbeat read-out of the meeting the night before, Jeremy was feeling considerably less optimistic on the Prime Minister's behalf. The Liberal Democrats had been keen to emphasise their policy differences, Gavin had told Jeremy, and he worried that they were only talking to Labour because it would help their negotiation with the Tories.

With the Prime Minister not yet back from Scotland, the war room was quiet. After sorting out the location for the Prime Minister's meeting, Jeremy spent his time making calls on the Greek crisis and ringing Christopher Geidt to assure him he was doing what he could to delay the Prime Minister resigning. Around him, people tapped at keyboards or talked in low voices. It felt calm for a change, though the evidence of the ongoing political storm was clear in the takeaway containers piled on tables and chairs, the ties draped everywhere, and the acrid smell of nervous men that hung in the air.

Early that afternoon, the Prime Minister reappeared. After making a few calls, he pushed back his chair and picked up his notes. 'Are you coming with me for this meeting with Nick?' he asked Jeremy.

Jeremy took a deep breath. He wanted to go – both because of his loyalty to Gordon and out of curiosity. But even though it was permissible, he felt that it wasn't the right thing to do. 'It's best if someone from your political team joins you,' he told the Prime Minister, 'because I don't want anyone to misunderstand my role.' As he watched the Prime Minister walk away, Jeremy felt guilty but he was sure this was the right decision.

When the Prime Minister returned a couple of hours later, he told his team that he'd discussed several issues with Nick Clegg, including Europe and electoral reform, where he'd offered to hold an early referendum. Overall, he thought the meeting had gone well and there were no obvious deal breakers.

More hours of kicking heels followed, during which the special advisers worried about the fact that the Liberal Democrats' working-level meeting with the Conservatives had been going on all day. Then a call came through proposing another bilateral between the Prime Minister and Nick Clegg later that evening and the mood shifted again.

At this point Jeremy headed home again – after all, the only role for the Civil Service in the negotiation process was fact checking, and no one seemed to need that. 'Even I'm finding the roller coaster of emotions in the war room exhausting,' he told me. 'I don't know how they'll keep going if this lasts much longer.'

Jeremy hoped that, by Monday morning, the situation would be clearer. But this time he arrived in Downing Street to find Andrew Adonis shaking his head.

'The meeting last night was difficult,' Andrew said. 'Nick handed over an ambitious wish list of policies, said he wanted immediate legislation on electoral reform, and made it clear that Gordon's departure had to be part of any deal.'

'What is the Prime Minister going to do?'

'He wouldn't commit to any specific timetable for leaving, which frustrated Nick, but I think he's ready to announce that he's standing down in October. Hopefully, we can then start negotiating.'

Andrew was right. That afternoon, after another meeting and two more calls with Nick Clegg, the Prime Minister stood up. 'Okay,' he said, 'it's time. They've agreed to start proper discussions after I've made my statement.'

When Gordon headed out into Downing Street, Jeremy and the rest of the war room fell silent, watching the TV. Gordon took his place behind the wooden lectern and told the assembled journalists that he intended to 'ask the Labour Party to set in train the processes needed for its own leadership election'.

When the Prime Minister reappeared a few minutes later, everyone applauded, Jeremy included. Several people were crying.

Gordon smiled. 'Thanks, but everything we achieved, we achieved together. Now back to work. Andrew, we need another draft of the policy document for Cabinet. We need to be ready to negotiate.'

'We're back in the game,' Alastair Campbell said.

At 6 p.m. Jeremy and Gus joined the start of Cabinet, which covered the euro crisis and Afghanistan. These topics were important, but the discussion was subdued – after all, no one knew whether the government would survive for long enough to take any action. The meeting felt odd in other ways too, with Jim Knight, the work and pensions minister who'd lost his seat, turning up in jeans and Chris Wormald, who was supposed to be doing the minutes, not turning up at all because of his role supporting the Liberal Democrats.

After fifteen minutes of discussing government business, Jeremy and Gus left and the meeting moved on to political issues. When that was over, the Labour team hurtled out for their first formal negotiating session with the Liberal Democrats.

On his way past Jeremy's desk, Peter Mandelson paused. 'Will you come with us?' he asked. 'It would demonstrate that we're serious.'

But again, Jeremy shook his head. 'I can't join a political discussion,' he said, even more sure, on this second time of asking, that this was the right decision.

On Tuesday morning we woke to reports that Labour's talks with the Liberal Democrats the previous afternoon had gone badly and a warning from David Blunkett on the *Today* programme that Gordon Brown shouldn't form a 'coalition of the defeated'.

Jeremy arrived in Number 12 to find the Prime Minister drafting an economic approach to share with Nick Clegg. After the Labour negotiating team left for another working-level meeting with the Liberal Democrats, Jeremy walked around the horseshoe to talk to James Bowler.

'We don't yet know what is going to happen, but I think it's time to dust down our plan for clearing out Number 10,' he said in a low voice. 'But don't touch anything yet. Gordon Brown is still Prime Minister and Number 10 is still his. However, if he does leave, we may have little time before Cameron and Clegg arrive.'

The Labour team again came back shaking their heads.

'It was scratchy,' Andrew told Jeremy. 'The Lib Dems want to go further and faster than we do on deficit reduction. They've completely changed their stance since the election and it's pretty clear why that is.'

After days in which little had happened, over the next few hours, time seemed to accelerate. More senior Labour figures made public statements criticising the possibility of a coalition, and when Gordon Brown returned from his meeting with Nick Clegg in the House of Commons early that afternoon, he said he was going to resign immediately – he couldn't wait for the Liberal Democrats any longer.

'You need to persuade the Prime Minister to stay put,' Christopher Geidt said when Jeremy rang him.

Jeremy looked across at Gordon, who was sitting under a TV screen that was predicting a Conservative–Liberal Democrat coalition. 'I'll try,' he said, 'but we're reaching the limit of what we can expect. It might help if you talked to him in person.'

By the time Christopher arrived an hour or so later, Jeremy was huddled with the Prime Minister and Alastair Campbell. It was ridiculous, Alastair was saying, for Gordon to be expected to hang around just to give Clegg more time to wring concessions out of Cameron. The Prime Minister nodded – he was only prepared to stay on, he told Christopher, if it was at the express wish of the Queen.

The war room was filling up. Sarah Brown and Sue Nye were there. Ed Miliband and Ed Balls were talking to Alastair Campbell and Andrew Adonis was huddled with Peter Mandelson and a group of other political advisers and civil servants.

The Prime Minister's phone rang. 'It's Tony Blair,' someone said and the room hushed while Gordon exchanged compliments with his predecessor. For the first time Jeremy began to think about the moment when all these people would be gone, bracing himself for the approaching loss.

Shortly after the Prime Minister finished his call, Jeremy's phone rang. It was Christopher Geidt – the Queen was willing to accept the Prime Minister's resignation if Gordon Brown believed he was unable to form a government.

'Thank you,' Jeremy said. 'I'll let him know. He just wants to have one final conversation with Nick Clegg.'

More time passed, some of which Gordon used to have a haircut in his office, while Jeremy and Ed Balls shared a few gentle reminiscences. Shortly before 5.30 p.m., Nick Clegg called again.

'I'm open to having a negotiation,' the Prime Minister said, 'but only if you break off your discussions with the Conservatives. The Queen is waiting, and the country needs clarity.'

'Nick is going to speak to his colleagues and let me know,' Gordon said after putting down the phone.

There was a collective groan.

'You need to leave in daylight,' Gavin said.

'I know.'

Ed Balls started telling old jokes, mixing up the punchlines. People were laughing. The phone rang and the room fell silent once more.

'You're a good guy, Nick,' the Prime Minister said, 'but I can't give you more time.' He paused, listening for a moment, before shaking his head. 'Nick. I have to do this now. Okay, thanks Nick. Goodbye.'

This time, when Gordon replaced his handset, everyone rose to their feet.

'Daddy, we're going to Grandma's,' John Brown said, running in with his brother Fraser.

Gordon smiled down at his son before looking up at the forty or so people who had crowded into the war room. 'I couldn't have done it without you,' he began, before going on to describe some of the things they'd achieved together during his time as Prime Minister. He took a deep breath. 'Thank you for your professionalism and your total commitment to public service.'

Many people were crying, and Jeremy felt close to it himself. Fraser and John had clambered on top of the horseshoe table to watch their father speak. Up on the wall, Sky News was predicting the Prime Minister's resignation, its camera trained on the front door of Number 10.

At 7.18 p.m., Gordon, Sarah, John and Fraser stepped into Downing Street and Gordon walked up to the lectern for a final time. 'Only those who have held the office of Prime Minister can understand the full weight of its responsibilities and its great capacity for good,' he said. 'I have been privileged to learn much about the very best in human nature and a fair amount, too, about its frailties, including my own.'

His few words said, Gordon turned and walked with his family down the road in the gathering dusk, a bank of flashing cameras turning to follow their progress. Jeremy, watching on the screen in the war room, felt a familiar ache. One by one the Labour advisers began to leave, the door of Number 11 opening to the sound of helicopters overhead and shouted questions from reporters.

When Gavin Kelly came to say goodbye, Jeremy could only manage a handshake. 'I've got under an hour to pull this lot, and myself, together,' he muttered.

Gavin nodded at this and smiled before picking up his bag and following the others out.

Jeremy took a deep breath. 'Okay,' he said to James and the other civil servants left in the war room, 'we need to get this place clean.'

At this, everyone began running around, pulling Labour Party mugs off shelves, collecting leaflets, clearing dirty crockery and gathering up policy papers. One act had just finished – an act dominated by a Prime Minister who, for all his frustrating working patterns, had proved himself able to understand and act on issues with a depth and passion that Jeremy had never seen before. And when that issue was a global financial crisis, this had enabled him to make a difference to Britain and probably to the world.

The duty clerk came to find Jeremy. 'The first Conservative special advisers are about to arrive,' he said.

Jeremy glanced at the clock. Only ten minutes had passed since Gavin had left and the next chapter in Britain's political history was about to begin.

34

'Upside Down You're Turning Me': A new form of government

May–June 2010

Jeremy reached the link door to the Cabinet Office in time to greet Kris Murrin, who was managing the transition for the Conservatives. Following her in were Ed Llewellyn, Kate Fall, Andy Coulson, the Conservatives' director of communications, Gabby Bertin, Andy's deputy, and at the back, Steve Hilton, the de facto head of policy – though he refused to be pinned down by anything so mundane as a job title.

Jeremy gave these new arrivals a short tour of the ground floor of Number 10, ignoring the still-scurrying civil servants. When reports came through, around an hour later, that David Cameron was returning from the Palace, the special advisers headed out onto Downing Street to watch his arrival. Meanwhile, inside Number 10, the Civil Service team threw the final items of Labour paraphernalia into bags and the last scraps of rubbish into bins, before assembling in two lines behind the front door.

Jeremy glanced across at Tom Fletcher, who was putting on a clean blue and yellow tie. He straightened his own. Outside they could hear muted cheers and shouted questions. Camera flashes lit up the windowpanes, the door of Number 10 swung open and David and Samantha Cameron swept in. Jeremy glanced around at his clapping colleagues, many of whom still had puffy eyes, and nodded.

The Prime Minister paused when he reached Jeremy. 'It's good to see a familiar face,' he said with a grin.

Jeremy returned David's smile before falling in next to Gus to follow the Prime Minister down the yellow corridor to the Cabinet Room, and on through the blue-felt covered doors into Tony Blair's old office. Although the previous five days had felt like an eternity, the truth was that this new coalition government had been formed remarkably quickly, particularly by continental standards. And aged only forty-three, David Cameron was not only Britain's youngest Prime Minister for almost two hundred years, he was also the first Jeremy had served who was younger than himself.

Over the next hour, David Cameron talked to other world leaders on the phone, including President Obama, who made everyone smile when he addressed him as Prime Minister. In the gaps between calls, while various special advisers and civil servants came in and out, the Prime Minister, George Osborne, the new Chancellor, and William Hague, the new foreign secretary, discussed the state of the coalition negotiations.

Many policies were already agreed. There was a commitment to Plan A – the Conservatives' deficit reduction plan – and a package of constitutional changes, including reforming the House of Lords and moving to five-year fixed-term parliaments to lock both parties into the Coalition. Most critically for the Liberal Democrats, there would be a referendum on an alternative vote system, which if agreed, would benefit smaller political parties.

Jeremy was concentrating hard, his temples throbbing. He needed to soak up not just the nuances of the policies, but also a new vocabulary. He was also observing the relationships between individuals and trying to understand what mattered to each one. All this information would be critical if he was going to make this new administration comfortable with a Civil Service team that, until a few hours before, had been serving their rivals.

After the Prime Minister returned from addressing his party in the House of Commons later that evening, they sat around the Cabinet table to discuss possible ministerial appointments, though nothing could be finalised before the coalition negotiation with the Liberal Democrats had been concluded.

After a while, David paused and looked at Jeremy. 'Has Ed told you I'm thinking of basing myself in the White Room upstairs?'

Jeremy forced a smile. 'Yes, we talked about that. We'll see what's possible, but we need to make sure that wherever you are based isn't just quiet but also secure and that it allows us to work in an efficient way.' He paused. Was he sounding too much like Sir Humphrey?

'But didn't Margaret Thatcher work upstairs?'

'She did – but we now also often use those rooms for functions.'

'Oh.'

Jeremy smiled. 'Why don't you start working down here, Prime Minister, in the office where Tony Blair ended up being settled? In the meantime, we'll figure out the practicalities.'

'Okay. But I want you to look at it properly.'

'Of course I will.'

At 9.30 a.m. on Wednesday morning, Nick Clegg shook hands with the Prime Minister outside of Number 10 before making his way inside. A modest team of special advisers followed him in including Polly Mackenzie, his chief policy adviser and Jonny Oates, his chief of staff.

Jeremy, Gus O'Donnell and Sue Gray spent most of that morning helping their new leaders finalise their ministerial appointments. This wasn't an easy process since the number of roles allocated to each party needed to be roughly proportional to the number of votes they'd won, which meant there needed to be one Liberal Democrat minister for every five Conservative ministers and five Liberal Democrat seats in Cabinet. As a result, some Conservatives who'd worked hard on their shadow briefs would be displaced, but despite this, the discussion was good-humoured. On the Civil Service side, Jeremy and Gus were being solicitous to their new ministers, but Sue Gray was undaunted, cutting across the conversation at one point to tell David Cameron that he would have to sack a Conservative if he wanted to make way for another Liberal Democrat.

When the Prime Minister stopped to take more calls, Sue took Nick Clegg for a tour of Number 10 to find him an office and Jeremy headed down to Number 12 in search of Oliver Letwin – the grandly, though accurately, titled minister for government policy. When he reached the war room, Jeremy paused. Only a day ago this had been the centre of power. Now it was deserted, the chairs around the horseshoe in disarray.

Almost deserted. Rohan Silva, Steve Hilton's deputy, was sitting with his back to one of the windows.

Rohan looked up and smiled. 'It's a quiet place to work,' he said. 'But I'm glad you're here because I found something on the printer addressed to you.' He rustled through some documents and handed Jeremy a sheet of paper. On it, printed in capital letters, was a message:

DEAR JEREMY. AS I LEAVE NO 10, I WANTED TO SAY IN WRITING HOW MUCH I VALUED OUR PARTNERSHIP AND YOUR GENIUS. YOU ARE A TOWERING INTELLECT AND POLICY MAKER. THE NATION OWES YOU THE GREATEST OF DEBTS. MY THANKS FOR EVERYTHING. GORDON.

Jeremy nodded at Rohan and made his excuses, sliding the note into his jacket pocket. He was touched by Gordon's words and already missed him. But just as in previous transitions, there was no time to think about that now – his focus had to be on his new ministers and their priorities.

Jeremy found Oliver leaning over the large walnut table in the office next to the war room talking to Danny Alexander, the Liberal Democrat Secretary of State for Scotland, James O'Shaughnessy, the head of the Policy Unit, and Chris Wormald. Laid out in front of them were the Conservative and Liberal Democrat election manifestos, together with the high-level policy document that had been put together during the coalition negotiation.

Chris Wormald handed Jeremy a copy of the draft Coalition Agreement. When it was finished, this would detail all the Coalition's priorities, including policies to transform the NHS, reform the banks, introduce a cap on immigration, and make various environmental and tax changes. In the process, a few policies loved by one side but not the other would be lost, like the Chancellor's inheritance tax change, but most would remain in some form.

'Are we getting Civil Service input on all these?' Jeremy asked, conscious of the dangers that could lurk in such an extensive list of policies.

'I'm trying to do that – though we don't have much time,' Chris said.

Jeremy nodded. This new government was moving at pace both because it was determined to address the deficit and because it didn't know how long the Coalition would last. But developing policy at speed was always dangerous.

Some of the highlights of the Coalition Agreement were outlined by the Prime Minister and Deputy Prime Minister in their Rose Garden press conference early that afternoon. They wanted, they said, smiling behind twin podiums in the spring sunshine, to create a 'seismic shift' in UK politics.

After the press dispersed, most of the rest of that day was spent making decisions on special advisers and committees. The new administration wanted fewer than fifty special advisers across the whole of government, and since only a few of these would be Liberal Democrats, this rarer phenotype had to be distributed with care. Oliver Letwin then proposed four new Cabinet committees, each chaired by one party with a deputy from the other and Jeremy and Gus added a fifth – a home affairs committee. Given that this would deal with all the domestic policies and constitutional changes in the Coalition Agreement, the Deputy Prime Minister decided to chair it himself.

All in all, Jeremy told me when he got home, it had been a very productive day.

On Thursday morning Sue Gray caught Jeremy on his way into Number 10.

'I couldn't find a suitable office for Nick Clegg in Downing Street yesterday,' she said, 'so he's decided to take Peter Ricketts's room in 70 Whitehall.'

Jeremy winced, realising that, in all their preparations for a potential coalition government, they'd overlooked the obvious question of where a deputy prime minister would sit. And though Nick Clegg had every right to choose whatever office he wanted, Peter Ricketts, who'd just become the government's first-ever national security adviser, was about to lose his elegant new room with its bow window overlooking Parade Square.

'Poor Peter. He thought that was the perfect place for the new national security headquarters.'

'Well, that's where Nick Clegg is going to be now,' Sue said, 'so I've shuffled Peter out into Shriti's old office.'

Later that morning, Peter appeared in Jeremy's doorway.

'I'm sorry about your office,' Jeremy said.

Peter shook his head. 'I'm not here about that. I've come straight from the first meeting of the National Security Council.'

'Good,' Jeremy said. The National Security Council was another Coalition innovation. It would bring together the relevant parts of Whitehall to discuss national security issues so they no longer had to rely on bilateral discussions with the national security departments and agencies. It was another example of a COBR-style process being used to develop policy.

'I'm not so sure. After the meeting, I gave the Prime Minister and Deputy Prime Minister a list of other potential security topics that we might discuss. The one they chose was sorting out the situation with the Guantanamo Bay detainees.'

'Oh,' Jeremy said. This was a particularly knotty issue. Now that they were back in the UK, many of the detainees had launched lawsuits against the government, claiming it was complicit in their alleged torture by the Americans. The problem was that Whitehall couldn't defend itself without having details of intelligence operations aired in open court.

'The Prime Minister says he wants to find a solution to this in the next six months before it becomes his government's problem,' Peter went on. 'In fact, he wants to see if there is a way to stop the detainees' cases, and, if necessary, he is prepared to legislate to make them illegal.'

Jeremy blinked at this. Trying to prevent the detainees from suing the government was probably impossible under the European Convention on Human Rights. 'Can you get Paul's view?' he asked, knowing that Paul Jenkins, the Treasury solicitor, could be relied on to provide wise counsel, 'and I'll talk to Gus.'

Jeremy spent the rest of that week and the weekend working

through a mound of documents. These included the Queen's Speech, which the European and Domestic Secretariat was coordinating, and a paper Oliver Letwin was drafting with Jim Wallace, Scotland's advocate general, on how the government would operate, which included the idea of creating a Coalition Committee to resolve policy disputes between the two parties.

What was incredible, Jeremy told me when he broke off for dinner on Saturday evening, was how quickly the new government was reaching decisions. This was why he was trying to read everything, looking for policy or procedural traps that might cause problems for the government later or make it difficult for the Civil Service to operate effectively.

I nodded and bit my lip. What Jeremy was saying made sense but it also meant that, after only a brief period of calm during the purdah period and Coalition negotiation, he was back to working as hard as ever.

It soon became clear that, whether I liked it or not, the Coalition had no intention of slowing down. Number 10's new daily rhythm, which was bookended by office meetings at 8.30 a.m. and 4 p.m., helped drive the pace. David Cameron and the Chancellor sat in the wing-backed armchairs in the den for these flanked by Jeremy, who laid claim to the upright chair beside the Prime Minister, and Rupert Harrison, the Chancellor's special adviser, who stood behind his minister, tapping away on a BlackBerry. There was then an unseemly rush for the other seats, which often left Ed Llewellyn standing when he came in late, brandishing the final copy of the agenda.

The Coalition Agreement and the document laying out how the Coalition would operate were both approved by Cabinet on Tuesday 18 May, one week after the start of the Coalition government. Jeremy joined this discussion, the first time since 1945 that ministers from two different parties had gathered around the long, curved table in the Cabinet Room.

After that, Jeremy turned his mind to his next priority – the Coalition's determination to cut that year's budget for public spending. In many ways this was a test, Gus told Jeremy when they discussed it during one of their commutes in from Balham in their shared government car – could the system respond at pace to political demands so different to the ones it was receiving before? It was a sentiment that Jeremy shared, though luckily the Treasury had done a fair amount of thinking about this issue before the election.

The Treasury's proposals for reducing the deficit were debated in a series of meetings between the four key Coalition leaders – the Prime Minister, the Chancellor, the Deputy Prime Minister and David Laws, the Liberal Democrat Chief Secretary, with Jeremy, Ed Llewellyn and Calum Miller, Nick Clegg's principal private secretary, also attending. These debates occasionally became heated, although the tension was rarely between the Chancellor and the Prime Minister or even between the Liberal Democrats and the Conservatives. Instead, the most difficult moments were when ministers in charge of spending departments were invited in to be told they needed to cut their budgets.

In late May the Prime Minister hosted a meeting at Chequers to debate the emerging set of in-year cuts. On their way back up to London, he told Jeremy that, prior to the election, he'd been dubious about the role of permanent secretary at Number 10. But now he'd understood what Jeremy did, he wanted him to stay.

'Are you disappointed about not getting the Treasury role?' I asked Jeremy when he told me this.

'A little,' he said, 'but it's interesting getting to know this new set of ministers. And we are getting a lot done. The Prime Minister takes boxes at night, works through his papers and chairs meetings well. We even have Cabinet committees that meet regularly.'

I smiled. 'But are you enjoying it?'

'Yes, of course. We discussed the Treasury's options for welfare cuts today, including making the BBC pay for the free TV licences for the over-75s. Whereas Gordon would have kept asking for analysis, the Prime Minister rattled through the items with rapid-fire "yeses", "noes" and "this won't fly in Witney's".'*

But despite this rush of activity, Downing Street and 70 Whitehall both felt quiet. As Ed had anticipated, the Strategy and Delivery Units had both been abolished after the election and the Policy Unit,

---

* Witney was the Prime Minister's constituency in Oxfordshire.

which was being headed by James O'Shaughnessy, a Conservative special adviser, had only a handful of people left in it. There was so much empty space that some people had taken to working at different desks on different days depending on their mood.

'It's similar to the structure that existed in 1985 under Thatcher,' Oliver Letwin told Jeremy when they discussed it. 'Maggie ran things with only five key people. If it worked then, there's no reason why it won't work now.'

Jeremy decided not to point out that Margaret Thatcher's agenda had been all about reducing the role of the state rather than reforming it. And unlike Oliver, he worried that there wasn't enough resource left in Number 10 to enable them to steer Whitehall effectively, particularly when the Coalition's honeymoon was over. But he also knew that having a fight about an issue like this early on in a new administration would achieve little – if the new team was wrong about what they needed, then they would find out soon enough.

35

'Jamming':
Churning out decisions

June 2010

Late on Friday 21 May, the government finalised its in-year spending cuts after the last minister, the home secretary Theresa May, agreed to change her budget. The massive £6.25 billion reduction that they announced on Monday morning would come from a range of measures including freezing Civil Service recruitment, reducing IT spending and abolishing child trust funds. It was, however, only the first phase in the Coalition's battle to reduce spending. The next would be to revise Labour's budgets for future years. These numbers, together with a new set of tax changes, would then be announced in an emergency Budget in June.

Jeremy and Rupert Harrison joined the Prime Minister's meetings with the Chancellor in the Number 11 flat to discuss the outline of this Budget. Their first decision was how aggressive they should be in tackling the deficit, with the options ranging from getting the debt-to-GDP ratio on a declining trend through to eliminating the entire structural deficit by 2015/16. Depending on what was agreed, this would mean a fiscal adjustment of between £30 billion and £60 billion by 2014/15, on top of the £75 billion already proposed by Labour.

In these discussions the Chancellor pressed for the most ambitious of these targets, arguing that this was still less aggressive than several of the Treasury's options. Around 20 per cent of this would be delivered through tax changes, including the Treasury's long-sought increase in VAT to 20 per cent, while the remaining 80 per cent would come from additional spending reductions.

Despite the Chancellor's conviction, Jeremy was concerned about the scale of benefit reductions and cuts in departmental costs that would be required to achieve this hugely ambitious target. There was a real risk, he advised the Prime Minister, that after announcing the numbers, they would be unable to deliver them. Jeremy wasn't the only one worried. But when the target was debated in the Quad – as the meetings between the Prime Minister, Deputy Prime Minister, Chancellor and Chief Secretary were by then being called – the ambition of eliminating the structural deficit by 2015/16 was approved with relatively little debate.

In the Quad meetings that followed this decision, while Jeremy didn't again challenge the deficit target, he did try to moderate some of the cuts being proposed to achieve it because he was concerned both about hitting public sector wages too hard and whether the private sector would step in with enough investment to prevent substantial deflation. The deficit could still be reduced, he argued, if the VAT increase was phased in – and it would also be possible to do other things to help achieve the target, like restarting the privatisation programme or persuading the Ministry of Defence to take on more of the reductions, that might have less impact on the real economy.

Some of the proposed actions were softened a little through these discussions. For example, after the Deputy Prime Minister also expressed concern about raising VAT to 20 per cent, arguing that this would hit the poor hardest and could kill off the first signs of recovery, the group agreed to accompany it with an increase in bank lending. They also decided to override the Treasury's qualms and create a regional growth fund. But given the government's determination to get all the changes needed to address the deficit agreed and legislated for while the Coalition was strong, these were minor changes to a hugely aggressive plan.

One of the departments most resistant to having its administrative costs reduced in the June Budget was the Department of Work and Pensions (DWP) because, alongside implementing these reductions, it was also being expected to put in place massive welfare cuts and to create an entirely new benefit – Universal Credit. This benefit would consolidate the complex patchwork of working-age benefits and tax credits into a single payment, making it possible, its advocates argued, to ensure that people's incomes would always rise if they took a job or worked more hours. But while it was hard to disagree with the theory behind it, there were reasons why Universal Credit hadn't been attempted before, in particular the complexity of bringing together multiple IT systems containing the details of the eight million or so households affected and the cost of compensating the losers that such a transition would create.

The idea of creating Universal Credit had been around for years, but because it hadn't been in the manifestos or in the Coalition Agreement, Jeremy had been surprised when it became a Government priority. In fact, it was only after Iain Duncan Smith had become the Secretary of State for Work and Pensions at short notice following Theresa May's move to the Home Office, that he had announced his intention to bring it in.

Despite this, when Jeremy had discussed Universal Credit with Leigh Lewis, the permanent secretary of the department, shortly after the election, Leigh had assured Jeremy that it was implementable from a technical point of view. Leigh also thought the timetable was manageable so long as the policy decisions were taken in good time and HMRC's separate real-time information system, which would track people's earnings, was delivered on schedule. The political commitment to Universal Credit was also clear. As well as being backed by Iain Duncan Smith, it was supported by Oliver Letwin and – subject to the costs being confirmed – also by Rupert Harrison. In addition, while at official level the Treasury was grumbling about the cost of implementing the benefit, the Chancellor, though he was no fan of Iain Duncan Smith's, saw its theoretical attractions, and of course, welcomed the longer-term savings being promised.

Since the Prime Minister was keen to have a narrative on welfare to put alongside the one about cutting benefits, Universal Credit soon became a totemic Coalition policy. By October it was being described by Cameron in the *Financial Times* as 'one of the boldest and most radical reforms since Beveridge'. It was, however, to become one of the Coalition's biggest headaches.

After concluding all the departmental negotiations, including the one with DWP, the Chancellor announced his 'tough, but fair' emergency Budget on 22 June 2010. This was the most dramatic deficit reduction Budget ever published in peacetime Britain. In addition to increasing VAT, it proposed that £83 billion would be taken out of annual government spending by 2014/15, of which about £52 billion had already been implied in Labour's projections. If that £83 billion was achieved, the new Office for Budget Responsibility (OBR) predicted that the Chancellor would meet his target of eliminating the structural deficit by 2015/16. However, although the scale of the required cuts was clear, the Budget only detailed the source of the first £30 billion of savings, with the remaining £53 billion due to be specified in the spending review in October. But that first tranche, which included an eye-watering £11 billion cut in welfare spending and a freeze in public sector pay – already gave a good indication of what was to come.

At the end of June, Jeremy went through the first draft of the National Security Strategy, which proposed prioritising risks from international terrorism, cybercrime, major accidents and natural hazards, including severe flooding or an influenza pandemic*, and international military crises. After this was agreed, the National Security Council started trying to figure out how the Ministry of Defence, whose forward budget was already overcommitted by £38 billion, an amount similar in scale to its entire annual spend, could pivot to address these threats – and Jeremy became much more involved.

This second part of the work, the Strategic Defence and Security Review, began with a series of meetings between the Prime Minister, the Chancellor, Ed Llewellyn and Peter Ricketts to establish a common position between Number 10 and the Treasury, at least on the Conservative side of the Coalition. This was critical, not least because of the Treasury's suspicion, based on years of experience, that all prime ministers were over-generous to the military and the intelligence agencies. When the Ministry of Defence then joined the discussions, they

---

* The report said, with some foresight, that there was a 'high probability' of a pandemic occurring that could result in between 50,000 and 750,000 deaths with 'corresponding disruption to everyday life'.

tried a new ploy: claiming that the cost of the nuclear deterrent shouldn't be counted as part of their budget because it was a 'strategic asset'. After this imaginative argument was dismissed, the group started looking for ways to spend less on conventional equipment so they could increase spending on things like the cyber programme, and the debate descended into the traditional fight between the air force, army and navy over who should be hit hardest.

These weren't easy conversations. As well as streamlining personnel, several major programmes faced the axe including the decade-long plan to rebuild the ageing Nimrod maritime patrol aircraft. Having already absorbed almost £4 billion, this was still not close to completion and there was increasing doubt that Nimrods would ever be effective. But the most difficult issue was left to almost the end of their discussions – did it make sense to spend more than £5 billion on the two new aircraft carriers that Gordon Brown had ordered back in 2008?

'Is it true,' Jeremy asked Peter Ricketts, 'that we don't have any aircraft that can land on the carriers even if we decide to build them?'

Peter nodded. To save costs, in addition to the Nimrod programme, one of the Ministry's fleets of fast jets needed to be scrapped. Jock Stirrup, the chief of the defence staff who was about to retire, was fighting to protect the Tornado fleet – which he used to fly – over the Harriers, arguing that their superior range made them useful in Afghanistan. But Tornados, unlike Harriers, couldn't land on aircraft carriers.

'So, what would we put on the aircraft carriers?'

'Ahh,' Peter said. 'Well, we were going to order the new Harrier-style F-35B jump jets, which can land and take off vertically. That's what the carriers were designed to carry.'

'Were?'

'Yes. The secretary of state now wants to switch to the F-35Cs, because they have greater range and can carry more weapons …'

'Okay.'

'… but if we do, we'll have to change the design of the carriers because the F-35Cs need catapults and arrestor traps to take off. They say this will be cost neutral because the F-35Cs are cheaper, but the planes won't be available in quantity until after 2020.'

'So, we'll have aircraft carriers with no planes on them for at least four years,' Jeremy said shaking his head.

Jeremy often played devil's advocate when it came to decisions like this. 'Is this a horse and tank moment?' he asked the department when they came in to discuss the F-35Cs. 'Wouldn't it be better if we invested in unmanned aircraft rather than in old technology? And is there any guarantee the new carriers will remain invulnerable to attack from anti-carrier missiles?'

But despite Jeremy's questioning, the Prime Minister and Chancellor were keen to confirm the carriers – and they accepted the department's plea to switch to the F-35Cs.

With this intent clear, Jeremy was tasked with finding a way to squeeze these purchases into the department's budget. He worked on this with Richard Freer, the new Number 10 defence adviser, and James Quinault, the Treasury's uncompromising defence team leader. They reviewed the budget line by line, looking for ways to free up resources, for example by speeding up the sale of spare land and unwanted radio spectrum, reducing the number of civilians employed and renegotiating contracts with the main defence suppliers. It was painstaking work, particularly because the Prime Minister had limited the amount by which the front-line forces could be shrunk. But the cost gap began to close, at least over the period of the spending review to 2014/15.

Alongside this review of the defence budget, Jeremy was also still working with Peter Ricketts to try to find a way to handle the lawsuits launched by the Guantanamo Bay detainees. After spending many hours exploring the options, including almost daily sessions with the Prime Minister and Deputy Prime Minister, Jeremy and Peter concluded that the only way for the government to avoid going to court was for them to negotiate an individual settlement with each detainee. They also recommended that the independent inquiry into Guantanamo Bay that had been proposed by both the Conservatives and Liberal Democrats before the election should go ahead as soon as the legal issues were settled.*

* Theresa May later decided that this inquiry was not needed.

Jeremy and Ciaran Martin, who was by then the director of security and intelligence, discussed these recommendations with the Prime Minister during his train journey up to Bradford to attend the first Cabinet awayday at the end of June. David Cameron was predictably unhappy, but Jeremy advised him that this was the only feasible way to address the issue. And after a lengthy debate, the Prime Minister agreed – the first time he'd shown his trust in the Civil Service on such a significant topic. When the train stopped at Leeds, Ciaran jumped off to write up the final conclusions at a workstation in the Department of Work and Pensions so they could review them on their way back down to London.

A few days later, on Tuesday 6 July, the Prime Minister announced these decisions, and that Friday, Jeremy sent the team implementing them an email to check how they were getting on. This was, as Whitehall knew, Jeremy's usual style. In fact, his 'where are we on this?' – or WAWOT – emails, had become something of a trademark. But on this occasion, the reply he received from Paul Jenkins, the usually jovial Treasury solicitor, was terse. 'Voluntary resolution of a dispute with sixteen angry individuals who've been detained without trial in Cuba in orange jumpsuits is likely to take longer than four days,' Paul informed Jeremy.

Jeremy smiled – and decided on this occasion to give the team a month before checking in again.

36

'(Nice Dream)':
A policy innovation machine

June–October 2010

In the early months of the Coalition, Jeremy had also been spending time with Steve Hilton and Rohan Silva. Steve and Rohan's 'compassionate Conservatism' themes – which included decentralisation, families, the Big Society and transparency – had been developed early on in David Cameron's leadership of the Conservative Party, well before the financial crisis had shifted the focus to the deficit. Compassionate Conservatism now sat somewhat uneasily alongside financial austerity, but Jeremy was still excited about having Steve and Rohan in the building since they were radical thinkers, unencumbered by Civil Service history, and the Prime Minister listened to their views.

'Copy me into all your emails and I'll try to help,' Jeremy had told Rohan shortly after his arrival in Downing Street, 'and I'll also get you and Steve along to one of Gus's Wednesday morning meetings so you can tell the permanent secretaries about these ideas yourselves.'

Jeremy had followed through on these promises, sending emails around Whitehall to drum up enthusiasm for Steve and Rohan's ideas and endorsing their proposals with his colleagues. But it was soon clear that progress was being hampered by both the nebulous nature of their agenda and Whitehall's resistance to novelty. Jeremy, therefore, decided to convene a series of discussions in Number 10's subterranean video-conference room on the different themes, hoping that the setting, which resembled a long-neglected municipal office in Slough, would inject momentum into the proceedings.

Unfortunately, however, for once the idea of bringing people together from across Whitehall to focus on a topic that the Prime Minister cared about largely failed. While the meetings on decentralisation initially made progress, the ideas fell apart under steady fire from the Treasury since the Chancellor couldn't see why, after having only recently gained power, the government would want to give it away. The families agenda, which was similarly ill-defined beyond Steve's view that all government policies should be tested for family-friendliness, also ran into quicksand. So, at Jeremy's suggestion, various reviews were launched, covering matters like urban regeneration, deregulation and child poverty, in the hope that these would unearth some policies that Whitehall could implement.

But for many people, Jeremy included, the most intriguing part of Steve and Rohan's agenda was the Big Society. The idea of giving communities additional powers and encouraging people to be more active in their local areas sounded promising. However, Jeremy also found it hard to help Steve and Rohan make progress on this since there were few details of how it would work beyond a proposal to create a National Citizenship Service for sixteen-year-olds and appoint local community organisers.

All of this meant that the only part of Steve and Rohan's agenda where Jeremy felt confident about making progress was their push for greater transparency. He, therefore, helped them draft a feisty letter for the Prime Minister to send out around Whitehall on this, which declared that the new default for public sector financial, resource and procurement data was to publish it, and listed, by department, what had to be released. After that Jeremy sat back and waited for his colleagues to respond, while encouraging Steve and Rohan to keep working on ideas that could more easily be turned into policy.

By late June, the other issue that had landed on Jeremy's desk was a proposal by Andrew Lansley, the new Secretary of State for Health, to reform the National Health Service. Unlike Universal Credit, this policy had been hinted at in the Conservative manifesto and in a few speeches before the election – and some of its aims had even been included in the Coalition Agreement. Jeremy, therefore, understood the broad intent of Andrew's changes, which was to push decision-making on health provision down to local communities and to take politicians out of the day-to-day management of the NHS. But in the frenetic early weeks of the new government, he hadn't had time to get underneath the jargon to understand the detail of what was involved.

For this reason, it wasn't until Andrew circulated a draft of his White Paper that Jeremy realised the scale of his vision. Despite the government's pledge in the Coalition Agreement to 'stop the top-down reorganisations of the NHS', and the fact that – following the huge funding increase that it had received under New Labour – public satisfaction with the NHS was high, Andrew was planning to launch the most radical overhaul of its structure and incentives in its 63-year history. At the centre of this was a proposal to separate the job of defining what the health service needed to deliver from the oversight of that delivery. Oversight would be carried out by a new NHS Commissioning Board, which would commission specialist services at national level, while clinical commissioning groups, made up of local doctors, would arrange services in local communities.

When Jeremy went through the White Paper, he struggled to see what the issue was that this scale of change was trying to fix. And even if there was something to resolve, he couldn't see how a solution that handed decisions on issues like closing hospitals to an arm's-length body would ever be politically acceptable. But although he knew that Chris Wormald and Gus were also concerned about the White Paper, Jeremy wasn't aware of any other unease within government until issues were raised at a rare meeting of the Coalition Committee in early July.

Unfortunately, Andrew wasn't at this meeting, so the questions posed by the Chancellor, foreign secretary William Hague and others about the political purpose of the reforms, how the financial controls would work, and the amount of power being handed to local doctors, went unanswered. When he later heard about it, Andrew was reportedly furious. He told his colleagues that they already knew his plans – and in one sense, they did, though Jeremy suspected he wasn't the only one who felt baffled whenever Andrew talked about the outcomes framework, primary care trusts and health and wellbeing boards.

When Andrew's White Paper was published on 12 July 2010, many commentators, including the King's Fund and the Nuffield Trust, also pointed out the scale of the change and the disruption it might cause. This did little to quell Jeremy, Gus and Chris's concerns so, through July and early August, they held a series of meetings with the Department of Health to try to find ways to soften the measures while still achieving Andrew's objectives. They also attempted to alert the Treasury to the financial risk that was being created by handing billions of pounds of spending to local doctors.

These discussions, however, achieved little. Andrew was set in his views and many of the special advisers and politicians, including the Prime Minister and Chancellor, had known him for many years and were unwilling to challenge his vision. At official level, the department was also reluctant to take on its new secretary of state partly because it remembered being accused by Labour after the 1997 election of being unwilling to let go of Margaret Thatcher's health agenda.

'But what about Number 10?' I asked Jeremy when he told me all this.

'There's little health expertise left in Downing Street,' Jeremy said, shaking his head, 'so we are finding it hard to mount a challenge. In any case, Steve Hilton likes Andrew's reforms because they align with his transparency and decentralisation agendas and so does Oliver Letwin, even though he normally agrees with my advice. Even the Lib Dems seem content to go along with the reforms because they want to show that the Coalition can make change happen.'

'So, what will you do now?'

'I'll raise it with the Prime Minister one more time, but I fear we're going to get a bill containing a very pure form of Lansleyism.'

After our summer break in northern Greece, Jeremy spent that autumn trying to get some of the Coalition's policies implemented, particularly those needed to tackle the deficit. By this time, though he was still working hard, Jeremy's hours had settled back into a more normal pattern – which was good because I was approaching the final promotion hurdle at McKinsey, which would take me from partner to senior partner. If I cleared this, I would be one of only a handful of women to reach that level in the fifty years that McKinsey had been in the UK.

That autumn, Jeremy was also helping to finalise the Treasury's spending review, in which they still needed to identify more than £50 billion of savings without reducing funding for the NHS, overseas aid and pensioners' benefits, all of which the government was determined to protect. With so much ringfenced, the remaining choices were limited, which meant that Jeremy was worried about how the next wave of cuts would impact the welfare and criminal justice systems.

With the search on for acceptable cuts, Steve Hilton decided to crowd-source ideas from public sector workers. There was a degree of cynicism about this in Whitehall, but when Steve sent out his emails, thousands of people responded. The Chancellor was shown the best two hundred ideas that emerged from this process and prioritised twenty. The exercise was was so successful that Steve and Rohan decided to create a Facebook page titled the 'Treasury Spending Challenge' to open it up to the whole country. This, however, turned out to be a step too far – the page attracted substantial abuse, and when a rival page featuring a goat was set up, it fast gained more followers.

Jeremy laughed when he told me this. 'If you're going to innovate,' he said, 'you have to accept that not everything will work. And good luck to the goat.'

Unfortunately, the thorny issue of defence costs, which also needed to be settled as part of the spending review, was probably even beyond the goat. Jeremy, Richard Freer and James Quinault had narrowed the gap between the Treasury and the Ministry of Defence's figures earlier in the year, but Nick Clegg and Danny Alexander, who had by then replaced David Laws as Chief Secretary, continued to think that the department was getting off lightly.

They also still needed to take a decision on aircraft carriers. Jeremy continued to find it hard to believe that buying two of these at vast cost was the best use of the defence budget, but Liam Fox, Secretary of State for Defence, was keen, and when Jeremy explored the option of cancelling them, it became clear it wasn't viable. HMS *Queen*

Elizabeth was already two-thirds built, and although HMS *Prince of Wales* was still on the drawing board, BAE Systems said that the charges for cancelling it were higher than the costs of going ahead – and halting the work would also destroy thousands of jobs. The Prime Minister, therefore, decided to build both carriers but to mothball the *Prince of Wales* once it was finished until it was needed. He also agreed to redesign both of them to include the catapults and arrestor traps needed for F-35C aircraft, having been assured again that this would be cost neutral.

The Strategic Defence and Security Review, which was published on 19 October 2010, included these decisions as well as the team's conclusions on the future size, shape and structure of the armed forces. In addition, after a painful last-minute haggle over the final tens of millions between the Prime Minister and Liam Fox – which had only been concluded after Jeremy convinced the Treasury that a 7.51 per cent budget cut could be rounded up to 8 per cent – it also settled the Ministry of Defence's budget for the following four years.

The 2010 spending review, which was announced the following day, outlined £52 billion of public spending cuts. In addition to the savings that had emerged from the Strategic Defence and Security Review, these reductions would be achieved by abolishing nearly half a million public sector jobs, raising the retirement age, cutting the budgets of unprotected departments by an average of 19 per cent over four years and shrinking the welfare budget by another £7 billion on top of the £11 billion proposed in June.

'It is a hard road,' the Chancellor told the House of Commons, 'but it leads to a better future.'

Ed Miliband, who'd recently beaten his brother David to become leader of the Labour Party, in response accused the government of taking 'the biggest gamble in a generation' with growth, jobs and livelihoods.

Despite the chanting protesters who crowded the end of Downing Street after the Chancellor's statement, Jeremy shared George Osborne's view that action was needed. After all, public sector debt was at its highest point since the Second World War, and without action, the OBR was predicting that it would reach almost 75 per cent of GDP by 2014/15. However, he continued to worry about how the public sector would absorb the huge cuts being proposed and that the pace of the spending reductions could cause the economy to stall.

After David Cameron returned from his first party conference as Prime Minister in October 2010, Andrew Lansley came into Downing Street to discuss his health reforms one final time. When he left, both Oliver Letwin and Danny Alexander declared their support for the changes, while Jeremy, Gus and Chris Wormald again raised their concerns. It was rare for the Civil Service to lock horns with ministers on such a fundamental government policy, but in this case, they were determined to make their reservations clear before a decision was taken.

At the end of another painful discussion, which was exacerbated by the complexity of the changes, the Prime Minister sighed before asking Oliver and Danny to review the thinking again. This was unpopular because it meant delaying the legislation. And though well intended, it ultimately achieved little because, although Jeremy and Chris kept suggesting ways to moderate the reforms, Andrew Lansley made it clear that he had no intention of changing his proposals in the absence of any explicit demands from the Prime Minister. Therefore, when Oliver and Danny reported back to David Cameron, it was decided that the department should keep working on the legislation while Number 10 focused on handling what was likely to be a difficult transition.

When Jeremy told me all this, I shook my head. 'Surely you can't let the bill proceed if you don't think the reforms will work?'

He shrugged. 'Sometimes you get to a point where you have to stop raising objections. If a minister prioritises a policy and has the Prime Minister's backing, then it's the Civil Service's job to make the best of it.'

Jeremy let the health reforms run after that, although they would, of course, become a priority again later. In the meantime, he turned his mind to another familiar, though no less controversial, issue – tuition fees for university students. In their manifesto, the Liberal Democrats had pledged to resist any attempt to raise these. But in one of its final acts before the election, Labour had launched an independent review of higher education funding, and when the report from this came out in October 2010, it said there was no evidence that tuition fees deterred poorer students from going on to higher education. It, therefore, recommended removing the cap on fees and letting universities charge whatever they wanted while expecting those that charged the most to show how they were widening access.

Jeremy was pleased by this endorsement of tuition fees given the role that he'd played in putting them in place. Despite this, he believed – as did most of the Prime Minister's other advisers – that removing the cap entirely risked charges spiralling out of control, even if poorer students received support. He did, however, see a case for raising the cap, as did the Prime Minister, though it seemed impossible for the Liberal Democrats to support this given their manifesto promise. For a while Jeremy assumed the issue would be deadlocked, but David Cameron was determined to act. And in the end, after asking Jeremy to look again at a graduate tax, and Jeremy having once more laid out why it wouldn't work, Nick Clegg agreed.

'But why?' I asked Jeremy.

'He's always been against his party's policy on tuition fees, which he tried to change before the election. And the case for raising the cap is clear,' Jeremy said.

I nodded. Higher education needed more funding, and if it didn't come from students, it would have to come from taxpayers, many of whom hadn't enjoyed the benefits of going to university themselves. The government was also increasing maintenance grants for poorer students to soften the blow. However, we both knew that none of these arguments would deter the students who were already descending on Whitehall to burn Nick Clegg's effigy.

37

'Karma Police':
The Civil Service's values

October 2010–March 2011

In the autumn of 2010, Jeremy's father's health declined, and in late October, he held our hands and smiled before closing his eyes for a final time. This is not the place to recount the hours we spent with Peter leading up to that moment, or the grief Jeremy felt at losing him. Perhaps it is enough to mention the eulogy, rich in love and memories, that Jeremy drafted in the days afterwards. His father had been, Jeremy wrote, 'a private person with simple tastes, intensely devoted to his loving family while also being fascinated by the great political and national events of the day, acutely observed and sharply critiqued from the vantage point of his beloved and increasingly ragged armchair'. And I knew how much Jeremy would miss all that, together with Peter's intense interest and pride in every aspect of Jeremy and Simon's lives.

On our way back to Jeremy's childhood home in York in the early hours of the morning after Peter passed away, his mother Brenda said she wanted to come and live with us in London. We said 'yes' – we were flattered that she wanted to be part of our lives and delighted that Jonny, Lizzie and Peter would get to know her better. But the prospect of Brenda's arrival was also daunting since I was still working long hours at McKinsey and it was becoming increasingly clear to Jeremy how challenging it was going to be to implement many of the Coalition's policies.

* * *

The effort that it was taking to set up the new Efficiency and Reform Group (ERG) in the Cabinet Office was a good illustration of these challenges. After the election, Francis Maude, the new Minister for the Cabinet Office and the Paymaster General, had taken up with relish the task of making the Civil Service more efficient. Alongside freezing all external recruitment and hauling suppliers in one by one to tell them that the government's procurement processes were going to be toughened up, Francis had set up the ERG in the Cabinet Office. Into this went the Treasury's 800-strong Office of Government Commerce, which supervised the purchase of more than £60 billion of products and services each year, the Government Digital Service, which oversaw Whitehall's 750 different websites and other digital activities, and a new Major Projects Authority, which would monitor the delivery of the government's most significant projects.

Jeremy was enthusiastic about the ERG, partly because it was planning to implement many of the ideas that had been developed by the *Smarter Government* team before the election. However, his enthusiasm wasn't shared by many of his permanent secretary colleagues, who worried about the disempowerment of their functional heads and the possible outsourcing, or even mutualisation, of their back-office functions.

The real difficulties with the ERG emerged, however, when it tried to impose its agenda on departments that were already struggling to deliver other major Coalition policies. This is why DWP, which was still trying to implement a slew of benefit reforms, found it so challenging. It wasn't long before Francis began complaining to Jeremy about the 'fortress mentality' that Robert Devereux, the new permanent secretary of DWP, was creating. However, Robert told Jeremy a different story. The risk was, he said, that for the sake of saving a few tens of millions in back-office costs, he might jeopardise billions in welfare savings. And since all his staff belonged to the same union, if some went on strike, they might take everyone else with them. But while Jeremy had some sympathy with this, he still urged Robert to cooperate because there was a risk of the entire ERG agenda stalling if the largest departments found excuses to opt out.

* * *

Despite accepting the need to increase efficiency within Whitehall, Jeremy was, however, still worrying about the impact of austerity on the real economy – so much so that, before Christmas 2010, he suggested a new set of measures to encourage growth to the Prime Minister, including further reducing the headline corporation tax rate, decreasing the capital gains tax paid by serial entrepreneurs and lifting personal allowances.

In February 2011, Jeremy's advice on this was followed by a note from Jonathan Portes, the chief economist in the Cabinet Office. But while Jeremy had suggested measures that would sit alongside the austerity programme, Jonathan challenged it head on and proposed switching to a more gradualist approach to reducing costs. When the Prime Minister received Jonathan's paper, he sent it on to the Chancellor, who was furious about this challenge to a core Coalition policy – and became even more so when its contents were leaked to the press. Jonathan's paper – which was soon dubbed the 'Plan B memo', in a cheeky reference to the Conservatives' Plan A austerity programme – was never discussed again. However, while never directly challenging Plan A himself, Jeremy did continue to advocate measures to stimulate the economy within its constraints.

Throughout 2010, Jeremy also continued to worry about the capabilities that Downing Street had lost after the election. The impact of this had been particularly clear when they'd tried to mount a challenge to Andrew Lansley's health reforms, but it was also affecting Downing Street's ability to work out whether Whitehall was effectively implementing the Coalition's priorities and to intervene when it wasn't. In the absence of a Delivery Unit, Jeremy had tried to use the Coalition's departmental business plans as a chasing device, but this had proved relatively ineffective in getting departments to act.

It took a crisis at the end of 2010 before the Prime Minister at last changed his view of the resources needed in Number 10. The trigger for this was the announcement by the Department for the Environment, Food and Rural Affairs of its intention to sell off large swathes of the UK's woodlands. This unleashed a surge of protest, with over half a million people signing a petition against what the

Guardian described as an attempt to 'asset strip' the nation's natural heritage. The policy was embarrassing for the Prime Minister, not least because it was at odds with his promise to create the 'greenest government ever'. In fact, after a tense Coalition negotiation, which Jeremy had helped resolve, the government was about to publish its fourth Carbon Budget setting out the next stage in the UK's path to achieving its target for reducing greenhouse gases.

With outrage over the woodlands policy continuing to mount, the Prime Minister called James O'Shaughnessy and Jeremy into his office. 'Why didn't the Policy Unit stop this policy before it was announced?' he asked James.

'We didn't know about it – my unit is far too small to track what's going on in every department,' James said – happily unprompted by Jeremy.

'Well, we need to make your team bigger,' the Prime Minister said.

'We can certainly do that, Prime Minister,' Jeremy said with some enthusiasm. And after that, they took the Policy Unit back up to ten to fifteen staff, which at least meant that, in the future, they were more likely to get advance warning about difficult issues, even if they still had limited capacity to sort them out.

The other team that they strengthened that autumn was the one in Nick Clegg's private office. Despite his huge brief, the office supporting the Deputy Prime Minister was smaller than those of most secretaries of state – an unintentional oversight that reflected the Civil Service's lack of experience of supporting a coalition government. Although it had taken far too long for this issue to be recognised, when it did become clear, Gus expanded the team and appointed Chris Wormald to be Nick Clegg's senior adviser, mirroring Jeremy's role for the Prime Minister.

We arrived back from our Christmas break in early 2011 ready to begin unpacking the first of Brenda's many boxes of archaeology books ahead of her arrival in Balham. Meanwhile, in Downing Street, they were coming to terms with an equally significant exit.

Rumours about phone hacking at the *News of the World* had been building for several years after Clive Goodman, its misnamed royal affairs editor, had been jailed in 2007 for breaking into the voicemail messages of Prince Harry and other members of the royal family. Now more people were coming forward to say they'd been the victims of phone hacking – including Gordon Brown, who'd asked Gus before the election if there was enough evidence to commission an inquiry.

Andy Coulson, the Prime Minister's director of communications, had been the editor of the *News of the World* while phone hacking had been taking place, but had always denied any knowledge of it. His position on this was, however, being increasingly challenged, particularly by a long piece in the *New York Times* the previous September. At that point the Prime Minister had taken no action, again accepting Andy's assurances that the allegations were untrue, but in January 2011, when the police began a new investigation, the noise about Andy became unmanageable and he handed in his resignation.

This first loss from the close group of advisers that had entered Number 10 back in May 2010 was a personal blow for the Prime Minister and also a political blow, since it raised questions over his judgement in appointing Andy.

Most other people in Downing Street, Jeremy included, were sorry to see Andy go, with the exception of Steve Hilton, who'd never liked Andy's focus on the tabloids. In the aftermath of Andy's departure, Steve seemed reinvigorated, returning with enthusiasm to his thinking on the Big Society. This became the basis for the Prime Minister's speech at Somerset House on 14 February, in which he announced the creation of Big Society Capital, which would invest in social enterprises, together with a mechanism to allow people to donate to charities through cashpoint machines, the creation of a National Citizen Service for teenagers and 5,000 Big Society community organisers.

Jeremy was keen to make maximum use of Steve's new momentum so he stepped in to help put together several elements of this plan, including recycling various earlier initiatives such as Ronald Cohen's Reclaim Fund, which they used to fund Big Society Capital. Steve and Rohan's enthusiasm about Jeremy's contribution might explain an article in the *Economist* that came out at about the same time hailing Jeremy as an 'unsung radical'.

Despite all this effort, however, progress on most of the rest of Steve and Rohan's agenda was still slow. As a result, Steve's enthusiasm soon began to fade and he took to walking around Number 10 in his socks, saying George Osborne had excluded him from the meetings of the Quad and people didn't understand the Big Society. Steve was right, but however difficult his views were to translate into tangible actions, Jeremy still believed the government would be poorer without his radicalism. He was, therefore, determined to keep trying to help.

38

'Viva La Vida':
The Coalition's durability

March–June 2011

By March 2011, Brenda had settled into our basement, the children had welcomed her into our world, and I was helping sort through the mass of documents she had brought with her on her family history and her archaeological research. I was worried, though, that something was wrong – Brenda was getting upset about small issues, like losing pairs of scissors, and kept forgetting where her new bedroom was. But moving to London had been a major change in her life, particularly so soon after being widowed, so we assumed these difficulties would pass.

At work Jeremy was again worrying about defence issues after the UK's decision, on Tuesday 19 March 2011, to help establish a NATO-led coalition to try to end attacks by Colonel Gaddafi against rebels in Libya. Reaching this decision had been a scramble because applying the lessons learnt from the Iraq war meant arranging a Cabinet meeting at short notice to review the legal advice before the Prime Minister could make a statement to the House of Commons. The decision also revealed some of the limitations of the previous year's National Security Strategy, which hadn't prioritised such humanitarian interventions.

They also, of course, no longer had a working aircraft carrier.

'If we hadn't mothballed the *Ark Royal*, we would have put it north of Libya in the Mediterranean,' Mark Stanhope, the First Sea Lord, told the Prime Minister. 'Instead we'll have to fly Tornados down from southern Italy, which will be more costly and riskier because we'll need to refuel in the air.'

Jeremy raised his eyebrows at this, and glanced over at Richard Freer. Despite the department's indignation about the previous cuts imposed on its budget, which had necessitated mothballing the Arc Royal, they needed to go through its numbers again because, beyond 2014, they still didn't add up.

This time when Jeremy, Richard and James Quinault went through the defence budget, the options for reducing costs were far more limited. However, one possibility did emerge, which was to take up the recommendation from a recent review of expanding the size of the Territorial Army, which in turn would allow them to reduce the size of the conventional army. They also brought forward to 2019 the date for taking Jock Stirrup's beloved Tornados out of service. When these measures were combined with giving the department a 1 per cent per annum real-terms increase through to 2020, the defence budget shuddered into balance for the first time in a decade. And when they also included military pensions in the figures, as other countries already did, this settlement maintained the UK's defence spending at above 2 per cent of GDP – an important NATO target.

This, of course, wasn't the end of the issue. Like all budgets, the defence numbers would continue to require regular maintenance. Jeremy also later had to chase up some of the actions they'd agreed, including sending Will Cavendish, the head of the Implementation Unit, out to interview reservists around the country in the spring of 2013 to find out what was delaying the expansion of the Territorial Army. Jeremy and Will presented the findings from this assessment to the military top brass when they turned up, resplendent in their regalia, to say that the work was on schedule.

Jeremy shook his head when they gave the Prime Minister this assurance. For the expansion to happen on time, he said, four separate ambitions would have to be achieved. And given the progress that had been made, that was like expecting four aces to be dealt first in a pack of cards. Which was never going to happen, was it?

In April 2011 we took the children to celebrate Prince William's marriage to Kate Middleton at David Cameron's surreal but joyous street party in Downing Street, which came complete with bunting, a brass band, a royal blue ice-cream cart and occasional glimpses of spring sunshine. After that, Jeremy returned again to the issue of Andrew Lansley's elaborate NHS reforms. By this point these had been transformed into a complex bill, which at 550 pages was three times the length of the legislation originally used to establish the NHS. There was still, however, little sign of any enthusiasm for the changes outside the department. In fact, Philip Stephens, the *Financial Times*' political columnist, was claiming they could become Cameron's poll tax, and Andrew Cooper, Number 10's new strategy director, told the Prime Minister they had the potential to undo years of work to detoxify the Tories on the NHS.

It wasn't yet time to fight Andrew's reforms again, Jeremy told me, but he did decide to reinforce his team by appointing a new health adviser in the Policy Unit. His lead candidate for this was Paul Bate, who'd been in the Delivery Unit before leaving government to set up a consulting firm.

'So what do you think of the Health and Social Care Bill?' Jeremy asked Paul at the end of their interview.

'It's doomed,' Paul said.

After Paul left, Jeremy turned to Chris Wormald, who'd joined him for the interview. 'I can't appoint Paul just because he thinks Andrew Lansley's bill is heading for disaster,' he said.

Chris raised his eyebrows.

Jeremy chewed the end of his pen. 'Why am I saying that? Of course I can – the man's a genius!'

The Health and Social Care Bill limped along for several more weeks before the Liberal Democrats' spring conference in March delivered the knockout blow by passing a motion calling for the reforms to be changed. Despite being widely disliked, however, the reforms had so much political momentum, and so much had already been altered at local level, that it was impossible to stop them entirely.

'But what you could do,' Gus and Jeremy advised the Prime Minister, 'is pause the bill to give everyone time to think.'

After some thought, the Prime Minister agreed with this – though he remained reluctant to criticise the changes. On 31 March he called Andrew Lansley and Nick Clegg into Number 10 for a private meeting, and when everyone else, including Jeremy, filed in an hour later, he said they were halting the legislation.

Andrew was sitting on the sofa shaking his head. 'Surely you don't mean we should stop the next round of the GP consortia expressions of interest?' he said.

Jeremy held his breath.

'I'm not sure I even know what that means,' the Prime Minister said, 'but yes, everything will stop.'

Andrew announced the pause in the House of Commons on Monday 4 April 2011 to jeers from Labour. And Jeremy told a pale-looking Paul Bate, who'd started work in Number 10 on the same day, that he would be in charge of negotiating a new version of the reforms with the Department of Health.

'It is, at last, an opportunity to change the proposals,' Jeremy told me with some enthusiasm that evening. But his optimism waned over the following days as it became clear that, although most people outside Andrew's circle hated the bill, there was no consensus about how to change it. The things Jeremy found intriguing – like increasing competition between health providers to drive up performance, promoting patient choice and ensuring clear political and financial accountability – were of little interest to most Tory MPs and weren't a meaningful part of the reforms. Indeed, many wanted to remove the NHS from the existing half-baked competition regime, reinforcing the position of the incumbent NHS hospitals. In addition, perhaps because the reforms had been developed over a long time in opposition, their main focus was on the historic problem of reducing waiting lists. They, therefore, did little to address more recent concerns like the dysfunctional relationship between the free, but expensive, care delivered in hospitals and the means-tested social care provided in the community.

David Cameron asked Jeremy to chair a weekly meeting to oversee the changes to the Health and Social Care Bill during the pause while the Department of Health created a 'Future Forum' to gather views from across the sector. Jeremy found these weekly meetings painful because the officials and advisers from the Department of Health spent them fighting for the purity of their original proposals while Jeremy, Chris and Paul tried to modify the most controversial elements. But by the end of the spring, Jeremy was able to tell the Prime Minister that, though he believed the reforms were still a missed opportunity, he thought they'd done enough to get the bill approved.

On 7 June 2011 David Cameron ended the pause and the bill resumed its legislative journey, clearing the Commons on 7 September and heading for the upper house. This second stage of its passage was no easier than the first, particularly after four hundred doctors wrote to the Lords urging them to reject the bill. But Jeremy was largely able to leave its management to the Lords whips and to Freddie Howe, the Department of Health minister in the Lords. Many twists and turns later, to an ongoing chorus of discontent from health professionals, with one small group of protesters chaining themselves to the gates at the end of Downing Street, the Health and Social Care Act received royal assent on 27 March 2012.

It had been a long and painful journey to approve a set of reforms for which few people had any enthusiasm. Indeed it had been so traumatic, Jeremy told me, that he doubted anyone would propose any significant new health legislation for at least a decade – a prediction that turned out to be remarkably accurate.

During the health debate, another piece of policy had been proposed that also made Jeremy uncomfortable. But this time, though he shared his frustration with me, he didn't attempt to intervene. The interim Vickers Report, published in April 2011, considered how, in the wake of the financial crisis, Britain should change the regulation of its banks. Its answer was far more profound than Jeremy had expected. In future, the universal banks – those that undertook wholesale, investment and retail banking – should ring-fence their UK retail operations from the rest of their activities to protect savers and small businesses.

Jeremy agreed the banks needed to be strengthened. He'd watched the financial crisis at close quarters, and in retrospect, had been amazed at how bankers' pay packages had soared while their institutions had taken on more debt and risky investments, with few of the benefits flowing through to shareholders. But rather than designing a bureaucratic and bespoke UK regime to address these issues, he would have toughened up the leverage and capital requirements for the banks while conducting regular stress tests to ensure the system could withstand major shocks. But there was little he could do about the Vickers Report because it was supported by both sides of the Coalition and because, with his investment banking background, he risked appearing partisan.

Until early 2011, although the Coalition had needed to deal with many controversial issues, there had been relatively little tension between the Conservatives and the Liberal Democrats. This all changed, however, in mid-February when the polls started to indicate that Liberal Democrats might win their cherished referendum on the alternative vote. In response, the cross-party, though heavily Conservative, 'No2AV' campaign launched adverts showing third-placed jockeys going on to win and put up posters suggesting that babies' and soldiers' lives would be put at risk if the voting system changed. As the vote neared, the claims became bolder. By April the Prime Minister was calling the alternative vote 'crazy' and 'undemocratic' and the No2AV campaign was saying it would cost £250 million to change the voting system – a figure the Chancellor refused to deny.

The tension this created within the Coalition exploded on 3 May when Chris Huhne, the Liberal Democrat energy secretary, marched into Cabinet and threw a stack of No campaign leaflets on the table. On the front of them was a picture of Nick Clegg holding up a sign saying he wouldn't vote for tuition fees. 'AV will lead to more broken promises,' read the caption underneath.

'Did George know about these?' Chris Huhne demanded. 'And will you sack whoever approved them?'

'This is a ministerial meeting, not some sub-Jeremy Paxman interview on *Newsnight*,' George Osborne retorted.

'I'm only responsible for the No campaign being run by the Conservative Party, not the all-party No2AV Campaign,' David Cameron said, shaking his head.

Jeremy studied his notebook. At least, he thought, they only had two more days to survive before the polls opened.

The electorate's verdict when the vote took place on Thursday 5 May was at least clear – though it wasn't good news for the Liberal Democrats. On a turnout of 42 per cent, they rejected the alternative vote system by 68 per cent to 32 per cent, and on the same day, the Liberal Democrats lost 748 of their council seats in the local elections, while the Conservatives gained 86.

The aftermath of these results was immediately noticeable within Downing Street. Coalition relationships became more transactional, and the business of governing more edgy. But because there was no appetite on either side of the Coalition for a general election, work continued on the policies outlined in the Coalition Agreement. The Fixed-Term Parliaments Bill also continued making its way through the House of Commons – although, in the aftermath of the referendum on the alternative vote, it had morphed from an orderly fantasy dreamt up in the heady days of coalition formation into a useful safeguard against a disorderly divorce.

39

'Life On Mars?':
Policies others neglect

June–September 2011

Far away from the limelight of these big political dramas, Jeremy was working on a host of far less prominent policies. He sometimes told me that he felt he made the most difference when he worked on these because at least some of them wouldn't happen without his backing.

Given Jeremy's concern about the economy, he was pursuing several initiatives focused on stimulating growth. These included a 'help to buy' scheme that Jeremy was developing with Paul Kirby, the new head of the Policy Unit, which would assist people who were acquiring their first homes or purchasing newly built properties. Although Paul had once been seconded to the Conservative Party, he was by this time a civil servant, so his appointment to replace James O'Shaughnessy symbolised the Prime Minister's intent, despite the dramas of the alternative vote, for the Policy Unit to continue working for both sides of the Coalition.

Although the Policy Unit was helpful in working up new policies like the Help to Buy scheme, in the centre of government the number of groups generating new ideas had again proliferated, with ideas also being generated by Steve and Rohan, by Oliver Letwin and by the Treasury. This time, however, there was more division between the different parties than there had been back in 2001, with Steve complaining that Paul wasn't copying him into papers and Paul struggling to accommodate Steve's radical thinking.

While Jeremy was keen to resolve these overlaps, he knew the Prime Minister wasn't ready to act. So, while he bided his time, he did his best to digest the output of these different teams, sitting in the Cabinet Office's basement café ploughing through papers while drinking coffee and munching one of the packets of crisps that I'd banned years before on health grounds.

In June 2011 Jeremy did, however, meet Steve and Rohan to try to at least get their bulging portfolio of initiatives under control.

'We've already got them down from forty to ten,' Rohan said, brandishing a list that included open public services, mayors, Somerset House, marketing Britain, Tech City, the pharmaceutical industry and sex trafficking.

Although these topics were all admirable and interesting, there was little or no connection between them. 'We've made a start on most of these,' Jeremy said, 'but we might make more progress if we concentrated on a couple and came back to the others later.'

After some debate, Rohan and Steve agreed to reduce their list with Rohan keen to make Tech City, a new hub for entrepreneurs in east London, one of their priorities. This hub would be accompanied by a set of policy changes to make life easier for start-ups, including additional tax incentives for angel and tech investors and a fast-track visa system for entrepreneurs.

Steve and Rohan were also both determined to continue their work on open public services. The next step on this was to prepare a second tranche of letters for the Prime Minister to send out to departments ahead of the publication of a White Paper. Jeremy worked with Rohan and Tim Kelsey, the new director of open data and transparency in the Cabinet Office, to prepare these. Given Tim's background as the CEO of Dr Foster, a company that assessed and published data on the health outcomes of people treated in hospital, he was keen to release data that showed the public sector's effectiveness as well as its efficiency. Jeremy agreed – after all, he'd championed choice throughout his career, but choice was only meaningful if it was based on good information. Releasing data on the effectiveness of public services would also enable entrepreneurs to develop new products to help citizens make these choices – something no one in the Civil Service had the incentive or time to do.

'We are planning to publish the White Paper in early July,' Tim told Jeremy when they met to finalise the letters. 'To promote it,

Steve wants to make the front door of Number 10 transparent for the day. He's down there now examining the hinges.'

Not everyone shared Steve's enthusiasm for transparency. For example, the Department of Transport worried that revealing the cost of different train tickets would encourage passengers to switch to cheaper routes, invalidating the economics of the rail franchise agreements. And the Department for Education was reluctant to publish data on education outcomes, even though they already released calculations based on them, because they thought that doing so might somehow endanger students.

Despite these difficulties – and the fact that the door of Number 10 stayed opaque because the Cabinet Office thought that changing it might indicate a willingness to publish the Cabinet minutes – the Open Public Services White Paper was another step forward in increasing transparency. Jeremy believed, however, that Whitehall could go further, and he, therefore, helped persuade the Chancellor to allocate £10 million in the 2011 Autumn Statement to set up an Open Data Institute to keep lobbying for further openness. He also championed the publication of another White Paper the following year, which required all departments to prepare a plan to make more of their information available to the world.

Despite his enthusiasm, there were limits to Jeremy's belief in transparency. And in a coincidence of timing, these were exceeded not long after the publication of the Open Data White Paper when the National Audit Office handed over to the Public Accounts Committee all the material it had been given on the government's major projects. Jeremy shared the Prime Minister's fury about this because he believed that the Major Projects Authority's blunt assessments of these projects had made the government far more effective in managing them – and there was a risk that, if the Public Accounts Committee succeeded in its demand to continue receiving these reports, the reports might need to be diluted and the Major Projects Authority could even be disbanded. It took several weeks of negotiation before they found a compromise – the committee would continue to receive the information but would discuss it in private and would keep the individual project ratings confidential.

One Whitehall department was also particularly anxious to preserve its confidentiality. After Tim presented his latest thinking at one of Gus' Wednesday morning colleagues' meetings, he was handed a small slip of paper. He opened it to discover a note written in the green ink favoured by the chief of the Secret Intelligence Service.

'Tim,' it said, 'while I admire your passion for transparency, there are some of us who must always remain in the shadows. C'

On 4 July 2011, the phone-hacking scandal exploded again after the *Guardian* accused the *News of the World* of accessing the voicemail messages of murdered schoolgirl Milly Dowler while the police had still been searching for her. Once again, the Prime Minister's judgement in hiring Andy Coulson was questioned. The suspicion was also raised – fostered by Labour – that the government had been slow to act on the rumours of phone hacking because it had become too close to the media, as demonstrated by the alleged favours paid to Rupert Murdoch, the chair and CEO of News Corporation, which owned the *News of the World*, during his £12 billion bid to buy 61 per cent of BSkyB.

In response to these new revelations, Nick Clegg argued that the government should announce an independent, judge-led inquiry and Jeremy agreed, as he had in the past with other inquiries. 'It's best to do it before you're forced into it,' he advised the Prime Minister, 'not least because your personal integrity is being questioned.'

But the Prime Minister hesitated because he still hoped the row would blow over and he was reluctant to open up the issue of press regulation. It would, of course, also be galling to hand Ed Miliband a political victory.

'I understand,' Jeremy said, 'but you don't want people to be thinking, "Well, maybe there was something in that". And the other papers aren't going to let this go, and nor is Labour.'

Craig Oliver – who had by that time replaced Andy Coulson as director of communications – tended to agree, as did Ed Llewellyn, though articles soon appeared in the press criticising Jeremy for advocating a full inquiry. Despite this, some combination of Jeremy and Nick's arguments together with pressure in the House of Commons and from Hacked Off, a group set up to represent the victims of phone hacking, made the Prime Minister relent. On 8 July 2011 he announced an independent inquiry that would begin by looking at the culture, practices and ethics of the press and making recommendations on its regulation. This would be led, it was announced a few days later, by Lord Justice Leveson.

We'd hoped to get away from Whitehall to spend the summer hiking up Cretan gorges with the children. But although we did some of that, after rioting had erupted in north London in early August following a police shooting in Tottenham, Jeremy also spent hours on his email and reading the newspapers on my iPad.

'It's very violent,' he said, shaking his head, 'and Craig Oliver is the only senior person left in the office.'

'Do you want to go back?'

Jeremy sighed. 'No. But I may have to.'

Things turned uglier over the next two days. Footage appeared showing stores being burnt and looted close to our house in Balham, including the party shop at Clapham Junction that had often provided supplies for our children's birthdays. But by this point, Gus O'Donnell was on his way home and the police had put every available officer on the street to calm the situation down. By the time we arrived back in the UK in late August, order had been restored with over three thousand people arrested and the prisons were again close to bursting.

'But what I really want to know,' the Prime Minister said when Jeremy went to see him, 'is what caused the riots and what we can do to prevent them from happening again.'

This was an almost impossible question to answer but Jeremy knew who might be willing to try – Louise Casey, the director of the National Anti-Social Behaviour Unit and the Respect Task Force.

'We need to focus on the 120,000 most troubled families in the country,' Louise told the Prime Minister when she surged into Number 10 to see him. 'If we do, I'm certain it will make a difference.'

The Prime Minister nodded – it was hard not to be carried along by Louise's enthusiasm. 'Let's get this started.'

At this point Jeremy glanced across the table to see Steve Hilton smiling. He knew what Steve was thinking – at long last the families agenda was about to start moving.

One of Steve's other priorities, the Beecroft Report, was also making progress that autumn. Steve had launched this work with Ed Davey, the employment minister, a few months previously. The aim was to find ways of making the UK labour market more flexible – despite the fact that, as Jeremy pointed out to Steve, the UK already had one of the most flexible labour markets in the world, together with relatively good industrial relations. Steve, however, was not to be deflected and had appointed Adrian Beecroft, a scientist and venture capitalist, to run the review, arguing that he was perfect for the job because, although he had no labour market expertise, he had a good understanding of what tied people up in red tape.

With Adrian's report due to be finalised in October, Jeremy called a cross-departmental meeting in the State Dining Room in Number 10 in late September to go through its emerging conclusions.

Rohan did most of the talking. 'Beecroft has covered a lot of ground and he thinks that, though we have a relatively competitive and flexible labour market, we could do more. In particular, he wants to make it easier for companies to remove underperforming employees.'

Jeremy fixed Rohan with a stare. 'How does he want to do that?'

Rohan glanced at his papers. 'Well, he has a range of ideas. But the main one is to introduce "compensated no fault dismissals" that would allow firms to sack employees without having to give a reason.'

There was low muttering around the mahogany dining table.

Rohan ignored this. 'Beecroft also wants to charge employees a fee if they appeal to an employment tribunal. And he thinks we should ignore EU labour laws that affect temporary workers.'

This time there was a surge of voices.

'But George and Dave told us to be radical,' Steve said, cutting through the noise. 'We have to get the economy going again.'

Jeremy focused on the easiest line of attack. 'We can't advise the Prime Minister to break EU law,' he told Steve.

'Well, I don't see why he has to obey it,' Steve said.

The room went quiet. Everyone watched Jeremy.

Jeremy straightened his shoulders. 'If you want to advise the Prime Minister to implement unlawful measures, you are welcome to do so,' he told Steve in what he hoped was his most stern voice, 'but the Civil Service cannot work on them.'

After the meeting, Steve – who seemed undaunted by Jeremy's lecture – headed around Whitehall drumming up support for the report from ministers. 'George is intrigued by Beecroft's proposals,' he told Jeremy, 'but the Liberal Democrats are much less enthusiastic.'

'Ah,' Jeremy said, hoping he was conveying surprise. 'Well, why don't we just wait and decide what to do when we get Adrian's final conclusions?'

40

'Call Me':
Becoming Cabinet Secretary

September 2011–February 2012

In the autumn of 2011 we were invited to join the Prime Minister for another barbecue with the Queen at Balmoral Castle. By this time I knew the drill so my wardrobe crisis was minimal. Instead, we were able to relax, enjoying a couple of days free of work or childcare responsibilities, particularly during the time we spent at Craigowan Lodge or roaming around the Balmoral estate with Christopher Geidt and his wife, Emma.

After we returned, David Cameron called Jeremy into his office. 'As you know,' David said, 'Gus is retiring. I've discussed it with Nick Clegg, and we would like you to succeed him so long as you can also continue to be my lead policy adviser.'

Jeremy knew about Gus's plans since they'd been talking about them during their morning commutes into Whitehall. Gus had originally thought that either Suma Chakrabarti from the Ministry of Justice or David Bell from the Department for Education could take over while Jeremy became the Permanent Secretary of the Treasury. And Jeremy had agreed, partly because he'd always wanted the Treasury role and partly because he'd never liked being the front man.

This preference for avoiding the limelight went back a long way. One of Jeremy's stories was of how he'd convinced his friend Keith to run for class president when they'd both been at the London School of Economics twenty-five years previously. With Jeremy managing his campaign, Keith had won. It was, though, a victory that Keith had regretted after Jeremy later convinced him to complain, on behalf of the year group, about Professor Michael Bruno's incomprehensible lectures on worldwide stagflation and this had brought the school's wrath down on Keith's head.

As the weeks passed, however, it became clear that neither of Gus's names was finding favour in Number 10. Jeremy, therefore, wasn't entirely surprised by the Prime Minister's suggestion that he should become Cabinet Secretary himself, though he still didn't know if he wanted to do it. In addition to his reluctance to be the front man, Jeremy told me he was worried he wouldn't be credible because he'd never run a department. He also thought it would be hard to ask controversial questions if he was the most senior person in the room. I understood the first of these new concerns, but I laughed at the second, telling him that he just needed to appoint a deputy who would stand up to him if he went too far.

In addition to wanting to make Jeremy his Cabinet Secretary and lead policy adviser, the Prime Minister also wanted to appoint a second person to oversee the Civil Service. This structure was unusual – in the past most Cabinet Secretaries had also led the Civil Service and had only intervened on policy issues during major crises, like Richard Wilson had done during the foot and mouth outbreak. But the Prime Minister didn't want to lose Jeremy's policy advice and Jeremy shared his view that, if he was going to continue providing this, then a second person would be required to lead the work on Civil Service reform.

Like Tony Blair before him, David Cameron was keen for this new head of the Civil Service to be appointed from the private sector. Jeremy was content with this, believing that it could accelerate change in Whitehall. But Gus told the Prime Minister that he wasn't convinced that an outsider could manage the Civil Service given its uniqueness.

David raised an eyebrow. 'Do you have an internal candidate who could really drive change?'

'No – but let me keep thinking about it.'

While Gus pondered, Jeremy became more enthusiastic about becoming Cabinet Secretary. 'Terry Burns and I discussed it over lunch in the Inn in the Park,' he told me one evening. 'He thinks I have all the skills to do the job and would be mad to turn it down if the Prime Minister is asking me to do it.'

I nodded, pleased that Jeremy's concerns seemed to be easing. 'But are you sure about the proposed structure? In all my time at McKinsey, I've rarely seen a co-leadership model work. It would be far better if the person leading the Civil Service reported to you.'

Jeremy frowned. 'George Osborne also thinks I should do the whole role. But I think it will be hard for the head of the Civil Service to be effective if they are seen as being junior to me.'

We went around this several times before I gave up. 'Okay,' I said, 'so which parts of Gus's job would you keep?'

Jeremy smiled, produced a PowerPoint sheet from his bag and spread it out on our kitchen table. 'I would keep all the Cabinet Secretary's responsibilities, including doing the Cabinet minutes and managing the Cabinet committees and Cabinet secretariats,' he said, running his finger down the page. 'That's at the heart of the job and it's closely linked to my policy role. I would also retain propriety and ethics, though I don't expect it to be fun, and responsibility for making sure Whitehall implements the government's priorities, since that's the biggest frustration for any prime minister.'

I laughed. 'So what would you let the head of the Civil Service do?'

'They would manage the departments day-to-day, including overseeing the reform programme, running the corporate functions, fronting big events like Civil Service Live and going to visit staff in far-flung places.'

'All the bits you don't like.'

He nodded. 'They're important, but I'm sure someone else will do them better than I would.'

Jeremy's appointment as Cabinet Secretary was announced in October 2011, with the intention that he would start his new role in January 2012 after Gus's retirement. 'He is,' the BBC declared, 'quite possibly the most important person in the country that nobody has ever heard of.'

After the announcement, Jeremy tidied up the structure he was leaving behind him in Number 10. He didn't refill his old role of permanent secretary, since he would continue to advise the Prime Minister on policy, but he appointed Chris Martin from the Treasury to succeed James Bowler as principal private secretary, since James was due to move on. Chris threw himself into his new brief, picking up, among other things, a project Jeremy had started to record Number 10's history. I was, however, less well behaved, telling Jeremy's new private office, when they sent me a long list of events they wanted me to host, that I already had a full-time job.

After this, Jeremy returned to thinking about the Coalition's policy priorities, including how to implement the Prime Minister's decision to allow same-sex marriages, something Jeremy strongly supported, and reviewing Steve Hilton's ideas for stimulating growth. The best of these ideas, including launching a national infrastructure plan and opening technology and innovation centres to create a bridge between universities and businesses, were swept into the Prime Minister's speech to the CBI on 'new economic dynamism' on 25 October 2011.

This speech didn't include Adrian Beecroft's proposals on labour market reform, despite Steve's continuing enthusiasm for them, although Adrian's idea of allowing firms to sack employees without giving a reason was leaked to the *Daily Telegraph* the day afterwards together with the suggestion that it had been approved by both sides of the Coalition. Nick Clegg and Vince Cable, the Liberal Democrat Secretary of State for Business, soon made it clear this wasn't true, after which the Prime Minister and Chancellor backed away. Tempers became frayed with Adrian labelling Vince a 'socialist' and Steve insisting that all of Beecroft's recommendations had to be implemented.

When Jeremy was, somewhat inevitably, sent in by the Prime Minister to negotiate a compromise, he managed to drag one proposal from the wreckage. In exchange for the Conservatives agreeing to a Liberal Democrat proposal for a British business bank to finance smaller enterprises, the Liberal Democrats would accept a proposal that allowed employees to give up some of their employment rights, including the right to claim unfair dismissal, in return for gaining tax relief on their company's shares. This idea survived long enough to allow the immediate drama to pass but had a troubled passage through the Lords and was scrapped by a later Chancellor.

Jeremy's in-tray that autumn contained reports from Louise Casey on her work with troubled families, regular updates on the Leveson inquiry, which had started interviewing its first witnesses, and drafts of the Life Sciences Strategy. This last piece of work was something Jeremy had argued for after Pfizer, a pharmaceutical company, had closed its plant in Sandwich, Kent in February, and it included a number of proposals that he supported, including investing over £300 million in biomedical research and commercialisation and making NHS patient data available for approved research unless patients opted out.

All of this was interesting, but Jeremy was conscious that he still needed to get the Prime Minister to appoint the new head of the Civil Service before Gus left in the new year. The problem was that, although David Cameron remained determined to appoint a business person, none of the names that had been suggested seemed plausible. A compromise was, therefore, agreed – the job would first be advertised internally and would only be opened to external competition if no suitable internal candidate could be found. To widen the field, they also decided that the role could be done part time alongside leading a department, as Gus had done with the Cabinet Office.

After several weeks of assessing candidates, the appointments panel, which included Jeremy, recommended two: Helen Ghosh, permanent secretary at the Home Office, and Bob Kerslake, permanent secretary at the Department of Communities and Local Government. There was then a further wait while the Prime Minister and Francis Maude interviewed both candidates before deciding on Bob, impressed by the fact that he'd been chief executive of two local authorities.

While Bob moved into his new quarters, up a narrow staircase next to the private office that he and Jeremy would share, and I kept muttering about the dangers of this double-headed leadership structure, Jeremy finalised his speech for Gus's leaving party in Admiralty House. 'As I know from Black Wednesday in 1992,' he told his audience, 'Gus is the consummate press secretary. He can convince anyone about anything. I should know. In 2007, when I was sitting happily in my office in the City, he convinced me that, even though Gordon Brown hadn't spoken to me for six years while I was in Number 10 working for Tony Blair, he really did like me.'

And the funny thing, Jeremy thought, while everyone laughed, was that Gus had been right. He was also conscious how much he would miss this man who, ever since Jeremy had first joined the Treasury back in 1984, had always been a reliable sounding board and supportive friend no matter how complex the policy issue or crisis.

After throwing our own party for Jeremy's fiftieth birthday in late December, with a mixture of work colleagues and old friends dancing until the early hours in the playroom of our house in Balham, we flew to Lanzarote with the children, leaving Brenda staying with Jeremy's brother Simon. We had many things to celebrate in addition to Jeremy's august age – his appointment as Cabinet Secretary, the children being well and happy and Jeremy's knighthood, which was announced in the New Year honours list. Those sunny days in the Canary Islands felt, even at the time, like a high point in our lives.

On 3 January 2012, Jeremy took up residence in the wood-panelled office in 70 Whitehall that he'd visited so many times over the years for meetings with his predecessors. A week later I went in to do an inspection, making my way along the gallery that had once formed part of Henry VIII's sixteenth-century tennis courts. Jeremy's new office was huge and was lined with floor-to-ceiling dark wooden cupboards. When I saw them, I remembered my curiosity as a young civil servant about what they contained and ran around opening each one, only to find they were empty. Jeremy laughed at my antics, and when I stopped, called me over to see the view out of the sash windows that overlooked Horse Guards Parade.

'And do you like the painting I chose?' he asked, pointing to the large canvas above the fireplace. 'It's by David Austen. We had a fight to get it because Penny in the Government Art Collection thought it wouldn't fit in here.'

I looked up at the large, bright picture. It was exactly what I would have expected Jeremy to choose: modern, warm and a little controversial.*

Jeremy had no time, however, for any further interior design because he needed to prepare for his first Cabinet meeting. This was held at the embryonic Olympic Park in Stratford, which was due to be finished in six months' time ready for the opening ceremony. The meeting was, however, focused on a very different issue after the Prime Minister's announcement on 8 January that he was ready to begin negotiating the terms of a referendum on Scottish independence with Alex Salmond.

This announcement had been brewing for months. The previous May, Alex's Scottish National Party had gained twenty-three seats in the Scottish Parliament and formed a majority government determined to make Scotland independent. In response, the Prime Minister had said that, while he didn't see the need for a referendum on this, he wouldn't stand in the way of one. After this initial flurry of words, progress stalled. In London the Quad, joined for these discussions by the Scottish secretary, Michael Moore, debated whether the Scottish Parliament had the right to decide the rules of a referendum. And if they didn't, but held one anyway, would the Scottish authorities be breaking the law if they spent money preparing for it?

In June 2011, Gus had then appointed Ciaran Martin, his former principal private secretary, to head the Constitution Group in the Cabinet Office. Ciaran's job was to get decisions made on the referendum, but this wasn't easy when the Chancellor was keen to move ahead while the Prime Minister and Deputy Prime Minister wanted to delay. Weeks had passed in limbo, while the noise north of the border grew. The impasse had, in the end, only been resolved after Jim Wallace, the advocate general for Scotland and a British minister, advised the Quad that the Scottish Parliament had no legal right to call a referendum, and the Quad realised that they'd asked the wrong question. It didn't matter whether Alex Salmond had the right – if he called a referendum and won it, he would still claim political and

---

* Jeremy is standing in front of this picture on the cover of this book.

moral authority. And the alternative of Westminster calling a snap referendum, which some were advocating, could result in Alex telling Scottish schools, where the polling booths would be located, and the Scottish police, not to cooperate.

All of this left only one option – negotiating the terms of a referendum with Scotland. While this wasn't ideal, the opinion polls suggested that the Scots would oppose independence, so doing this quickly might allow the Prime Minister to show respect to the Scottish government while at the same time seeing off independence for a generation.

When Jeremy came home after this Cabinet meeting, he pulled a sheaf of paper from his briefcase and sat in our playroom marking it up. 'It's going to take me hours to get the Cabinet minutes done each week,' he said after a while.

'Are you being too pedantic?' I asked, knowing his tendency in that direction. He was, after all, the son of an English teacher.

He frowned. 'No. This is the first draft of history. I can't have it littered with bureaucratic acronyms.'

'Well, you'll have to teach the Cabinet Secretariat how you want history recorded. And how was the Olympic Park?'

'It looked like a gigantic construction site. I don't know how it's going to be ready in time. But they seemed remarkably calm.'

By the spring of 2012, almost two years after the start of the Coalition government, the Prime Minister was becoming increasingly frustrated about how slowly his policies were being implemented. Jeremy and Oliver, therefore, agreed that it was time to see if they could convince him to recreate more of Downing Street's old capabilities.

Jeremy took a deep breath at the start of the meeting. After waiting for so long, he didn't want to mess this up. 'None of us would like to see a return to New Labour-style PSA targets,' he said.

The Prime Minister narrowed his eyes. 'Indeed.'

'They can distort departmental behaviour and cut across the system-wide reforms and bottom-up incentives you've been implementing,' Jeremy said before pausing, wondering if he was laying it on too thick. 'But you said you were worried about implementation and I share that concern.'

'Okay. Where are you going with this?'

Jeremy squared his shoulders. 'I recommend we establish a properly staffed unit in the Cabinet Office to track implementation, Prime Minister.'

'Or delivery,' one of the private secretaries added, rather unhelpfully.

Cameron ignored this. 'Oliver, what's your view?'

'I agree. Right now, too much depends on Jeremy or me – or you during your briefing for Prime Minister's Questions – spotting that something isn't happening.'

The Prime Minister nodded, and by the end of the meeting he had agreed to create an Implementation Unit – which confirmed Jeremy's view that, in the end, all prime ministers would realise they needed this capability within Number 10.

But while Jeremy was confident that the Implementation Unit would help get Whitehall moving, he knew there would always be some things he would have to help sort out himself. One of these came back into his in-tray in the spring of 2012 after Philip Hammond was appointed Secretary of State for Defence and started looking again at whether the two new aircraft carriers that they had ordered should really be fitted with the 'cats and traps' needed to handle the longer-range F-35C planes.

When Jeremy joined Bernard Gray, the chief of defence materiel, to review this decision they discovered that, in contrast to the department's assurances, fitting the cats and traps wouldn't be cost neutral after all because it would require the almost-complete HMS *Queen Elizabeth* to be cut apart. In fact, if they were essential, the best option would be to build HMS *Queen Elizabeth* without them and then scrap or sell her while completing HMS *Prince of Wales* to the new design. But since this would mean paying £8 billion for a single carrier, rather than less than £6 billion for two without the cats and traps, it wasn't long before Philip Hammond decided that they should cancel the modifications and revert to using the shorter-range F-35B planes.

Jeremy was relieved that, after fourteen years, this extraordinary aircraft carrier saga had at last been settled. Through a combination of vested interests and a lack of imagination, a vast amount of time had been spent on it. As well as being wasteful, this had also crowded out discussion of things like cyber warfare and drones, as well as the wider security threats posed by corruption, money laundering and tax havens, all of which he believed would be more important in maintaining international order than building a couple of massive new ships.

At least though, Jeremy told me, with the aircraft decision made, he could move on to more productive discussions – like helping the Prime Minister work out what his legacy on health should be beyond the toxic memory of the Health and Social Care Act. After convening several meetings to discuss this issue, the Prime Minister decided to focus on dementia, a growing, devastating and hugely neglected disease. It was also one that, by that time, we knew a lot about because Brenda, who was still living with us, had been recently diagnosed with Alzheimer's disease – something that we had surmised for some time even if we hadn't wanted to admit it.

Following the Prime Minister's decision, Jeremy and Paul Bate worked with Jeremy Hughes from the Alzheimer's Society to come up with a plan that included a doubling – and later a tripling – of the dementia research budget alongside changes to the health and social care system to make it more dementia-friendly. They also arranged a 'dementia friends' session for Cabinet to give people a sense of what it was like to live with the disease, after which ministers were asked to find ways within their briefs to help.

Jeremy wore his Dementia Friends badge with pride for weeks after this Cabinet session and told me he hoped this would be a turning point for the disease. However, he was also conscious that he only had time to work on issues like aircraft carriers and dementia because Bob Kerslake was leading the thinking on the Civil Service reform programme. But while the benefits of Bob's role were clear to Jeremy, the Public Accounts Committee was less convinced – as they made clear when they called Jeremy and Bob in to explain themselves in late February 2012.

'In this Pinky and Perky division of roles …' Austin Mitchell, one of the MPs on the committee, began, 'Sir Jeremy is responsible for policy and great thoughts; he is the chap at the top. Sir Bob, being the rough engineer from Sheffield, has a spanner with which he occasionally hits the machine.'

More seriously, Margaret Hodge, the chair of the committee, asked Jeremy how he would measure the success of the new arrangement.

'I don't have an answer off the top of my head,' Jeremy said, though he added that, if at the end of four years, people said their fears about it had been misguided, that would be good.

This would turn out to be a tough test, though Jeremy and Bob's first joint appearance in front of the 200 most senior civil servants a few weeks later went well. While 'two jobs Bob' provided a reassuring presence on stage, Jeremy outlined his priorities as Cabinet Secretary. The new government had, he said, a set of novel policy ideas including payment by results, partnerships with new providers and transparency. But there was no reason why this should only be a set of innovative policies owned by one set of political masters – it was a fresh, modern agenda that the whole Civil Service could own.

41

'Video Killed the Radio Star': A fresh, modern agenda

February–July 2012

To deliver the government's 'fresh, modern agenda', Jeremy was determined to make full use of the Behavioural Insights Team or 'nudge unit'. This had been set up by Gus after the 2010 election to test the power of the behavioural economics popularised by Richard Thaler, later a Nobel prize winner, and Cass Sunstein. Not long after it had been established, Jeremy had gone to meet the CEO of the unit, David Halpern, and had found him standing in his office in Admiralty House waving a small tube.

'It's an e-cigarette,' David said. 'I brought it back from Japan. I think it could be revolutionary.'

Jeremy smiled. Given that the purpose of the nudge unit was to find small interventions that could change people's behaviour, it made sense for David to be excited about something like this. 'Why?'

'Because substitution is one of the best ways of getting people to quit an addictive habit. And if e-cigarettes can tempt people away from real cigarettes, which are packed full of carcinogens, that has to be a good idea.'

This discussion with David, and the others that followed after Jeremy joined the nudge unit's board, convinced him that behavioural economics could be used to make public policy more effective, often at next to no cost. After he became Cabinet Secretary, Jeremy, therefore, invited David to present his work to the permanent secretaries from across Whitehall, knowing that many were more sceptical, particularly at a time when they were implementing large cost reductions. David took the group through examples of the unit's insights, including the fact that, if people were told that most citizens paid their tax on time, they were more likely to pay their own. The mandarins were rapt, and afterwards, nudge thinking went mainstream.

Following that first meeting with David, Jeremy had also become convinced about the potential benefits of e-cigarettes. However, by 2012 the battle to make them easily accessible had gone into reverse after rumours began to circulate of companies selling e-cigarettes to children outside schools in eastern Europe.

'If a pill could be invented to save so many lives,' Jeremy told me, 'the government would do everything in its power to promote it. But with e-cigarettes we seem determined to do the opposite.'

'Then you need to intervene,' I said.

Neither of us said the thing that I was thinking – that if e-cigarettes had been available in the past, they might have stopped Jeremy inhaling toxic smoke for a decade himself – though I consoled myself with the fact that he'd quit smoking well over fifteen years before.

After this conversation, Jeremy set up a meeting with the Prime Minister to go through the potential benefits and risks of e-cigarettes. When David Halpern reached his final page of his presentation, Cameron nodded.

'I tried an e-cigarette once and it was like inhaling a damp cloud of raspberry,' he said.

David blinked. 'Oh.'

'But I still buy your argument,' the Prime Minister added.

Jeremy also kept urging Sally Davies, the Chief Medical Officer, usually over one of their dinners at the carnivorous St. John restaurant in Smithfield, to say something about the relative safety of e-cigarettes. Over time, as the evidence accumulated, Sally's position mellowed, and by 2013, with David Cameron also lending his support, the government was considering allowing e-cigarettes to be sold in petrol stations and supermarkets. Two years later, Public Health England said e-cigarettes, while not harm free, were likely to be at least 95 per cent safer than cigarettes. And although a series of later deaths in the US showed that e-cigarettes could be dangerous, particularly if tampered with, this fundamental view has since remained unchanged.

While the nudge unit provided a rich seam of innovative policies, Jeremy was always on the lookout for ideas from other sources, finding them in meetings, at dinner parties or during chance conversations in the Cabinet Office's basement café where he often still retired at lunchtime to eat a sandwich and another packet of *verboten* crisps. Rohan and Steve were particularly good at generating new policies, so when Rohan suggested in mid-2012 that the UK should map the genomes of 100,000 patients to help researchers assess the causes, diagnosis and best treatment of their cancers, Jeremy listened.

'The UK could become a world leader in this space,' Rohan said, 'because we can combine genomic data with NHS patient records, something that's only possible in a country with a single-payer health system.'

Despite the daunting ambition – Rohan's proposed target was two orders of magnitude greater than what had previously been achieved – the Prime Minister was enthusiastic. And this time both Sally Davies and the Department of Health were also supportive, though they resisted Jeremy and Rohan's push to make the database accessible, with appropriate safeguards, to companies wanting to use it to build apps.

The Prime Minister announced the genome mapping target in December 2012, although it took Jeremy later banging the table with frustration during a meeting with the Secretary of State for Health, before real progress was made. After that John Chisholm, an engineer and businessman, was appointed to lead the work, and in July 2013, Genomics England, a company wholly owned by the Department of Health, was created to get the sequencing under way.

Jeremy was thrilled by this new ambition. 'But my real goal,' he told me, 'isn't just to find individual policies that I can champion. What I really want to do is to make the whole of the Civil Service better at creating policy.'

I nodded, and in the months that followed, watched him collecting more ideas, magpie-like, to bring this about. From the National Institute of Clinical Excellence, he stole the methodology to do real-world testing and evidence gathering, setting up a What Works network to do the same thing within government. From McKinsey, where I was still working, he took the idea of publishing a *Civil Service Quarterly* magazine highlighting the best policy thinking. And inspired by academia, Jeremy and Chris Wormald, who was by then head of the Civil Service Policy Profession, created a master's programme at the London School of Economics to teach thirty high potential civil servants a year how to become experts in policy creation.

As a final step, Jeremy told me he wanted to find a way to tap into the millions of pounds of research that was being funded each year by the Economic and Social Research Council. The problem here was that departments were reluctant to admit what they didn't know, so it was no surprise that the academics being funded by the council weren't trying to fill their knowledge gaps. It took time to convince Whitehall to share this information, but from 2016, most departments were doing so and a new Open Innovation Team was helping them collaborate with researchers.

Jeremy loved finding these ways to get the Civil Service to change. However, even with Bob leading on public sector reform, he was struggling to find time to do this alongside his other responsibilities. These included answering the hundreds of emails he received each day from civil servants wanting to know what he thought about their areas of policy. He tapped out responses to these on his BlackBerry, often just a few terse words to make a connection or to offer encouragement. There were also, of course, the set-piece events like helping the Prime Minister and Deputy Prime Minister prepare for the March 2012 Budget. With the economy contracting in the first quarter, putting the economy officially back in recession, the Quad's early Budget discussions again explored measures to kick-start growth. Reducing VAT, which Jeremy supported since he'd seen it work before, was debated before being rejected by the Chancellor who instead wanted to reduce the top rate of tax from 50 per cent to 40 per cent to encourage investment.

Jeremy raised his eyebrows at this idea but kept quiet. This was partly since he was unsure of the Prime Minister's views and also because, in contrast to his predecessor, David Cameron generally deferred to his Chancellor on Budget decisions. The Deputy Prime Minister, however, felt no such reticence, saying he didn't want to cut taxes for the wealthy and would only do so if it were balanced by something that had the opposite impact, like increasing the taxation of expensive properties, a measure that the Liberal Democrats had included in their manifesto.

Jeremy was also enthusiastic about increasing property taxes. House owners in the UK, including us, had benefited from a huge increase in property values. Taxing that gain was reasonable and might reduce housing costs for the less affluent. It would also be relatively easy to implement. The Chancellor and his team were likewise sympathetic, arguing that housing was undertaxed. But the Prime Minister cut through this emerging consensus to say he didn't want to introduce a new tax on wealth.

The Prime Minister and Chancellor continued this debate in a series of private bilaterals over the following days. In addition to the technocratic arguments in favour of taxing housing wealth, the Chancellor thought Labour might propose something similar and pointed out that it would be difficult to find equivalent revenues from other sources. But the Prime Minister remained opposed, saying it was against his political principles to put additional burdens on those who'd worked hard to buy their own homes. His resistance, though disappointing, didn't surprise Jeremy since taxing houses was one area where, at least in the UK, he'd always seen middle-class vested interests get in the way of reform.

Back in the Quad, after the Chancellor and Prime Minister ruled out a tax on property, the Deputy Prime Minister said that, if this was the case, he would only support a cut in the top rate of income tax to 45 per cent. He also wanted it to be implemented with a year's delay and accompanied by a substantial increase in personal allowances to help the less well-off.

After this was settled, it felt like they were getting somewhere. However, all they'd agreed was a set of tax decreases – which meant that, by the time the Chancellor and Prime Minister flew to Washington to meet President Obama eight days before the Budget on 13 March 2012, the numbers were a long way from being balanced. To make things worse, the OBR said that, with growth still subdued, public sector net debt was likely to peak a year later than previously expected and the Treasury stopped sharing its thinking with Downing Street because they said the Chancellor was worried about confidentiality.

Two days later, Chris Martin called Jeremy. 'A journalist has just rung Oliver Letwin while he was being pedalled in a rickshaw across Times Square. He asked if we were about to cut the top rate of tax.'

'What did Oliver say?'

'He tried to brush them off. But do you know what's in the Budget?'

'Only some elements – and they may have changed since I was last allowed to see it.'

'Great. How are we supposed to handle this?'

From there things spiralled. News of the income tax reduction appeared in the *Guardian* on 16 March, and details of the increase in personal allowances were leaked to the BBC's *News at Ten* on the eve of the Budget.

The Treasury was understandably furious at these suspected Liberal Democrat leaks. As well as spoiling the drama of the Chancellor's speech, they also meant that, on the day, the press focused on some of the tax-raising measures that had crept in to make the numbers add up. These included a freeze in additional tax allowances for pensioners, the imposition of VAT on heated-up foods, taxes on hairdressers' chairs and on stationary caravans, and a cap on tax relief for charitable donations. Multiple noisy constituencies – from grannies to Cornish pasty bakers, holiday makers and charity donors – were soon making their annoyance clear. And Damian McBride, Gordon Brown's old spin doctor, added to the din with a blog post about how George Osborne must have been fooled by the Treasury's Budget process, which repeatedly served up innocuous-looking but politically dangerous options until someone failed to ask enough questions and they snuck through. These were, of course, the 'smelly rats' that Gus O'Donnell had once warned Jeremy about.

'It's a millionaires' Budget,' Labour cried. But the press, already irate over the Leveson inquiry, came up with a better title, dubbing it the 'omnishambles Budget'.

To be fair, tax rises are always hard, and the majority of them survived the outcry. There was also, at least for Jeremy, one positive consequence of all the fuss – the Prime Minister's determination that, in the future, Number 10 should always have a substantial role in preparing the Budget.*

While the Treasury started cleaning up their shambles, and the Prime Minister dealt with the revelation that the co-treasurer of the Conservative Party, Peter Cruddas, had been caught offering access to senior politicians in exchange for cash, Jeremy hoped to get back to work on the Coalition's policy priorities. But instead, at the end of what was turning into a torrid March, the Unite union started threatening to call tanker drivers out on strike over health and safety issues. Francis Maude, who'd been reading up on the previous fuel crisis, then made matters worse by telling people that, while a strike wasn't imminent, it might be best if they kept their petrol tanks full – and maybe stored a little extra fuel in a jerry can in their garage. Panic buying ensued and one woman suffered terrible burns when she tried to decant fuel from her jerry can in her kitchen.

Jeremy went to see the Prime Minister. 'We need COBR to manage this', he said. 'We can't afford to wait for the department to act – I've seen this before.'

To his surprise – since David Cameron had previously claimed that, unlike Gordon Brown, he wasn't going to spend his time managing crises through COBR – the Prime Minister nodded. It was a good decision because, after COBR took charge, they were able to orchestrate enough contact with employers and unions to hold off a strike.

After Bob Kerslake's appointment in January, Jeremy had largely left him to push forward the work on Civil Service reform. Bob had set up groups of permanent secretaries to brainstorm ideas, from which he'd fashioned a long list of priorities that Jeremy regarded as sensible but incremental. But by mid-May, Francis Maude was becoming

* 'Yeah – right,' George Osborne scrawled here when he read a draft of this book.

frustrated, telling the Prime Minister, when they met to discuss progress, that the reform plan was 'turgid and unspecific'.

'What about the Somerset House option?' Steve Hilton asked, glancing at Jeremy.

Jeremy tried not to roll his eyes. Oliver Letwin and Francis Maude had encouraged Steve to pursue the idea of cutting the Civil Service from 450,000 people to around 4,000 – the size some argued it had been in the nineteenth century when everyone could have fitted into Somerset House, a large neoclassical building perched next to the Thames. The idea wasn't turgid or unspecific. It was just completely undoable.

Jeremy was about to cut in when the Prime Minister spoke.

'I'm all in favour of radical reform. But that isn't practical. So go and find an achievable compromise.'

While this intervention was helpful, it became clear after the meeting that a 'compromise' for Steve still meant reducing the Civil Service by 70 per cent. While Jeremy and Bob fought this, Rohan decided he would make more progress if he focused on reforming a single department, the Department for Education, which had already pushed many of its activities down to schools. Unlike the Somerset House option, Jeremy supported this initiative, and so did the department's permanent secretary, Chris Wormald, since a preliminary review had suggested there was significant scope to reduce costs.

The final draft of the Civil Service Reform Plan included this 'zero-based' review of the Department for Education, together with 'snapshot' reviews of Bob's department – the Department of Communities and Local Government – and the Department of Work and Pensions, to see if policy officials' time was aligned with ministerial priorities. While the plan didn't include a target for shrinking the Civil Service, it estimated that, by 2015, it would be around 23 per cent smaller than in March 2010 – which seemed reasonable to Jeremy, who was certain there was scope for improvement. The only issue was whether, two years into the Coalition government, Cabinet ministers who were concentrating on delivering the manifesto priorities would be willing to make this a priority.

* * *

In early June 2012, we celebrated the Queen's jubilee, the highlight of which was a flotilla of over a thousand rowing boats, tugs, dragon boats and kayaks that we went to watch weave its way up the Thames one rainy Sunday afternoon. A few days afterwards, the Cabinet met to approve the Civil Service Reform Plan. Jeremy, sitting as usual on the Prime Minister's right-hand side, flipped through his copy while recording the main points being made. The plan was still complex, but some of the most difficult proposals had been taken out and it contained many things that Jeremy supported, including ending Whitehall's monopoly on policy thinking by making more use of academics, think tanks and others, getting rid of bureaucracy and making the government's services 'digital by default'.

Most ministers shared this view, though a few wanted the proposals to go further, saying the Civil Service spent too much time on things that weren't priorities and that ministers should have more power to hire and fire civil servants. Steve Hilton would certainly have shared their view. But by that time, he'd decided to abandon Whitehall for California and Jeremy, at least, was missing him because, despite the challenge of managing his creativity, and his occasional negative press briefings, Steve had also been the source of the Coalition's most original and bold ideas.

Jeremy glanced at the Prime Minister. With his permanent secretaries already under pressure to deliver austerity, if the conversation spiralled and the Reform Plan became more aggressive, Jeremy worried that he would struggle to maintain morale. But a minute or two later, Cameron brought the discussion to a close, thanked everyone for their input, and Jeremy breathed out. The Prime Minister was happy with the overall intent of the plan and probably didn't want to open a new flank with his Coalition partners, the Civil Service, or his more radical Cabinet members. And though not perfect, the plan still envisaged major reform.

42

'The Guns of Brixton':
Coalition crises

July–September 2012

When Philip Rycroft, who'd just become Nick Clegg's senior adviser, came to see Jeremy in early July 2012, he was shaking his head. 'The Liberal Democrats are furious because the Prime Minister isn't backing the House of Lords Reform Bill,' Philip said. 'While the Conservatives took a different view on the substance on the alternative vote, the Liberal Democrats see this as different – after all it's a government Bill.'

Jeremy nodded. In the 2010 manifestos, which had been written in the shadow of the MPs' expenses scandal, the Conservatives and Liberal Democrats had both pledged to remodel the House of Lords. But while the Liberal Democrats were passionate about making the Lords fully elected and reducing its size – with nearly 800 members it was the second largest parliamentary chamber in the world – the Conservatives were far less enthusiastic, and it increasingly looked like they were heading for a major Coalition row. Jeremy hoped Philip wasn't regretting exchanging his well-paid private sector role for a front row view of this drama.

'The Liberal Democrats may block the boundary changes if the reforms are defeated,' Philip added.

This time Jeremy winced. The boundary changes, which were designed to make the parliamentary constituencies more equal in size, would also make around twenty seats easier for the Conservatives to win. There was no link between those changes and the reform of the House of Lords, but it was a way for the Liberal Democrats to take revenge. 'Well, that would be toxic for the Prime Minister,' he said. 'Jesse Norman is rallying Conservative opposition to reforming the House of Lords, and as far as I can see, the Prime Minister is doing his best to resist that. But this has always been a difficult issue for Tories. They really would be turkeys voting for the proverbial.'

Philip had been right to warn Jeremy about this issue. On 10 July, only a few days after their conversation, there was a gruelling debate in Parliament on House of Lords reform. Many Conservative MPs raised objections while the Deputy Prime Minister was speaking and ninety-one voted against the bill. As result, the government was forced to withdraw the programme motion. Since this defined the timetable for progressing the legislation, it left the government facing a situation in which defiant backbenchers could clog up parliamentary business for weeks, if not months, by debating House of Lords reform, just as they'd done with the Maastricht Bill.

If House of Lords reform had been the government's only problem, that would have been bad enough. But in addition, after the economy shrank by more than expected in the second quarter, the IMF declared in mid-July that, if there was no recovery by early 2013, the government would need to moderate its austerity programme. Rumours began to circulate that the Coalition might collapse, though Jeremy didn't believe them because neither the Prime Minister nor the Deputy Prime Minister had much to gain by an election.

However, while it seemed unlikely that the Coalition would end, a large amount of trust had disappeared. As a result it became more difficult to get anything agreed and tempers became short. After this translated into another burst of prime ministerial exasperation about Whitehall's slow delivery, Jeremy and Bob proposed more measures to accelerate progress. These included producing weekly reports on stalled policies, refocusing permanent secretaries' objectives on implementation and recreating the National Economic Council.

The Prime Minister agreed to all these apart from the last, given its Gordon Brown overtones. But he did agree to Jeremy's alternative suggestion of a Growth and Enterprise Cabinet Committee, which would do essentially the same thing, bringing together the relevant bits of Whitehall, and occasionally outside experts, to identify ways of stimulating the economy.

The instability caused by the floundering House of Lords Bill was particularly noticeable in the Coalition's more difficult policy discussions. One example of this was the debate about whether prisoners should be allowed to vote.

The issue of prisoner voting had arisen back in 2004 when the European Court of Human Rights had ruled against the UK's blanket ban and British governments of all colours had been dodging it ever since. In October 2010, David Cameron had felt forced to announce that he would allow prisoners sentenced for fewer than four years to vote – though he'd added that the thought of this made him feel 'physically ill'. But even after that concession, the government had managed, through various foot-dragging and legal procedures, to avoid doing anything. By mid-2010, however, the UK was facing a looming December court deadline for implementing the ruling with the risk that, if they failed to act, they could be forced to pay tens or hundreds of millions of pounds of compensation to prisoners.

'I need advice on the consequences of non-compliance with the European Court's ruling,' the Prime Minister declared during one of his morning office meetings.

Jeremy glanced around at the nodding heads. With Nick Clegg not present, there were roughly twenty people in favour of breaking international law against one Cabinet Secretary who saw it as his job – indeed was obliged under the Civil Service code to make it his job – to comply with the law. The Prime Minister might just as well have asked for advice from the patrons of his local pub.

Then Oliver Letwin spoke. 'The politics are ghastly. But we have to obey international law. So our best approach is to do nothing.'

Jeremy nodded. 'Oliver is right,' he said in his most soothing voice, 'we should continue to try to stop this coming to a head – after all, we've managed to do that for over eight years. But the Civil Service is not allowed to advise you on how to break international law.'

'You're being a ridiculous bureaucrat,' the Prime Minister declared.

Jeremy blinked, trying to resist reacting. 'I'm sorry you feel like that,' he said, straightening up, 'but my strong advice is that, while continuing to delay, we should explore what minimum compliance would look like.'

'Well you can do that, but Oliver, can you do me a note on non-compliant options, since Jeremy won't help?'

The meeting ended on a tense note, with Jeremy telling the Prime Minister that the Ministerial Code also prevented ministers from acting illegally and the Prime Minster threatening to change the code. In the following days, Jeremy worked up a number of minimum-compliance options, including allowing prisoners to earn their right to vote, something Nick Clegg favoured. But the Prime Minister remained opposed to any compromise.

None of this helped the Prime Minister's mood – even though, in the end, his government managed to keep stalling the decision on prisoner voting, first by asking a joint committee of both Houses of Parliament to review a draft bill and then by sending the attorney general out to Strasbourg periodically to assure the court that the UK was doing everything it could to comply – it was just taking time. In the end it wasn't until December 2017, under a new prime minister, that prisoners released on temporary licence or home detention curfew were given the vote. The Council of Europe noted this long-delayed compliance 'with satisfaction', and back in London, Jeremy sent twelve years of paperwork off to be filed.

Away from this Coalition stress, one of the highlights of 2012 came in July when we attended the rehearsal of the opening ceremony for the London Olympic Games – Danny Boyle's glorious tribute to industrialisation, the National Health Service and British pop music. Jeremy also joined me a few weeks later, this time clutching tickets I'd won in a raffle at work, to watch the athletics on Super Saturday, 4 August 2012 in the beautiful – and by then completed – Olympic stadium. It was, he told me afterwards, the most marvellous night of sport he'd ever experienced, being part of an 80,000-strong crowd seeing three British athletes win gold medals within an hour.

Despite his enthusiasm for attending the Olympics – and following it back home on TV – Jeremy had stayed out of most of the preparations for the Games, leaving these to Simon Case, the head of the Olympic Secretariat in the Cabinet Office. There had been a few moments when he'd become involved – for example when G4S, the private sector company hired to guard the Olympic stadium, had declared it couldn't meet its commitments. But for the most part, Jeremy tried instead to focus on issues where his involvement was needed to unstick a policy discussion, to chase progress or to give the Prime Minister a message he didn't want to hear.

It was odd that the glorious 2012 Olympics should come in the middle of such a difficult year. But that's the way of government – things turn up piecemeal, often with little connection between them. In another illustration of this, when Jeremy returned to work after our summer break in Turkey, he found an entirely different crisis waiting for him. This one was signalled by a request for a meeting from Philip Rutnam, permanent secretary at the Department for Transport.

Jeremy expected that Philip wanted to discuss the allocation of the franchise for the West Coast Main Line railway. Jeremy had first become aware of dispute over this in late July after Richard Branson, the head of Virgin Rail, had written to Justine Greening, the Secretary of State for Transport, accusing her department of mismanagement. At the time Jeremy had asked Philip, Justine's new permanent secretary, to take a look at the process, and after Philip had confirmed there was no evidence that Virgin Rail had been unfairly treated, the Chancellor had passed this message back to Branson.

The issue hadn't, however, gone away. When the West Coast Main Line franchise had been awarded to FirstGroup in mid-August 2012, Branson denounced the department for accepting FirstGroup's 'absolutely preposterous' bid and Virgin Rail applied for a judicial review. But the look on Philip's face when he walked into Jeremy's office suggested that things were far worse than that.

'In putting together the evidence to contest the judicial review, we have unearthed a flaw in our model,' Philip said.

'What sort of flaw?'

'We miscalculated the amount of risk associated with each bid and, therefore, the amount of capital each bidder needed to provide. I think we'll need to scrap the whole contest.'

Jeremy felt sick. He spent some time questioning Philip, making sure he understood the details. When Philip left, he picked up his pen. After apologising to the Prime Minister, he said he would commission an independent review of what had gone wrong and an assessment of every other black box analytical model in Whitehall. He would ensure the Civil Service was held to account and wouldn't tolerate the level of professional incompetence that appeared to have taken place.

'But I've let the Prime Minister down,' Jeremy told me when he got home. 'And it's the worst possible time for it to happen, when he's already under pressure from the Leveson inquiry, the unravelling of the Budget and Lansley's health reforms.'

I nodded. Jeremy couldn't monitor every process being run by the Civil Service, but that didn't lessen his accountability. And the rest of the story played out as Philip had anticipated: the franchise competition was scrapped on 3 October, multiple inquiries followed, and three officials were suspended, though they were later reinstated. Action had been taken, just as Jeremy had promised – though it had arguably been relatively mild given the gravity of the error.

In his reshuffle on 4 September 2012, the Prime Minister tried to address some of the government's issues by appointing Jeremy Hunt, who had just finished overseeing the Olympics, to replace Andrew Lansley as Secretary of State for Health. Andrew Mitchell became the new Chief Whip and David Laws returned from a period of exile following an earlier scandal to become a minister of state for education. Jeremy expected to spend time with all these appointees – and particularly with David Laws, who was going to work with Oliver Letwin on the Coalition's agenda for the second half of the Parliament. But it was Owen Paterson, the new Secretary of State for Environment, Food and Rural Affairs, whom Jeremy spent time with first, during what became known as 'badger weekend'.

Years of research had shown that badgers, despite their endearing looks, were probably responsible for spreading tuberculosis to cattle and other animals through droplets in their breath and the urine they used to mark their territories. With around 30,000 tuberculosis-infected cows being slaughtered each year in the UK, David King, of historic foot and mouth fame, was once again advocating a cull.

For two years Jeremy had left the department to develop their plan for implementing this cull, which proposed starting with pilots in the west and south-west of England where tuberculosis was rife. Culling badgers was always going to be controversial and it needed to be done both humanely and precisely, not least because, if badgers were allowed to spread out into newly emptied territories, this could increase the spread of the disease. But Mark Walport, the chief scientific adviser, told Jeremy he agreed with the department's planned approach and Bronwyn Hill, the permanent secretary, confirmed that the economic case was positive so long as the farming industry contributed to the cost.

Jeremy and the Prime Minister were, therefore, both expecting the pilot culls to take place in the autumn of 2012, but when Owen Paterson arrived in the department, he found that the preparatory work was woefully behind schedule, with the National Farmers' Union lacking sufficient specialist ammunition and little pre-baiting having been done. One of the companies contracted to carry out the cull then pulled out, saying that, with the mornings becoming misty, it was too late to start that year.

One Sunday morning in late September, Jeremy picked up the phone at home to find an agitated Prime Minister on the other end of the line. 'Owen Paterson rang,' David Cameron said. 'He says he wants to postpone the badger culls for another year.'

'A year?'

'Yes. How hard can it be? I asked him if he wanted me to go down and do them myself.'

'Please don't! I'll look into it.'

'I thought you might call,' Jeremy Marlow, the head of Owen Paterson's office, said when Jeremy rang. 'Unless we start the pilots soon, Natural England is saying they will withdraw the licence for this year. So we're calling everyone in for a meeting today to decide what to do.'

Jeremy sighed. He knew nothing at all about badgers, but he did know he would only get to the bottom of what was going on if he was in the room. So, an hour or so later he was in the secretary of state's office, still in his weekend jeans and battered brown leather jacket, quizzing Peter Kendall, the president of the National Farmers' Union, on every aspect of the cull. This included Peter's intention to use peanut butter as bait, which Jeremy nicknamed 'badger heroin'.

On the Number 10 stairway, 2001.

With Tony Blair, 2000.

With Gordon and Sarah Brown and the rest of the private office, 2008.

Meeting with David Cameron and Nick Clegg, 2010.

With David Cameron in
his Downing Street office,
2011.

Receiving a knighthood,
2012.

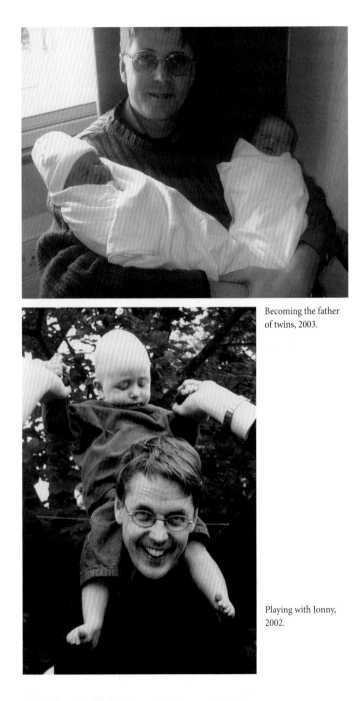

Becoming the father of twins, 2003.

Playing with Jonny, 2002.

Meeting Santa with me, an unimpressed Lizzie, Jonny and Peter, 2005.

Supporting David Cameron
in Cabinet, 2012.

Welcoming Theresa May
to Downing Street, 2016.

Becoming Baron Heywood of Whitehall, 2018.

With the family in Malta, 2017.

Jeremy's memorial service, 2019.

Jeremy's questioning couldn't, however, change the facts. Despite Owen and Peter's determination to begin, it was clear the culls would have to be postponed. With this decided, the secretary of state rang the Prime Minister, receiving an earful of frustration before passing the phone on to Peter so he could get the same.

After badger weekend, Jeremy asked the Implementation Unit and the Ministry of Defence to go through the plans for the 2013 and 2014 culls in detail and he dispatched Jeremy Marlow and other senior officials to Gloucestershire and Somerset when the culls began to ensure that only badgers were shot. The culls went well, although the badger population was smaller than expected, leading Owen to declare, to general ridicule, that the badgers had 'moved the goalposts'. Maybe they had, but by 2018, there were early indications of success with the incidence of tuberculosis in cattle halving in both of the pilot areas.

Back in the office, the political mood worsened after the House of Lords Bill was abandoned in early August 2012 and the Liberal Democrats again threatened to withdraw their support for the boundary changes. With the Coalition on edge, the Quad, which had expanded over time, was pared back to its core – the Prime Minister, Deputy Prime Minister, Chancellor and Chief Secretary, together with Jeremy, Philip Rycroft and the two chiefs of staff.

Despite the tension, the Quad still worked. It, therefore, became – just like Jeremy's meetings with Ed Balls in Churchill's Cafe years before – the main place where decisions could still be made. For this reason it was also where Jeremy decided to raise the thorny topic of airport expansion.

Jeremy knew, of course, how politically difficult this issue was. A new runway had been ruled out in the Coalition Agreement, it didn't fit with the Prime Minister's aspiration of creating the 'greenest government ever', and several senior Liberal Democrat and Conservative ministers had parliamentary seats under potential flight paths. The debate was made more complex by the fact that the Mayor of London, Boris Johnson, was determined to build a new airport on an island in the middle of the Thames. But the economic benefits, which Jeremy was familiar with from all the work that had taken place under Labour, were also clear.

'What we need,' he told the Quad after taking them through the arguments, 'is an independent review to go through the issues once and for all, including the mayor's proposal.'

And despite the politics, at the end of a long discussion, the Quad agreed, because the benefits were substantial enough to make rejecting the possibility feel irresponsible. On 7 September the transport secretary, Patrick McLoughlin, announced the creation of an Airports Commission. This would look at the economic, social and environmental costs and benefits of different runway options and report back by the summer of 2015 – a date that was conveniently after the next election, so no manifesto commitments would be broken.

By this time, Labour – the only major party to have supported airport expansion in its manifesto – had also ruled it out. But Jeremy knew that his old friend Andrew Adonis also understood the economic benefits of more runway capacity and was, therefore, confident that Andrew would convince his colleagues to accept the government's plan. After the Commission had been announced, Jeremy sent his airports papers to file and waited, like everyone else, to see if Howard Davies, the chair of the new commission, could finally resolve the issue.

43

'How Deep is Your Love':
Plebs and Europe

September 2012–January 2013

In the run-up to the 2012 Autumn Statement, Jeremy put rail franchise agreements, badgers and runways aside to join the Prime Minister for a Coalition Cabinet meeting at Chequers. The mood was downbeat after the declaration by the Office for National Statistics in April that the economy had fallen back into recession – a so-called 'double-dip recession', since it had only just emerged from the previous one. What this meant, the Chancellor told the Quad, was that they needed to find further cuts of around £6 billion in 2015/16 and £10 billion in 2016/17 to meet their deficit reduction targets. In the debate that followed, the Chancellor proposed delaying the introduction of Universal Credit and the Liberal Democrats suggested a wealth tax. After a day of intense discussion, they left Chequers with their different positions at least clear, but with little alignment on which actions to take.

Back in the office, Francis Maude came to complain to Jeremy about the lack of progress on Civil Service reform, pointing out that even the 'snapshot review' of Bob's department seemed to have stalled. After intervening to get this work accelerated, Jeremy decided that, since Bob and Francis seemed to be struggling to work together effectively, he would have to start attending their meetings on the next phase of the reform plan since this had the potential to change the Civil Service dramatically. In those discussions, Jeremy supported many of the changes that were being proposed, including publishing permanent secretaries' objectives and strengthening the Civil Service's accountability to Parliament for major projects. However, he resisted others that he felt could politicise the service, like giving ministers the right to choose their permanent secretaries, to carry out their performance reviews, to sack them and even to remove their pay.

But there was one proposal that both Jeremy and Francis supported even though it was also controversial. This was the idea of giving the Prime Minister a choice of suitable candidates when permanent secretary posts were being filled, rather than a single name. The Prime Minister also strongly favoured this, so Francis was asked to broach it with the independent Civil Service Commissioners who oversaw these appointments.

That autumn there were several issues hanging over Downing Street that Jeremy could do little about including finding a way forward on the Scottish referendum and trying to anticipate what might emerge from the ongoing Leveson report on phone hacking. In mid-September 2012, Jeremy was, however, distracted from these worries by a massive row over a single word.

Jeremy's part in this saga began with an email from Chris Martin on Wednesday 19 September. This said that Andrew Mitchell, the new Chief Whip, had been caught up in an altercation on Downing Street after a police officer had asked him to dismount from his bike to go through the gate. According to the *Sun*, which splashed the story two days later, Andrew had called the officer a 'pleb' – a word that underlined for many the chasm between a government made up of posh, privately-educated ministers and the people who were being beaten up by their austerity programme.

The policeman involved, PC Toby Rowland, was a well-respected and long-serving officer, but the story was Andrew's word against his. At the Prime Minister's request, Jeremy, therefore, spoke to the Metropolitan Police Commissioner, Bernard Hogan-Howe, who agreed that, since Andrew had apologised for losing his cool and no criminal offence had been committed, there was no need for any further action.

Chris Martin came to see Jeremy a few days later. 'There's been a development,' he said. 'The deputy chief whip says he's had an email from Keith Wallis, one of his constituents, who claims he was standing outside the gates with his nephew when the row happened – and he says that he heard Andrew use the word "pleb".'

'Oh.'

'And since the email arrived before the incident became public, it seems genuine. So the Prime Minister wants you to look into it.'

Jeremy blanched. 'Really?'

'Yes. But without contacting the police. He doesn't want to prompt them into an investigation that will stir this story up any further.'

The following day things became more complex after Andrew Mitchell reported that he had received his own email. This sender, James Reynolds, also claimed to have witnessed the incident, but said Andrew hadn't used the word 'pleb'. However, since James wouldn't make or receive calls, and didn't want his email address shared, Jeremy couldn't see any way of confirming his account.

That afternoon Jeremy, Chris Martin and Sue Gray headed down into the basement of Number 10 to see if they could at least verify Keith Wallis's story. They huddled around a small screen to watch grainy black and white footage of Andrew pedalling down Downing Street. The bike paused, but since there was no audio recording, they couldn't hear what Andrew was saying and the images were too fuzzy to allow lip reading. On the far side of the gates they could see a bald man in a pale jacket who they presumed wasn't Keith Wallis since he was on his own.

'But there's a blind spot by the gates,' Jeremy said. 'Can we get any more footage?'

'There's another camera on the lamp post outside the MoD,' Sue said. 'But that belongs to the Met – which means we can't use it.'

They watched the film again. There was only one thing for it, Jeremy decided – Chris would have to stand on Downing Street and pretend to be Andrew Mitchell while Sue stood in the blind spot to see if she could hear Chris talking. When they did that the result was clear – from the blind spot Sue couldn't hear Chris. Therefore, since there was nowhere else that Keith could have been standing, his evidence was unreliable.

Jeremy rang the deputy chief whip, John Randall. Given their findings, he said, they needed to talk to Keith Wallis. John agreed with this, though he said he needed to have the conversation himself since Wallis was one of his constituents.

The following day, John was back. 'Keith refused to see me,' he said, 'so I turned up at his house unannounced. He repeated his story and he assured me that he has no connection with the police or the media. But he's refusing to talk to anyone else.'

Jeremy picked up a picture of the balding man taken from the CCTV footage. 'Did he look like this?'

John shook his head. 'No, nothing like that.'

Jeremy completed his report on 27 September. Keith Wallis's evidence was unreliable, he told the Prime Minister. And, if that was the case, then it raised questions about how he could have found out about the incident on Downing Street before it had been reported in the press. They should, therefore, consider giving the results of their investigation to the police.

Chris Martin rang Jeremy the following day to say that the Prime Minister was grateful for his report. He'd decided that, since Keith's evidence was unreliable, Andrew Mitchell would carry on as Chief Whip. However, neither he nor Andrew wanted to involve the police and nor did they see any need to refer the issue to Alex Allan, the independent adviser on ministers' interests.*

'Okay,' Jeremy said. He didn't feel strongly about involving Alex since Alex wouldn't have access to any new information, but as he'd said in his report, he would have preferred to involve the police. However, his main concern was that Keith Wallis's evidence shouldn't affect Andrew Mitchell's position. He also assumed – wrongly – that this would be the end of the affair.

By the time Jeremy finished his report on the Andrew Mitchell saga, things were at last progressing on the Scottish referendum. The big political issues, like the wording of the referendum question, were being mulled over by the Scotland Cabinet Committee, which was being supported at official level by Philip Rycroft. Philip was the

---

* After being resisted for many years, this role had been created by Gordon Brown after he became Prime Minister. After being appointed Cabinet Secretary, Jeremy frequently relied on Alex's advice on proprietary issues.

perfect person for the job, Jeremy told me, because, in addition to advising Nick Clegg and overseeing the Constitutional Unit in the Cabinet Office, he lived near Edinburgh, and unusually for Whitehall, had experience of working for the Scottish government. If anyone could maintain channels of communication through the impending storm, it was Philip.

While the ministers pondered, Jeremy focused on drafting guidance on the referendum for the Civil Service. This turned out to be more complex than he'd anticipated after the Prime Minister argued that civil servants should be able to support the campaign.

'Civil servants have always supported government campaigns like promoting recycling or persuading other countries to sign arms trade treaties,' David Cameron said. 'Surely, it's only party-political campaigns that civil servants have to avoid, not any campaign that is in any sense political?'

But Jeremy shook his head at this, and dug in. Although the two parties at odds with each other were largely geographically separated, he said, the Scottish referendum was clearly political. And after some debate, the Prime Minister conceded this point, which meant Jeremy could finalise his guidance.

But while this tidied up one issue, less progress was being made at ministerial level on the terms of the referendum. The Prime Minister's main concern was to make the question one that could be answered by a simple 'yes' or 'no' because offering a third choice, like the 'devo max' option of giving Scotland full taxation powers that Alex Salmond had been suggesting, would muddy the answer and split the unionist vote.

In early September 2012, Jeremy met Ciaran Martin, who was supporting Philip Rycroft.

'The Scottish government is ready to settle the outstanding issues,' Jeremy said.

Ciaran stared at Jeremy. 'How do you know?'

'I can't say,' Jeremy replied, though Ciaran knew that Jeremy talked regularly to the senior officials in the Scottish Civil Service. 'But I gather that, now Nicola Sturgeon has been put in charge of their constitutional portfolio, they're ready to discuss terms.'

After that, work on the referendum accelerated in Whitehall, and in mid-October, the Edinburgh Agreement was signed. The Prime Minister would get his single question and the referendum would take place by autumn 2014, after which, in a little-noticed twist, the powers being delegated to allow Scotland to call it would expire.

While these talks between the Scottish and English government were coming to a conclusion, another negotiation – between EADS, a Franco-German company which owned Airbus, and the UK's BAE Systems – was falling apart. The talks between EADs and BAE about a possible merger to create a £28 billion aerospace and defence company had started positively. From the UK's point of view – as Jeremy had advised the Prime Minister – it would have allowed BAE, a critical supplier to the Ministry of Defence, to benefit from growth in Airbus' commercial plane and helicopter businesses. The deal, however, collapsed when the Germans refused to back it, despite Tom Enders, the former German Army paratrooper who was the CEO of EADS, flying to Berlin to make the case. There just wasn't enough in it for them, particularly given BAE's involvement in the UK's nuclear deterrent and the fact that some German manufacturing would become part of the new UK-led defence division.

The merger was called off on 10 October 2012. But the questions it had raised in Jeremy's mind about the challenges facing BAE Systems hadn't gone away. In the weeks afterwards he, therefore, asked a team in the Cabinet Office to find other ways of strengthening the company, such as by reducing the amount it spent on its ships and submarine business, for which the UK government was the only major customer, and reinvesting the savings in its aerospace business, where there was more export potential. These discussions weren't easy but ultimately Jeremy knew – as did the Ministry of Defence – that the interests of the government and BAE Systems, its largest defence supplier, were inextricably linked.

Jeremy was also dragged into a far more politically difficult issue that autumn when a row exploded over the price of energy bills. This began after David Cameron announced, without the agreement of his Coalition partners, that he intended to pass legislation to force energy companies to give their lowest tariffs to all their customers. This prime ministerial coup – of a kind familiar to Jeremy ever since Tony Blair's statements on issues like street crime and health funding – infuriated Ed Davey, the Liberal Democrat Secretary of State for Energy and Climate Change, who instructed his officials to down tools on the energy package they'd been in the process of preparing.

The next step was predictable – Jeremy was called in to find a way through a dispute in which the battle lines were already clearly drawn. The Prime Minister, under pressure from Ed Miliband to reduce bills, was frustrated because the existing policy assumed that consumers would switch to lower energy tariffs if they were available, but few people – particularly if they were poor or elderly – actually did. Meanwhile, the Liberal Democrats worried that additional regulation would decrease investment in renewables, undermine their 'Green Deal', and stifle competition by reducing the number of tariffs available.

The compromise that Jeremy presented to the Quad in late October 2012, after lengthy negotiations with both sides, had something in it for everyone, though it was perfect for no one. For the Liberal Democrats, it included a commitment to spend £7.6 billion on renewables, enabling the UK to meet its 2020 target, though only by purchasing 10 per cent of its renewable energy from abroad. There was also a commitment to setting a new carbon emissions target for 2030. In exchange, the Prime Minister would legislate to require suppliers to offer a single price for each tariff type and to switch consumers to that price as soon as possible.

With the Chancellor and Ed Davey at odds over the size of the commitment to renewables, finalising this package hadn't been straightforward. Jeremy was, therefore, relieved when the measures were announced on 20 November and broadly welcomed – particularly by new energy providers who said it would be easier to enter the market if the large companies were forced to offer their lowest tariffs to existing rather than only to new customers.

* * *

Jeremy had largely managed to put thoughts of the Leveson report out of his mind while he'd been working on these other issues through the autumn of 2012, but by early November its imminent arrival made it harder to forget. After all, if Lord Justice Leveson decided that David Cameron had given Rupert Murdoch preferential treatment, it would be difficult for the Prime Minister to survive – and some would see Jeremy, who'd pushed for this public and judge-led inquiry, as partially to blame.

An advance copy of the 2,000-page Leveson report was at last delivered to Number 10 early on Wednesday 28 November 2012, twenty-four hours before its publication. While David Cameron prepared for Prime Minister's Questions, Jeremy, the Number 10 team, and departmental experts from the Home Office and Ministry of Justice gathered around the table in his office go through it. They flipped through the pages in silence, but within minutes, the mood relaxed. The report was tough, but it focused on the conduct of the press and on data protection, not on the government or even – to Jeremy's surprise – the failure of the police to investigate the phone hacking allegations with vigour.

After the departmental officials left, the remaining group discussed the implications of the report for the Prime Minister. Although the conclusion that the UK's political parties had become too close to the press was uncomfortable, it was relatively benign. More difficult was the report's rejection of the press' proposed new approach to self-regulation, which it regarded as too weak. Instead, Lord Justice Leveson wanted to set up a new body under legislation to approve press regulators. Jeremy thought that this recommendation was a clever one because the proposed legislation wouldn't directly establish a press regulator or give the government or Parliament any right to constrain what newspapers published. It wouldn't force papers to join a regulator, although approved regulators would be able to offer relatively inexpensive arbitration services to their members, but it would oblige the government to protect the freedom of the press.

Having ensured he'd understood the subtleties of the report, Jeremy went with Ed Llewellyn, Kate Fall and Craig Oliver to see the Prime Minister and the Chancellor.

'Well, this could hardly be any better for us,' David Cameron said after they summarised the conclusions. 'And even if Labour and the Lib Dems decide to back Leveson's proposed legislation, I don't think we should.'

The others nodded, but Jeremy didn't. If it had been his choice, he would have implemented Leveson's recommendation since it was hard to see how the tiny role for Parliament that it envisaged would have made the slightest difference to the quality and fearlessness of the British press. But Cameron and George Osborne didn't see it that way – after being cleared of wrongdoing, they saw this as an opportunity to take a more newspaper-friendly position than the other two main parties.

'If the Lib Dems disagree and want a legislative solution, we'll have to hold a Coalition Committee meeting to suspend collective responsibility on this issue,' Jeremy said.

'Okay,' the Prime Minister said.

Jeremy studied his papers. This was going to be difficult because, if they suspended collective responsibility, the Civil Service would need to provide separate advice to the Conservatives and Liberal Democrats on this hugely political issue while somehow ensuring that everyone felt they were being fairly treated.

This Coalition split soon became clear to the rest of the world. At 3 p.m. the following day, the Prime Minister told the House of Commons that, while he accepted Lord Justice Leveson's principles for effective press self-regulation, he had serious misgivings about the proposed statutory involvement. Immediately afterwards, Ed Miliband said he supported setting out the principles of press regulation in statute. And later that afternoon, the Deputy Prime Minister outlined his own position, which was broadly aligned with Miliband's.

This was a political quagmire, Jeremy told me. Members of the government's front bench were expressing conflicting views in Parliament and one half of the Coalition had aligned itself with the Opposition. The Civil Service could do little to resolve this political row, but it could search for acceptable technocratic compromises to the issue of press regulation. Jeremy, therefore, handed over this challenge to the unflappable Treasury solicitor, Paul Jenkins, and Helen

MacNamara from the Department of Culture, Media and Sport, telling them to pull him in if required.

While Paul and Helen started work, Jeremy returned to the 2012 Autumn Statement. After announcing in April that the UK was in a double-dip recession, the OBR had increased the economic gloom in mid-November when it had worsened its forecasts for 2012 and 2013. Given this deteriorating outlook, the Chancellor had at last been forced to accept in his Budget in March that the structural deficit wouldn't be eliminated until after the end of the Parliament in 2016/17. They were sticking to Plan A, but it had been eased, just as Jonathan Portes had recommended almost two years before.

This relaxation provided a little more leeway in the Autumn Statement, but they were still struggling to agree what actions to take to address the economic deterioration, with the Liberal Democrats again wanting to increase personal allowances, the Chancellor and Prime Minister wanting more welfare cuts, and Jeremy arguing for more measures to kick-start the economy. When it was announced on 5 December 2012, the Autumn Statement somehow managed to reflect all these views. It included an increase in allowances alongside another tranche of spending cuts, though these had been spread over several years. Using some Treasury magic, the Chancellor had also transformed the expected windfall from the auction of the 4G mobile spectrum, which was due to be completed early the following year, into a package of growth measures including cancelling a planned rise in fuel duty, reducing corporation tax and increasing investment in infrastructure and science.

A few days afterwards, however, Ed Llewellyn turned up in Jeremy's office with news that made all these measures feel insignificant. Ed told Jeremy that he was working on a speech for the Prime Minister – and at the heart of it was a promise to include a referendum on Britain's membership of the EU in the next Conservative manifesto.

Jeremy was aware of the pressure for this. Throughout his career, starting from John Major's 'game, set and match' rhetoric at the end of the Maastricht Treaty negotiations, the Eurosceptic tide in Britain had been rising. In 2009 the Prime Minister had attempted to stop his party 'banging on about Europe' by guaranteeing a vote on any future transfer of power to the EU. But this hadn't been enough to turn the tide. Too much frustration and mistrust had built up, exacerbated by the eurozone crisis, the Labour government's refusal to hold a referendum on the Lisbon Treaty, and David Cameron's failed attempt to veto a new European treaty the previous year. On top of this, the Conservative Party was worried about the Ukip party, which was demanding an in/out vote on Europe and threatening to attract both defecting Conservative MPs and many voters at the next election.

But while Jeremy understood these issues, he still felt that people were too negative about Britain's position in Europe, probably because little was said about the things that had been achieved, for example the agreement to reduce greenhouse gas emissions. And though the growth in Euroscepticism was clear, this didn't reduce his disquiet about opening up the question of Britain's EU membership. This is why, after discussing it with some of his permanent secretary colleagues, he made an almost unheard-of trip into the office on 30 December to write a personal memo to the Prime Minister.

Jeremy didn't question David Cameron's decision to hold a referendum. That was a political choice, whatever his own views. Instead, he began by saying that he understood the Prime Minister's wish to see a fresh settlement between the UK and the rest of the EU, including the repatriation of some powers. However, since failure to achieve this could lead to the UK's exit, it would be essential to show the government had understood and prepared for such an eventuality.

He also wanted to stress three other points.

First, the Prime Minister should be conscious that, once the content of his speech became public, businesses would assign a 25 to 50 per cent probability to the UK's exit, which would impact investment in the UK.

Second, while the Prime Minister's negotiation with the EU ahead of a referendum might end up as a UK-specific repatriation of powers, it would be better to start by trying to reform the EU more broadly.

And finally, while the starting point for the debate, and the focus of the Prime Minister's speech, was the eurozone's economic and growth crisis, a referendum could only be won if the issues relating to immigration, welfare, extradition and the European Court of

Human Rights that dominated the newspapers were addressed. However, the Prime Minister should be aware that none of this would be easy since free movement of people was fundamental to the EU, and concerns relating to the European Court of Human Rights largely sat outside the EU's jurisdiction.

Jeremy continued to worry about the Prime Minister's forthcoming pledge during our New Year's break. If the Prime Minister called a referendum, he might open up a Pandora's box of problems he couldn't solve. The issue of immigration was particularly frustrating because, for years, governments of all colours had been reluctant to talk about its benefits, David Cameron had then increased the tension by making an impossible promise, before the 2010 election, to limit net immigration to 'tens of thousands'.

Our holiday in South Africa was at least a distraction from such concerns. It was, however, a trip with highs and lows. Glorious dawn safaris watching a pride of lions with their cubs contrasted with the agonising pain I had in my leg after spinning out of control and crashing on an ice rink before Christmas and Jeremy's devastation when both his BlackBerrys were stolen in the crowds in Cape Town on New Year's Eve. Back in London, Jeremy was issued with new gadgets and I found out that my leg was broken, despite my doctor's previous assurances that it was fine.

On 15 January 2013, the Prime Minister replied to Jeremy's note. He'd taken time to digest the advice, he said, and he hoped Jeremy could see that it had influenced the drafting of his speech. To some extent this was true – for example the final version declared an intent to make change happen 'for the entire EU, not just for Britain'. But the bulk of the speech still focused on issues like the crisis of EU competitiveness and the gap between the EU and its citizens, while the more troubling topics that Jeremy had raised, such as the role of the European Court of Human Rights, were either mentioned in passing, or in the case of immigration, not at all.

'It is time,' the Prime Minister said when he took the stage in Bloomberg's office in London on 23 January, 'for the British people to have their say. It is time to settle this European question in British politics.'

44

'You Can't Always Get What You Want': A new beginning

January–July 2013

For a while, the Prime Minister's pledge to call a referendum on Europe changed very little. After all, it was a commitment that would only kick in after the next election, and only if the Conservatives were returned to power, presumably with a majority. So, after the Bloomberg speech, Jeremy, like everyone else in Number 10, put it to the back of his mind and focused instead on more immediate issues like helping to finalise the Coalition's mid-term review.

The Coalition: Together in the National Interest, which was published on 7 January 2013, was intended to signal a fresh start after a torrid 2012. This time, however, the Coalition's intentions weren't announced in a rose garden and the review couldn't fix the government's underlying issues. The Liberal Democrats, who'd campaigned to scrap tuition fees and re-inflate the economy before switching their position once in government, were particularly scarred. As political parties in other countries had often discovered, it's hard to be the junior party in a coalition government.

This ongoing stress continued to reveal itself in unexpected ways, for example, during the appointment of a new permanent secretary to the Department for Energy and Climate Change. Jeremy had left Bob Kerslake managing this process, only to find that the candidate put forward by the panel was David Kennedy, the chief executive of an independent body that advised the government on preparing for climate change. For all David's strengths, it was clear that this would never work within a government that was far from aligned on the importance of environmental issues. After the Prime Minister blocked David's appointment, Jeremy, therefore, stepped in to restart the process.*

But these small spats were easier to deal with than the decision by the Liberal Democrats to act on their threat and vote against the parliamentary boundary changes on 29 January 2013.

'This is a car crash: we need to put on our hard hats, and get ready to hit the wall,' Jeremy told me. 'Though, more practically, I've asked my office to dig out the papers on how to serve a minority government.'

Luckily neither the hard hats nor the files were needed. After the boundary changes were defeated, several Conservative ministers called for an election. But it soon became clear that the party leaders weren't willing to dissolve the Coalition, at least not yet. Quad meetings continued, the relationship between the Prime Minister and the Deputy Prime Minister remained respectful and largely collaborative, and Jeremy returned his papers to the files.

'Plebgate', the name that had been bestowed on Andrew Mitchell's outburst on Downing Street, resurfaced towards the end of January. After Jeremy had given his report to the Prime Minister the previous September, he'd initially thought little more about it. In October 2012, however, after the Conservative Party turned against him, Andrew Mitchell resigned. After he did, he demanded copies of the Downing Street CCTV footage, and released them to the press.

While most journalists moved on, Michael Crick, Channel 4's veteran political correspondent, kept digging. His efforts were rewarded when he discovered that Keith Wallis, the man who claimed to have witnessed the incident, was a police officer. This raised suspicions – which it turned out were correct – that a disaffected group of police officers had conspired to embarrass Andrew and the government.

Bernard Jenkin, chair of the Public Affairs Committee in the House of Commons, summoned Jeremy to a special hearing on 10

---

* Jeremy also apologised to David, and later supported his appointment to a role in the Department for International Development.

January 2013 to grill him on his failure to uncover Wallis's identity. After running through the steps Jeremy had taken to produce his report, the committee started probing.

'Have you done a lot of assessing CCTV footage, or is this your first time?' Jenkin asked.

'No, this is my debut,' Jeremy admitted.

The committee then wanted to know why Jeremy hadn't raised with the police the inconsistencies he'd found between Keith Wallis's emails and the CCTV footage, and why he hadn't demanded to see the police log or involved Alex Allan.

Jeremy braced himself. He'd been asked, he said, to investigate whether Keith Wallis's account was reliable. He'd concluded it wasn't and had advised the Prime Minister to disregard it in coming to a decision about Andrew Mitchell's position. He continued to repeat this statement in various forms for several hours, coming home exhausted.

The Prime Minister swung in to support Jeremy, saying he was right to have asked him to investigate the incident and thought he'd done a good job.

'Which is the least he could do,' I said.

'It was a difficult situation,' Jeremy said.

The Plebgate saga continued to ebb and flow for months after that, while four police officers were sacked for misconduct and Keith Wallis was found guilty of lying and jailed for a year. Andrew Mitchell, meanwhile, continued to insist that he'd never said 'pleb', a battle he only ceased in November 2014 after losing an expensive libel case against News Group Newspapers. Although this ended this fight, the length and extent of Andrew's campaign had a long-term impact because it set a precedent for future arguments about ministerial propriety and, therefore, made this aspect of Jeremy's role much more delicate and time-consuming. It also underlined the importance of involving the independent adviser, Alex Allan, in these investigations both to provide wise counsel and to offer some protection if there was subsequent criticism of either their outcomes or how they had been conducted.

* * *

Our home life had by this time become more complex after the symptoms of Brenda's dementia morphed from mild confusion into midnight wanderings, kettles filled with boiling milk, and an afternoon of panic after we lost her in the crowds during a trip to Bath. For the time being we could cope, though only with Maggie, our ever-dependable nanny, watching Brenda for most of each day. But of course, this wasn't just a practical issue – for Jeremy it was also the gradual loss of his mother, who was withdrawing from our world.

It would have helped if things were getting easier in Number 10. But although the pace had slowed after the initial post-election sprint, the economy was still stuttering and both sides of the Coalition continued to nurse lists of perceived injustices and broken promises. This meant that, although the Quad was still functioning, and joint policies were still being progressed, the parties were beginning to separate. One symbol of this was the Prime Minister's decision in April 2013 to shift the focus of the Policy Unit so that it supported only the Conservatives rather than both sides of the Coalition. Jo Johnson, a Conservative minister, was appointed to replace Paul Kirby and start work on the party's 2015 manifesto, while the Liberal Democrats began working on their own manifesto with the help of the Deputy Prime Minister's office.

When the first draft of the March 2013 Budget papers arrived, Jeremy went through them in detail, keen to avoid the omnishambles of 2012. Yet again it seemed that the economic conditions were worsening after the Office for National Statistics' declaration back in January that, following a better third quarter, the economy had shrunk again in the last quarter of 2012. This meant that the UK was on its way to an almost unheard-of triple-dip recession. In response to this, the IMF declared in late January that the government should tone down its austerity plans and Moody's stripped the UK of its triple-A credit rating.

Although these economic numbers later turned out to be wrong – the UK hadn't even experienced a double-dip recession the previous year let alone a triple-dip – in that moment it felt like the economy was collapsing. The increasing, though largely unspoken, fear in the Quad was that the IMF might be right that the Coalition had gone too far with austerity, and by doing so had plunged the economy into a downward spiral.

But rather than caving in to this pressure and further easing his targets, the Chancellor said he was determined to keep going, and would reduce departmental budgets for 2015/16 by £11.5 billion rather than the £10 billion he'd declared in the June spending round. While Jeremy didn't argue against this, he again pushed for further action to stimulate the economy. He was, therefore, relieved when, alongside these additional spending cuts, the Chancellor also announced in his Budget a £3 billion boost in infrastructure spending, a further reduction in corporation tax and a new Help to Buy scheme for homeowners.

Throughout this period, Francis Maude and Bob Kerslake had continued to work on the next instalment of the Civil Service Reform Plan. As part of this process, Francis had commissioned the Institute for Public Policy Research (IPPR) to identify lessons that could be learnt from overseas. Jeremy had known about this project – in fact, it was being paid for by a new Contestable Policy Fund that Jeremy had championed as a way of bringing more outside expertise into Whitehall. But he was surprised to find, when we returned from a short break in Amsterdam in May 2013, that the IPPR had finalised its recommendations without asking for his views or sharing the draft findings with him.

Jeremy's surprise morphed into irritation when he opened the IPPR's report to discover that it echoed many of Francis Maude's proposals to increase ministers' control over the Civil Service. These included introducing four-year fixed-term contracts for permanent secretaries and allowing ministers to appoint 'extended offices' of staff outside of the normal Civil Service recruitment processes. This was, Jeremy realised belatedly, the risk of the new fund – rather than bringing challenging voices into Whitehall, it could be used to reinforce opinions that people already held.

In mid-June, Jeremy, Bob Kerslake and Francis Maude met the Prime Minister to discuss the recommendations. By this point, emotions were running high with many of Jeremy's permanent secretary colleagues claiming that Francis was 'waging a war' against the

Civil Service and that his reforms threatened to make it impossible for them to serve future administrations impartially.

They began the meeting by discussing the idea of fixed-term contracts for permanent secretaries. Francis was strongly in favour of these, while Jeremy argued that it would be better to avoid complex contracts and instead make all permanent secretary appointments for five years, with the possibility of extending them for another two.

'I agree with Jeremy,' the Prime Minister said.

Francis frowned at this before turning to the next item. 'I think the idea of appointing extended ministerial offices is an excellent one,' he said.

'I'm less convinced,' George Osborne said, and Jeremy nodded – he'd hoped the Chancellor would be a moderating influence. 'If we appoint many more people outside the standard processes, we could be accused of politicising the Civil Service. Why don't we just allow ministers to have a few more special advisers?'

'Bringing in a few more expert advisers could be helpful if they're not political cronies,' Jeremy said. 'But I agree that we should be cautious about going further. The best departments are those where ministers work closely with their officials, which is how Number 10 works today.'

But Francis was shaking his head, and on this point he wasn't budging. Giving ministers the flexibility to appoint more advisers was essential, he argued, since ministers were accountable to Parliament for ensuring that their departments delivered. And after a long debate, David Cameron decided to side with Francis so long as he retained the right to approve each appointment.

For Jeremy the outcome of the meeting had been mixed, and it became worse when Francis adjusted the conclusions to say that permanent secretary appointments should be for four rather than five years and to remove the requirement for the Prime Minister to approve new special advisers. But after the Prime Minister readjusted these, Jeremy decided he could live with the outcome. It wasn't ideal, but nor would it fundamentally endanger the Civil Service's impartiality.

* * *

While Jeremy was finding some of the Coalition's reforms challenging, he was still championing others, in particular their push for more openness. His support for this even extended to one of the most controversial debates at that time – whether the documents that the government had shared with the Chilcot inquiry into Iraq, including the Joint Intelligence Committee papers, should be declassified.

Back in late 2010, Gus O'Donnell had written to the inquiry to say that some of these documents, including Tony Blair's notes to George Bush, couldn't be made public because doing so could damage the UK's international relations. When he became Cabinet Secretary, Jeremy had challenged the advice Gus had received on this because he believed there was little chance people would accept the inquiry's findings if significant documents were concealed.

It had taken huge effort to change Whitehall's stance on the declassification of the Chilcot inquiry papers – including Sue Gray negotiating with the deputy US ambassador, Jeremy speaking to Tony Blair and a letter from the information commissioner confirming that this wouldn't be taken as a precedent. But by June 2013, they'd agreed to declassify virtually everything with only a few redactions remaining relating to diplomatic relations with other countries on non-Iraq issues.

When Jeremy told me this, I asked him whether it meant that the Chilcot Report would soon be finished. The inquiry's timetable was causing huge frustration, with the papers often blaming Jeremy for its sluggish pace. Jeremy said he hoped so – after all, although Chilcot had never set a firm deadline, the government had originally understood the inquiry would be concluded by 2012. The problem was that they could do little to speed Chilcot up since the inquiry was independent and Chilcot had said he didn't need extra resources.

Jeremy's support for openness, however, had its limits – as his earlier battle to protect the reports produced by the Major Projects Authority had revealed. Another situation where Jeremy stepped in to preserve confidentiality began that June when Olly Robbins, who was by then deputy national security adviser, came to see Jeremy.

'We believe that the *Guardian* has many of the Snowden files,' Olly said.

Jeremy knew about Edward Snowden, a former CIA subcontractor who had leaked vast amounts of classified information from the US National Security Agency, but this was the first time he had heard that those papers might be in Britain. 'How much UK material do they have?' he asked.

'Possibly tens of thousands of highly classified intelligence documents.'

'Really? What's the worst-case scenario? And I mean the actual worst case, not the agencies' general aversion to people seeing intelligence material. We can't overclaim the damage to ministers.'

Olly shook his head. 'It's not good. The documents could reveal the identities of intelligence officers and possibly their contacts. They could also expose the techniques we use against hostile states.'

'Okay,' Jeremy said with a sigh. 'We'll have to find a way to get the papers back. But I don't know how. I can't see Nick Clegg, or even David Cameron being willing, after Leveson, to issue an injunction against the *Guardian*.'

While Olly and Jeremy pondered how to proceed, events progressed by themselves. On 6 June, the *Guardian* claimed that the National Security Agency in the US had hoovered up the records of telephone customers, and on 17 June, it alleged that the UK's security forces had bugged foreign leaders at Gordon Brown's London G20 summit.

Craig Oliver, who was ironically with the Prime Minister at the G8 summit in Northern Ireland when this second story broke, rang Alan Rusbridger, the *Guardian*'s editor.

'Craig told Alan that, while the government would neither confirm nor deny the allegations about the G20, printing such stories could damage the UK's national security,' Olly reported to Jeremy afterwards.

'What did Alan say?'

'He says they're working on a number of further articles based on the Snowden papers. But they'll act in a responsible manner and won't reveal details of individual operations.'

'They can't possibly be the best judge of what could damage

national security,' Jeremy said, exasperation creeping into his voice. 'We'll have to try to persuade him to cooperate.'

'I'm going to see if I can get a meeting with Paul Johnson, Alan's deputy.'

'Good. But it will be a tightrope. If you threaten them too much, they'll call our bluff and ask why the police aren't getting involved. But if you threaten them too little, they won't agree to let us work with them, even if it's only to edit out particularly damaging bits of stories. Even the Liberal Democrats would support us doing that.'

A few days later, Olly returned. 'It didn't work,' he told Jeremy. 'Paul refused to cooperate even though I told him that we're worried that their systems could be hacked by foreign states.'

'What did he say?'

'He assured me the data was secure. Though it helped that, while we were talking, a window cleaner abseiled down outside the windows of their glass edifice at King's Cross, presumably enjoying an excellent view into their offices on his way down.'

While Jeremy smiled at this, he knew that, if Olly had reached an impasse, he would have to step in himself. So, after consulting the Prime Minister and Deputy Prime Minister, he headed up to King's Cross on the morning of 21 June with Barry Wells, his ever-cheerful Civil Service driver, at the wheel. Jeremy knew it wouldn't be easy to find a solution – not least because his predecessor Robert Armstrong, when he'd gone on a similar mission to Australia in 1986, had notoriously failed to stop the publication of *Spycatcher*, the memoir of an ex-spy – but he still had to try.

'I'm grateful for the responsibility you've shown so far,' Jeremy told Alan Rusbridger when they were seated in the *Guardian*'s office, 'but the Prime Minister, the Deputy Prime Minister, the foreign secretary and the attorney general are all concerned that sensitive information, like the location of our troops in Afghanistan, will become public. You've had your debate – it's not in the public interest to publish more articles.'

'I don't see the point of this,' Alan said. With his untidy mop of hair, he looked, Jeremy thought, more like one of his Hertford College professors than a newspaper editor. 'Other papers overseas also have the Snowden material. Even if you restrain us, the material will still be published.'

'Yes, but you have stolen British material on British soil. And as Olly has said, we believe you're a potential target for hostile foreign powers. I know you don't intend to put lives at risk. But you can't guarantee that you can keep the material secure.'

'Yes, we can. The data is being held in five hard drives, offline from the rest of our system. And the hard drives are in a bunker that is being kept locked with the blinds drawn and a guard stationed outside twenty-four hours a day.'

'It sounds like you've thought the security through,' Jeremy said, again deploying his soothing voice, 'so perhaps you wouldn't mind if we assessed it?'

After Alan somewhat grudgingly agreed to this, Jeremy sent a team in to review the *Guardian*'s bunker. Their work revealed – as he'd expected it would – significant security flaws, including the fact that no one had checked the nationality of the guards or knew how many keys there were to the room.

When the report was shared with Alan, he at last agreed to destroy the files.

'Though he's insisting that the *Guardian*'s staff should do it themselves,' Olly told Jeremy. 'They're going to do it using angle grinders and drills, under the supervision of two GCHQ technicians.'

Jeremy smiled. 'It's a good outcome,' he said. 'The *Guardian* has had its debate about surveillance and press freedom, but no British lives have been put at risk and we didn't have to resort to the law.'

45

'If Not for You':
The biggest change since Beveridge

July–September 2013

During Jeremy's first year and a half as Cabinet Secretary he'd spent most of his time resolving Coalition rows or dealing with crises. Despite this, when he stood up in front of the 200 most senior civil servants in early July 2013, his main message was about the need to reform Whitehall. What he wanted to create, Jeremy told his audience, was a Civil Service that was better able to address new challenges because it was unified, could work across departments and had strong commercial and digital skills.

To generate momentum behind this agenda, Jeremy invited Mike Bracken, the head of the Government Digital Service, to share with Cabinet his plan to put twenty-five of the most frequently used government services online, including prison visit bookings and applications for agricultural payments. If this worked, Mike told them, it would affect more than half of the transactions people made with the government and create savings of over £1 billion a year.

Under Mike's leadership, this 'digital by default' agenda was soon being adopted across Whitehall. Generally Mike was right that it created services that were both more cost effective and more efficient. However, it started to create problems when it was applied to Universal Credit.

By this point it was clear that, in the heady months after the 2010 election, ministers had been over-ambitious about the timetable for setting up Universal Credit and that the Civil Service, hampered by its desire to be helpful to the incoming government, hadn't been clear enough about the challenges it posed.

The original plan for Universal Credit had been to pilot it in a few jobcentres in April 2013 before rolling it out across the country. But this timetable soon began to look optimistic. The Welfare Reform Act, which defined the policy, only received royal assent in March 2012, and it took another year after that to complete the regulations. This meant that the details of how Universal Credit would operate were still being defined while the software for it was being coded. Even if the policy had been clear, there was then the challenge of integrating the multiple existing benefit systems that would form part of Universal Credit. When, on top of all that, the government also decided to apply Mike's Digital by Default agenda and make it possible for people to apply for the new benefit online, the timeline for delivering this already tough project became almost impossible.

Jeremy was conscious of how challenging Universal Credit was, but the Prime Minister was reluctant for him to get directly involved in monitoring it because he trusted his secretary of state, Iain Duncan Smith, to deliver the changes. So, instead, Jeremy started taking Robert Devereux, the department's permanent secretary, out for a regular plate of pasta at the Gran Paradiso restaurant in Victoria – not least because he knew that Universal Credit was only one of twelve major projects that Robert was implementing, alongside reducing his department's running costs by more than a quarter.

Through 2012, the traffic lights for Universal Credit on the reports from the Major Projects Authority began turning from amber to red. The situation worsened in September when Terry Moran, the highly respected but massively overloaded civil servant responsible for the project, suffered a breakdown that led to his early retirement. Terry was replaced by Philip Langsdale, who brought experience from Heathrow and the BBC. For a few weeks it felt like things were back on track until, in a tragic turn of events, Philip died just before Christmas. The shock of this, coming so soon after Terry's departure, was immense, the ripples fanning out across Whitehall.

In January 2013, David Pitchford, the head of the Major Projects Authority, came to see Jeremy. 'We've reached a turning point,' he said. 'Francis Maude has asked us to undertake another review of

Universal Credit. And if that shows we need to, we are prepared to take over the project.'

As David anticipated, this time the review's conclusions were severe – every area of the programme required urgent action – and it was, therefore, agreed that he should take charge.

At this point, Mike Bracken stepped forward with an even more radical proposal – rather than approving the next phase of the department's IT spend on Universal Credit, the Government Digital Service should build the new benefits system itself. If they used an agile IT method to do this, developing the solution in an iterative way, he thought it would only take about six months.

'The idea is absurd,' Robert Devereux told Jeremy over a tense dinner in the Gran Paradiso. 'Particularly since no one in government has any experience of agile IT. And I don't know anyone who has tried to use it for a project of this scale.'

Jeremy, though he knew nothing about IT, suspected Robert was right. 'But given where we are, there's nothing we can do,' he told him. 'They have to show us that it's possible or prove it isn't.'

But while Jeremy was willing to let Mike set up his thirty-person team of coders in an old police office in Victoria to try to build a new benefits system from scratch, he wasn't willing to go along with Iain Duncan Smith and Francis Maude's next proposal, which was to sack Robert.

'They believe it's in his best interests to go now rather than hanging around for a bad National Audit Office report later in the year,' Bob Kerslake told Jeremy when they discussed this in March 2013.

Jeremy shook his head. Sacking a civil servant was an easy way to allocate blame but it would be unfair to Robert and hugely demotivating for the Civil Service. So, before the 'Sack Devereux' campaign could build momentum, he set up a meeting with the Prime Minister, the Chancellor and Oliver Letwin.

Robert had faced unprecedented bad luck, Jeremy told this group, before going on to underline the many challenges of the Universal Credit project, including the fact that its timetable had been agreed before Robert's appointment. Robert had also delivered a raft of other changes in his department, including a remarkable increase in jobcentre productivity.

'I agree,' George Osborne said. 'As you know, I've always been sceptical about Iain's plan.'

The Prime Minister also agreed. However, while he was content to keep Robert, by this point he was worried enough about Universal Credit to ask Jeremy and Oliver to start monitoring its progress more closely. They, therefore, began attending Iain Duncan Smith's weekly progress review meetings, in which it soon became clear that Mike Bracken's dream of building a new benefits system in six months had been just that. Rather than six months, Mike now said he needed a year and a half.

'Can we do anything with the old system that we were going to use for the pathfinders?' Iain Duncan Smith asked Robert with a note of panic in his voice – after all, an eighteen-month timeline meant that Universal Credit wouldn't be operational until after the election.

'I don't know,' Robert said, 'but I'll find out.'

The answer that Robert brought back a few days later was remarkably positive. Despite all the disruption, the work on the pilots had continued, and the system was in good enough shape to be expanded nationally for single claimants and to the north-west for family claimants by December 2015. This meant that the initial roll-out would use different software to the one being coded by Mike's team. But as well as demonstrating progress, using the original system would give the department an opportunity to trial the implementation of Universal Credit. Both Jeremy and Oliver, therefore, thought that this was the right approach, though it took a turbulent meeting of all the key ministers and officials from the department and the Cabinet Office before it was agreed.

On 5 September 2013, the National Audit Office published its much-feared report. This contained plenty of criticism – for example, the department hadn't produced a detailed blueprint or operating model for the new system – however, the project wasn't over budget and was still on track to meet its 2017 deadline. Robert was then called in front of the Public Administration Select Committee to defend the work, with rumours circulating of ministers giving the committee difficult questions to throw at him. However, if this were true, the attack failed because the session, though gruelling, was respectful.

After Robert's hearing, the press briefings eased, as did the calls for him to resign. It seemed to Jeremy that Iain and Robert had realised that their fortunes were intertwined. If Iain sacrificed Robert, he would have no one to blame if the timetable slipped again. And Robert knew that, to be successful, he needed Iain's support. They also both agreed on at least one other point – while the department could have done a better job, it had more understanding of what was required than anyone in the Cabinet Office.

That autumn, Mike Bracken decided to let his coders move out of their old police office and into the department to work alongside the rest of the Universal Credit team.

'They found out how complicated the benefits system is,' Robert told Jeremy over a calmer plate of pasta. 'But we're not going to waste their work. We'll put our more conventional platform in place while we keep working on their all-singing, all-dancing, digital front end.'

Progress was steady after that. By February 2014, five thousand simple Universal Credit cases were being handled by the pilot offices, and in November 2014, the first trial of the new digital front end took place in Surrey.

Setting up Universal Credit had taken far longer and had been more difficult than anyone had anticipated. Jeremy was also conscious of the challenges ahead – for example it was likely that the government would have to find ways to compensate the most vulnerable of those who would lose out in the transition to the new benefit. Some of the details of how Universal Credit was implemented – for example the 42-day wait initially imposed before the first benefit payment was made – would also later become hugely controversial. But despite all this, Jeremy still believed that simplifying the benefits system to remove the disincentives to working remained a major Coalition achievement.

46

'Give a Little Bit': Energy troubles

August–November 2013

We were on holiday in York on Wednesday 21 August, taking Brenda to visit some of her old haunts, when Syrian government forces launched a chemical weapons attack on hundreds of its own civilians in Damascus. Horrific photos of injured and dead children flooded the news.

After several days punctuated by calls, Jeremy told me he needed to go back down to London for an emergency Cabinet meeting and a vote in Parliament on possible military action.

'Okay,' I said, trying to conceal my disappointment, particularly because by that stage Brenda needed as much, if not more, care than our three children. But Jeremy said he had no choice – he needed to ensure that the Cabinet materials on Syria, including the legal advice and intelligence materials, were accurate, just as he had before the government's decision in 2011 to join the NATO-led coalition in Libya.

'But beyond that,' he said, 'it's down to the politics.'

Jeremy was right – but this time the politics were problematic. Even though it seemed incontrovertible that the Syrian regime had used chemical weapons against its own people, a large number of MPs were opposed to the idea of the UK participating in targeted strikes. The Prime Minister, therefore, changed the vote to make it about the principle of intervention, with the intention of holding another vote the following week after United Nations weapons inspectors had confirmed Syria's use of chemical weapons. But even after this concession, the government was still defeated by 285 to 272.

The aftermath of this lost vote contributed to the subdued mood in Downing Street when Jeremy returned after our summer break – and the mood worsened after Ed Miliband promised to freeze UK gas and electricity bills until January 2017 if he was elected in 2015. This energy commitment was part of a Labour Party campaign focused on the 'squeezed middle' – those too rich to receive benefits but too poor to feel financially secure – which was gaining momentum because, although the economic news was improving, average disposable income was still lower than it had been before the financial crash. The tabloids loved Ed's pledge, and Labour surged in the polls.

The Coalition's first response to this was technocratic – freezing UK gas and electricity prices was a 'gimmick' from a 'Marxist universe' and one that wouldn't work long term in the real world of global energy markets. But after being beaten up twice at Prime Minister's Questions, David Cameron decided that looking like he was defending the energy companies wasn't good for his image when their popularity was roughly on a par with that of the banks. His next move was, therefore, predictable – he instructed Jeremy and Simon Case, who was by then the Number 10 energy private secretary, to go and find a better answer.

This was a challenge that Jeremy thought he might enjoy since it was likely to combine a little digging around with some tricky negotiation. The initial analysis that he did with Simon confirmed that energy bills were increasing, driven in part by world oil prices, which were again touching $100 a barrel. But it was difficult to justify a windfall tax on the energy companies because there was no evidence they were making excess profits. Nor was it clear that such a tax would reduce consumer prices – it might even have the reverse effect. Their best bet, therefore, was to convince the energy companies to compromise.

Over the following days, Jeremy and Simon talked to the CEOs or chairs of the six major energy companies, most of whom Jeremy knew from his time at Morgan Stanley. What they said was that government policies, like the warm home discount and the requirement to provide poorer customers with loft insulation and to install smart meters, were adding about 10 per cent, or £130, to the average bill. The companies were, however, all willing to work with Jeremy and Simon to find a way to lower their bills, since this would be a better outcome from their point of view than the government deciding to adopt Labour's policy.

When Jeremy reported these discussions back to the Quad, there were smiles around the room.

'I want them to reduce their bills by an average of £50 and for their prices then to remain stable through to 2015,' the Prime Minister said.

'While still meeting all their green commitments,' the Deputy Prime Minister added.

'And without removing their support for the fuel poor,' the Prime Minister said.

Given that Jeremy had no authority over the energy companies, and would have to negotiate separately with each one to avoid any suggestion of collusion, this was a tall order, but he promised to do his best.

Jeremy was still deep in papers on energy prices when Francis Maude appeared in his office wanting again to talk about Bob Kerslake. The complaint this time was that Bob had circulated a paper on strengthening the Civil Service's functional leadership to all permanent secretaries without consulting Francis. In itself, this wasn't a big issue, but for Francis it was the last straw. He wanted Bob either to become head of the Civil Service full time or to allow someone from the private sector to take on the role.

Jeremy protested, still believing that Bob was doing his best in difficult circumstances. But Francis was on a roll. In addition to his fury at Bob, he was frustrated that the Civil Service Commissioners had refused to give the Prime Minister a choice of qualified candidates for each vacant permanent secretary role.

'They argue that it would be the start of a slippery slope towards politicisation,' Francis said.

Jeremy raised his eyebrows. He'd been worried the commissioners might dig in on this issue, particularly because there was little support for this change outside government. But he thought it was the wrong thing to have a fight about because it was essentially how they already operated. In any case, he didn't believe they could ever say to the Prime Minister, 'Sorry, here is the deep state's choice – take it or leave it.' He sighed. 'I'll always defend the Civil Service from improper political interference,' he told Francis, 'but I've never believed the best way to do that is to defend our old ways of doing things regardless of their merit.'

'Well, what are we going to do?'

Jeremy smiled, unable to resist a little dark humour. 'I wonder if the commissioners know that we're about to launch the triennial review of the Civil Service Commission?'

'Good point. We need to get someone good to lead that. How about John Birt?'

Jeremy grinned even more at this mention of his old friend. 'You might find John's views bracing, Francis. The last time I talked to him, he thought permanent secretaries should be appointed by a technocratic board with no ministerial involvement.'

'Really? Well not John then!'

'How about your friends at the IPPR?' Jeremy said. 'Or maybe not. And whomever we appoint, we need to keep talking to the commissioners to see if we can get them to understand that this is not the threat they seem to think it is – after all they'll still approve all the candidates.'

Jeremy pondered all this during a weekend that we spent in Morocco with my work colleagues that autumn to celebrate my appointment as a senior McKinsey partner. Somehow, through both the financial crisis and the Coalition government, I'd continued to work, though at times it had felt impossible. Indeed, at one point, when Jeremy had announced that, yet again, he needed to go into work early, I'd told him we couldn't decide who got to get into their office on time based on who was doing more to save the country because it was a battle I'd always lose. To be fair, Jeremy had agreed. And as the prospect of global financial meltdown had receded, he'd often managed smaller crises from home while adjudicating Lego competitions or supervising baths, which had helped us muddle through.

In Marrakesh, Jeremy was amused to be put on the spouses' programme, one of two husbands in a sea of wives. Their agenda included a group session with a therapist who asked them to draw lines on charts to represent their lives, an exercise that Jeremy abandoned in favour of his BlackBerry after about twenty minutes. More interesting was a discussion with Dom Barton, the global head of McKinsey, during which Jeremy cut through the complaints about the firm's working hours to point out that McKinsey was almost unknown to senior politicians and needed to be more thoughtful about its press relationships – the days in which powerful global organisations could hide behind a wall of secrecy were coming to an end. This provoked a lively discussion, and when I later went to find Jeremy, I discovered him in a colonnaded courtyard continuing the debate with a table full of new admirers.

While we sunned ourselves in North Africa, the Prime Minister was still fighting his way through the aftermath of the Leveson inquiry. Early in 2013, Paul Jenkins and Oliver Letwin had come up with an ingenious way of resolving the argument about legislation. The solution, they said, was to use a royal charter to set up the new body that would approve press regulators, copying the approach that had been used to establish the BBC. Everyone had fallen on this compromise, but it still took until mid-March for a draft charter to be agreed by all three political parties and by Hacked Off, the victims' group. Along the way there were many more fights and fallings out, multiple attempts by backbench MPs to amend pieces of legislation going through the House of Commons with Leveson-style provisions and a final late-night pizza-fuelled negotiation in Ed Miliband's office in the House of Commons.

Jeremy assumed that the matter was effectively concluded after that – and so did everyone else until Helen MacNamara attended a charity event in late March. Halfway through the dinner, the woman sitting next to Helen, who'd said she worked for a publisher, apologised for needing to leave early.

'I have to go to an emergency meeting about a royal charter,' she explained.

Helen peered at her. 'What royal charter?'

'The press's one.'

After Helen rushed back into the Cabinet Office bearing this news, Jeremy advised the Prime Minister that the government's process had to be delayed – they couldn't risk asking the Queen to approve their charter before the press's charter had been considered. This wasn't popular advice, but in the end it was accepted. When the competing charter later materialised, no one was surprised to find that it contained a very weak regulatory power. It was, therefore, rejected by the Privy Council before they at last approved the cross-party royal charter on 30 October 2013.

While the outcome of this long and painful process seemed like a win for the government, in reality all they'd done was to create an answer almost identical to the one that Leveson had proposed over a year before. And all the effort turned out to be largely pointless in any case because none of the national newspapers joined one of the new regulators. Instead, one group clubbed together to join an unrecognised regulator, Ipso, and the *Guardian* and *Financial Times* chose to self-regulate.

Jeremy was making more meaningful progress that autumn on his efforts with Simon Case and Stephen Lovegrove, the head of the Department of Energy and Climate Change, to chip away at consumers' energy bills. He kept the Quad updated on their progress, although these discussions often became difficult with Ed Davey, the Secretary of State for Energy and Climate Change, refusing to compromise on the government's green commitments. Eventually, the Prime Minister stopped inviting Ed to the meetings and even held one particularly controversial discussion in his office in the House of Commons, leaving one of the private secretaries to guard the door in case Ed tried to break in.

By the middle of November 2013, Jeremy had found a way to achieve the Prime Minister's target of taking £50 off consumers' energy bills. As Ed had feared, this would require the government to compromise on the timing of some of its green commitments like the need to insulate solid-walled homes, though it didn't change the requirements themselves. The details were described in an article by the Prime Minister and Deputy Prime Minister in the *Sun* ahead of the Autumn Statement, after which several of the energy companies made positive statements about their dialogue with government.

Jeremy was pleased with the progress he'd managed to make in this complex, multi-party negotiation. However, his satisfaction faded when it became clear over the following weeks that, despite their promises, the energy companies' fixed-rate tariffs had barely changed. Since these were being paid by around 20 per cent of the population, this mattered. There was no easy way to force the companies to behave so instead, based on Jeremy's advice, the Prime Minister agreed to give the Department for Energy and Climate Change powers to compel the energy companies to at least reveal the different tariffs that they were imposing on consumers.

Although this was frustrating, Jeremy felt that most things were going well that autumn. In addition to his work on energy bills, in mid-October he also helped conclude the sale of 60 per cent of Royal Mail to private investors, raising £2 billion and giving the company better access to capital, just as was already being enjoyed by its competitors Deutsche Post DHL in Germany and Bpost in Belgium. The belief that Royal Mail would fare better in the private sector had sustained Jeremy through a seven-year struggle to get this deal done, which had included abolishing its terrible regulator, sorting out its indebted pension scheme and conducting two government reviews, both of which had shown how inefficient the Royal Mail was.

'But this,' he told me, 'is why I love this job. Because there's always something we can do. The easiest answer is always, "No, Minister – it's not possible". But I prefer, "I think we can do it, Minister, but it's not going to be easy and it will require some compromise".'

47

'Moonlight Mile':
Juggling policies and reviews

November 2013–June 2014

By the time of the Civil Service Awards on 21 November 2013, Jeremy was able to list many Coalition achievements including helping more than 60,000 'troubled families', privatising the Royal Mail and shrinking the Civil Service to 415,000 people. All this, together with the stronger growth that was by then being predicted for 2013 and 2014, contributed to the jubilant tone of the Chancellor's Autumn Statement in early December.

'I'm hugely relieved,' Jeremy told me on our drive back to London after spending our Christmas break in Cornwall.

I nodded, focused on the road. After heavy rainfall had caused flooding all the way along the south coast, I was worried about whether our car, loaded with holiday paraphernalia, was going to make it through the deepest puddles.

'We even managed to include some more stimulus measures in the Autumn Statement,' Jeremy continued, before pausing while I negotiated another oily lake. He sighed, looking out at the sloshing water. 'I guess I'd better try to work out whether the stories on the radio about the government failing to dredge the waterways around here are true and, if so, what we're going to do about it. But don't worry, whatever happens, I still think we should plan on getting away for a couple of weekends in the next few weeks.'

* * *

Getting away was a nice idea, but it didn't last long. Shortly after the Prime Minister finished trundling around Britain in his wellies, assuring people that the flooding was under control, he summoned Jeremy to his den. He was about to hand over the first of a series of mini crises and reviews that neatly illustrate the diversity of problems faced by a Cabinet Secretary.

David Cameron told Jeremy that he'd just found out that a secret Whitehall letter had been put in the National Archives by mistake. This revealed that, in 1984, the British government had responded 'favourably' to an Indian request for advice on how to remove Sikh extremists from the Golden Temple in Amritsar. Shortly after this, the Indian government had stormed the temple, the holiest site in the Sikh faith, killing around 400 people in the process, though Sikh groups said it was thousands. Now the Prime Minister needed Jeremy to try to find out what had really happened.

Jeremy started this work by holding several meetings with the Sikh community to understand their concerns. He then asked Hugh Powell, Jonathan Powell's nephew and a member of the National Security Secretariat, to help him search through around two hundred highly classified files, containing more than 23,000 papers, to see what they could discover. What they found was that an SAS officer had gone to Delhi to advise the Indian government, but their subsequent operation hadn't reflected the officer's advice. And beyond this, there was no record of the UK providing any further help or of its advice being linked to any policy or commercial issues.

Jeremy wrote up these findings in a report, which was made public. It didn't answer every question or contain the answers that everyone wanted, but it did at least mean that the government had put as much as it could into the public domain.

Jeremy picked up his second remit while he was still finalising his Golden Temple investigation. This time the Prime Minister wanted some thinking on how to help 16- to 24-year-olds find sustainable long-term employment. This was an issue that everyone agreed was important, but no one could agree how to address. David Cameron wanted to reform the benefits system to ensure all young people were 'earning or learning', while Nick Clegg and Danny Alexander wanted careers advice improved and were sceptical of further benefit cuts. Meanwhile, Matt Hancock, the Conservative minister for skills and enterprise, Vince Cable and others were pressing for reforms to allow young people to develop their expertise while finding employment, though their proposals were being resisted by the Department for Work and Pensions.

The review became interesting when Jeremy realised that, in addition to assessing the underlying evidence base and beginning to negotiate a compromise between these different positions, he could also deploy some of his favourite policy innovations. These included the social impact bonds that he'd helped accelerate back in 2007. By this time fourteen bonds had been set up and the evidence was that they were working – for example, young people in the ThinkForward programme in Tower Hamlets, which was being supported by one of these bonds, were achieving significantly better GCSE grades than would have otherwise been expected.

Jeremy outlined the conclusions of this review in a Quad meeting in early 2014. His proposed package included a new training offer, better careers advice in schools, enforcing local authorities' duty to ensure that young people were either in education or employment and launching social impact bonds to support mentoring.

At the end of his presentation, Jeremy smiled – he was sure the new measures would make a difference. But the discussion that followed was far tougher than he'd expected. The Chancellor declared that he wouldn't provide more funds for training without a cut in benefits and Michael Gove, the Secretary of State for Education, said he was opposed to any new requirements being placed on schools. Pretty soon everyone was fighting their own corner and Jeremy's proposal, which he'd worked so hard to stitch together, was torn apart.

It took several weeks to piece something back together, but on 12 March, the Quad at last agreed a new set of measures. This package was far more muted, although it still included social impact bonds, an online application portal for young people looking for post-16 learning and employment opportunities, and more mandatory training for those on jobseekers' allowance.

'The process was immensely frustrating,' Jeremy told me when we escaped to Madrid that April for one of his promised weekends. 'And there's so much more to do in this area – for example we haven't yet found a way of persuading people who become unemployed later in their lives to retrain.'

We were back in London for the start of Jeremy's next crisis, which this time was signalled by a call from Ian Read, the CEO of Pfizer, a large US drugs company, on Saturday 26 April. Ian had last come to Number 10's attention back in 2011 when he'd announced the closure of his plant in Sandwich, so he wasn't a popular figure in government. This time Ian said he was intending to merge Pfizer with AstraZeneca to create the largest pharmaceutical company in the world and he wanted to know whether the government would support the deal.

On Monday morning, Jeremy gathered together the lead officials from the Department of Health, the Department of Business, Innovation and Science and the Treasury to consider Ian's question.

'If Pfizer bought AstraZeneca, it would be the largest foreign take-over yet of a British firm,' Jeremy told them. 'Or, more accurately, of an Anglo-Swedish firm that has expanded by taking over foreign companies. But never mind that. AstraZeneca is British now and we don't have long to decide on our advice.'

'We can't stop a merger if AstraZeneca's shareholders agree to it,' one of the officials said. 'We can only stop deals on national security grounds, financial stability or media plurality grounds …'

'… not just because we don't like them,' Jeremy said. 'Okay, I know that, but if Pfizer is prepared to give us some written commitments in exchange for our blessing, what would we want those to cover?'

'We would want them to base their European operations in the UK,' one official said.

'And to remain committed to AstraZeneca's new research base in Cambridge,' another said.

'Keeping the facility in Macclesfield will also be important,' said a third.

At the end of the meeting, Jeremy sent the experts away to prioritise their requests. He was conscious that the government had never previously asked for commitments like these during a takeover and it was unclear how enforceable they would be. But when he briefed the Prime Minister, the Deputy Prime Minister, the Chancellor and business secretary Vince Cable, they were adamant they were needed to protect the UK's pharmaceutical sector.

After AstraZeneca rejected Pfizer's initial approach on 28 April, Pfizer increased their offer on 2 May and wrote to the Prime Minister to say they would make the commitments that the government had requested. But AstraZeneca's board refused to be swayed, and instead started trawling around its investors explaining the case for remaining independent. The deal was also opposed by Labour, and within government by Vince Cable, with both arguing that a non-binding letter from Pfizer wasn't enough, particularly from a firm that had cut more than two thousand jobs at Sandwich.

With questions being tabled in Parliament, and the Science and Technology Select Committee launching an inquiry, Jeremy worked with John Kingman from the Treasury to try to find ways to make Pfizer's promises watertight – for example by putting AstraZeneca's UK research and manufacturing operations into a trust that Pfizer could operate but couldn't sell or move out of the country. But on 19 May, before anything could be agreed, AstraZeneca rejected Pfizer's final offer and Pfizer walked away.

Within government the immediate reaction to this was relief, but the experience had made Jeremy realise how hard it was for the government to intervene in deals that threatened important British companies. Since creating powers to block takeovers was incompatible with EU law, Jeremy and John, therefore, instead persuaded the Takeover Panel to amend its rules to make acquisition commitments binding – although, since it would be a year before these amendments could be put in place, they knew they would still be vulnerable if Pfizer returned before then.

The next problem to hit Jeremy's in-tray, like Pfizer's attempted takeover, also enabled him to strengthen the British system. This time the issue was triggered by the European Court of Justice's decision to strike down the data retention directive. This created a crisis because the directive gave internet and telephone companies a legal basis for keeping data such as logs of their customers' calls, though not the details of the content of those calls, for twelve months in case they were needed by the police or security services. According to Charles Farr, the head of security and counterterrorism in the Home Office, unless this legal basis could be reinstated, many current investigations would have to be stopped.

The only viable solution to this, Jeremy and others advised the Prime Minister after a series of intense policy discussions, was to rush through emergency legislation to fill the gap. However, after the home secretary Theresa May's failed attempt two years previously to pass the Communications Data Bill, which would have established far wider powers than the directive, doing this was hugely controversial. At the time the press had dubbed Theresa's bill a 'snoopers' charter' and the Liberal Democrats had opposed it – a position that, for once, Jeremy had been unable to change when he was sent by the Prime Minister to negotiate with Nick Clegg.

All this meant that, to get their emergency legislation – the Data Retention and Investigatory Powers Act (DRIPA) – agreed this time around, they had to insert a 'sunset clause' stating that it would be repealed at the end of 2016, by which time the government needed to have found a long-term solution. At Nick Clegg's request, Jeremy then briefed groups of Liberal Democrat MPs on the bill. And at the Prime Minister's request, he rang the big Silicon Valley tech companies to try to get them onside.

All this preparation meant that the government was able to race DRIPA through the House of Commons and the House of Lords in a week. Two years later – after many more dramas – it was replaced by the Investigatory Powers Act, which at last made all of the government's powers in this area clear, put them in one place and made the UK system more US-friendly by introducing judicial oversight.

While the Pfizer and DRIPA issues had eventually reached satisfactory conclusions, Jeremy's final crisis that spring revealed a more endemic issue within the UK system. In fact, the issue of Birmingham schools revealed a weakness within the Civil Service that Jeremy would spend the rest of his career trying to fix.

Jeremy first became aware of this issue in March 2014 when Birmingham City Council announced that, having received an anonymous letter talking of 'Operation Trojan Horse', it was investigating an attempt by Muslim extremists to take over various schools. Over the next few weeks it became clear that the council had been sent hundreds of similar warnings over the years, the Department for Education tried to get a grip on what was going on and Ofsted, the schools inspectorate, rushed in to assess the schools under suspicion.

The timing of this crisis was terrible for the education secretary, Michael Gove, whose relationship with the National Union of Teachers had already deteriorated to the point where they were calling for him to resign. This might explain why an article in *The Times* on 4 June 2014, that quoted 'sources close to Gove', tried to shift the blame by accusing the Home Office of failing to 'drain the swamp' of extremism. In response, the Home Office published a letter from Theresa May to Michael Gove, which said that the education department hadn't acted on threats to schools dating back to 2010.

At this point, the Prime Minister again called Jeremy in. The situation was out of control, he said – and as a first step, Jeremy needed to work out how a letter between two Cabinet ministers had found its way onto the Home Office's website, which was a breach of the ministerial code.

Jeremy spent a couple of days assembling the facts. In contrast with some of his investigations, this one was straightforward. Michael Gove and his advisers had behaved in a provocative and non-collaborative fashion, but the Home Office had published a Cabinet letter. By Friday afternoon, the only unanswered questions were which one of Theresa May's three special advisers had leaked the letter and whether the leak had been authorised by the home secretary.

'I need to talk to Fiona,' Jeremy told his private secretary, Rachel Hopcroft, though it wasn't a call he wanted to make – not least because Charles Farr, the official whom Michael Gove and his advisers had singled out in their attack, was Fiona's partner.

A tearful Fiona took the call.

'I need to know if you leaked the letter,' Jeremy said, 'because publishing Cabinet correspondence is a breach of the special advisers' code – and we have the terrible situation of two Cabinet ministers warring with each other in public.'

After Fiona took responsibility for the leak, Jeremy turned to the second question. This required another difficult conversation, this time with the home secretary, Theresa May, which took place late that night after she returned from Brussels.

'I need to know if you authorised the leak. If you did, it would be a breach of the ministerial code,' Jeremy said.

'I didn't authorise it,' Theresa said.

After that, the next steps were preordained. On Saturday morning, Theresa rang Fiona, who duly resigned, and Michael Gove wrote a letter of apology.

But all of this, though dramatic, did nothing to solve the more fundamental issue of tackling extremism in Birmingham's schools. So, after declaring that protecting children was one of the first duties of government, the Prime Minister set up a taskforce to do this and asked Jeremy to chair the committee that would prepare for its discussions.

By this point Jeremy's approach to addressing crises like this was well established, with his first step being to assemble the known facts.

'Do we know which mosques are willing to cooperate with the government and which are being run by radical imams?' he asked Melanie Dawes from the Economic and Domestic Secretariat, whom he'd asked to corral the available information from across government.

Melanie shook her head.

'Okay, let's start with an easier question – how many mosques are there in Birmingham?'

But even this turned out to be difficult to answer, because no one in Whitehall had thought to gather the data. And other critical information that had been known in the past, like how people felt about 'Britishness', was no longer collected because the government had cut back on its public opinion surveys to save money.

On the education side, Chris Wormald at least knew how many state schools there were in Birmingham, though he knew less about independent schools, Sunday schools or children who were being home educated. And it was impossible to tell what the Home Office knew because they refused to divulge anything, claiming the risk of leaks was too great.

What Jeremy and his team did know was that, as in other areas of the country, some diverse groups in Birmingham were isolated from mainstream British society. If these became more integrated, they might challenge hard-line schools that they often didn't regard as extreme. Beyond this certainty though, the details of what was driving the extremism in Birmingham were vague. So, on the basis of little information – though having made lots of demands for more – Jeremy, Melanie and Chris developed a set of interventions for the nudge unit to test. This was all sensible, but Jeremy still came home more disturbed by this crisis than he'd been by any of the others so far that year.

'It made me realise,' he told me, 'that barely anyone in Whitehall comes from these diverse groups or knows anyone who does. If the Civil Service is going to be effective in the future, that is something we have to change.'

48

'Stay':
Our friend and neighbour

June–September 2014

Michael Gove's perceived demotion from education secretary to Chief Whip was the biggest news of the July 2014 reshuffle though it was widely expected after his public battles with other Cabinet ministers and the backlash against his education policies. Nicky Morgan took over from Michael, while Owen Paterson – who'd never fully recovered from his comment about badgers and goalposts – was replaced in the Department for Environment, Food and Rural Affairs by Liz Truss.

Within Whitehall, the Prime Minister also abolished Bob Kerslake's role as head of the Civil Service. This decision had been triggered by one final spat, this time concerning the replacement of the permanent secretary at the Department for Culture, Media and Sport. In this case, through a series of mix-ups, Bob had arranged for the outgoing permanent secretary, Jonathan Stephens, to be posted to an interim role in the Treasury without it being clear who would pay Jonathan's salary. When this emerged, and tempers started to fray, Jeremy stepped in to find a face-saving formula. His proposal – that Jonathan should become the permanent secretary for the Northern Ireland Office – made sense given Jonathan's Northern Ireland expertise, though it came at a cost, since the role had previously been done at director general level. After that, Bob and Francis Maude had barely spoken, and newspaper articles had appeared deploring Bob's performance.

Once he had decided to abolish Bob's role, the Prime Minister began debating different ways of restructuring the top of the Civil

Service. When Chris Martin rang to get Jeremy's thoughts on this, Jeremy told him that, within reason, he was happy for the Prime Minister to decide. Having looked at the issue many times in the past, he believed many options were possible – the important thing was to choose one that suited the way in which the Prime Minister wanted to work.

David Cameron made his decision in mid-June. A new role – the chief executive of the Civil Service – would be focused on Civil Service reform and managing the Civil Service's central functions. Unlike the head of the Civil Service, this would be a full-time position and it would report to Jeremy, recognising that, as Cabinet Secretary, with his close relationship with the Prime Minister and the Cabinet, he was always likely to have the most authority within the system.

The following week, Bob went to see the Prime Minister to discuss these changes. However, because he still didn't want to take on the Civil Service role on a full-time basis, he decided instead to focus before his retirement on his work in the Department of Communities and Local Government. After that the search commenced for someone else who could take on this new role, with the Prime Minister again keen to make this appointment from the private sector.

The biggest consequence of this restructuring for Jeremy was that he was about to become the head of the Civil Service in addition to being Cabinet Secretary. However, he told me during our holiday that summer in Japan that, somewhat to his surprise, he was looking forward to it. He wouldn't enjoy making more speeches, though people seemed to appreciate them, but he was looking forward to using his new position to strengthen the Civil Service. His only concern was how he would manage when, in addition to his existing responsibilities, he also became responsible for more than 400,000 civil servants and had thirty people reporting to him.

Jeremy's concern about his looming workload was one of the reasons why he came home smiling when John Manzoni won the competition to become the first chief executive of the Civil Service that autumn. It was an ideal appointment, Jeremy told me, because John brought private sector experience from his time as an oil and gas executive while also understanding the public sector from his time as head of the Major Projects Authority in the Cabinet Office.

One of the first things that Jeremy and John worked on together after John's appointment was the simplification of the Civil Service Reform Programme. Jeremy had been loath to interfere with this while Bob had been leading it, but now they streamlined its thirty or so objectives and sub-objectives to make it easier to implement. The three priorities they selected, with the help of the Civil Service board, were ones that Jeremy had long cared about – improving commercial capabilities, accelerating the digital agenda and increasing diversity.

While John focused on the first two of these priorities, Jeremy took a personal interest in the third. He felt strongly about diversity, he told me, not only because of the legal and moral case but also because of the business case. The challenge the government had faced in understanding the growing extremism in Birmingham had underlined the dangers of homogeneity. A more diverse Civil Service would create better policies, serve citizens more responsively and be more engaged.

Jeremy tackled diversity like he addressed any other policy issue – by demanding data, asking questions and creating a plan. In the past, he'd championed apprenticeships, which had helped diversify the Civil Service's intake. His focus now was on improving the flow of diverse candidates up through the ranks. Doing this – for example by having equal numbers of men and women in the Civil Service's talent development schemes, publishing diversity targets for each department and demanding that his senior colleagues sponsor diverse colleagues – would take longer than making symbolic appointments at senior levels. However, if it could be achieved, it would permanently change the service.

Alongside developing this reform plan with John, the most significant policy issue on Jeremy's desk in the run-up to the summer of 2014 was the looming Scottish referendum. Earlier that year, the Treasury had begun work on the Scotland Analysis Programme. The output of this programme, which detailed the benefits of the Union, had been published in fifteen papers covering everything from energy to science and banking, culminating in a summary document released in June.

Of all these papers, Jeremy believed that the first – *Scotland Analysis: Devolution and the Implications of Independence* – was the most important. Largely written by Professor James Crawford, one of the world's leading lawyers on the issue of statehood, this argued that, if Scotland left the United Kingdom, the UK would retain its previous legal personality, but Scotland wouldn't. This simple statement had profound implications – it meant the UK would still be a permanent member of the UN Security Council and would stay in NATO and the EU whereas Scotland would lose all these memberships. It also implied that everything other than the fixed assets within Scotland belonged to the UK.

Although the Scottish government had contested this paper, they couldn't rebut it. But despite the importance of Crawford's paper, it was another document, which relied on his thinking that had become far more controversial when it was published in February 2014 – Nick Macpherson's advice to the Chancellor that Scotland shouldn't be allowed to keep the pound if it became independent.

Jeremy hadn't known that Nick's note would be made public, and though he welcomed transparency, would have advised against it. While he wanted to keep the Union together as much as anyone, he worried that the Civil Service's reputation would be damaged by the release of advice that could be seen as partisan. This is why he spent hours checking the leaflets that the government sent out to every household in Scotland explaining the benefits of the Union, making sure that every statement was factually correct and could be verified.

The Prime Minister was keen to have the Civil Service's support in preparing documents like the Scotland Analysis Programme and these information leaflets, as well as in monitoring the press and opinion polls on the referendum and providing factual briefing for ministers. But he told Jeremy he didn't want the Civil Service to do any work on the consequences of Scotland deciding to leave. A decision by Scotland to leave wasn't government policy, and no matter how remote the risk of leaks, if news of such work was revealed it would undermine the government's No campaign.

Westminster wasn't, of course, the only administration preparing papers ahead of the Scottish referendum. In November 2013, the Scottish government had published *Scotland's Future: Your Guide to an Independent Scotland*, which made the case for leaving the Union. This had ignited another row because many saw the document, which laid out the policies that the Scottish National Party would pursue if it were re-elected, as a political manifesto.

Things became more difficult when the press began to ask why Peter Housden, permanent secretary to the Scottish Government, had allowed the Scottish Civil Service to work on *Scotland's Future*. Jeremy agreed that the paper was on the outer edge of what the Civil Service should support, but he was also always inclined to support his civil servants, particularly when, like Peter, he believed they were doing their best in difficult circumstances. He, therefore, gave Peter his backing and offered him advice on how to handle the press and parliamentary criticism.

As the referendum date of 18 September 2014 drew near, Jeremy was often on the phone to Gordon Brown. Though not part of the official Better Together campaign, Gordon strongly believed in the Union. As a highly respected Scottish Labour MP, he was also listened to in Scotland. So, with the Prime Minister's agreement, Jeremy ensured Gordon received Philip Rycroft's factual briefings and set up discussions for him with the Prime Minister and Chancellor.

In their calls, Gordon told Jeremy that he was frustrated by the Better Together campaign because its focus on the economic cost of Scottish independence made it look like it was talking Scotland down. In his view, the campaign should instead be highlighting the advantages for Scotland of being in the Union, for example the benefits of being able to pool resources to deliver free healthcare and a strong welfare state. Above all, Gordon believed the Scots wanted change. And although all three pro-Union parties were in favour of devolution and had, therefore, supported the Scotland Act, which had given Scotland more financial powers, and the establishment of the Strathclyde Commission, which was considering changes to Scotland's governance, this wasn't the perception in Scotland.

Despite Gordon's concerns, there seemed little appetite to change the campaign – at least there wasn't until 7 September 2014 when the *Sunday Times* published a poll that put the Yes campaign for an independent Scotland in front for the first time, overturning the twenty-point lead enjoyed by the Better Together team only a year before.

'The Yes campaign couldn't win, could they?' I asked Jeremy.

'They could,' he said. 'We may be about to see the disintegration of the United Kingdom. The Better Together campaign has managed to get some business voices to speak out, but their campaign is all over the place and the Yes campaign has all the momentum. God knows how the government has got itself into this position.'

Jeremy spent a lot of that day on the phone. He had heard, he told me, that his hero Alex Ferguson, the former manager of Manchester United, would come out for the No campaign. But after watching J.K. Rowling and Andy Murray being attacked in the press and on social media for pledging their support, Alex refused to say anything in public. More fundamentally, it was becoming clear that Gordon was right – what the Scottish people wanted was more clarity on the additional powers Scotland would get if it stayed in the Union.

'I've spoken to Gordon Brown,' Jeremy told the Prime Minister on Monday morning. He'd seldom seen David Cameron looking so tense. 'Having spoken to the *Daily Record*, he thinks we need to make a credible commitment to give more powers to Scotland, signed by all three party leaders.'

While the Prime Minister considered this, Helen MacNamara from the Economic and Domestic Secretariat and Philip Rycroft came to see Jeremy. Although the Prime Minister had said no work should be done on the consequences of a vote to leave, and Jeremy hadn't requested any, Helen and Philip took him through a possible plan for the day after a Yes vote including a draft statement for the Prime Minister to give in the morning, a list of the calls he would need to make and the agendas for Cabinet and the National Security Council. Many of the issues raised by a vote in favour of independence would take months or years to resolve, so their thinking beyond day one was more about setting up processes than proposing answers. After looking back to 1922, when the Irish Free

State separated from the United Kingdom, and at the 1992 break-up of Czechoslovakia, they thought it would be helpful to create a Yes Cabinet committee and to launch a constitutional convention to debate how relationships would work between Westminster and the devolved parliaments.

Jeremy, Helen and Philip spent some time discussing this. Their most fundamental realisation was how much power the United Kingdom would have in the divorce negotiations. Effectively, they could choose to turn the lights off north of the border if they wanted to.

'But none of us wants that,' Philip said.

'Yes,' Jeremy said. 'My strong advice to ministers, whatever the emotions after the vote, would be to play nice rather than to punish the Scots for wanting to leave.'

Over the following days, the draft of a potential commitment to Scotland began to circulate within a tight circle of ministers and officials. Once it was agreed by the Coalition, they shared it with Gordon Brown who discussed it with Ed Miliband. On Tuesday 16 September 2014, 'The Vow' was printed on the front page of the *Daily Record* alongside pictures of the party leaders. 'We are agreed,' the vow said, 'that the Scottish Parliament is permanent and extensive new powers for the Parliament will be delivered by the process and to the timetable agreed by our three parties, starting on 19 September …'

Following a mass rally the following day, at which Gordon gave what Jeremy considered to be the finest speech of the campaign, and possibly of Gordon's career, the polls opened on Thursday morning. The Prime Minister had taken a massive gamble that more than three hundred years of history, partnership, loyalty and blood ties, together with many economic benefits, would prevent Scotland from leaving. After a record 84.6 per cent of the electorate voted – the highest percentage recorded in the United Kingdom since the introduction of universal suffrage – the result was unveiled. Scotland was staying in the Union.

49

'One of Us':
Another referendum

September 2014–January 2016

The sense of relief across Whitehall after the Scotland vote was palpable. The government had risked the integrity of the United Kingdom and had won – though only after teetering on the brink of disaster. Of course, everyone knew that another roll of the dice, this time to determine the UK's relationship with Europe, might be coming, but that wasn't imminent, and in any case, it depended on the outcome of the next general election.

In the aftermath of the referendum, Jeremy strengthened the Civil Service's ability to advise ministers on the Union. One of the things that the referendum had highlighted was that, historically, Whitehall hadn't paid much attention to Scotland or to the details of the devolution settlement. Therefore, with the Prime Minister's agreement, Jeremy combined the Constitutional Unit in the Cabinet Office with the Scotland and Wales offices. This new group, headed by Philip Rycroft at permanent secretary level, would advise the Prime Minister on constitutional issues and deliver policies to sustain the long-term integrity of the United Kingdom.

It wasn't long after that before the politicians became absorbed in preparing for the approaching general election. This moved the Coalition into a new phase in which less time was spent delivering common commitments and more was spent highlighting their differences. This often left Jeremy feeling like he was working for two political parties rather than for a single government – as he did, for example, when the Prime Minister used his party conference speech in October 2014 to promise another increase in the personal allowance, one of the Liberal Democrats' favourite policies.

The Autumn Statement that December was similarly competitive, with the parties racing each other to be photographed in hi-vis jackets while claiming the credit for an increase in infrastructure spending. Far more contentious, however, was trying to decide whether again to push back the deadline for eliminating the structural deficit. With tax revenues falling, meeting the Chancellor's existing target would require the government to reduce spending as a percentage of GDP to its lowest level since before the last war. But Osborne was unswayed – partly because Labour's perceived weakness in addressing the deficit had recently been underlined by Ed Miliband's failure to mention it in his party conference speech. The government would 'stay the course', the Chancellor told the House of Commons in his Autumn Statement on 3 December.

The increased separation between the Coalition parties was also evident when they debated the so-called 'West Lothian question' – the voting rights that Scottish MPs should have on English issues in Westminster – a subject that, much to Gordon Brown's fury, the Prime Minister had felt obliged to reopen after the Scottish referendum. After substantial debate in the new Cabinet committee set up to discuss this issue, it became clear that there was no possibility of aligning the Coalition. So instead, Jeremy suggested laying out all three of the Conservative options and the one Liberal Democrat option in the White Paper they published that December. Since this made the paper a smorgasbord, the Labour Party was asked if it also wanted to contribute a delicacy – an offer it refused.

Jeremy did his best to remain even-handed in these discussions and he put together guidance for his permanent secretaries on how to navigate these tensions in the run-up to the election. He also worked with Philip Rycroft on a paper laying out the process for running a coalition so that the Civil Service would be ready if, as was widely expected, that was again the election outcome. This included guidance on issues like the rights one party had to request policy advice from a department in which it had no ministerial representation and the proposal that, in the closing period of a Parliament, there should be 'private space advice' – advice from the Civil Service on long-term policy issues to one party that wouldn't be shared with the other.

Despite these tensions, one issue at least was resolved that autumn after the Civil Service Commissioners at last agreed to give the Prime Minister a choice of qualified candidates for permanent secretary roles. After their initial discussions with Francis Maude over a year before, the Commission had launched a consultation on how it might change its recruitment principles in which, somewhat bizarrely, it had failed to include the Prime Minister's proposal as an option. Jeremy knew the commissioners were keen to avoid any change that might politicise the Civil Service, and that some of his permanent secretaries were also keen to maintain the status quo – if only to win a totemic victory over the Maude agenda. But he still felt this was an odd issue to have a huge mandarins versus ministers row about since any overly political candidate would always be rejected – that was one of the points of the process.

The Prime Minister felt the same way. He told Jeremy that he thought the Commission's position was ridiculous. In fact he was so frustrated that he also agreed – despite Jeremy pointing out that it reversed his previously held view – to Francis Maude's proposal that they should only consider internal candidates for permanent secretary roles since, according to the rules, the commissioners could then be excluded from the appointment process.

In November, David Normington rang Francis. On reflection, he said, the commissioners had decided to agree to the Prime Minister's request. This was good news – and it also meant that, when Sir Gerry Grimstone and Olly Robbins later completed their Triennial Review of the Civil Service Commission, which highlighted a number of failings, Jeremy was able to block Francis Maude's suggestion that David Normington should step down.

'The choice issue was badly handled,' Jeremy told the Prime Minister, 'but behind the scenes, David has been trying to get the commissioners to be pragmatic. I don't think there's any need for further action.'

The Prime Minister nodded. 'We can let this one rest.'

* * *

After celebrating the New Year with me and the children in the midst of a snowstorm in Naples, Jeremy returned to London in January 2015 to face yet more rows as the political temperature continued to increase ahead of the election.

The most painful of these was an argument over the application of the special advisers' code. This had been triggered by the Rochester and Strood by-election in November 2014 – a high-stakes contest because it had resulted from MP Mark Reckless's decision to resign from the Conservatives to join Ukip. With the Conservatives keen to throw everything they could at Rochester, Sue Gray, the head of propriety issues in the Cabinet Office, came under pressure to allow special advisers – who were political appointees – to campaign. Unusually, this had an effect. Sue agreed they could, though only by phone and from Conservative HQ. When some of the special advisers then refused to do this because they were busy supporting their ministers, the Conservative Party deselected them as parliamentary candidates.

After news of these deselections leaked, Sue's ruling became controversial, and at the end of January, the Public Administration Select Committee called Jeremy in to explain himself. The situation was particularly frustrating because Sue hadn't consulted him on her decision, and it clearly wasn't aligned with the special advisers' code. But Jeremy was determined to protect Sue – after all, she'd spent years defending the propriety rules, even when that had required taking on senior ministers.

'You need to consult the government's law officers,' the chair of the committee, Bernard Jenkin, concluded after they had gone around the issue several times with Jeremy pointing out some of the ambiguity within the code that might – but probably didn't – justify Sue's ruling.

'I will,' Jeremy said, feeling sure Bernard understood his predicament. 'What this has highlighted is a need to clarify the code.'

And that is, therefore, what they did. The code was amended to allow special advisers to campaign so long as they did it in their own time and out of office hours. It wasn't the outcome that Jeremy or many of the special advisers wanted, but they had no choice.

The one positive conclusion from this incident, however, was that it showed the power of the various codes of conduct that were by then in place. Since they could soon be facing another set of coalition negotiations, Jeremy decided to update one of the most critical of these – the Cabinet Manual. This document, though relatively new – Gus had dreamt it up on a flight back from New Zealand in 2010 – had already proved invaluable in multiple sticky situations, and within the Civil Service, was treated somewhat like a sacred text. But despite its importance, it left many issues unclear, for example whether the purdah rules applied during coalition negotiations. After the previous set of these negotiations, during which some of the Labour politicians claimed that the Treasury and the Bank of England had endorsed the Conservatives' austerity programme, Jeremy, therefore, wanted to underline how important it was for the Civil Service to limit its role to providing facts and answering procedural questions.

The manual was, however, only valuable if permanent secretaries understood it. So, just like Gus had done before the 2010 election, Jeremy arranged another series of role plays, though this time, rather than being focused on the politics of forming a coalition, these concentrated on the Civil Service's role, including what they should do if there was a policy crisis during the negotiations such as a collapse of the eurozone.

As the election drew near, and Coalition relationships became even more fraught, Jeremy found that he was spending almost all his time trying to get decisions made. Even a simple issue like whether to have a spring Budget became difficult to resolve – so much so that, even after they agreed to hold one, the Liberal Democrats still decided to produce a follow-up Budget of their own encased in a canary-yellow box.

Alongside this, in the final days of the Coalition, Jeremy ploughed his way through a list of more practical issues that needed to be resolved before the possible start of another set of cross-party negotiations. These included things like checking that the rooms being prepared for the different political teams were located so that the parties couldn't see each other, and ensuring the sandwich menus included vegetarian options – an oversight that had irritated the Liberal Democrats back in 2010.

* * *

After the government at last went into purdah on 30 March 2015, Jeremy turned with some relief to the tasks he'd saved for this time, like completing the annual performance reviews of his permanent secretaries and joining a series of presentations in the Pillar Room in Number 10 on topics like behavioural economics, open government and the Government Digital Service. In addition, triggered by a letter to the Prime Minister from a group of business leaders calling themselves the Productivity Leadership Group, he convened a series of meetings to try to work out why the UK had such a long tail of companies with low productivity.

However, before Jeremy could make much progress on any of these issues, the leaking of a Scottish Office memo to the *Daily Telegraph* on 3 April put his purdah holiday on hold. The note claimed that, in contrast to her public position, Nicola Sturgeon, the leader of the Scottish National Party, had told the French ambassador that she wanted David Cameron to remain in Downing Street. The Labour Party leapt on this, claiming that Nicola was a Tory supporter in disguise – a handy attack given Scotland's aversion to the Conservative Party.

Nicola Sturgeon rang Jeremy. 'I want a leak inquiry. The content of the memo is false and it's outrageous for it to be released at any time, let alone during an election campaign.'

'I agree. I'll do everything I can to get to the bottom of it, and rapidly,' Jeremy said, and meant it – if a civil servant was responsible, it would be a sackable offence.

This time, when Jeremy worked through the evidence with Sue Gray, the answer was clear. Euan Roddin, one of the Scottish secretary's special advisers, had rung the *Daily Telegraph* on his government mobile two days ahead of the story appearing, as well as before and afterwards. When he was confronted with these facts, Euan confessed to leaking the document – though he said his Liberal Democrat secretary of state, Alistair Carmichael, had told him to do it.

'I need to talk to Alistair,' Jeremy told Sue.

Sue shook her head. 'That's not possible. He's in the Shetlands campaigning and is refusing to be interviewed.'

'Then we need to publish our report without talking to him. The election is only a week away.'

'Jonathan Jones and Philip Rycroft both say we can't do that.'

Jeremy paused. This made things difficult. Jonathan had taken over from Paul Jenkins as the head of the government's legal service and Philip knew the views of the Liberal Democrats, who would want to protect one of their own. It was, he decided, time to ring Nick Clegg.

'I have compelling evidence that Alistair authorised the leak,' Jeremy told Nick. 'If Alistair's refusing to take our calls, there's still a case for publishing before the election. Can you or Jonny Oates put pressure on him to talk to us in the next couple of days?'

'I'll do what I can,' Nick said. 'But you can't publish until you've talked to Alistair. If you do, it will be a hugely political act.'

After that, the Liberal Democrats went silent, and despite further chasing, Alistair Carmichael remained uncontactable. This meant that, to his immense frustration, Jeremy was trapped – the report couldn't be released until after the vote.

When Big Ben chimed 10 p.m. on 7 May 2015, David Dimbleby's exit poll predicted a small majority for the Conservative Party, their first since 1992, with the expected Ukip surge muted by the Prime Minister's promise to hold an in-out referendum on Britain's membership before the end of 2017. The Liberal Democrats, meanwhile, seemed to have done terribly, slumping from fifty-seven to eight seats. As the results tumbled in, and these predictions were confirmed, Ed Miliband, Nick Clegg and the Ukip leader, Nigel Farage, all resigned as the leaders of their parties.

Jeremy spent the next few days helping the Prime Minister shape his new Conservative-only Cabinet and helping Whitehall assess the likely changes in policy direction. He also went to see the staff in Nick Clegg's private office to assure them they would all be found new roles. What was noticeable, he told me, was the change in the style of government. This new era already felt less formal and less focused on the middle ground. The government also had no excuse for dropping any of its manifesto pledges, so Whitehall would need to try to implement all 517 of them.

After the election, Alistair Carmichael was the only Liberal Democrat MP left in Scotland. On 22 May, after he confirmed that he had authorised the calls made by Euan Roddin, Jeremy published his report on the leaked letter. His conclusions were clear, but the consequences of them were frustrating because, although Alistair agreed to forgo his ministerial severance payment, he refused to step down as an MP and Parliament wasn't able to force him to do so because he'd become aware of the memo through his ministerial role.

Three weeks after the election, the government introduced the EU Referendum Bill. Apart from his memo to the Prime Minister back in December 2012, Jeremy hadn't provided any advice on the decision to hold a referendum since this was a political choice. But after the bill was introduced, he began to think through how the Civil Service should operate during the referendum campaign.

One of the first issues to resolve was whether the Civil Service should abide by the purdah rules that would normally apply during a general election, which would restrict its support to providing factual briefing. Jeremy thought that, since the referendum would be highly political, these rules should apply. But David Cameron disagreed. It would be ridiculous, he told Jeremy, if on an issue so significant, the elected government was unable to make its case to the people as effectively as possible.

The Prime Minister's view was echoed, for different reasons, by the government's lawyers. They told Jeremy that, if the normal purdah rules were applied, there was a risk of business-as-usual activities, like EU ministerial councils in Brussels, falling foul of them. In theory, if UK ministers secured a good outcome at one of these councils with Civil Service support and wanted to talk about it, this could be seen as an attempt to influence the referendum. The lawyers also worried that, taken literally, the purdah rules might prevent ministers from negotiating effectively in Brussels, for example by publishing statements on the UK's position.

With everyone lined up against him, Jeremy felt he had no choice but to try to change the rules. He was sceptical, though, that Parliament would agree to anything other than the normal practices, which were laid out in statute, even though there was a case to be made.

Jeremy was right to be sceptical. In late July 2015, after an angry debate about the issue during the second reading of the Referendum

Bill, Jeremy was again summoned in front of the Public Administration and Constitutional Affairs Committee. In the days before this, he spent hours sitting on the sofa in our playroom going through his briefing. At least being there, he could look out at our garden through the glass folding doors, play some Dylan and allow the espresso cups to pile up on the table in front of him.

This process ended, as it always did, with Jeremy facing an arc of MPs in a wood-panelled committee room in the Houses of Parliament, determined to be helpful and respectful while supporting the government's public position and trying to avoid creating any headlines.

Bernard Jenkin, who wanted the UK to leave the EU, made his view clear at the start of the session. Purdah should be imposed as usual during the referendum campaign and doing so shouldn't affect government business.

Different lawyers would take different views, Jeremy said, but the advice he'd received was that, unless the rules were changed, there was a risk that people might launch legal suits against ministers conducting normal work in the EU.

After that the hearing became heated. Committee members dredged up whatever they could to throw at Jeremy, including his failure to conclude the Alistair Carmichael investigation speedily, the publication of Nick Macpherson's advice against sharing the pound with Scotland, the decision to allow special advisers to campaign during elections and the delays in the Chilcot inquiry.

Facing this onslaught, the minutes lingered. Jeremy concentrated on each word he uttered, knowing that the smallest slip would cause the MPs to fall upon him. I found these sessions, which I usually watched remotely on my computer, painful viewing. But Jeremy was more sanguine, telling me it was part of his job, though it was one that had become far tougher over time.

On this occasion Jeremy was, however, fighting an unwinnable battle, particularly because the Electoral Commission had already supported the committee's position. More fundamentally, easing the purdah restrictions required Members of Parliament, including those in favour of leaving the EU, to believe that a government that wanted to stay in wouldn't abuse the Civil Service's support. No matter how reasonable Jeremy was, in the absence of this trust, the committee would never support a change in the rules.

Bernard Jenkin wrapped up the session by thanking Jeremy and telling him that he'd been very forthcoming.

'That worries me,' Jeremy said, unable to restrain his sense of humour after hours of concentration.

Later that day, after dissecting various other witnesses, the committee concluded that the purdah rules shouldn't be changed – a ruling that was confirmed in early September when Tory rebels aligned with Labour MPs to defeat the government in a vote on the issue.

A potentially more productive debate resumed within Number 10 in July 2015 when the Airports Commission made its final recommendation on increasing runway capacity. After twice considering and rejecting Boris Johnson's proposal to build a new airport in the middle of the Thames, the commission had assessed two options at Heathrow and one at Gatwick. To Jeremy's relief, it hadn't fudged its conclusion. Having analysed all the issues and consulted interested parties to the point of exhaustion, the commission declared that a new runway to the north-west of Heathrow would be best placed to provide additional capacity for long-haul destinations and business travellers.

In his foreword to the report, Howard Davies urged the government to make an early decision based on its recommendation. It was a exhortation that Jeremy took seriously, immediately commissioning work on a national policy statement, which would need to be approved before work at Heathrow could move ahead.

Jeremy was also by then working on the July 2015 Budget. The Prime Minister wanted this first fully Conservative Budget in almost twenty years to underline his 'compassionate conservatism', which meant including policies like the Chancellor's National Living Wage alongside reducing inheritance tax and increasing the personal allowance. What felt less compassionate were the £12 billion of additional welfare cuts that had been promised in the March 2014 Budget. On the Prime Minister's behalf, Jeremy, therefore, urged the Treasury to spread these over four rather than two years – even though this partly triggered the decision to push back the timeline for addressing the deficit again, this time to anticipate a surplus in 2019/20. This was, Jeremy felt, a good thing. The Conservatives had needed to tackle the deficit, but he felt more comfortable if they did this at a pace that lessened the impact of austerity on people's lives.

With the Budget settled, Jeremy also had time to return to the productivity issue that had caught his attention before the election. He called in some of the members of the Productivity Leadership Group, who told him they were willing to take a lead on this if the government could provide them with a small amount of support. They then trialled a set of interventions that became the basis for a new charity, Be the Business, that would go on to develop measures to improve business productivity.

That summer we flew to San Francisco, and from there drove down the west coast of the US and inland to the Grand Canyon. Things had changed in Number 10, Jeremy told me. The Cabinet committees that had proved so valuable in resolving policy issues during the Coalition were meeting less frequently and more was being decided by letter. However, the eleven cross-departmental implementation taskforces that he and Oliver Letwin had set up to track the delivery of the government's manifesto commitments were making progress.

Given that the tension within government had significantly reduced, Jeremy's workload was less intense that autumn and he was rarely being bothered at weekends. But he was still busy with various pieces of policy work including finalising the new Strategic Defence and Security Review, which would allocate defence resources ahead of the 2015 Autumn Statement. Despite announcing in the July Budget that defence spending would be maintained at 2 per cent of GDP, efficiencies still needed to be found if they wanted to increase their ability to address state attacks following Russia's invasion of Ukraine. The Prime Minister also wanted to find enough funds to replace the cancelled Nimrods with new Poseidon maritime patrol aircraft. Squeezing savings out of the defence budget was never straightforward but they again managed it through a range of measures including replacing military roles with civilian ones, selling off more of the Ministry of Defence's extensive estates and reforming its pay system.

Despite this success, the autumn of 2015 was overshadowed by the news that Chris Martin, the Prime Minister's principal private secretary, who had been fighting cancer for some time, was ill again. Jeremy visited Chris many times in hospital during that September and October trying to cheer him with tales of the office and stories from the past, like when they'd huddled in the basement of Number 10 trying to work out if Andrew Mitchell had said the word 'pleb'. But fate wasn't to be diverted. During a Wednesday morning colleagues' meeting in late November, Jeremy was told that Chris had died. He cut the meeting short and spent the rest of the day visiting some of the many civil servants who'd been close to Chris, coming home pale and hollow-eyed. He later wrote an obituary in *Civil Service World*, in which he described Chris as 'quite simply, one of the finest civil servants of his generation'.

Jeremy told me he didn't want to discuss Chris's death, and in its aftermath, he seemed drained. I started pressing him to rest but his workload was increasing again, with the Prime Minister keen to launch new thinking on how the government could help the lives of the poorest and saying that, if he managed to negotiate a new settlement for Britain in the run-up to the European Council in mid-February 2016, he would call the in-out referendum that he'd promised in his manifesto. In anticipation, one Remain and two Leave campaign teams had already been set up, with Vote Leave activists disrupting the Prime Minister's speech to the CBI in November. Within government, the politicians and special advisers began preparing for the referendum campaign while the EU policy officials, including Tom Scholar who was heading the European and Global Issues Secretariat and Mats Persson from the Policy Unit, supported the Prime Minister's discussions with other EU country leaders.

Jeremy was, meanwhile, beginning to worry about some of the other implications of the looming referendum. How, for instance, should the government handle ministers who wanted to argue in public against its policy of staying in the EU? There were, he advised the Prime Minister, three options. Dissenting ministers could be asked to resign, they could be allowed to campaign against the government without resigning, or the government could be neutral and allow ministers to campaign however they wished.

After debating these different approaches, David Cameron chose the second. 'Which is,' Jeremy told me, 'the most difficult one for the Civil Service to manage because we will need to find a way of supporting ministers who think we should stay in Europe and those who want us to leave. It will be even trickier than serving the Coalition government because the Coalition was – at least most of the time – trying to pursue a single set of policies.'

Jeremy was still worrying about how to handle the referendum campaign when we trekked up Lantau Peak in Hong Kong a few days after Christmas. In the light of what happened, I later felt guilty about that walk. I love a hike, and to please me, Jeremy had agreed to do one, adding that he had fond memories of following the same path with Terry Burns back in 1993.

During the first part of our climb up the long green slope, I let the children wander ahead while I stayed back with Jeremy. We talked about the Prime Minister's negotiations with other European leaders – he'd been spending a huge amount of time flying around the EU pushing for his new settlement, Jeremy told me, and seemed increasingly keen to call the referendum in January.

Later in our trek, while I caught up with Jonny, Lizzie and Peter, Jeremy dropped further behind. He was horribly unfit, he said when I went back to find him. But by the time we reached the Buddhist temple on the far side of the peak, and settled down for an almost inedible vegan lunch, it was clear there was more to it than that – Jeremy's knees and ankles were so swollen that he could barely walk. The pain lasted for the rest of our week away and made it virtually impossible for him to go up or down stairs.

By the time we arrived back in London in January 2016, Jeremy was more mobile, but still shuffling. In Number 10, he appointed Simon Case to replace Chris Martin as principal private secretary and I made my own move – leaving McKinsey to become a managing director of Exor, a holding company partly owned by the Agnelli family. Jeremy embraced this new Italian element in our lives and even cheered me on when, in the short break that I had between jobs, I flew to Fiji to try to find *Wavewalker*, the boat I'd grown up on, determined to confront some of the complexities of my childhood. While I revisited my past, ringing each morning to give Jeremy an update on my quest, he stayed behind in London, worrying about the approaching referendum.

50

'Hung Up':
Another end game

January–June 2016

No one knew what the outcome of the February EU Council would be. But many, including Jeremy, worried that any concessions the Prime Minister managed to wring out of Europe as part of his new settlement were unlikely to meet the heady expectations he'd allowed to build up.

This was particularly the case on immigration. At his party conference back in October 2014, the Prime Minister had promised to 'get what Britain needs' on free movement. The political pressure to make this promise had been huge and it wasn't going away – during the summer of 2015 the papers had been full of stories of refugees trying to storm their way through the Channel Tunnel to Dover, and the Office for National Statistics had recently released figures showing that Britain's net migration figures had soared from 177,000 in 2012 to 318,000 in 2014.

But while gaining concessions on immigration was a priority for Britain, giving them wasn't a priority for the European Union, particularly since many of Britain's migrants were EU citizens taking legitimate advantage of one of the European Union's founding principles. And it also didn't help that, while the UK was complaining about immigration, the EU was dealing with its own migrant crisis, after vast numbers of refugees arrived on its southern shores to take shelter from the Syrian civil war.

But one thing was clear by early 2016 – if the Prime Minister returned from the European Council with enough change agreed to call a referendum, the best date for the vote would be in late June. Achieving this timetable would be difficult given the amount of preparatory work required, including bringing forward two statutory instruments, giving the Electoral Commission six weeks to designate the lead campaigns and allowing ten weeks for the campaign itself. But politically it made sense. There was no guarantee that delaying would strengthen the government's case – and every possibility that another summer migration crisis or an economic downturn would worsen voter sentiment.

While Ed Llewellyn, Simon Case and others began this preparatory work, Jeremy prepared advice for the Prime Minister on the issue he'd been pondering during our Christmas break – how the Civil Service should serve dissenting ministers during the referendum campaign. What he needed were clear rules, ideally backed by precedent, so he dug out the principles used in 1975, ahead of Britain's last referendum on Europe, and a letter from the then Prime Minister, Harold Wilson, to his Cabinet. In most areas, Jeremy found that the 1975 approach was aligned with the modern Civil Service code. However, there were others where it was more generous – for example civil servants had been allowed to provide dissenting ministers with factual information on European Community issues and dissenting ministers' special advisers had been permitted to support them even when they were campaigning against the government's position.

On both these points, after some debate with his team, the Prime Minister chose to go with the 1975 precedent, determined to avoid giving his opponents grounds for complaint. For the same reason, he also resisted using the precedent of the Scottish referendum to extend the referendum vote to sixteen- and seventeen-year-olds and decided not to set a turnout threshold for a vote to leave to have legitimacy. Jeremy didn't argue against these political choices – he just hoped the Prime Minister was right in his confidence that, even without such advantages, the government would still win its case.

Jeremy was also worrying about who would approve the various referendum documents that the government had committed to publishing, including the details of whatever new settlement emerged from the EU Council and an economic analysis of EU membership.

The existing Europe Cabinet Committee couldn't do this because it contained ministers from both sides of the debate, so instead Jeremy suggested setting up a new EU Referendum Cabinet Committee composed only of ministers who supported the government's position.

'While you are busy doing all this it must be easy to forget what it could all mean,' I said one evening when Jeremy was describing these preparations.

'I know. But the decision to hold a referendum was a political one,' he said, thumbing through his documents.

'You always say that. But was it wise?'

'That is for the Prime Minister to judge,' Jeremy said. 'But there is one area of the 1975 precedent that I hope we can retain – Harold Wilson's instruction to his Cabinet ministers that they should show good manners to each other.'

We exchanged smiles – that already seemed unlikely.

Late on Friday 19 February 2016, the Prime Minister emerged from two days of meetings in the massive granite and glass Justus Lipsius building in Brussels brandishing commitments to strengthen the single market by cutting red tape, to restrict in-work benefits for new arrivals from the EU for four years, to protect Britain's financial institutions and to exempt Britain from the commitment to form an ever closer union. It wasn't as much as he'd wanted – for example migrants would still have their tax credits phased in over four years and could claim other benefits, like child benefit. But given that the EU had made concessions on some of its core principles, the settlement had been hard won, and David Cameron's judgement was that it was enough.

The special Cabinet discussion the following morning was tense but civilised. The Prime Minister invited comments from his colleagues based on a little-used order of precedence that Jeremy had dug out of the files. And afterwards he stood at a podium on Downing Street to call – after voting reform and Scotland – the third major constitutional referendum of his premiership. It would be, he said, the biggest decision 'in our lifetimes'.

Within days it became clear how ferocious this third throw of the constitutional dice was going to be. Michael Gove, the Prime

Minister's hitherto ally and friend, had declared his intention to campaign against the government even before the Prime Minister arrived back from Brussels. More unexpected was Boris Johnson's decision to join Michael, since Boris's position on the referendum had until then been unclear. In total, five Cabinet ministers and over a hundred Tory MPs decided to campaign for Britain to leave the European Union.

Less than a week later, on 29 February 2016, Jeremy was again called in front of the Public Administration and Constitutional Affairs Committee, this time to be grilled on how the Civil Service would operate during the referendum. Jeremy was particularly apprehensive about this – not because he hadn't done his preparatory work, which he had, but because the politics were so fraught that everyone was looking for someone to blame.

'Where is the precedent … for the extent of denial of information to dissenting ministers that is proposed in your guidance?' Bernard Jenkin demanded this time when Jeremy took his seat.

'There has been a misunderstanding,' Jeremy said before going on to explain that the Civil Service would only deny dissenting ministers referendum briefings and speech material, not anything they needed to run their departments.

Another member of the committee wanted to know whether dissenting ministers could ask civil servants to check if their speeches in favour of leaving the European Union were factually correct.

This was within the guidance, Jeremy said.

'But this is marvellous,' Bernard said. 'What a breath of fresh air. This is so straightforward. We might be able to shorten this whole session.'

Jeremy gave Bernard a tiny smile. 'That would be a pleasure.'

After negotiating this hurdle, Jeremy stepped back from the referendum – though he continued to follow the news of the ever more personal attacks and counter-attacks between Leave and Remain Conservative ministers. There was work to be done, even in the middle of a political war, like negotiating a compromise on the Department of Health's efficiency review between Patrick Carter, the Labour peer leading the thinking and Jeremy Hunt, the secretary of state.

There was also the March 2016 Budget to finalise. Here, when some of George Osborne's pension reforms fell away, Jeremy suggested that the gap could be filled by a levy on sugary drinks. This was a measure that he had been advocating for some time with little success, despite the clear evidence that it would help reduce obesity, perhaps because of the wall-to-wall negative coverage that had greeted the Strategy Unit's suggestion back in 2004 of a tax on unhealthy foods.

'I don't understand why everyone is going so sugartastic,' the Prime Minister exclaimed when they discussed this. But in the end, he came around, partly helped by a meeting with David Halpern in which David had stacked a pile of sugar sachets on the Cabinet table to demonstrate the amount of sugar in a bottle of Pepsi.

While Cameron's nervousness was understandable, the reaction was fine on the day, with the TV chef, Jamie Oliver, turning up outside Westminster on his scooter to tell the press how great the measure was. And over the next two years, sugar levels in soft drinks fell by 11 per cent in the UK while their sales by volume slightly increased. In any case, the sugar tax was overshadowed in the Budget by the Chancellor's decision to tighten access to disability payments, which prompted Iain Duncan Smith, the architect of Universal Credit, to resign, saying this wasn't defensible within a Budget that benefited the better off.

After the excitement of the Budget, the media returned to its wall-to-wall coverage of the referendum campaign. Within Whitehall it also seemed strange to focus on anything else, but the government was still in power and work needed to continue on those 517 manifesto pledges.

One of these pledges, in particular, was occupying a lot of Jeremy's time – the £50 billion project to build the High Speed 2 (HS2) railway from Euston to Birmingham and from there up to Leeds and Manchester.

'The cost of HS2 has spiralled out of control,' the Chancellor said when he discussed the project with the Prime Minister in early March. 'According to PwC, the unit costs for the second phase are twice as high as those for similar projects overseas. And we're running out of time because the NAO's report in June will show that the work is over budget. If we don't get the costs back in line, the politics of this are going to get worse and worse.'

The Prime Minister glanced at Jeremy, who sighed and agreed to take a look. Given how little he knew about railways, he put together a team of major project specialists and officials from the Department of Transport and the Treasury to help him do this, appointing Will Cavendish, the former head of the Implementation Unit, to lead it.

'We're not asking whether HS2 should happen,' Jeremy told them – 'just whether, given the benchmarks, there's scope to reduce the cost.'

Two weeks later, Will was back. The team had probed each major element of the project and identified many excess costs including extensive tunnels and expensive rolling stock and stations. Most critically, the price per kilometre for constructing the line was far higher than for similar projects in Europe.

After absorbing this analysis, Jeremy began to dig into the detail. One of the things that was driving the cost was the depth of the track. People wanted the line to be invisible, but this required more earth to be removed. So, what were the trade-offs, Jeremy asked, between the depth of the track, the angle of the banks on either side, the speed the trains could run at, the avoidance of curves and the number and length of the tunnels? And what was being optimised through each of these choices, since it clearly wasn't cost?

In some cases, Jeremy concluded there were valid reasons for the higher prices. But in others it was less clear, perhaps because the HS2 team had been more focused on the politics of the project and getting its legislation approved than on its budget. With Will's help he chipped away at different elements of the costs, making suggestions as he went – for example proposing that part of the line should be rerouted so that it ran through Sheffield, which would be less expensive and make it easier for travellers to connect to other trains. Through this process they identified savings of around £8 billion from within the £56 billion programme – an outcome that delighted the Chancellor, though they all knew they would have to keep challenging the costs as the project moved from concept to delivery.

* * *

From early April the referendum began to absorb more of Jeremy's time. As he'd done before the Scottish decision, the Prime Minister told Jeremy that he didn't want the Civil Service to do any work on the consequences of a 'no' vote since the government wasn't obliged to work on something that wasn't its policy. In any case, if such preparations were leaked, they would be seized on by the Leave campaign.*

What the Prime Minister did want, however, was any support the Civil Service could legitimately provide to the government's side of the debate. To do this, Jeremy set up a Referendum Unit composed of around thirty civil servants in the Cabinet Office. Though the unit was within the rules, its work was always going to be controversial, which is why it took a steely-eyed session in Jeremy's office before he could convince Matthew Gould, a former British ambassador to Israel, to lead it.

The Referendum Unit produced several papers including one on Article 50, the mechanism in the European Union treaty that would need to be triggered to enable the UK to leave, and another on the options for the UK outside the EU. Their most controversial publication, however, was the leaflet that the government wanted to send out to all 27 million British households on the case for remaining in the EU. Jeremy crawled through the text of this, just as he'd done with the leaflets sent out before the Scottish referendum, telling Matthew and his team, that if they imagined the most pernickety person in the world, then he was going to be ten times more pernickety than that.

The timing of the leaflet was as tricky as its content. Jeremy advised the Prime Minister that it should go out on 11 April, two weeks earlier than the Number 10 political team wanted, so it would be delivered before the start of the ten-week referendum purdah period. The Royal Mail screamed about this change of date, and it didn't stop the leaflet being controversial because it cost £9.3 million and still

* Jeremy's compliance with this request may puzzle some readers. But as he explained to me, the Civil Service works for the ministers of the crown rather than directly for the British public. It is, therefore, ministers who decide what work the Civil Service should do.

went out within the purdah period for the local elections. But Jeremy was satisfied it was within the rules.

Jeremy also spent time stress-testing the Treasury's comprehensive analysis of the long-term economic impact of leaving the EU, and once his amendments were included, felt comfortable with the conclusions. These ranged from a 3.4 to 4.3 per cent loss in GDP after fifteen years if Britain became a member of the European Economic Area, like Norway, through to a 5.4 to 9.5 per cent loss if the UK traded with the EU on World Trade Organisation terms, like Russia or Brazil – although this subtlety was lost after the work was published in April with pro-Remain ministers highlighting the more extreme outcomes.

The other issue Jeremy needed to resolve was what to do about the government websites that set out its pro-EU position. Under the purdah rules, the government wasn't allowed to publish new material during the campaign, but it wasn't clear what this meant for material already online. Unsurprisingly, Leave campaigners thought that everything should be taken down, while Remainers demanded that nothing should change. Jeremy, therefore, took advice from multiple colleagues before setting out a central course – no new pro-EU material should be put online, and links to the government's referendum website should be removed from other government websites, but material already online was effectively published and should be left alone.

As the start of purdah on 26 May neared, the political battle intensified. Boris Johnson claimed the EU was pursuing 'a similar goal to Hitler' in trying to create a superstate while David Cameron gave a speech that many interpreted as suggesting that Brexit could lead to war in Europe. But just before Jeremy stepped back from the fray, he heard that the Treasury was about to publish another document, this time on the immediate economic impact of leaving the EU. When he tracked down a copy of this, he was startled by its conclusion – a vote to leave would push the country into recession and destroy between half a million and 800,000 jobs. This felt extreme, particularly since this impact was based only on a decision to leave, not by the exit itself. But this time, when Jeremy rang the

Treasury to discuss their analysis, he was told it was too late to make any changes.

Jeremy told me he was incredibly frustrated by this. He agreed with the Treasury that leaving the EU would harm Britain's economy and that people should understand this – even though they might still want to leave for reasons of sovereignty or to reduce immigration. But if the government put out material that was seen as being too dramatic, it risked making the Civil Service look political and made it easy for pro-Leave campaigners to dismiss it – as they did after this second paper was published, labelling it 'Project Fear'.

When purdah at last began, a degree of peace descended on Whitehall. Jeremy, as usual, used this time to catch up on his in-tray and tried to get some rest. By then he was no longer complaining of pain in his legs although, despite my nagging, he was doing little real walking – the three or four steps from the house to his government car were the only ones I saw him take most days. Over the following weeks, he kept out of the campaign as much as he could, only intervening when he had to – for example to adjudicate on whether the annual population estimates for the UK and its regions, which were due to be published by the Office for National Statistics on the day of the referendum, breached the purdah requirements. They didn't, he advised, since the ONS was independent, though their new net migration figure wasn't helpful to the government.

Jeremy was, however, following the ongoing twists and turns in the campaign in detail both in the press and on Twitter and it was clear that things were going badly for the government. Many of the right-leaning newspapers were going all-out for Leave, while those that supported Remain were ambivalent about endorsing a Conservative prime minister. But it wasn't just this – the Remain campaign was struggling to present a positive vision of Britain's place in Europe, had tried to frighten people with worst-case scenarios on the impact of leaving, and faced an uphill battle against the anti-EU sentiment that had been nurtured for years by both the press and politicians. Meanwhile, the Leave campaign was waging a more effective campaign under the slogan 'Take Back Control', although it had also rubbished the views of experts and given people misleading facts about the cost of the EU and Britain's rights within it.

By Friday 9 June, it was clear that the Leave campaign had almost closed the gap with Remain. It wasn't Jeremy's job to get involved, but since he was conscious that there was something the government could do that might turn things around, he went to talk to Ed Llewellyn.

'This is only a personal view,' he told Ed. 'But what if you made a vow, just like you did at the end of the Scottish campaign? This time you could pledge to reduce immigration by, say, 50 per cent in five years – effectively giving the EU a yellow card – and offer a second referendum if that wasn't achieved.'

Ed frowned, and Jeremy hoped he wouldn't dismiss the idea. Jeremy had always felt that immigration was Remain's weakest point. Successive governments had thought that if they didn't talk about the issue, it would go away. But that had never worked. Nor were people impressed by the fiddly changes David Cameron had negotiated on the welfare entitlements of EU migrants. But if the eurozone began to recover, the number of immigrants would naturally begin to fall – and of course Whitehall could also come up with a series of measures, just as it had on asylum seekers for Tony Blair years before, to make sure it did.

But Ed was shaking his head. 'It's too late. I'm going to ask George and Dave if we should try to get Merkel to make a helpful statement. But even that could be counterproductive. We need to stay calm and keep fighting.'

On Monday 13 June 2016, with only ten days before the vote, the *Financial Times* published a poll of polls that showed Remain and Leave neck and neck. After that, the government did act – though not in the way that Jeremy had suggested. On 15 June, the Chancellor announced that, if the vote was lost, he would rush through an emergency Budget to increase income tax and cut funding for health, defence and education to fill a £30 billion 'Brexit hole'. In response, four Tory grandees, including Norman Lamont, accused the government of trying to scare the electorate. The following day Jo Cox, a Remain-supporting Labour MP, was murdered in her constituency by a man shouting 'Britain first!'

This escalation of rhetoric, culminating in human tragedy, was frightening. Society's norms were fracturing and any referendum outcome seemed possible. Two nights before the vote, Jeremy asked Olly Robbins to come and see him. Having worked with Olly for years, he believed that, whatever the task that might lie ahead, Olly would be the best candidate to lead the work.

'In the unlikely event that we vote to leave,' Jeremy told Olly, 'I would like you to lead the negotiation with Brussels at official level.'

Olly studied Jeremy. 'It would be an amazing job, but the campaign has been so divisive that I'm worried about how it would affect my family.'

'Well, a lot of the venom will disappear once we're past the vote,' Jeremy said, hoping he sounded more confident than he felt. 'But only if we convince ministers that the Civil Service is working to secure a successful exit. I'm sure we can – it's no different to managing the transition from one party to another.' He took a breath. 'But I need you to do this job. You can handle all the Treasury, justice and home affairs issues and I trust you to be a total professional.'

51

'Deacon Blues':
Begin again

June–October 2016

The EU referendum vote took place on Thursday 23 June 2016.

I rang Jeremy after landing at Heathrow in the early hours of Friday morning. 'Is that really what we've decided?'

'Yes. Over 50 per cent voted in favour of leaving on more than a 70 per cent turnout,' Jeremy said. He was still lounging in bed, half kidding himself he was dozing while catching every new announcement and comment in his emails or on Twitter.

'What happens now?'

'God knows. Despite the Prime Minister's protestations before the vote, I can't see him wanting to stay on. And we need to decide how to make an exit happen, which I fear will be harder than anyone has appreciated.'

'What does it mean for you?'

Jeremy sighed. 'I don't know. I'm trying to work out if I should talk to the Leave campaign to find out what work they want to commission. But I've no idea how I'll build the confidence of Leave-supporting ministers and backbenchers after the vitriol of the campaign.'

After our call, Jeremy took a deep breath and jumped out of bed. There was no point in hiding from the world – he was the head of the Civil Service and he needed to present a strong and confident face to his team.

At 8.15 that morning, David Cameron announced his intention to resign.

'He had to – he would get a wall of hostility if he tried to stay,' Craig Oliver told Jeremy. 'Anyway, he felt he couldn't credibly lead our negotiations on exiting the EU after campaigning so fiercely in favour of staying in.'

'I guess you're right,' Jeremy said – though as he listened to Cameron's short speech to his Number 10 staff thanking them for 'an incredible journey', he felt a familiar sense of loss. Some of this was personal. Jeremy respected David and they had a relationship that stretched back over twenty years. It was also professional. While they waited for a decision on who the next Conservative leader would be, all the in-flight initiatives across Whitehall would be frozen. A few might survive, but many wouldn't. However, even putting aside all these considerations, this prime ministerial ending was particularly bittersweet because, despite his many achievements, it was already clear that David Cameron would only be remembered for one thing: the spectacular failure of his final constitutional gamble.

That afternoon, Jeremy wrote a message to the Civil Service:

You will have seen the Prime Minister's statement this morning. Our duty as civil servants is clear. The task falls to us to support the government, and the new Prime Minister when appointed, in carrying forward the clear decision of the British people to leave the EU and set a new direction for the country. And we'll do so while ensuring other business continues as usual, serving the public with professionalism and pride.

I got home that evening to find Jeremy already immersed in practicalities.

'At least the Prime Minister hasn't yet triggered Article 50 as he stated he would during the campaign,' he said looking up from his papers. 'It's just as well. We have a massive amount to do. For a start, we need to get ready to negotiate agreements with every trading bloc in the world. And the pound has plummeted, so we need to find a way to reassure the markets. But do you know what the most difficult issue is?'

'What?'

'Ireland.'

'Really?'

'Absolutely. If Northern Ireland is out of the EU and Southern Ireland is in, then we'll need a hard border between them. But that would demolish the Good Friday Agreement. I don't yet see how we will solve that.'

'Do we have to have a hard border?'

'Yes – unless we can come up with a clever technological solution to stop goods flowing across the border with no customs checks, but no one seems to know how that might work.'

While the Conservatives worked on finding a new leader, Jeremy, Camilla Cavendish, the head of the Policy Unit, and Oliver Letwin met in Oliver's small, panelled study in Number 9 Downing Street to start preparing for Brexit. It was going to be hard to make much progress when they didn't know who the next prime minister would be, but they could at least start to lay out the questions. They also needed to confirm who would lead the thinking at official level. When Jeremy proposed Olly, Oliver was enthusiastic, having seen Olly in action at the National Security Council. However, since Olly had only just moved to the Home Office, it took most of the weekend for Jeremy to convince him to take the role and for Oliver to convince the home secretary to release him.

'Which means,' Oliver said, after Theresa May finally agreed to this, 'that she thinks she will become Prime Minister.'

Olly's appointment to lead the small and somewhat demoralised European and Global Issues Secretariat in the Cabinet Office was announced on Wednesday 29 June 2016. While Olly started recruiting more staff, Oliver Letwin talked to each of the Conservative Party leadership candidates and various other Brexit opinion formers. There was little overlap in their views of how Brexit should be handled, he told Jeremy. However, the central conundrum was clear – how could the UK maximise trade flows with the EU while controlling immigration and making free trade deals with the rest of the world? Being able to make these deals was important since this was the biggest potential upside of leaving – after all, despite the decades of anguish about Brussels bureaucracy, no one had identified much opportunity to deregulate after Britain's exit.

'I don't see how we balance all these needs,' Olly told Jeremy on their way back to the Cabinet Office after another long working session in Oliver's office, crowded in by stacks of well-thumbed global free trade agreements.

'Neither do I,' Jeremy said. 'And we have no idea how UK companies will be affected if we move to World Trade Organisation rules. Sometimes our job feels like playing sixteen-dimensional chess when you don't know what the solution looks like. But even if we don't know our destination, we can still help the government take the next step, which right now means laying out the possible options.'

In this odd hiatus while the Tory Party squabbled over its next leader and Oliver read free trade agreements, the Chilcot report on the Iraq war was finally published. After seven years of work, the report concluded that the decision to go to war was flawed because it had happened before all the peaceful options for disarmament had been exhausted and because its judgements about Iraq's weapons of mass destruction had been presented with a certainty that wasn't justified. A critical procedural conclusion from all of this, Jeremy told the Public Administration and Constitutional Affairs Committee a few weeks later, was the need to avoid groupthink by ensuring senior officials, ministers and external experts felt they could offer an alternative view to the prevailing wisdom.

Jeremy hadn't been asked to give evidence to the Chilcot inquiry, and wasn't mentioned in the report because he hadn't attended any of the key meetings on Iraq. This, though, didn't stop Peter Oborne dubbing him 'Sir Cover-Up' in an article in the *Daily Mail* the day after it was published. I found this offensive, but Jeremy was sanguine. Peter had long believed that, as principal private secretary, Jeremy should have attended and minuted all the meetings on Iraq. But plenty of qualified advisers had been part of those discussions, so Jeremy still believed he'd been right to focus instead on domestic policy issues, particularly the euro decision and public sector reform.

Meanwhile, back in 2016, the internecine race to become the leader of the Conservative Party was speeding up. Before the first round of the ballot on 5 July, Michael Gove killed Boris Johnson's campaign by declaring that Johnson wasn't fit to be prime minister.

In revenge, Michael's own pitch for the leadership was curtailed in the second ballot by angry Conservative MPs. When Andrea Leadsom dropped out on 11 July after implying she was a stronger contender because she was a mother, Theresa May became the only candidate still standing.

After six days, a contest that had been expected to go on until after the summer was over and we were about to get our second female prime minister. However, few people knew what Theresa May would be like as prime minister or were certain of her views. Even Jeremy was unsure. Theresa had been a half-hearted Remain supporter but had avoided the limelight during the campaign. Beyond that, the things that stood out were her attempts to create a 'hostile environment' for illegal immigrants while she'd been home secretary and her fights with Michael Gove. The only thing that did seem certain was that, with a new prime minister about to arrive in Downing Street, Jeremy would have to pull out of the first half of our summer holiday in Australia, though he promised to join me for the second half.

David Cameron chaired his last Cabinet meeting on the morning of Tuesday 12 July. The mood became increasingly emotional as individual ministers made tributes to his premiership, which Jeremy dutifully recorded in his notebook until the Prime Minister ended the discussion and walked out.

That afternoon, Theresa May's special advisers Nick Timothy and Fiona Hill* came to see Jeremy in his office. He smiled a little nervously when they sat down, hoping they wouldn't hold the past against him. He respected both of them – Fiona for the media expertise that she'd demonstrated in the Home Office and Nick, a committed Eurosceptic with a Solzhenitsyn beard, for his political brain. It was just a pity that Fiona had only just been reappointed as a special adviser by the Prime Minister after her resignation two years before following the leaking of the Birmingham schools letter and that Nick had been one of the special advisers deselected as a parliamentary candidate after Sue Gray's liberal interpretation of the special advisers' code.

---

* Previously Cunningham.

Thankfully, this tension didn't seem apparent in their conversation. They started by discussing the reshuffle, in which Mrs May was planning to replace George Osborne with Philip Hammond. What was less clear was whether she would give Michael Gove a role after he'd campaigned against her in the leadership race. But since these were political decisions, they spent more time discussing the new Brexit and trade departments that Theresa May had promised during her campaign – with Nick and Fiona making it clear that this commitment couldn't be unravelled despite the additional complexity it would create. They also reviewed some of Jeremy's preliminary Brexit thinking and debated whether, to reduce duplication in Whitehall, it might make sense for Olly Robbins to head the Brexit department alongside his role in the Cabinet Office.

Nick was watching Jeremy. 'The Brexit vote is a mandate for change,' he said. 'It's not only about leaving the EU, it's also about taking a more active role in the economy, sorting out markets that lead to unfair outcomes for consumers and addressing issues of race and social disadvantage.'

'I agree,' Jeremy said, nodding. 'And what role do you two want to play in making that happen?'

'We're a partnership,' Fiona said, 'so we don't know who should be chief of staff.'

Jeremy chewed the end of his pen. 'Why don't you become joint chiefs?'

Theresa May spent the morning of Wednesday 13 July working with Jeremy in his office, having agreed she would take possession of Number 10 after David Cameron finished Prime Minister's Questions. While they waited, they discussed various issues including her view on the possibility of Japan's Softbank buying ARM, a major UK technology company that designed chips for smartphones, and whether she wanted to delay the impending vote in the House of Commons on renewing the Trident nuclear deterrent. But her big message was one Jeremy was delighted to hear – after the disruption of the referendum, she wanted stability. That meant no snap election or emergency Budget.

When the newly-minted Prime Minister returned from Buckingham Palace that afternoon, she paused to give a speech outside the door of Number 10. Her words echoed Nick Timothy's the day before – her government would be about fighting 'burning injustices' to make Britain a country that worked for everyone, not just for the privileged few.

With her speech over, the door of Number 10 swung open, and Theresa and Philip May swept in. Jeremy followed them, together with Nick and Fiona, between the columns of clapping staff down the yellow corridor towards the Cabinet Room. This was the third time he'd done this with a new prime minister and he knew it was the moment when every previous assumption about how the centre of government worked, including his own role, might be about to change. When they reached the den, Jeremy took a deep breath and tried a slight smile. It was time for the office conversation again.

'This, Prime Minister, is where you sit,' he said, indicating the office with a sweep of his hand.

Theresa May glanced around. 'Fine,' she said, putting her handbag on the desk, 'though could you get me a meeting table?'

With a legally binding contract for a new nuclear power station at Hinkley Point in Somerset due to be signed on 29 July, Jeremy's most urgent policy task in the days after the Prime Minister's arrival was finding out whether she supported the deal.

Although the Civil Service was conscious of the criticisms being made of Hinkley Point – in particular the price the government had committed to pay for the energy it would produce and the fact that some of the funding was coming from a state-owned Chinese firm – everyone assumed the Prime Minister's support wasn't in question. After all, she'd been in Cabinet and in the National Security Council during many of the critical discussions. But when Jeremy sent her a submission outlining the background to the deal and requesting permission to sign the contract, she summoned him in to say she wasn't sure it should go ahead.

Jeremy blinked. 'Of course, Prime Minister. What are you concerned about?'

'I'm not sure we need new nuclear power stations. And even if we do, I'm worried about the level of foreign involvement in Hinkley Point.'

Jeremy told himself to stay calm, a message he knew he would soon be repeating to his colleagues. His next step, though, was clear – he needed to give the Prime Minister the best possible advice on the issues that concerned her, and to keep doing that until all her questions were answered and she was ready to make a decision.

In their first meetings on Hinkley Point, the Whitehall experts took Theresa May through the background to the deal, which had been agreed back in October 2013. It had been a difficult negotiation because, although the Coalition Agreement had ruled out public subsidies for new nuclear projects, there was little chance of EDF, a French electric utility company, building a nuclear power station without them – after all, the plant would cost £18 billion and wouldn't produce any power until the mid-2020s, even assuming that it came in on time and budget.

Despite these issues, the Coalition, and in particular the Conservatives, believed nuclear power was a vital part of the UK's energy mix – as did Jeremy, who was familiar with the case for nuclear power since he'd assessed the plans for Sizewell B when he'd been in the Health and Safety Executive at the start of his career. Nuclear had challenges, but it was able to churn out low-carbon energy even in the middle of a windless night. However, the only way for the government to make a new nuclear power plant feasible, without offering direct public funding or taking on project risk, was to agree a high enough price for the plant's future power to make the economics work. After several months of negotiation, this had been set at £92.50 per megawatt-hour – generous enough to allow the project to go ahead but lower than the £140 per megawatt-hour that they had offered for offshore wind.

The Prime Minister soon agreed with the general case for nuclear power and was largely reassured that the Hinkley Point deal offered value for money. But she remained concerned about the national security risk created by the involvement of China's state-backed General Nuclear Power Corporation, which was providing 33.5 per cent of the investment and which was also due to invest in a second reactor at Sizewell and build a third at Bradwell in Essex.

By this point it was apparent they would miss the July deadline for agreeing the contract for Hinkley Point. At the Prime Minister's request, Jeremy, therefore, apologised at length to the Chinese ambassador, because he knew that the lead Chinese businessman was already on his way to Somerset for the signing ceremony. Given the French government's ownership of EDF, the Prime Minister meanwhile spoke to President Hollande of France, whom she was keen not to offend just before the start of the Brexit negotiations.

Over the following couple of weeks, after waving me and the children off on holiday, Jeremy organised further meetings on Hinkley Point and compiled mountains of Whitehall briefings on the subject, including a full national security assessment. With the press speculating daily about the Prime Minister's deliberations, some of these discussions became heated, including one in which Theresa May turned towards Jeremy, narrowed her eyes and accused him of conspiring with the French.

Jeremy said little for the rest of that meeting, bundling up his papers and walking stiffly back to the Cabinet Office at the end. He told Simon Case, who went with him, that he'd never been spoken to like that before and would resign if the Prime Minister didn't withdraw her words. There were many things he could tolerate, but not an accusation about his loyalty to his country. But the Prime Minister did apologise, and to be fair, tempers were generally running high, with the Chancellor, for example, telling Jeremy not to piss off the Chinese, while at official level the Treasury was making it equally clear that they opposed the deal.

Jeremy left Whitehall working on Hinkley Point while he fulfilled his promise to join me and the children for the final part of our holiday in Australia. He was generally able to put the tensions in Downing Street behind him while he was away, exchanging his suits for his beloved cardigans and jeans, and enjoying our visit to the Blue Mountains. But it was clear to me, when I saw him away from our normal life, how unwell he still was. He was struggling to walk far and his left shoulder was so sore that he could barely raise his arm.

While I'd been away in Australia, he'd been referred by his doctor to a rheumatologist, who'd sent him off for various tests including a chest X-ray to try to find out what was wrong. But the only thing that had been suggested at the end of these investigations was that he should reduce the quantity of the steroids that he'd been taking since 2009 to manage his colitis.

By the time we returned to London, most of the additional work on Hinkley Point was finished, and in mid-September, the Prime Minister decided to let the project go ahead with the government taking a special share that it could use in the future if EDF tried to sell its controlling stake to an unsuitable buyer. The UK was still open to new nuclear if the terms were right. And the Prime Minister had shown that, though she took decisions in a very different way to her predecessor, she still trusted advice from the Civil Service.

New nuclear had dominated the first few weeks of Theresa May's premiership, but the far bigger issue on everyone's mind was Brexit. Jeremy thought, even then, that Brexit would be the biggest challenge of his career – in fact he told the first meeting of the top 200 civil servants after the referendum that he believed it was a more significant international relations challenge than Iraq, a more profound constitutional challenge than the Coalition, a more challenging policy issue than the financial crisis and a more substantial economic challenge than the ERM. And he added later to me, having been involved in every one of those, he felt he'd been training for it all his life.

In September 2016, Olly Robbins became the Prime Minister's sherpa to Europe, making him her lead adviser on Brexit. In theory he'd been carrying out this role ever since he'd become the head of the European and Global Issues Secretariat back in June but the Prime Minister had hesitated before confirming his appointment because, since then, Olly had also become the permanent secretary of the new Brexit department, the Department for Exiting the EU (DExEU). Jeremy had remained unenthused about creating DExEU, but if it had to exist, he believed it would help align Whitehall's thinking if Olly performed both roles. And after pondering the matter for several weeks, the Prime Minister had agreed.

Olly and his DExEU team had a mountain of work to do. For a start, Brussels was insisting that both Britain's 'divorce bill' from the EU and the consequences of Brexit for EU citizens living in Britain had to be resolved before any future arrangements could be discussed. Earlier in the year the UK had tried to resist this, proposing that 'nothing should be agreed until everything was agreed'. But by the time Jeremy had left for Australia, Michel Barnier, the EU's lead negotiator, had ruled that out. DExEU was also trying to answer the question Jeremy had posed shortly after the vote – how different business sectors would be affected if Britain left the customs union – which meant sifting through the claims people were making to decide which were over- or understated.

DExEU's most difficult challenge, however, was working with the Treasury to detail the potential options for the UK's future customs arrangement with the EU, beyond the Prime Minister's somewhat cryptic statement that 'Brexit means Brexit'. There were multiple possibilities. In their initial discussion with the Prime Minister, the DExEU officials described five. The last of these, the 'hybrid option', was, at least to Jeremy, the most intriguing. Under this approach the UK would continue to impose EU tariffs at its borders, though these could be reclaimed if goods stayed in the UK and the UK had a lower tariff regime for them than the EU did. This was attractive for two reasons – it removed the need for a customs border between Northern Ireland and the Republic of Ireland and it would be relatively easy to implement.

While DExEU developed these options – and the Treasury worried about the impact they would have on economic growth and on the movement of goods through British ports – Jeremy tried to help Whitehall adjust to the new Prime Minister's way of working. Since Theresa May liked to mull over issues, at ministerial level he also set up three new Cabinet committees covering the main elements of her agenda – trade, industrial strategy and social reform.

Despite Whitehall's preoccupation with Brexit, Jeremy was also determined to keep other policy issues moving. One of these was the long-running debate about airport expansion. After the Airport Commission's report had been published in July 2015, Heathrow had started working on runway designs while Whitehall prepared a National Policy Statement for Cabinet and Parliament. But the government still needed to decide whether it supported the commission's recommendation.

The Prime Minister, as the MP for Maidenhead in Berkshire, was familiar with the issues around airport expansion but hadn't revealed her hand, and after Hinkley Point, Jeremy was taking nothing for granted. What he did know was that the government's verdict would be subjected to considerable scrutiny and that, if they could, both sides of the debate would resort to legal challenge to reverse or slow down a decision they didn't like. With David Cameron's agreement, he'd, therefore, already set up a new Cabinet committee, the Economic Affairs (Airports) Sub-Committee, to consider the issue. This contained, alongside the Prime Minister and Chancellor, seven other ministers, none of whom had been so outspoken in the past that they could be seen as having already made up their minds. Fortunately, they also represented all the departments with a policy interest.

In advance of the committee's meeting in October 2016, Jeremy went through the voluminous documentation prepared by Whitehall, covering every possible question that the group might ask. In the event, however, the discussion was straightforward, with the members of the committee unanimously agreeing the commission's recommendations. And when the decision was announced on 25 October 2016, although one MP, Zac Goldsmith, resigned his seat, broader reaction was muted. This meant that Heathrow was free to keep working up its designs ahead of the next stage of government decision-making in another two years' time.

52

'Lost Ones':
Article 50 and another election

October 2016–June 2017

In late October 2016, our phone rang while I was cooking dinner.

'Mum is dead,' my brother Jon said when I picked it up.

'Dead?' I felt light-headed and slid down to sit on the floor, closing my eyes.

'Yes,' Jon said before going on to explain that my mother had been at a drinks party with my father when she had said she felt unwell, sat down on a chair and tipped over. My father had caught her before she hit the carpet, but it was already too late.

We drove down to the Cotswolds several times to help my father prepare for my mother's funeral, and again for the day itself. Each time we visited, I walked alone along the Bristol Canal early in the morning. I was shocked and grieving, though my sorrow was for a maternal love I'd always craved but had eventually given up trying to win, whereas my father's grief at losing his lifelong companion was acute and sharp.

My father asked if Jeremy would help carry my mother's coffin.

'He can't,' I said. 'He would if he could, but his shoulder hurts when he lifts his arm.'

So our older son, Jonny, stepped in to take Jeremy's place while our younger son, Peter, sang the Ave Maria, which years before my mother had requested at our wedding. Our family had become smaller and a little sadder, and another piece of the past had disappeared.

* * *

In between joining me on these trips to support my father, Jeremy was worrying about the Autumn Statement. By then it had become clear that the change of regime in Downing Street had refrozen the relationship between Number 10 and Number 11, so Jeremy again started holding official-level meetings with the Treasury to try to negotiate funding for the Prime Minister's domestic agenda. These discussions were painful since there was little willingness to compromise on either side, but he managed to extract enough to fund some new productivity and innovation measures together with some additional affordable homes.

Alongside the Autumn Statement, Jeremy was also working with the Policy Unit and Ben Gummer, the new Cabinet Office minister, to try to wrestle the 2015 manifesto pledges into alignment with Theresa May's determination to fight 'burning injustices'. However, no matter how important all this work was, it still felt like a sideshow to Brexit. Each Sunday evening, Olly shared with Jeremy a draft of his note to the Prime Minister summarising the latest thinking in Brussels and Whitehall. These notes then formed the agenda for the Prime Minister's midweek Europe strategy meetings with Olly and Jeremy, Nick and Fiona, the deputy chief of staff, Joanna Penn, the head of the UK's representation in Brussels, Ivan Rogers, and the director of communications, Katie Perrior.

These discussions were important to Theresa May because they were her chance to debate the Brexit options with a close group of trusted advisers. They sometimes became bad tempered, however, as the group tried to reconcile what Brussels wanted with what the Conservative Party would tolerate. Nick and Fiona were often particularly intolerant of Olly's reports, but beyond occasionally stepping in to ensure Olly had the space to give the Prime Minister honest advice on what could be negotiated, Jeremy generally ignored this – after all, they were all under pressure to find a solution and he knew from experience that difficult behaviour would resolve itself over time.

After Christmas 2016, we flew to Cuba, which had recently reopened to tourists. We stayed in Havana, mesmerised by the old Buicks and Mercedes in ice-cream colours that made us feel like extras in a 1950s Hollywood film. We even tried our hand at salsa dancing, though Jeremy's innate rhythm couldn't overcome his lack of coordination, which frequently left him facing backwards while the children and I faced forwards. But despite the cars and the dancing, it wasn't the easiest of holidays. I felt that Jeremy and I had slipped, almost without noticing it, into the age-old trap in which any sense of 'us' as a couple had become subsumed by friendship, parenthood and work.

'We can fix this,' Jeremy had assured me when I'd raised it with him that autumn. 'It's just we've both been so busy, and I've been so tired.'

I knew that was true. Jeremy's exhaustion had changed the shape of our life. His naps on the weekends were longer and our evenings out were rarer. That holiday he made more of an effort, spending time talking about our plans for the future. But he was still plagued by ailments, and for the first time since I'd known him, he was also complaining of headaches.

We celebrated the New Year by compiling our usual lists of 'best ofs', with the children this time joining in. Surviving his third prime ministerial transition that decade was Jeremy's biggest achievement of the year and Brexit was his biggest surprise. Two days later, we boarded our flight back to London via Paris. When we landed ten hours later at Charles de Gaulle airport, we discovered both that we had missed our connecting flight and that Ivan Rogers had resigned. We, therefore, spent the next few hours hauling ourselves, the children and our luggage across Paris to Orly Airport while Jeremy negotiated a replacement to fill the hole – Tim Barrow, Britain's former ambassador to Russia.

Between calls to try to resolve this, Jeremy told me that he'd known it might happen. Although Ivan had stayed in post in Brussels after the referendum, he'd made it clear he thought Brexit was a bad idea and that the negotiations with the EU would be more difficult, and take longer, than anyone expected. In retaliation, he'd been briefed against in the press in a campaign many attributed to the chiefs of staff. Nevertheless, Ivan's departure was still a shock, and it was made more difficult by the parting email that he sent to his staff telling them to 'never be afraid to speak truth to those in power'.

Although Jeremy regretted losing Ivan's European expertise, he told me he'd also struggled with Ivan's negativity about the Brexit process. However great the challenges of leaving the EU were, the British people had voted, and that decision couldn't be changed. And while it was right for the Civil Service to offer advice on how best to interpret the referendum, it was the Prime Minister's job to decide.

Theresa May had begun laying out her thinking on the Brexit decision in her party conference speech the previous October. In this she'd stated two of her 'red lines' for the exit negotiations – ending the jurisdiction of the European Court of Justice and taking back control of immigration. These red lines, which pleased the more extreme Brexiteers in her party, had significantly narrowed the UK's leave options. Although she didn't state this at the time, to comply with them, the UK would have to leave the single market. In addition, if Britain wanted to negotiate its own trade deals with other countries, it would probably also have to leave the full customs union.

The Brexit negotiating challenge had become even tougher after the Prime Minister's next speech, which she gave in the gold-leaf-embossed long gallery in Lancaster House in mid-January 2017. This time, as well as launching her 'Plan for Britain', which summarised the results of Jeremy and Ben Gummer's work to align her thinking with the 2015 manifesto pledges, she added another red line – there should be no new barriers within the United Kingdom.

The political rationale for this new pledge was clear. A hard border between Northern Ireland and the Republic of Ireland would jeopardise the Good Friday Agreement and a border in the Irish Sea separating Northern Ireland from the rest of the UK would be unacceptable to Unionists. But though understandable, it further narrowed the UK's leave options. If borders weren't allowed, it wasn't clear how any differences in product regulations or tariffs between Britain and Europe would be managed – or indeed how any of this could be reconciled with the Prime Minister's desire, which she also expressed in her speech, for 'tariff-free' and 'frictionless' trade with Europe.

'But what concerned me most about the Lancaster House speech,' Jeremy told me when we discussed all this, 'was the Prime Minister's statement that "no deal for Britain is better than a bad deal". Based on everything I've seen, that can only be true politically.'

Jeremy kept worrying about this throughout January 2017. Although the Prime Minister's red lines had ruled out many future customs solutions, a few remained. The hybrid option, which Jeremy still favoured, was one. Another was the 'third-party customs option', which involved streamlining trade barriers and inventing a techno-logical solution to secure the Irish border without using a physical barrier. But both of these depended on the EU agreeing to let the UK develop its own trade agreements while at the same time allow-ing it to retain preferential access to the EU's markets – and for the Eurosceptics to be satisfied that the UK would become sufficiently sovereign.

While the Treasury worked up these options, Jeremy focused on other things, including attending the Public Administration and Constitutional Affairs Committee, which was planning its next inquiry into the relationship between ministers and officials. He also visited various doctors for blood tests and brain scans. No new expla-nation for his multiplying ailments emerged from this, however. So we instead continued to rely on short-term fixes – Jeremy's shoulder was injected with cortisone, which made little difference, we stocked up with paracetamol, which kept the worst symptoms at bay – and we soldiered on.

In the run-up to the March 2017 Budget, Jeremy focused on trying to find resources for the Prime Minister's industrial strategy and for her push to rebalance the economy away from the south-east. These were both important elements of her Plan for Britain but Jeremy still made limited progress because, despite the strengthening economy, the Chancellor was determined to stick to his predecessor's austerity target. Jeremy did, however, convince the Treasury to release some money to support research and development on biotech, robotic systems and driverless vehicles.

Jeremy was also trying to persuade the Treasury to increase fund-ing for adult social care. This was an issue he'd worried about for years, but despite multiple reviews and Green and White Papers, the social care system had remained fundamentally unchanged while demand continued to escalate, with many people forced to sell their homes to pay for care. The Treasury was unwilling to provide more money for this in the absence of a wider review, so Jeremy decided to conduct a review of social care himself using a team of experts in the Cabinet Office, led by Paul Kissack.

Ahead of the Budget, Jeremy shared the preliminary thinking from this team with the Prime Minister. There were several long-term approaches to solving the social care crisis, he said, but regardless of which was chosen, the short-term funding issue still needed to be tackled. This wasn't about eye-catching initiatives, it was about addressing years of underfunding that was revealing itself in multiple ways, like in the fragility of residential care providers. After the Prime Minister accepted this advice, they managed to negotiate a further £2 billion for social care from the Treasury, together with the promise of another Green Paper on long-term solutions.

What Jeremy couldn't influence, however, was the Chancellor's determination to increase National Insurance for the self-employed to bring them in line with other workers. Although this issue needed to be dealt with, Jeremy argued – as did most of Number 10 – that it would be better to do it after Matthew Taylor, the chief executive of the Royal Society of the Arts, finalised his report on modern employment practices in July. Jeremy had high hopes for Matthew's review partly because it had been set up using the lessons learnt from the Beecroft report. This meant, for example, that a panel of experts, including an employment lawyer, had been involved in the thinking from the start and the team had conducted several public consultations. The intention was that the work would clarify the rights and benefits of self-employed workers, after which the government could debate their taxation.

But despite this pending review, the Chancellor was in no mood to wait. In his final Budget meeting with the Prime Minister he, therefore, agreed that, in exchange for providing another £320 million to help fund up to 140 more free schools – something Nick Timothy wanted – he would widen Class 4 National Insurance contributions to include the self-employed.

When the Chancellor announced this National Insurance change in his Budget speech on 8 March, there were howls of protest. It was, the papers cried, a breach of the Conservatives' 2015 manifesto, which had ruled out increasing National Insurance, income tax or VAT. The Treasury fought back, arguing that this pledge hadn't applied to this variant of National Insurance, but unsurprisingly, this technocratic defence didn't stop the onslaught. In fact, it became clear over the next few days that, unless the measure was changed, the Finance Bill might not make it through Parliament. Faced with no other alternative, a week after the Budget, the Chancellor, therefore, decided to withdraw it.

For the government to be forced into a U-turn on a central Budget measure was hugely embarrassing. But three days after this humiliation, Jeremy was told something that made this feel irrelevant – the Prime Minister was about to trigger Article 50, giving notice of Britain's intent to leave the EU.

Jeremy had known this was coming – the Prime Minister had announced the previous October that she would do it no later than March and the legislation that she needed to trigger Article 50 had just finished its tortuous journey through Parliament. He asked her for a couple more weeks to prepare, but didn't push for more since he knew that the European Commission was refusing to start the Brexit negotiations before the UK fired the starting pistol and he was conscious of the huge political pressure the Prime Minister was under to get the process started. He knew, of course, the game the EU was playing – they wanted to force the negotiation into the two-year period dictated by Article 50, believing that the threat of failing to agree a deal would weigh heavier on the UK than it would on Europe – but it was unclear how Britain could change those terms.

However, the political drumbeat was by then too strong for the Prime Minister to concede even Jeremy's requested short delay. Instead, on Monday 20 March 2017, she announced that Article 50 would be triggered in nine days' time. After that the government would have two years to negotiate the terms of the UK's withdrawal, and ideally also its future partnership with the European Union.

After pulling this trigger, the Prime Minister embarked on a tour of European capitals to start the discussion about Britain's future relationship and the Brexit effort ramped up. Olly Robbins, in particular, was juggling a massive workload, with DExEU overseeing 313 Brexit workstreams, all tracked in a huge colour-coded spreadsheet that Jeremy regularly brought home to pore over. This, though, was only part of Olly's challenge – he was also dealing with the intensifying demands of his two bosses: the Prime Minister, who liked going through every issue in detail, and the Secretary of State for Exiting the EU, David Davis, who, while less exhaustive, was more passionate about Brexit. But despite these challenges, Jeremy wasn't keen to split Olly's role, and neither was Olly, because they both still saw the benefits of having DExEU closely connected to the negotiations in Brussels.

In any case, by this time the Prime Minister was too busy thinking about the possibility of a snap election to worry about much else. Theresa May had made it clear when she launched her bid to lead the Conservative Party that she didn't intend to hold an early election and she had confirmed this several times since – including in her conversation with Jeremy shortly before she became Prime Minister. But it was becoming clear that Westminster wasn't coming together on Brexit. A successful election would help the Prime Minister get the Brexit legislation through the House of Commons and give her a personal mandate in her negotiations with Europe. In addition, since the Fixed-Term Parliaments Act dictated that the next election was due in May 2020, there was the risk that, if one wasn't called early, the Brexit endgame – and any post-Brexit economic downturn – would take place squarely in the run-up to the vote.

By the time we returned from our short Easter break in Greece, the Prime Minister had made up her mind, announcing on 18 April 2017 that an election on 8 June would enable her to provide the country with the 'strong and stable leadership' required to deliver both Brexit and her social reform agenda. This decision was endorsed by Parliament the following day, as required under the Fixed-Term Parliaments Act.

Many members of the Conservative Party were shocked by May's decision – including her Cabinet, which was only told on the morning of her announcement. But since the Conservatives were twenty points ahead in the polls, there seemed little doubt about the outcome. It also appeared that, even if they were unenthused about the prospect of another election, the electorate had warmed to their unflashy and reserved Prime Minister, since Theresa May's personal ratings were far stronger than those for Jeremy Corbyn, the Labour Party's new hard-line socialist leader.

Unfortunately for the Tories, this advantage didn't last. After the local elections on 4 May, where the Conservatives did remarkably well, the mood changed, and it became clear that Theresa May was struggling to communicate her vision. With knife crime soaring, she was criticised for her decision as home secretary to reduce police numbers, a view that intensified after horrific terrorist attacks took place in Manchester and London. A *Mirror* reporter dressed as a chicken began following her around after she dodged the head-to-head television debates with other party leaders. And in early May, the president of the European Commission, Jean-Claude Juncker, claimed she was 'living in a parallel universe' after a dinner they had to discuss the Brexit negotiations. The Labour Party, in contrast, experienced a surge of popularity, especially among younger voters, partly due to the support Jeremy Corbyn was receiving from Momentum, a digitally savvy left-wing activist group.

The hefty Tory Party manifesto, which was published on Thursday 18 May after a mad scramble to get it ready, could have helped turn the campaign around, but instead did the opposite.

In an attempt to define how May would deliver social reform, the manifesto included a host of new policies including a controversial proposal to ask people to contribute more to the cost of receiving state-funded social care in their own homes, with the payments being collected after their death. This policy was one of the ones that Paul Kissack had been considering with his team in the Cabinet Office. Jeremy, however, had always been more intrigued by the simplicity of the solution that had been proposed by the economist Andrew Dilnot in his 2011 report. Andrew had argued that the best way to fund social care was through insurance cover, but since this wouldn't work if the cost of receiving care was too high, the government should cap the lifetime cost of social care. The problem was that, while logical, this cap would be expensive to implement, and because it would mainly benefit the middle classes, it would have to be balanced by other measures. Dilnot's recommendation had, therefore, been endlessly debated before being deferred by George Osborne after the 2015 election.

Given this background, Jeremy read the details of Theresa May's manifesto commitment with mixed feelings. Although this wasn't his preferred solution, he was pleased that a way forward on social care was at last being proposed. However, he was surprised to see something so controversial announced in the middle of an election campaign, particularly because it needed more work. No one had figured out, for example, how to fund care for people with early-onset diseases like multiple sclerosis. But the press was much less forgiving – in fact the papers wound themselves up into such a fury about this 'dementia tax' that, four days later, the Prime Minister reversed her position and said the government would consider capping the cost of care – though she somewhat oddly claimed that this wasn't a change in policy.

While the Prime Minister fought to maintain her lead in the election campaign, Jeremy spent the purdah period filling his briefing folders for incoming ministers and working with Ronnie Cohen to detail a £1 billion outcome fund to support social impact bonds. With all the politicians out canvassing for votes, Jeremy was getting more rest, but his tiredness wasn't easing, he was still breathless and his headache had become permanent. With only a week to go before the election, he went to see our local GP, Dr Patel, who, after listening to his chest, told him he needed to go for blood tests and a chest X-ray because one of his lungs might have collapsed again or he might have pneumonia.

'Do you think Dr Patel's right?' I asked that evening. I felt uneasy, though I didn't say so. Over the years I'd become used to Jeremy's ailments, his pill bottles accumulating in the corner cupboard in the kitchen. But this felt different, with new pains appearing without obvious cause or resolution.

'I don't know,' Jeremy said. 'Dr Patel says both are unlikely, particularly a collapsed lung. But I know this isn't me. I'm ghosting through each day, timing my painkillers for when I have to perform. But next Friday the election will be over and I need to be back. I can't live like this.'

So I hugged him and said it would be okay. It was good to do the tests, and afterwards we would do whatever it took to make him better.

When the polls closed on Thursday 8 June 2017, the Conservatives still seemed set for victory, though by that time no one thought it would be spectacular. But the 10 p.m. exit poll changed all that – suggesting instead that the Conservatives had lost their majority. After watching some of the media commentary, Jeremy texted Jeremy Corbyn's office in case they needed to talk later and went to bed to try to get some sleep. By 5 a.m. we were back up and the results were clear – rather than winning more seats, Theresa May had lost thirteen, together with eleven of her ministers and her parliamentary majority. The pound was plummeting and we again had a hung Parliament. However, this time only the Conservatives – if they could persuade the Democratic Unionist Party (DUP) to lend its support – could realistically form a government.

Jeremy arrived in Number 10 to find the Prime Minister sitting at her glass-topped meeting table looking pale and exhausted. Peter Hill, who had taken over from Simon Case as her principal private secretary, James Slack, her official spokesman, and Sue Gray were also there, but because there was no sign of Nick and Fiona, she still looked oddly alone. Jeremy wasn't surprised by the chiefs' absence since he knew they were being blamed for the election outcome. Some of this criticism was fair – after all Nick Timothy had written most of the manifesto. But others had also been involved in preparing the election thinking, and though the chiefs' overbearing style had made them few friends, they were loyal to the Prime Minister and Nick had been pivotal in developing her policies during the first year of her premiership.

But none of this was the immediate issue. Jeremy took a deep breath. After consulting Christopher Geidt on his way in, it was again time to fulfil his role as a member of the Golden Triangle. 'I know you must be disappointed, Prime Minister,' he said, 'but have you considered your own plans?'

'Yes. I'm going to stay on,' Theresa May said, and they exchanged smiles.

With this constitutional point settled, the meeting turned to the more immediate issue of the Prime Minister's timetable for the morning – a rest, calls to check the loyalty of her key colleagues, a visit to the Palace to signal her intent to remain in office, a short statement outside Downing Street and the appointment of her Cabinet.

Jeremy got back to 70 Whitehall to find a message on his desk telling him to ring his GP.

'The scan is back,' Dr Patel said after they were connected, 'but there's something on it.'

'What's on it?'

'It's not clear. But I want you to see an oncologist next week.'

Jeremy rang me after that and time stopped. It couldn't be true, I cried. Of course, it couldn't be true. Meanwhile Emma Southard, Jeremy's diary secretary, scrambled to make an appointment with a consultant, Dr Landau, who said he could do a scan on Tuesday. We had four days to wait.

At home that weekend, Jeremy lay on the sofa in our playroom talking to Fiona, who wanted his advice on whether, after Nick's resignation on Friday, she should also resign, and reviewing papers on how a confidence and supply arrangement with the DUP might work.

'I feel awful,' he said, going on to describe his raging headaches, breathlessness and exhaustion.

While he took another call, I dug out the results of the lung scan he'd had the previous year while I'd been in Australia.

'The attached report says there is a suspicious nodule in your lung,' I told Jeremy when I walked back into the playroom a while later holding the papers, which I hadn't seen before. 'But the covering letter from the rheumatologist didn't suggest any follow up.'

Jeremy didn't look at me. 'Yes, I know.'

'Well, this should be the same.'

'Yes,' he said and I wondered if his stomach was churning as much as mine.

At 3.30 p.m. on Tuesday 13 June, I met Jeremy in the blue glass and white brick Platinum Medical Centre in north London. He'd already been there for several hours, having left the office to begin taking his scans after the Prime Minister had gone to France to meet President Macron. I found him in the café on the ground floor scrutinising his BlackBerry, his face pale against his long black raincoat, nursing an espresso in his other hand. We took the lift to the first floor where we hunched on moulded plastic seats in the waiting room, the sun streaming in through a tall glass window on our left.

I took Jeremy's hand and he looked at me.

'There could be any of six outcomes,' he said before itemising each, starting with 'it's nothing' and ending with cancer rampaging through his body.

'Don't,' I said.

'The doctor is ready to see you now,' said the woman at the desk.

53

'I Don't Want to Talk About It': Diagnosis

June 2017–June 2018

We followed a nurse down a nondescript corridor and she ushered us into a small white office. A man was sitting with his back to us, staring at a screen. He twisted around and indicated for us to sit down.

'I'm Dr Landau,' he said.

We gave him weak smiles.

'So, who do you have at home?' he asked.

While Jeremy answered, I felt my face flush and reached out to take his hand. It was the oddest question in the world.

'I'm afraid you may have lung cancer,' Dr Landau said when Jeremy paused. He kept talking, but I wasn't hearing his words. Something about not being certain, something about seeing us again on Friday. I blinked, trying not to cry.

My bravery didn't last. That night, when Jeremy turned over in bed, I flung my arms around him and sobbed. I wanted to talk, but discussing the past was too painful, contemplating the future unthinkable and the present overflowed with darkness.

'It's not fair,' I cried.

'I know. But I need to rest. I'm so tired.'

While we slept that night, a fire started in Grenfell Tower in Kensington, the exterior cladding catching alight and flames engulfing the building. We woke to reports of eight casualties and claims that the fire brigade had wrongly advised victims to stay in their flats and wait for help. The Prime Minister tried to do the right thing by visiting the site the following day, but this went terribly wrong after the police advised her not to meet survivors because of security concerns. With public anger mounting, Jeremy stepped in, asking Melanie Dawes, the calm and pragmatic permanent secretary at the Department of Communities and Local Government, to lead the Civil Service's response. That Friday, he joined COBR to check the right work was under way.

How Jeremy kept focused, I don't know. He knew he might have an incurable and possibly terminal disease, but while the Prime Minister's popularity plummeted, and rumours swirled of a coup against her, he continued to provide calm leadership. In contrast, I was finding it hard to function. I wanted to go back in time to Havana, when my only concern had been Jeremy's headaches and wanting us to spend more time together. Now I just wanted him to stay alive.

At 6.30 p.m. on Friday, 16 June I met Jeremy in another waiting room. 'The Prime Minister is still ashen-faced at the election results,' he told me.

I nodded – our crises were unfolding in parallel, although I would have traded ours for Theresa May's in an instant.

'It's definitely lung cancer,' Dr Landau told us this time when we filed into his office, 'though I need to consult more of my colleagues before I can advise you on the best treatment.'

'We need to talk to the kids,' I told Jeremy when we emerged, blinking, back onto the street. 'They'll all be at home after lunch tomorrow so we can tell them together.'

He shook his head. 'Let's wait until we know what we're going to do about it.'

But I wasn't compromising. I wanted to be able to say that we'd told them as soon as we'd known. And in the end, Jeremy gave in, though he said I would have to share the news on my own. So that weekend I did. Jonny, Lizzie and Peter listened to me in silence, their faces pale. They asked few questions – those would come later – and afterwards they went to find Jeremy to hug and cry.

On the evening of Monday 19 June, Jeremy rushed out of the debriefing on the first day of the Brexit negotiations to meet me again. He was frustrated, he told me, that the EU was refusing to discuss the UK's future trading relationship until 'sufficient progress' had been made on Britain's divorce bill, the Northern Irish border and European citizens' rights.

I frowned, trying and failing to focus on Brexit.

'You can go up now,' the receptionist said.

This time we found Dr Landau sitting at an almost bare desk. Beneath his hands, a glass screen showed images of lungs. 'The scans are complex,' he said, 'but I think I've understood what's going on. The tumour is squeezing the arteries in your chest and part of your left lung has died.'

The room was quiet. Outside I could hear cars passing, carrying people who were having normal days.

Dr Landau was still talking, his voice oddly calm. 'We can't operate on the tumour, so our best bet is chemotherapy and radiotherapy, but I'm confident they'll make a difference.'

'We need to tell our family and some of our close friends,' I told Jeremy this time on our way home. 'They care about you.'

'Okay. I'll give you a list of who you can speak to, but they must keep it secret or I won't be able to keep working,' he said, looking down at his iPhone.

During the following days, I worked my way through Jeremy's list. The worst call was with his brother Simon, who rang me while I was in a work meeting. I crawled back into the discussion afterwards hoping the lines of dried tears on my cheeks weren't visible. And while I did this, Jeremy spoke to the Prime Minister, who fully supported him continuing to work.

When Jeremy had his first dose of chemotherapy on Friday 23 June, I shared this news with the WhatsApp group I'd created to keep our friends informed about his treatment. 'He's in hospital today for his first chemotherapy session and is complaining of being bored ...' I typed, wondering where this string of messages would end.

After a weekend spent feeling tired and nauseous, Jeremy was back in work on Monday morning. Although he didn't feel well, the distraction helped. There were also things that needed to be done – like bringing together the overlapping Grenfell Tower investigations into a single inquiry and proposing that Martin Moore-Bick, a retired judge, should lead it; and finalising the confidence-and-supply agreement with the DUP. At the price of £1 billion of extra funding for Northern Ireland, this gave the government a majority of thirteen on confidence motions, the Budget and any Brexit legislation. This was an extraordinary cost, but at least it meant that the government could move ahead, beginning with confirming a date for the Queen's Speech that had been scheduled and rescheduled several times.

That Wednesday we met Dr Landau. 'You attended Cabinet four days after chemotherapy?' he asked, eyebrows raised after Jeremy described his two days back in the office.

I smiled – Dr Landau had a lot to learn about his patient.

In addition to Cabinet, Jeremy was also still attending the Prime Minister's meetings on the Brexit negotiations. By this time the cast list for these had changed. In addition to Tim Barrow taking over from Ivan Rogers, Gavin Barwell, a hard-working minister who'd lost his seat in the 2017 election, had become the Prime Minister's chief of staff and Robbie Gibb had replaced Katie Perrior as director of communications.

But though the group was different, the purpose of the meeting – allowing the Prime Minister to test her thinking with a small group of trusted advisers – remained the same. They were also still circling the same set of Brexit options. With the parliamentary arithmetic more difficult, the Prime Minister had reconsidered staying in the full customs union – something her Chancellor and many of her more pro-EU MPs wanted. But she'd soon ruled it out because she was unwilling to have a fight with the hardline Brexiteers. Support for the hybrid option was also waning because it would make it look like little had changed after Brexit. That left the third-party customs option in the ascendant – though no one had yet managed to devise a way to stop goods leaking across the Irish border without building a physical barrier.

This, at least, was the opinion at adviser level. In late June it became clear that the Prime Minister felt differently. 'Where,' she demanded, 'is the work on the hybrid option?'

Jeremy squirmed. 'HMRC hasn't done much work on it because it would be so difficult politically.'

'Well, I want it worked up,' the Prime Minister said, and after this, HMRC rose to the challenge and the hybrid option rejoined the race.

Jeremy told me he was relieved by this because he'd always thought that the hybrid option was the most attractive solution within the limitations imposed by the Prime Minister's red lines. But the question was still whether this, or any other bespoke customs option, would be acceptable to both Brussels and Parliament.

Jeremy's second chemotherapy session was scheduled for Friday 14 July. It came at the end of another long week, some of which Jeremy had spent on stage with the Prime Minister in front of thousands of civil servants during Civil Service Live, the government's annual learning and networking conference. We dubbed that Thursday 'peak health day' and marked it with a dinner in our local Italian, during which we played at being normal, discussing the gloom still pervading Downing Street after a spate of newspaper articles had speculated that the Prime Minister might be forced to resign.

The following days played out as before. On Friday morning Jeremy made his way up to the third floor of the London Clinic by Marylebone Road, where he was given the end bed by the window. The nurses hooked him up to a drip and he checked his emails while receiving a series of visitors. Among them was Robert Devereux, who had by then retired from the Department of Work and Pensions and was happy to sit chatting to Jeremy for hours. While we later waited downstairs for Jeremy to finish, Robert told me he was still grateful for Jeremy's kindness during the Universal Credit crisis – and he knew many others had also felt protected by Jeremy when they had found themselves in difficulty.

The worst days were the two following each treatment. That's why Jeremy scheduled his chemotherapy appointments for Fridays, crawling through the weekend exhausted and nauseous, before pulling himself together in time for Cabinet on Tuesday. If he could still be in those meetings, sitting beside the Prime Minister and offering her his support, then anything was possible.

We cancelled our summer holiday, which would have had us flying out to New York and Hawaii in early August. That was another life, a trip we would never take. Instead, we would create a different summer, one the children would still enjoy, but which could also be fitted in between hospital visits.

In the meantime, with the Brexit negotiations deadlocked in Brussels, Jeremy worked on a series of papers detailing the UK's options on issues like customs, fisheries and agriculture. This felt productive, though he was conscious that, with Number 10 engulfed by Brexit, little progress was being made on the rest of the Prime Minister's agenda.

Back at home, while Jeremy read papers, I hunted for lost friends that he'd asked me to find. People re-entered our lives, shaking their heads over missing time. And when I wasn't doing that, I investigated treatments or read papers about cancer trials, each nugget of knowledge creating the need for more.

Jeremy had his third dose of chemotherapy in early August, after which Dr Landau told us that the main lung tumour had shrunk by about a third.

That evening Jeremy gave me a card to mark our wedding anniversary. 'Thank you for 20 wonderful years,' it read, 'always full of love, support and truth. And then *this* comes along. You are the reason why it is worth me fighting with every ounce of my being for another 20.'

We spent the rest of that August juggling chemotherapy and radiotherapy treatments with short trips to stay in friends' houses in the countryside. Along the way, Jeremy attended a series of Brexit meetings, including an awayday at Chequers with Olly Robbins and the rest of the Number 10 team on 24 August to brief the Prime Minister ahead of the third round of the Brexit negotiations.

At the start of September, Jeremy faced two decisions. He needed to decide whether to split Olly's role, which by then clearly wasn't working, with David Davis frustrated about being excluded from Olly's private advice to the Prime Minister. And with his chemotherapy treatments almost complete, Jeremy also needed to decide whether to start immunotherapy.

The first decision was simpler. The benefits of combining Olly's two positions had become outweighed by the irritation it was creating, so Olly moved into the Cabinet Office to focus on the negotiations in Brussels and supporting the Prime Minister while Philip Rycroft, Olly's deputy in DExEU, was promoted to become its permanent secretary. The second decision was more difficult because taking a drug that would stimulate Jeremy's immune system might activate his colitis, an autoimmune disease. So he decided to delay making a decision until he'd finished his chemotherapy treatment and knew how effective it had been.

By this point, backache had joined Jeremy's list of ailments – which was to be expected, Dr Landau assured me, after his long hours on the radiotherapy couch. But as the days passed, and the pain didn't fade, I became anxious.

'Stop fussing,' Jeremy said. 'I have enough to do – I need to help finalise the Prime Minister's speech for Florence. She's going to agree to pay our Brexit divorce bill, which I hope will at last unblock the negotiations with Brussels.'

So I did – at least for a while. But by the end of September, Jeremy was still wincing every time he moved, and I wasn't prepared to wait any longer.

Jeremy was still shaking his head at my interference on the morning of Monday 2 October.

'I wish you wouldn't get involved. And have you seen this?' He was pointing at an article in *The Times*, which accused him of exerting an 'iron grip' over Number 10.

I shook my head.

'It doesn't feel like that. And now I have to go into work for two major meetings and won't be able to rest this afternoon because of the scan you've forced into my diary.'

I spent most of that day feeling guilty. I hated Jeremy being upset – my job was to make his life easier, not worse. And as the time of the scan approached, my guilt became mixed with fear as I started worrying about the news it might bring.

I was due to meet Jeremy at the clinic at 5.30 p.m., but at 4.53 he sent me a text. 'Seeing Landau. He says not good news. Seems to have spread. Where are u now?'

I burst out of the door of my office. 'I'm coming,' I texted back, as I ran through the Burlington Arcade and up Bond Street, bumping into people and dodging cars, the world blurred with tears.

'Ok ml. Bleak news. But maybe does not change what we do next. This other patch may have been there all along or maybe it has spread despite chemo. The best case is just one patch and we can do radio-therapy. But my life expectancy has just been cut dramatically.'

I arrived to find Dr Landau pacing the hospital foyer while Jeremy finished his scans. There were two new tumours on Jeremy's spine, Dr Landau said. They could use radiotherapy to treat them, but we now needed something else to fight the cancer that was swirling around his body, looking for places to land. And despite its potential side effects, immunotherapy was probably our best bet.

I listened and murmured agreement. But my brain was only focused on one thing – less than four months after his original diag-nosis, Jeremy had Stage 4 lung cancer.

Jeremy had his first dose of immunotherapy on 9 October while reading about the Prime Minister's disastrous conference speech during which she'd been handed a P45 by a prankster. In the days after the treatment, he felt fatigued and spaced out. His knees, his elbows and even his fingers hurt. But paracetamol, our wonder drug, kept most of these symptoms at bay and he told me he wanted to keep working, supporting the Prime Minister while she fought off an ineffectual coup by a backbench MP. Meanwhile, I took on the hospital, which despite my specific request had only carried out limited genetic testing on Jeremy's cancer. I needed to find out what mutation had triggered his disease. If I knew that, I could find the best medical trial for him to join, which might be the only option we had left if the immunology failed. In any case, I had to keep moving. The world was closing in and, if I allowed myself to pause, or even worse to think, I might give way to panic.

In mid-October, events again forced our hand after a journalist asked a member of the Number 10 press team whether Jeremy was ill.

'Not as far as I know,' he said before ringing Jeremy's office to ask if it was true.

'We'll get back to you,' they said.

Later that afternoon, Sam Coates from *The Times* rang the Cabinet Office to ask if the Cabinet Secretary was having tests and might need time off. The press officer who took the call said he hadn't heard anything.

'I don't want to make this public,' Jeremy told me that evening, 'I really don't.'

This I understood. It was hard enough for Jeremy to work while being treated for cancer – it would be doubly hard if everyone was watching him.

There was a long pause. 'I don't think this is going to work,' Jeremy said.

'What do you mean?'

More silence. 'People don't live long with Stage 4 lung cancer.'

I got up to hug him. 'But we're doing everything we can. The immunotherapy. More genetic testing. We have to believe.'

'And try not to think about the future,' he said.

Shortly after that conversation, we agreed to start work on this book. The process began with two stilted interviews on the sofa in our playroom. The words 'You're only doing this because I'm dying' hung in the air between us, though neither of us said them, and in any case, they weren't true – I'd wanted to write Jeremy's story for years. But the third evening when we talked, we laughed at his reminiscences, and the words disappeared.

Afterwards, Jeremy told me he was glad we were doing it. He'd been hesitant at first, but now we'd begun, he'd realised how much he wanted to share his stories, and through them, a little of how he got things to change. He also worried that few people remembered what had been done in the past on issues that only flared up occasionally like welfare reform, defence spending, social care and energy pricing.

Another week passed. Olly was trying to convince the other EU member states that, after three rounds of Brexit negotiations, sufficient progress had been made to let the Brexit talks move on to the next stage, while Jeremy concentrated on the domestic politics and helped Olly connect the two. There was a huge amount to do. In addition to the negotiations, they had to process all the Brexit legislation including the main European Union (Withdrawal Agreement) Bill, about ten other Brexit bills and 800 to 1,000 statutory instruments.

Despite Olly's efforts, when the European Council met on 19 October, it decided that not enough progress had been made. It was clear, Jeremy told me, that the EU and the Republic of Ireland were going to stand side by side, which meant that, unless a solution was found to the border issue that the Irish would accept, Britain wouldn't be allowed to move forward.

On 24 October 2017, Sam Coates rang the Number 10 press office to say that several people had told him the Cabinet Secretary was ill. By this time, the press officer knew this was true, but he still managed to dodge the question. For Jeremy, though, it was the deciding moment – he couldn't expect people to lie for him. He prepared a statement that said he'd undergone treatment for cancer over the summer and early autumn, which had 'gone well', and he was continuing his normal duties for the Prime Minister and Cabinet and as head of the Civil Service.

'Gone well?' I asked raising an eyebrow.

'Well, some of it did.'

Jeremy's statement was released at 10 a.m. on Friday 27 October 2017. We were on a train at the time, travelling up to Edinburgh for a weekend away with the children. To our relief, though it briefly led the news, the press reported it straight, and no one speculated further. In any case, I was preoccupied by the fact that Jeremy was again wincing whenever he tried to move.

Back in London, I arranged another scan for Tuesday morning, while trying to ignore Jeremy's furious texts. This revealed that one of the tumours had left behind a squash ball-sized hole in his spine. The cavity was making Jeremy's back unstable, the doctor told us, but it might be improved if they filled it with something that sounded like concrete.

'Shall we do the operation tomorrow?' I asked Jeremy.

He shook his head, still angry at my meddling. 'Don't you realise how busy I am? We'll have to do it on Saturday.'

'Okay,' I said, because it wasn't worth the fight. In any case, Jeremy was already changing the subject, telling me about the meeting he'd joined that morning during which they'd discussed the implications of a no-deal Brexit. At the end, he said, Michael Gove had initiated a round of applause for his bravery. I smiled at that, knowing how embarrassed Jeremy would have been at being singled out.

On Wednesday morning, after taking two steps into his office, Jeremy's back buckled. He reached out to clutch the wall, sliding his hands along the polished wood panels as he inched towards his desk. When he reached it, he sat down and texted me.

While I scrambled to pull forward his operation, the Prime Minister called Jeremy. 'I need you to investigate Damian Green,' she said.

Jeremy sighed. He'd been worried he might be asked to do this ever since reading the allegations in *The Times* that morning that the First Secretary of State made a pass at a journalist called Kate Maltby back in 2015. There were also historic rumours that the police had found pornography on his computer when they'd raided his parliamentary office in 2008 as part of a leak investigation.

'It's not my role to investigate this. Both incidents happened before Damian became a government minister,' Jeremy said, conscious, apart from anything else, of how close the Prime Minister was to her First Secretary of State.

'Jeremy. I need you to do this to clear the air.'

Jeremy sighed. 'Okay,' he said. After the buckling episode, he wasn't going to risk standing up, so he rang Sue Gray to ask her to see if she could obtain the police files.

That afternoon, when I got in the car to join Jeremy for the drive to King's College Hospital, he didn't look up from his iPhone. 'You couldn't have picked a worse day to do this,' he said, scrolling through his emails. 'There's so much going on.'

I bit my lip. Jeremy's ability to pretend he wasn't ill was his way of coping, but even for him, this was surreal. However, the façade dropped when we reached the hospital and had to go through the agony of getting him changed for the operation. Two hours later, he was back on the ward and ready to recommence the pretence, trying to convince the nurse to let him have a glass of cold white wine and catching up with the news that Michael Fallon, the defence secretary, had been forced to resign over allegations of sexual misconduct.

* * *

The concrete-reinforced Cabinet Secretary was back in his natural habitat the following morning, worrying about the Budget which was due to be presented on 22 November. With the economy growing more slowly than expected, Jeremy was again fighting to get funding for the Prime Minister's priorities, including investing in new technologies and supporting more housebuilding. He was also trying to persuade the Treasury to agree to make government-owned geospatial data available to the private sector.

Jeremy was also making progress on his investigation into Damian Green. It was clear by then that, despite his denials, the Metropolitan Police had informed Damian that they'd found pornography on the computers in his office. But the Kate Maltby story was less clear-cut – effectively it was her word against Damian's. In the end, Jeremy wrote in his report, his words chosen carefully, that her account was 'plausible'. And his overall conclusion, which was endorsed by Alex Allan, was that Damian had breached the ministerial code. Jeremy feared the report would become a repeat of Plebgate. But two days after it was finalised on 18 December, Damian Green resigned and the moment passed – perhaps because the public had changed its view of sexual misconduct.

On Friday 8 December 2017, the European Commission at last agreed that enough progress had been made for the UK to begin the next stage of the Brexit negotiations in January 2018. The joint report that they published to mark this step included the idea of an Irish 'backstop' – if the Irish border question couldn't be solved through a trade relationship or technology, then the whole of the UK would need to maintain 'full alignment' with the rules of the EU single market and customs union. This backstop was something that Downing Street knew the Brexiteers would hate – but without it, Brussels would have refused to allow the UK to move to the next stage of the talks.

On the same day, after completing his third and final round of immunotherapy, Jeremy had another scan. We were due to get the results on Monday, a fact that hung in the air throughout that weekend even though we tried to ignore it. It had been a difficult week, Jeremy told me. He'd spent hours on the phone to Martin Fraser, secretary general to the Irish government, after the DUP had rejected the original version of the backstop, which had only included Northern Ireland. It had taken days of negotiation before they'd found an acceptable compromise – broadening it to include the whole of the UK – though the DUP still didn't like it.

'Difficult' to Jeremy meant 'horrendous' in anyone else's vocabulary. But I was more concerned about how tired Jeremy was. When he went upstairs to rest, I helped the children decorate our Christmas tree before continuing to ring doctors, narrowing down the list of global cancer trials to the ones focused on the mutation that by then I knew was causing Jeremy's cancer.

After a weekend of not discussing Jeremy's scan, we met outside the Chelsea and Westminster Hospital early on Monday evening to hear the results. We made our way up in a metal lift to an empty waiting room where I fiddled around getting water and operating the coffee machine.

When Dr Tom Newsom-Davis, Jeremy's lean and serious chemo-therapist, came to collect us, he avoided meeting our eyes. 'It's not good news,' he said when we reached his office.

I glanced across to see Dr Landau sitting on the far side of the room. For once David wasn't smiling.

Tom indicated for us to sit down in two chairs, which were placed with their backs against the wall. Jeremy studied Tom and I slipped my hand into his.

'How bad is it?' Jeremy asked.

Tom grimaced. 'There are many tiny tumours across your lungs, you have a tumour on your liver and one on your pelvis.'

'How many?'

'Too many to count.'

'How long do I have?'

Tom blinked. I felt nauseous. There was a long silence.

'I don't know. To be honest, I'm surprised you look so well. Weeks? Months? But it's clear the immunotherapy isn't working, and the chemotherapy wasn't either. We need to start looking at trials.' Tom turned to his computer and pulled up a document. 'There's a trial in Sutton that might work.'

Now I was focused. 'Is that trial looking at the KRAS mutation? I

thought the most promising trials were at UCL and MD Anderson.'
My voice sounded shrill, panic and emotion mixing with
frustration.

Another pause followed my outburst. Dr Landau leaned forward.
'I think you know more about this than we do, Suzanne,' he said, his
voice level. 'It's probably best if you go through the options with
Tobias Arkenau who heads our research facility.'

We went down in the same lift and walked out of the same door,
but everything had changed. For the first time Jeremy was talking
about resigning. I told him we could both stop work. We could
travel around the world. We could take the children with us and do
whatever we wanted. I could hear my voice rising again so I stopped.
But the offer was genuine. I didn't know how much time we had left,
but I knew it wasn't long. If Jeremy wanted to do this, I would do it
willingly.

But Jeremy frowned and shook his head. 'Jonny is doing his
GCSEs this year and I can't leave the Prime Minister in the lurch
over Brexit.'

The following morning, Jeremy talked to Theresa May. If he needed
to stop, she said, she would support that without hesitation. But if it
wasn't harming his treatment, and if it was what he wanted, she was
happy for him to keep working.

'She was incredibly kind,' he told me that evening.

I nodded. Throughout our crisis Mrs May had been kind, never
forcing Jeremy to do more than he wanted to, but also never pushing
him to stop work, which was the last thing he wanted to do. But I
was more focused on the latest calls I'd been doing about trials. 'It's
clear that the most promising trial is at MD Anderson,' I told Jeremy.

He narrowed his eyes. 'I'm not going to Texas. I don't want to
spend the remaining time I have away from my family. And I want
to keep supporting the Prime Minister.'

I went to make more calls. If Jeremy wouldn't go to Texas,
Texas would have to come to Jeremy. I didn't know anyone who'd
managed to move a trial around the planet, and I had no idea how
to make it happen. But there had to be a way, and there was –
though I was lucky to have our old friend, Ara Darzi, guiding

me through the maze of permissions that were required. Three days later, the last form was signed, and by 21 December, Jeremy was clutching two bottles of trial drugs.

'This,' Dr Landau told us, 'is the most bespoke oncology care I've ever seen.'

'They're magic pills,' I told Jeremy. 'Let's hope they work.'

We flew to Malta the day after Christmas, the first time we'd left Britain since Jeremy's diagnosis. There were times when Jeremy wheezed and needed to lean on me or one of the children to get around. But there were also times that he spent playing air guitar with Lizzie, talking football trivia with Peter, debating politics with Jonny or falling about laughing when, due to a mix-up, he ended up with two huge chocolate cakes for his birthday on New Year's Eve. And while I watched him, back in his comfy cardigan, engaged with the children, I wondered how we would cope with the void that he was going to leave behind.

After we returned, the days took on an individual quality. On Monday 8 January, Jeremy came home exhausted after helping the Prime Minister orchestrate a reshuffle in which several ministers had refused to move. By then he was struggling to walk even short distances and again talked about resigning. On Tuesday he perked up, despite having to edit the Cabinet minutes. Then on Wednesday he woke up feeling so nauseous that he had to go into work late – though he still managed to get through a lengthy afternoon meeting on Brexit. But every day, regardless of how he felt, he kept churning out memos and emails, taking calls and chairing discussions.

That was, however, a normal week. Jeremy worried most about the times when he had to be on show, such as when he was called in front of the Public Administration and Constitutional Affairs Committee in mid-January to be questioned on everything from Hinkley Point to the Brexit preparations. The session felt neverending to me, watching it on my computer. I wondered if they could see Jeremy's paleness and worried that he might not make it through to the end. It was two and a half hours before the grilling ended, after which Bernard thanked Jeremy for a very good dialogue and Jeremy gave Bernard a very small smile.

It wasn't clear how much longer Jeremy could keep going – though I didn't want him to stop because I knew that, when he did, he would be accepting the end was near. In the meantime, he was working hard on both Brexit and the Prime Minister's domestic agenda, doing things like appointing Philip Augar, the writer and former banker, to lead a study of post-18-year-old education. And when Jeremy saw Theresa May at the end of January, she said his country needed him and she'd seen no reduction in his contribution.

Like the Prime Minister, the *Daily Mail* clearly hadn't noticed any change in Jeremy's output since it printed another rant in early February about his supposed determination to derail the Brexit process. *Private Eye* parodied the *Mail's* tirade, saying Jeremy should be 'arrested and tried for treason' and, when found guilty, strung up 'as it's the only language he understands apart from Belgian, probably'.

Unfortunately, someone else took the *Mail's* rant more seriously. One morning in mid-February, my assistant Tara came into my office holding a padded envelope.

'The writing is odd,' I said turning it over in my hands.

'Like a child's,' Tara said.

I sliced off the end of the envelope with a pair of scissors. It wasn't what I would normally do, but something about the parcel bothered me.

Inside there was a sheet of paper. I pinched one corner and slid it out. *Remind your fucking husband how the country voted. This is serious …*

In the shadows at the bottom of the envelope was a matchbox. I left it where it was, placed the parcel on a chair in the hall and called the police.

Two officers arrived within minutes, all thick black vests and burly chests. 'This is it?' they asked, pointing at the envelope.

'Yes,' I said, feeling like I was over-reacting. 'I think it contains a bullet.'

One policeman turned to face me, eyebrows clenched. 'How do you know?'

'Because the letter contains a death threat.'

My office was evacuated and I was called back a while later to find out that my suspicion had been correct. I walked home that evening wondering who was following me.

'Are you worried?' I asked Jeremy that night.

'Yes,' he said, 'but what can we do?'

Jeremy turned back to his papers and I didn't raise it with him again. As the Prime Minister had said, his country needed him. And, if allowing Jeremy to keep working, ploughing his way through the final report of Project After, which had clarified the immigration and industrial implications of a no-deal Brexit, and attending a Brexit Cabinet at Chequers, meant living with a threat, it was what we would have to do.

The days running up to Jeremy's next scan on Friday 2 March 2018 were a familiar blur of tension and tetchiness. Jeremy, as usual, distracted himself with work – two Cabinet meetings, a conventional one on Tuesday and a bonus Brexit one on Thursday, and a speech on the UK's future economic partnership with the EU that he was helping to finalise for the Prime Minister.

'She'll be giving her speech while I'm inside that machine,' he told me.

'I know you hate scans.'

'It's like playing Russian roulette.'

'It is,' I said. But this time I felt optimistic – since he'd begun taking his magic pills, Jeremy hadn't obviously deteriorated, despite Tom's words before Christmas.

Later that afternoon, I found Jeremy in another bare waiting room flipping through Twitter on his iPad and sipping a glass of water. His face was pale – his usual afternoon exhaustion combining with the lack of food that the hospital demanded ahead of the scans.

Dr Landau came to meet us, and we followed him back into his office. This time David was smiling. 'It's good,' he said. 'There's been no progression. I've never said that before. The trial drugs seem to have stopped the cancer growing.'

On our way out, we stopped by the lift to hug.

'Let's have a party,' I said, and Jeremy nodded. This wasn't a cure, but it was a precious piece of good news to share with our WhatsApp group. Diaries were cleared, and within hours, acceptances were pouring in and one of Jeremy's friends was working on a party tape.

Jeremy went back to work after that with renewed determination. He helped set up an investigation into the poisoning of a former Russian military officer and rumoured double-agent, Sergei Skripal, and his daughter in Salisbury, which many thought had been ordered by the Russian government. He was also doing what he could to manage the Brexit fireworks that exploded after the DUP declared that the European Commission's draft withdrawal agreement was 'constitutionally unacceptable' because it contained a Northern Ireland-only backstop. Despite this, at the EU Council meeting on 22 March, the other member states broadly endorsed the Prime Minister's thinking and confirmed that the next stage of the negotiations could begin. In a remarkable show of solidarity, they also condemned the Salisbury poisoning and several countries expelled their Russian diplomats.

The following day, Jeremy put out his quarterly blog to the Civil Service. 'There are few, if any, peace-time precedents for the scale and complexity of the constitutional and organisational challenge of withdrawing from the EU,' he wrote, 'and the Civil Service is rising effectively to that challenge.' This was, I knew, what Jeremy wanted to spend his time doing – celebrating and coaxing the Civil Service as he helped the Prime Minister find a way through the toughest policy challenge of his career.

What Jeremy didn't want to do became equally clear after we arrived in Spain on 1 April for a short Easter break and he announced that he hadn't brought enough of his magic tablets with him.

'I didn't count them properly,' he said, sitting on the bed in our hotel room surrounded by empty bottles and piles of tablets.

I said nothing though I was clenching my hands so hard that my nails were biting into my palms.

Jeremy rang Toby Arkenau, the doctor who was supervising his trial. Toby's view was that skipping a couple of days of tablets wouldn't make much difference – and in any case, there was no way to ship unlicensed drugs from Britain to Spain.

After that we continued our holiday. Jeremy couldn't carry anything, and in the afternoons he had to sleep. But he could still shuffle around churches and museums, read out chunks of Spanish history, do his emails and indulge in tapas.

We had one bad moment and that came in Ronda, where Jeremy wanted to see the thirteenth-century Arabic baths.

'But they're at the bottom of a slope and we can't get down there in the car,' I said.

'I'm still going to see them,' Jeremy said.

'You can't walk down there and back up,' I said, but Jeremy's jaw was set.

We stumbled downhill for a few minutes with Jeremy leaning on Jonny, moving slowly and not talking. The lane was steep, curving down around buildings. After a few minutes, Jeremy stopped and leant against a wall. I paused, and so did the children. We all looked at him.

'I can't do it,' Jeremy said. 'But I want you and Jonny to go and see them for me while the rest of us walk back up.'

'Let's stay together,' I said, but Jeremy shook his head. So Jonny and I trudged down to the baths, though all we did when we reached them, besides buying tickets as proof of our visit, was to slump on a low wall holding each other and crying for a while before climbing back up the hill again.

Back in London, our WhatsApp group was feverish with excitement by the day of our party on Saturday 14 April. The food was ordered and the playlist had been agreed. But Jeremy was nauseous. There was so much going on at work, he told me. The government was preparing to launch an air strike against Syria and the EU had made it clear that it hated the third-party customs option – now renamed the 'max-fac' option – since, in the absence of a technological solution, they thought it would create a leaky Irish border.

'They also weren't keen on the New Customs Partnership,' Jeremy said while I bundled him into the taxi – this being the new name for the hybrid option. 'They think it will give British firms a competitive advantage. But they're at least willing to keep it on the table because it would keep the border secure. The problem is that the Brexiteers hate it.'

Jeremy was quiet after that, and glancing at his pale face, I worried we would have to turn and leave as soon as we arrived at the party.

However, seeing our friends seemed to infuse Jeremy with energy. He found a chair in one corner of the room and held seated court. And before long, those who weren't lining up to talk to him were mainly grooving. Gus O'Donnell was dancing with Shriti Vadera, who had some excellent low moves, and Olly Robbins, fresh back from Brussels, also displayed remarkable rhythm. At one point, Jeremy even broke off himself to sit on the floor and lead the dancing to 'Oops Upside Your Head'. At the end of the evening, Jeremy's old school friend Camilla unveiled a drawing, which showed all of us clustered around him, woven in, around and through four big, red letters: L O V and E.

The following week was again tense. Not only were there rumours that the 1922 Committee of backbench Tory MPs might move against the Prime Minister to stop her pursuing the New Customs Partnership, but there was also a scandal developing about the UK's aggressive deportation of the so-called Windrush generation – people who had legally come from the Caribbean to settle in Britain decades before but hadn't been given paperwork to prove their immigration status. Jeremy came home drained, though he told me he was making progress on NHS funding and was hopeful the Prime Minister would be able to announce a big new settlement in time for its seventieth birthday.

I was hoping for a quiet weekend; one where Jeremy could relax and allow the sun to chase away his pallor. In the end he did manage some rest, though he also had to spend several hours orchestrating an inquiry into whether Amber Rudd, the home secretary, had known about her department's targets for deporting immigrants when she'd assured the House of Commons they didn't exist. Jeremy asked Sue Gray to go to the Home Office to work through the paperwork and compile a chronology. Following this, Amber decided to resign – although a later review by Alex Allan showed that she had been poorly supported by her department.

We kept going through May. The magic tablets were buying us time and we were determined to use it well. For Jeremy this meant trying to find an acceptable version of the Irish backstop, finalising a speech for the Prime Minister on improving cancer diagnosis, and spending time with me and the children. For me it meant being with Jeremy whenever I could, using this book as an excuse to talk. The good news, Jeremy told me, was that the Civil Service was flourishing despite Brexit. Engagement had increased in 2017 and the service had set new records for the number of senior women, disabled staff and ethnic minorities within its ranks. The next challenge was to attract more civil servants from working-class backgrounds and to do more to reveal and address bullying and harassment.

On Friday 1 June 2018, Jeremy was again inside the white metal tube he hated so much, moving forward inch by inch while the machine hunted for tumours. We had no results that day but this time, rather than spending the weekend worrying, I contacted Dr Landau who promised to ring us at around lunchtime on Sunday.

Sunday morning was bright and sunny, and when I opened the doors to the garden, the birds were singing outside. But neither of us could settle. Towards midday Jeremy's phone buzzed.

'Hi David,' he said. 'Yes, I've seen the emails.'

My heart thumped. 'Landau?' I whispered and Jeremy shook his head. It was, he told me afterwards, David Davis, who was upset about a *Sunday Times* article featuring a 'Doomsday' Brexit scenario supposedly drawn up by the Civil Service.

'Where are we on all that?' I asked, desperate for distraction.

'Nowhere,' he said. 'No one is willing to move. Though we might make one decision this week.'

'Which one?'

'Heathrow. I've tried to keep the possibility of expanding airport capacity alive for over a decade. If we decide to go ahead, it will be a major step forward.' He paused and looked at me. 'And whatever we find out today, they can't take that away from me.'

After Jeremy went upstairs for a rest, the other David called. 'The scans aren't great,' he said.

The room was still. I could still hear the birds. 'How not great?'

'The tumours have doubled in size. The one on his liver is particularly problematic. He needs to come in for another blood test tomorrow. In the meantime, look into his eyes and watch for jaundice.'

54

'Don't Think Twice, It's All Right':* At home

June 2018–

On Monday 4 June 2018 we were sitting in the chairs in Dr Tom Newsom-Davis's office with our backs again against the wall. This time, Tom was succinct. Another round of chemotherapy was the best next step, though the drug he would use, which was derived from the Pacific yew tree, would make Jeremy even more tired and would probably make him go bald. It would also decimate his white blood cells.

'We have a plan,' I told Jeremy afterwards and he nodded but didn't smile.

The following night, though, the smile returned. Cabinet had approved the 91-page Airports National Policy Statement, he told me. The UK was also close to sequencing 100,000 genomes and the Government was planning to announce a new ambition of mapping five million genomes over the next five years.

'Great. But have you told the Prime Minister your news?'

'Not yet. I will when I know when the chemotherapy will start.'

Unfortunately, starting turned out to be the issue. The following day, Jeremy's blood tests showed that his liver was malfunctioning. What he needed, Dr Landau said, was an operation to drain it – and until it was working, he couldn't begin chemotherapy.

Jeremy struggled through the rest of the week with nausea and pain. At different points, I found time to speak to each of the children. 'I don't know if Daddy is going to get better,' I told them.

---

* Jeremy's favourite song, which was sung by Cerys Matthews at his memorial.

'I know,' they each replied.

That Friday night, Jeremy had the same conversation with me. 'I'm not a well person,' he said.

'I know.'

'It can't go on like this.'

'I know.'

Jeremy looked at me. His eyes weren't jaundiced. They were pale, almost translucent blue, the whites watery and streaked with scarlet.

'I don't want to lose you,' I said, my own eyes stinging. 'I want to make you better.'

Now it was his turn. 'I know.'

We didn't say anything else. We rarely had these conversations because there was no need. We weren't concealing anything, so all the talking did was uncover the pain.

On Saturday 9 June, we rushed back into hospital after Jeremy woke me before dawn with a raging fever. Nurses came in and out doing tests.

'His oxygen is 91 per cent,' one said.

'His early warning score is eight,' said another.

'You should expect him to be here for several days,' a third told me.

On Sunday afternoon, Jeremy emailed the Prime Minister. His cancer had progressed, he told her, and it looked like he had an infection in his liver. This would require him to be in hospital for a week so he wanted to know if he should take a leave of absence.

'There's no need to take a leave of absence,' Theresa May replied.

More days passed. Jeremy was still trying to agree the NHS settlement, swapping phone calls with Department of Health and Treasury officials. 'I need the Treasury to understand that the NHS clearly needs more – it's had little in recent years compared to its historic increases.'

I smiled. 'The Blair–Brown health race.'

'Indeed.'

Jeremy was still in hospital on Sunday 17 June when the Prime Minister announced the final health settlement. The NHS would get another £394 million a week by 2023/24, giving it clarity over its funding for five years, although over half of that money would come from raising taxes and borrowing rather than from the 'Brexit dividend' that had been promised by the Leave campaign.

I managed to get Jeremy home on Tuesday, but we were back in hospital with another temperature spike the following weekend. The tumours on Jeremy's liver were growing, Dr Landau said, and for the first time his voice, normally mellow, was edged with panic. We had to start the chemotherapy urgently – but that would only be possible if we could deal with the infection.

After Dr Landau left, I sat by Jeremy's bed. He lay with his eyes shut, occasionally rousing himself to smile at me and reach out his hand to check his phone. It was, though, time to face reality. On Monday 25 June, he put out a statement saying he was taking a leave of absence over the summer 'for some more cancer treatment and to deal with a related infection'. While he was away, Mark Sedwill, the national security adviser, would stand in for him.

'This time I didn't give the Prime Minister a choice,' Jeremy said. 'But you know you've taken the right decision when you feel no regret after it's been made. Now it's not my problem that Cabinet secretaries from around the world are flying in for a meeting on Thursday, or that we need to prepare for another Brexit Cabinet next week. I hope, though, that I can be back by the autumn because I think the real fight will begin when people focus on the reality of the Brexit options.' He picked up his book on the Victorians, though his phone was still on his knee.

That week Jeremy had two more liver operations, returning from each in significant pain. But there were also better moments, including when friends came in to join him in watching England play Belgium in the football World Cup, while I handed around beers and nachos. England lost that match, but after they beat Colombia on Tuesday 3 July, Dr Landau brought us more good news – Jeremy was at last well enough to have the first dose of his new chemotherapy drug.

By Friday we were back home again, and Jeremy was sitting in his favourite, red armchair watching reports of the Brexit discussions at Chequers. It would be one of the most important meetings for years, he told me, particularly since the two ministerial sub-groups that the Prime Minister had set up to work through the rival future customs proposals had got nowhere.

'Do you wish you were there?'

He looked at me, his eyes puffy. 'No. Not now. But I worry about where we're going. We have a referendum result and we have what our elected MPs want. And in the gap between the two, our democracy is ripping itself apart.'

After the Chequers meeting concluded, Jeremy emailed the Prime Minister to congratulate her on the outcome. Somehow she'd managed to get her Cabinet to align around a deal that consisted of a version of the New Customs Partnership combined with maintaining common standards with the EU wherever possible to reduce border friction.

This unanimity didn't last. Within days, Boris Johnson, David Davis and David's parliamentary under-secretary, Steve Baker, had resigned and Jeremy was helping deal with the ramifications, typing emails with his left hand during his chemotherapy session while his right lay entangled in tubes.

Another week passed, punctuated by more spells in hospital fighting soaring temperatures. At home again, watching Jeremy settle back into his armchair, I was conscious of how much thinner and older he looked.

'I'm still here,' he said, noticing my gaze, and I leant forward to hug him.

For a few weeks after that, Jeremy stayed stable and the sun remained out. A stream of visitors made their way down to Balham. Olly Robbins came to tell Jeremy how much Brussels disliked the Chequers deal and the Prime Minister created a flutter when she was photographed with Jeremy on our doorstep. 'Does the Prime Minister have a secret lover?' the tweeters speculated before realising she was visiting the Cabinet Secretary.

'In any case,' Jeremy pointed out to me afterwards, 'if you were going to have an affair, you wouldn't bring a fleet of police protection vehicles with you.'

Once again we were playing pretend, but this time it was Jeremy who called it out. 'I'm not deluding myself,' he said one evening. 'I know we might only have until the next scan before we start going downhill again.'

It turned out we didn't have that long. Early in the evening of Saturday 11 August, while we were sitting at our kitchen table discussing whether to take the children out for pizza, Jeremy said he felt unwell. Less than half an hour later, he began convulsing. He couldn't stand up, and I couldn't get him out to the car, so I had to call an ambulance.

After a blue light ride and several hours in St George's crowded accident and emergency department, Jeremy's ever-loyal driver Barry swooped in at midnight to drive us back up to our usual hospital in Marylebone where I knew Jeremy would be more comfortable. I connected my phone to the car stereo and Jeremy lay across the back seat humming along to 'My Old School' by Steely Dan, 'Jamming' by Bob Marley and Van Morrison's 'Brown Eyed Girl'. In the front, Barry and I giggled, in the way you do when everything is wrong, but life has, for a moment, paused for long enough to let you smile.

Following this downhill skid, Jeremy's health stabilised again. His next scan, on Thursday 20 September, showed that his lung tumours had shrunk, although his liver was, Dr Landau said, still 'complex'.

'So, what do we do next?' Jeremy asked.

'Keep going. Three more cycles of chemotherapy.'

That takes us to Christmas, I thought. I hadn't been sure we would get another Christmas.

'What about work?' Jeremy asked and I thought about the political maelstrom outside, with ardent Brexiteers turning on the Prime Minister in the run-up to the EU Council meeting in October.

'That isn't a medical question,' Dr Landau said. 'You could work if you wanted to, but you're going to feel like this for several more months – or maybe even more tired, as the chemo accumulates. And in your job …'

We both looked at Jeremy.

'I'll leave it for a while,' Jeremy said.

We emerged out of the hospital to find Barry waiting for us.

'The lung tumours have shrunk,' Jeremy said.

Barry grinned, opened his arms and enveloped Jeremy in a massive bear hug.

'But it's not been such a good day for the Prime Minister,' Jeremy said when he started going through his emails in the back of the car. 'She's been beaten up in Europe.'

'Indeed,' I said. Donald Tusk, the president of the European Council, had used an informal summit of heads of state in Salzburg to attack the Chequers plan, declaring that it wouldn't work because it risked undermining the single market. He'd also stated that the EU wouldn't accept a withdrawal agreement unless it contained a 'solid, operational and legally binding' Irish backstop.

'Donald Tusk has been unbelievably rude,' Jeremy said. 'But the fundamental problem is that the EU thinks that, if we implement the New Customs Partnership, we won't be rigorous in applying the tariffs on our borders. And now we only have three weeks left to get all this sorted or risk a no-deal Brexit.'

'What will you do?'

'I'll do what I can, but I can't go back in.'

Another week passed. The twins turned fifteen and we celebrated with lemon drizzle cake.

At 4 a.m. on Wednesday 26 September, Jeremy shook me awake. 'I feel awful,' he said. He was pale, but his forehead was scalding.

'Okay, hospital,' I said.

This time the doctors were certain the infection was in Jeremy's liver and said he needed two weeks of intravenous antibiotics. But after a week of ferrying Jeremy back and forth to Marylebone, his temperature shot up again. Now the infection was exploding while Jeremy was still on antibiotics and I was frightened. Another liver operation was needed, the doctors said, and in the meantime, Jeremy had to stay in hospital.

Jeremy was still in the ward on 3 October when the Prime Minister gave her speech at the Tory Party conference. He watched it on TV, telling me he was proud of her for being bold and dancing, counteracting the trauma of her speech a year before. After that the days merged, though on Sunday 7 October, I obtained permission from Dr Landau to take Jeremy out for lunch. We sat in the courtyard of the Courtauld Gallery discussing Brexit while I ate and Jeremy poked at his food, his face ghostly even though he'd had a blood transfusion that morning. But I still found myself smiling because, if I didn't look too closely, the moment almost felt normal.

'I think we'll end up with a second referendum,' Jeremy said. 'The parliamentary numbers won't allow the Prime Minister to agree a Brexit deal in the House of Commons that Europe will accept. But I don't fancy trying to agree the purdah rules for another vote.'

I smiled. 'Do you think you will go back?'

'I don't know. However, right now, when so much is uncertain, no one is pressing me to decide.'

Back in the hospital, that peaceful hour soon felt distant. Jeremy seemed lost within himself, and before his next liver operation that Wednesday, talked for the first time of fading away. But I kept bringing him back, tempting him with sections of this book to debate, or with news of the children, who came in most days to see him. The operation went well – so well that he was soon back in his cardigan at home, attempting to finalise details of the £20.5 billion for the NHS that the Prime Minister had promised in June and trying to interest Whitehall in the UK Atomic Energy Authority's plan to put fusion power into the grid.

It was a brief respite. On Friday 12 October we were back in hospital with another escalating infection. In the days that followed, I sat beside Jeremy when he slept, watching the drip and the flashing numbers. When he woke, I tried to get him down to the hospital café in a wheelchair, marshalling all the cheer I could.

'I want to go and help her,' he said on Tuesday. He was watching the news of Mrs May's statement to Parliament on the Brexit negotiations ahead of the October Council, which was accompanied by more speculation about Brexiteers marshalling themselves to stand against her. 'She came into office wanting to fight injustices, but the reality is that we've been able to do little but Brexit, and even that is stuck.'

This was true but I was watching the next news item – an announcement by the energy firm Cuadrilla that it was about to start fracking. 'But you must be pleased about this?' I asked Jeremy, knowing he'd been interested in fracking for years – ever since he'd read a Policy Unit report about how it was enabling the US to be energy independent and making its energy-intensive industries more competitive.

Jeremy knew, of course, how controversial fracking was in Britain, not least because two of his old teachers from Bootham often lobbied him about it. But all the scientific evidence indicated fracking was safe, so with the Prime Minister's endorsement he'd championed work to clarify the regulatory framework and to prepare thinking on a possible UK sovereign wealth fund to protect fracking revenues.

Jeremy returned my smile. 'Some people believe civil servants shouldn't have views; but if you aren't proactive, you will achieve little.'

Our days had by then formed a new pattern. Most mornings, when I arrived on the ward, Jeremy would smile at me. 'Hi, Pearl,' he would say, 'I'm so glad to see you,' and it was clear he was. But other times, I found him lying in silence in the dark.

My job, whatever I found, was to bring brightness. Turn on the lights. Chat about the world. Produce small gifts of books or apples. Make sure the pain was under control. Assure him we had a plan. Get him down to the café for an espresso, even if he didn't drink it anymore. And while Jeremy slept, I would dash back to my office, returning with papers to read sitting next to his bed.

On Saturday 20 October, Dr Landau came to see us. 'The tumours in your liver are still growing,' he said. 'I'm afraid they're not being affected by the chemotherapy and they're in a difficult position.'

Jeremy didn't ask any questions, so neither did I. But later, while Jeremy was sleeping, Dr Landau met me downstairs in the hospital café.

'How long do we have?' I asked, the words inadequate for so profound a question. Around us, people chatted and sipped tea. I felt like screaming at them to shut up.

'I don't know, but it could be sudden. And he's so weak it might not even be the cancer.'

Before I fell asleep back at home that night, my eyes swollen with tears, Jeremy sent me a text. 'My darling Pearl. You have been an unbelievable rock through the last few months. I simply cannot have survived without your love and strength. Take care. J'

The following day marked a change. For the first time since they'd been unboxed, Jeremy's iPhones lay untouched beside him. But he laughed when at last he did pick one up to find that Alastair Campbell had emailed him a photo of Olly Robbins at the People's Vote march against Brexit the previous day.

'Is that Olly??' Alastair demanded.

'Looks like it. Finally doing a runner after constant provocation ...'

After agreeing it was unlikely that Olly was on the march itself – which Olly later confirmed – Alastair asked how Jeremy was.

'I am in poor shape I am afraid,' he replied, 'and certainly in no state to turn around the Brexit liner.'

Jeremy was right that it was unlikely he could do more. I arrived in the ward on Monday morning to find him lying on his side staring at me. I ran forwards, but before I could reach him, he started crying out in pain. I hit the button to call the nurses, who came first with tablets, then injections.

'Wait,' they said, 'it will get better.'

But it didn't. I opened the door and screamed down the corridor.

After the second set of painkillers, Jeremy lay on the bed, occasionally making odd statements, but otherwise sleeping. Sitting beside him, for the first time I felt lonely. Until that moment we'd been fighting this together. Now all I could do was watch over him, wait for him to come back and hope that our conversation about Whitehall, which we'd continued for over twenty-one years, was not yet over.

The next morning, in one of his brief periods of wakefulness, Jeremy decided to retire. After his statement was issued on Wednesday 24 October, the Prime Minister nominated him for a life peerage.

I stayed by Jeremy's bed through the rest of that day. In the early afternoon, Dr Landau came to tell me what I already knew – there was little more he could do. Jeremy's iPhones were filling up with tributes as the shock of his departure radiated out across Whitehall. But that world felt disconnected from mine, sitting listening to Jeremy's breathing and holding his hand.

When I arrived at the hospital on Thursday morning, Jeremy told me he'd had the worst night of his life, during which he'd struggled to call the nurses and to communicate what he needed after they'd arrived.

'I won't leave again,' I said.

'What do you mean? You must leave. The kids, your work,' Jeremy said, his voice raspy.

'I won't leave,' I repeated. 'Maggie will stay with the kids and they will come in to see us. My work will understand.'

Then Jeremy smiled, his first in days. 'The ultimate comfort blanket,' he whispered.

Messages were still piling in, but he answered only one more, which was from Barry. It was the last message he sent on his Cabinet Office phone.

Barry. Am really not well enough to text or speak. But you have been such a wonderful friend and support over the 11 years that there is an exception to every rule! I have had a terrible decline and feel seriously unwell – tired, lacking all energy and sick. May well be close to the end. Thanks again my friend. No one could have done more to help me. J xxx

After that I lost track of time. Each day the children came in for a short while, and Jeremy's brother Simon visited for long enough to allow me to walk down Marylebone High Street in the sun for an hour. Friends brought in food parcels and handed them over in the hospital lobby with tears and snatched hugs.

As a consequence of his life peerage, Jeremy would become a lord. 'You need to decide what you want to be the lord of,' I told him during one of his brief wakeful periods.

'Whitehall,' he said.

So I relayed this to the Cabinet Office, who later told me that getting this agreed had taken three calls to Garter, the extraordinarily titled person who makes these decisions, and a promise that the Civil Service would never ask for the title again.

The tributes continued. Ray, our ward assistant, brought in chocolates to thank Jeremy for everything he had done. And Barry brought in piles of letters, which I flipped through. One friend said that Jeremy's brilliance was the first issue for years on which Labour and the Conservatives had agreed. 'I never once saw you lose your temper,' another wrote. 'You never raised your voice. My abiding picture is of you sitting in Gordon Brown's open-plan office, day after day during the crisis while you, quietly, but with great insistence and authority, put the wheels back on the coach.'

While Jeremy slept, I talked to him, telling him that I wanted him to live to enjoy all the honours he'd earned and all the friendships he'd built. But it was clear I was losing him. He was going to disappear and none of this mattered. I would trade everything for time, but there was no one to accept my deal. And the future, rather than being full of promise, of all the things we'd planned to do together, was full of … well, nothing really.

On Saturday 27 October I had another email. The Queen had awarded Jeremy a Knight Grand Cross or GCB, the highest honour in the Order of the Bath. Jeremy winced when I told him this during one of his increasingly rare moments of consciousness.

'Why?' I asked.

'Because I've told them not to waste knighthoods on people who already have them.'

'Will you say no to the Queen?'

He shook his head. And secretly, I thought he was pleased.

The Palace graciously agreed to award the GCB at the hospital on Tuesday 30 October, condensing what would normally be a wait of weeks or months into a matter of days and turning a ceremony in the Throne Room in Buckingham Palace into one in a hospital meeting room.

Our preparations before the ceremony mimicked the moments before a wedding, with Simon and Jonny buzzing around Jeremy's wheelchair checking each other's ties. When I wheeled Jeremy into the room downstairs, the Deputy Lord Lieutenant was already there, his sword gleaming. Jeremy smiled and didn't say much, but he raised his chest when the Lord Lieutenant gave him his medal and they shared a salute.

Afterwards, when the family crowded around to have their photo taken with him, Jeremy frowned. 'This is for the Civil Service,' he whispered when I leaned in close. 'This is an official Civil Service ceremony.' He took a breath. 'And when you tell them about it, I want you to say how proud I was to be their leader.'

* * *

Soon after that, Jeremy said he was tired, so I took him back upstairs. For most of the rest of that day, he slept while I conducted a one-way conversation, sharing stories and asking his advice on issues. I knew we were close to the end, that the effort of receiving his award had absorbed his last few ounces of strength. But it was what Jeremy had wanted, so I had no regrets – and nothing was going to change this ending. In the following days, I focused on making sure Jeremy had the pain relief he needed, trying to interpret his expressions and sharing an occasional word, though even those stopped on Thursday.

On Friday 2 November, I contacted Jeremy's closest friends. It was time to say goodbye. Jeremy had been clear while he'd been awake that he didn't want visitors. But now he was sleeping, and I needed to consider the needs of those who loved him. It also helped me. Sitting in that room for day after day I'd become disconnected from the world and overwhelmed with grief. Others brought bits of life into the hospital with them. The children were best at doing this. Jonny would eat a muffin while reading the papers, Lizzie would sort our piles of letters and Peter would hoover up any spare chocolates he found lying around. Next to us, Jeremy slept. I hoped he could hear us.

On Saturday I wrote my own statement about Jeremy. There was nothing else left to do. Before I went to sleep that night, I hugged him. 'If you need to go, you should,' I told him. 'I'll look after the kids and we'll do you proud.'

I kissed him and lay on my camp bed watching his silhouette in the half-light. The nurses were doing their regular rounds. At 3.20 a.m., one of them came in and stood and listened. I sat up and listened too. Jeremy's breathing was regular. She went away and I lay back down. A little after four, a second nurse paused in the doorway.

'He's stopped breathing,' he said.

I listened, and indeed he had. It was too much – Jeremy had gone.

55

'Blame It on Me':
Greensill Capital

2021

When Jeremy and I sat together discussing this book in 2017 and 2018, we had no idea that one topic – Greensill Capital – would come to occupy so many columns of newsprint or that, in the aftermath of the collapse of Greensill Capital in 2021, there would be attempts to scapegoat Jeremy to distract attention from the actions of others. But this is what happened.

When I was interviewing Jeremy for this book, we discussed Lex Greensill, the man who went on to found Greensill Capital. Jeremy had met Greensill while working at Morgan Stanley in 2005, though they'd worked in separate parts of the bank – Jeremy in the investment banking division and Lex Greensill in the fixed income division. We didn't discuss Greensill's later appointment as an unpaid adviser to the Cabinet Office in 2012, probably because Jeremy didn't see it as a particularly interesting matter – and I didn't mention Lex Greensill in my chapter on Morgan Stanley because they hadn't worked together there.

On 8 March 2021, over two years after Jeremy died and five years after Lex Greensill had left the Cabinet Office, Greensill Capital filed for insolvency. Its collapse caused a scandal in the UK because David Cameron had started working for the company as a highly paid adviser after standing down as Prime Minister. He'd then lobbied the government and the Bank of England intensively via emails, texts and WhatsApp messages to try to secure support for Greensill Capital during the Coronavirus pandemic in 2020.

Although Cameron's lobbying didn't break any rules, the extent of his interactions with serving government ministers caused understandable public concern and was widely criticised in the media. I was surprised, therefore, when, in early April 2021, the *Sunday Times* turned its attention to events that had taken place almost a decade earlier, publishing two articles criticising Jeremy for supporting Lex Greensill's appointment as an unpaid adviser to the Cabinet Office in early 2012. Despite the headlines, it was hard to see what the issue with this was, particularly when helping small and medium-sized enterprises (SMEs), including those supplying government, had been a stated coalition priority at the time and when a government report – the Breedon Review – had suggested using supply chain finance to do this. Francis Maude, who'd been the Minister for the Cabinet Office (MCO) at the time, had also made clear his support for this work, telling the Procurex Conference on 14 March 2012, 'We will also consider the role of structured finance products, such as Supply Chain Finance, which have the potential to allow tier 2 suppliers to access payments early.'

Given the Coalition government's interest in this topic, it also didn't surprise me that Jeremy had supported Lex Greensill's appointment. It was Jeremy's job to find new ways of doing things to advance the government's policy agenda and he would have wanted to consider the idea properly. In the case of supply chain financing – a tool widely and effectively used in the private sector then and now – this work required expertise that wasn't available in the public sector, which was presumably why it made sense to bring in Lex Greensill, who'd worked on this topic at both Morgan Stanley and Citibank, although he was no longer connected to either institution.

The *Sunday Times* articles had been based on leaked documents, including some of Jeremy's personal emails, but when I approached a senior Cabinet Office official to ask if they would conduct a leak inquiry, he said they had no intention of doing so as the chances of finding the leaker were 'minuscule to non-existent'. I found this strange since the leaked papers would only have been available to the small group of people who'd worked on supply chain finance in the Cabinet Office between 2012 and 2015. However, whether or not we discovered the source of the leak, the episode made me nervous as it showed that someone was deliberately releasing documents which, taken out of context, and with the connivance of the *Sunday Times*, could create the perception that Jeremy had somehow done something wrong.

In mid-April 2021, with no sign of the noise over David Cameron's lobbying abating, the government announced a review into its use of supply chain finance. The decision to do this was politically understandable, but I was concerned when the Cabinet Office (which was responsible for setting up the review) said that it would be looking not only at the controversial lobbying that took place in 2020, but also at Lex Greensill's time in Whitehall almost a decade before. I told my senior contact at the Cabinet Office that it was possible people might use the review to distract attention from the lobbying row and to distance themselves from a now 'toxic' Lex Greensill by conveniently blaming their decisions and actions on someone who couldn't defend himself. His response was, however, reassuring: 'The whole thing needs to be done fairly to all involved – and that we make sure J, in particular, and his motivations are fully and properly represented.' I agreed with this, but told him that, being 'properly represented' meant having someone who was able to go through Jeremy's papers and 'prepare his position'. 'I completely agree,' my contact said. 'I had assumed we would do just this when I told you that we would make sure J was properly and fairly represented.'

Unfortunately, when I was introduced by email later that month to Nigel Boardman, the man who had been asked to lead the review, it became clear that he held a different view. Boardman is a solicitor from the firm Slaughter and May and his appointment had generated substantial criticism. This was both because he'd previously led a review of the procurement of personal protection equipment during the early stages of the Coronavirus pandemic that many believed had whitewashed the actions of government ministers, and because he had multiple conflicts of interest, including having been a member of the Conservative Party and being on the board of a department (Business, Energy and Industrial

Strategy) that had allowed Greensill Capital to access one of the government's Coronavirus loan schemes.* Some also questioned why a solicitor, someone more used to prosecuting a case, had been appointed rather than a judge, who would be more professionally neutral in weighing the evidence.

I'd never met Nigel Boardman, so I hoped for the best. However, before I had a chance to engage with him, two senior Cabinet Office officials appeared before the Public Administration and Constitutional Affairs Committee (PACAC) in Parliament on 26 April to discuss the work of the Cabinet Office. During that session they were asked about Lex Greensill's time in government in 2012 and stated that they were 'reasonably clear that Jeremy Heywood was seeking to bring Lex Greensill in to work in the Cabinet Office'. They then added that they were 'alarmed' by this and had been unable to find a 'contract' for Lex Greensill – despite also admitting that an 'appointment letter' setting out 'conditions on his appointment', covering things like the Official Secrets Act, confidentiality and using the Business Appointment Rules, existed.

I contacted the Cabinet Office after this hearing to say I was distressed by the comments that had been made about Jeremy. In particular, given that a detailed appointment letter existed, I couldn't understand why they'd said they were unsure how conflicts of inter-est were being managed. 'That's fair,' my contact replied, before promising me that, when the Cabinet Office wrote to the committee on various points of follow-up, they would 'include this correction'. He also assured me that all Greensill's appointment letters would be shared with PACAC.

Again, I felt somewhat comforted by this, but when I was contacted by Nigel Boardman's review team three days later, on 29 April, I realised that these comments in Parliament were only the start of a process that was being stacked against Jeremy. The team

* The government's decision to allow Greensill Capital to access this fund through the British Business Bank (which the Business, Energy and Industrial Strategy department directly oversees) was strongly criticised by the Public Accounts Committee (PAC) in its report on 20 November 2021. In this the PAC said that the decision had put up to £335 million of taxpayers' money at risk and it criticised the department for repeatedly chasing the bank on the progress of Greensill Capital's accreditation.

informed me that Boardman would only conduct formal interviews with those who had 'a direct role' in the issues within the scope of the review. This, rather conveniently, excluded Jeremy, and Jeremy alone, from the process. I was also told that Boardman was happy to meet with me informally, but it might not be 'possible or appropriate' to include any point I made in the review's findings. They were also not prepared to share any materials with me 'or any information about the content of the review, at any stage in the process'.

I was deeply distressed by this proposed approach, which as well as being obviously unfair was also in complete contradiction to the assurances I'd been given. I therefore wrote back to Boardman the following day to say that we needed to discuss how Jeremy would get a 'fair hearing'. I added that the Cabinet Office had told me that I would 'have access to the review on his behalf like others'. My preference, I told him, was 'to have access to papers and the report (if others do)', but if this wasn't possible then someone needed 'to review the report and provide input on [Jeremy's] behalf or this work will be uniquely unfair on a dead man'.

This time Nigel Boardman personally sent me his uncompromising reply. There were no papers he could send me, he said, because I did not have direct involvement in the events he was reviewing. He also claimed that it would not be 'appropriate' to share with me 'any extracts if they contain criticisms of Lord Heywood'.

I tried again after this to reach out to my Cabinet Office contact, but this time he didn't respond. Given that I had no other option, I therefore accepted Nigel Boardman's offer of an informal meeting, which took place virtually on 5 May. In this I emphasised I did have knowledge that would be relevant to his review (for example, I was the executor of Jeremy's will, was his biographer and had relevant papers) and asked again for Jeremy to be properly represented. Boardman, however, seemed uninterested in what I had to say. He remained silent for most of the meeting and offered no follow-up.

At this point, I felt like I'd hit a dead end. Boardman was clearly not going to offer me anything else, and the Cabinet Office wasn't responding to my messages. I continued to worry that others would blame Jeremy for their own actions, but (perhaps naively) still wanted to believe that Nigel Boardman, whom my Cabinet Office contact had assured me was a 'fair and decent' person, would conduct a balanced review.

For a month after that I continued to hope that things would not be as bad as I feared. Then, on 8 June, Francis Maude and several senior ex-civil servants were interviewed by PACAC about their involvement in the Greensill affair. In their testimony they all – to greater or lesser degrees – tried to shift the blame for their own decisions onto Jeremy. The most egregious of these was Maude, who initially claimed that he couldn't recall authorising Lex Greensill's appointment to the Efficiency and Reform Group (ERG), a unit he'd personally established and which he'd overseen as the responsible minister. He then admitted he 'might have agreed' Lex's appointment, but if he had, it was only to avoid a 'row' with Jeremy.

I wrote to PACAC after this hearing to share my concerns about this attempted scapegoating. But the incident also made me realise that if Maude and others were doing this in Parliament, they were almost certainly doing the same in front of Nigel Boardman. And when this was combined with the earlier document leak, it looked increasingly like Jeremy was being set up. If I'd been confident that the Boardman review was being conducted in a fair way, this wouldn't have mattered so much, but instead it looked like, by silencing Jeremy, the review was at best providing people with an easy opportunity to blame him for their own actions, and at worst was deliberately allowing this to happen. My anxiety then increased further when, on 14 June, a friend in the Cabinet Office contacted me to say they were 'horrified about where [the Boardman review] is all going', that 'some people' were 'rewriting history' and there was 'lots of unfairness'. On the same day I was also told by PACAC that the Cabinet Office was still refusing to release Lex Greensill's appointment letters. This is when I decided I had to act: if no one else was willing to defend Jeremy, I would have to fight back against Boardman's attempt to silence me and defend him myself.

Having decided this, my first step was again to reach out to my contact in the Cabinet Office. This time my message was far more emotional. 'Jeremy would have defended you or others if you were not here to defend yourself,' I told him after explaining how

Boardman had blocked me from participating in the review, 'but no one is defending him. It's horrible and distressing.'

My emotion at last elicited a response. 'I have already told Nigel that he must share papers with you,' my contact replied, 'and he has agreed.' He then promised he would 'follow up with Nigel'.

This time, however, with the delivery date of the review at the end of June fast approaching, and with so many previous promises having been broken, I wasn't reassured. So, on 16 June, I wrote directly to Nigel Boardman, titling my letter 'Natural Justice for Jeremy Heywood'. In this I said I was 'deeply concerned that if I continue to be denied any access to the papers being considered by your review, to be given any right of representation or any opportunity to see and respond to its conclusions as they relate to my late husband, it will be impossible to afford him the natural justice he deserves'.

Boardman didn't reply to this, but on 17 June I received an email from his team informing me again that Boardman would only engage with those with 'first hand knowledge of the relevant events'. On the same day, after I made another appeal to my Cabinet Office contact, he arranged for me to be sent extracts of Boardman's near-final report. I was grateful for this since it was the first time I'd seen anything coming out of the review. But, when I read the material, I was appalled. My worst fears were justified: Boardman was uniquely targeting Jeremy – the person he'd deliberately gagged – while letting past and serving ministers and special advisers off as lightly as possible. The report was so biased that I found it hard to read, and when I did so I became overwhelmed by the hopelessness of fighting back against what had all the hallmarks of an organised campaign to scapegoat Jeremy.

After I'd calmed down, I became more analytical and spent some time reading through the draft report several times. As I did this, it became clear that, as well as being unpleasant (for example, Boardman stated baldly in his introduction that he hadn't been able to speak to Jeremy, making it sound like Jeremy hadn't bothered to show up rather than explaining that he'd passed away), and being written in a highly subjective and biased way, most of Boardman's conclusions were – to the limited extent to which they relied on any evidence at all – based on post-hoc, one-sided testimonies and not supported by contemporaneous documents. I went through the extracts, highlighting places where Boardman had used subjective language, where his conclusions were not based on contemporaneous evidence and where he'd drawn conclusions that were clearly unfair. On 18 June, I sent Boardman these comments and repeated my concern about natural justice. I also pointed out the many flaws of the draft review, including its failure to acknowledge its heavy reliance on hindsight – after all, at the time of Lex Greensill's appointment in 2012, Greensill Capital had been a small Australian start-up whose later rapid growth, over-reach and then demise lay many years in the future.

I received no response from either Boardman or his team to this letter, so on 22 June I wrote again. This time I tried to draw Boardman's attention to the multiple precedents in the context of such an inquiry for how to treat people who had passed away. In particular I highlighted the approach that had been taken by Lord Dyson in his investigation into Martin Bashir's *Panorama* interview with HRH Diana, Princess of Wales, and specifically how he'd treated Steve Hewlett, the late editor of the programme. During Dyson's inquiry Mr Hewlett's widow had made detailed representations about the allegations relating to her husband, which Lord Dyson had considered carefully, and when post-hoc, unproven allegations were made against Mr Hewlett, Lord Dyson had dismissed them.

On Friday 25 June, Boardman at last decided to respond, sending me another short and devastating email. In this he stated that 'the evidence relating to all of the people involved in the issues I have been asked to review is now clear' and informed me that in coming to these conclusions he had 'not read' my representations and did 'not propose to do so'.

I barely slept that weekend. It was hard to accept that Jeremy had been let down so comprehensively by the institution to which he had dedicated his life or that people could have such little honour that they would try to shift responsibility for their own actions onto someone who was dead. The promises I'd been given by the Cabinet Office had been false and Nigel Boardman had reached his conclusions having comprehensively blocked any representation for Jeremy. I felt – and still feel – that it is very easy for people whose principal concern is to protect their own positions, or for those who are appointed to run a review in the way Boardman was, to ignore the impact of their actions on someone who is no longer here, and to waive away the concerns and distress of families left behind.

Given that Boardman clearly had no intention of giving Jeremy a fair hearing despite all my attempts to make him change his position, during that weekend I decided I had no option left but to take the government to judicial review. This was not an easy decision, but I felt I'd been left with no other choice and that I owed it to Jeremy to do whatever I could to make the government treat him with decency. On 30 June, the stated end-date of the review, a legal letter was sent to the Cabinet Office advising them of my decision. It was, this letter stated, an essential requirement of any review that it should be procedurally fair, and this requirement of fairness applied even when someone was deceased. Given this, Boardman's repeated refusal to allow Jeremy any representation was unlawful.

Nothing happened for several days after that. Then, on 6 July, I received another email from the review team: Boardman had changed his mind and decided to grant me a formal meeting. In advance of this, I would be allowed just forty-eight hours to access Jeremy's papers – though there were 150 pages of these, and no one was allowed to help me.

It was, of course, clear that Boardman (presumably following legal advice from the Cabinet Office's lawyers) was hurriedly ticking boxes to avoid being taken to court and was still intent on making it as hard as possible for me to represent Jeremy.* Not only was this meeting taking place after he'd already stated in writing that he had

---

* My suspicion that Boardman was only seeing me because of my legal challenge was confirmed when he testified in front of PACAC on 2 November 2021. During this session, Boardman confirmed that he had been a member of the Conservative Party although he didn't address any of his other conflicts. He was also criticised for including 'tittle tattle' in his report. Boardman claimed three times in his testimony that he'd changed his mind about allowing me to represent Jeremy, but omitted to say that this was at the eleventh hour, after the due delivery date of his review. He told the committee his change of view was because he'd decided that doing so would be 'fair'. But, when confronted on this point by the committee chair, Boardman was forced to admit that in reality he'd done so only after I'd threatened legal action following his shocking communication to me that his mind was made up and he would not even read my representations.

reached all his conclusions, it was also being done in a way that placed me under extreme time pressure, particularly given that, in contrast to every other participant in the review, I hadn't lived through these events, so this would be the first time I'd seen any of the papers. But I had little choice – no matter how much the process was stacked against me, if I didn't accept, Boardman would say I'd refused the opportunity to contribute. So I did accept, though under protest, telling him in my response that the meeting was coming at a point at which the fundamental flaws of his report were 'irremediable' given that the other individuals being considered by the review had been involved since its outset and that the review was all but finalised. I also asked again how his many personal conflicts of interest were being handled, though I had scant hope that this question, which I'd posed several times before, would be answered.

On 8 July, I was given temporary access to Jeremy's documents. These were a revelation because, when I compared them to the extracts of the draft report I'd seen before, it became apparent that Boardman was being highly selective in his use of evidence.* For example, the draft report I'd seen had stated that Jeremy had brought Lex Greensill into 'the very heart of Government without Ministerial authority'. However, there was ample documentary evidence that Francis Maude, as the responsible minister, had approved the appointment and no evidence whatsoever of any sort of 'row' between Francis Maude and Jeremy over the decision. For example, a submission sent to Maude's office in December 2011 proposed that Lex should be appointed to work on 'Project Bank Account and Supply Chain Finance (potentially 1 day per week)' with 'administrative support' and said this would be put to a 'Commissioning Board'. Since Maude was a member of the Commissioning Board (though Jeremy wasn't), he would have been part of the appointment decision, something that was confirmed by an email in which it was noted that Ian Watmore (the permanent secretary of the Cabinet Office) was intending to 'get MCO [Francis Maude]'s view at the commissioning board' on the submission.

---

* Because the review selectively quoted evidence to try to frame Jeremy, I have quoted some of the other documents here that were not revealed to give a more balanced picture.

The plan had been for Lex Greensill to be appointed to the Efficiency and Reform Group, a unit Maude had created after the 2010 general election to assess ways to reduce costs in government. This was headed by Katharine Davidson, who reported to Maude and who had worked for the Conservative Party for two years prior to the election. Davidson's office emailed Lex Greensill twice to say that she was getting Maude's permission for this appointment. The first of these, sent on 5 October 2011, said, 'her next steps will be to take this to Ian Watmore and Francis Maude so that she can be sure they are content', and the second, on 14 October, said, 'Hopefully she will receive a positive response from both MCO and COO Ian Watmore sometime next week.' Davidson's letter appointing Lex Greensill, which she signed on 21 February 2012 after the Commissioning Board, then stated that 'This arrangement has been agreed by both the Minister for the Cabinet Office [Francis Maude] and the Permanent Secretary for Cabinet Office [*sic*].' Given all of this, Maude's denial of his involvement in Greensill's appointment was shocking – as was Boardman's biased conclusion.

After an intensive weekend of work, I met Boardman on the afternoon of Monday 12 July. The meeting was held in a nondescript government building on Great Smith Street. When I walked in, I found myself facing Boardman, two members of his team and a Cabinet Office lawyer. I was accompanied by my own lawyer, but unlike Boardman's team, he hadn't been allowed to see Jeremy's papers and had been banned from speaking in the meeting.

After I'd sat down, Nigel Boardman smiled and started reading out his conclusions about Jeremy, pausing after each point. Each time he did, I responded, quoting the documents I'd seen that contradicted his views and highlighting the multiple papers he cited that hadn't been disclosed to me. Each time I did this, Boardman smiled again and moved on to his next conclusion. When he reached the end of his list, Mr Boardman said he had nothing more to say – but I did. I asked why he'd systematically excluded me from his review. Boardman said nothing in response to this, he just kept smiling. I then read out a list of his conflicts of interest (which took some time) and asked how they were being managed, but Boardman again remained silent.

Two days after this meeting, the review team sent me two emails containing some of the documents they'd failed to disclose before the meeting because of 'administrative oversight'. The following day they sent me a new set of extracts from the draft report, giving me two working days to respond. I opened these to find, unsurprisingly, that although some of the wording had changed, in substance the conclusions were the same as those I'd seen in June – thus again demonstrating that my last-minute meeting with Boardman had only been granted to avoid being taken to judicial review.

To go back to Lex Greensill's original appointment, the amended report stated, 'There is some evidence, albeit not conclusive, that this three-month appointment was formally approved by Lord Maude.' The report thus dismissed all the documentary evidence that indicated Maude's approval. It then went on to say that 'A covering memo to the Prime Minister in 2012, copied to Lord Heywood, points to Lord Heywood as the person primarily responsible for Mr Greensill being given a role in government.' This conclusion wasn't just biased, it was objectively unfair. As well as not quoting any of the extensive documentary evidence showing Maude's approval of Greensill's appointment, and only quoting the one document that mentioned Jeremy's involvement, the report also failed to mention that this passing sentence in a covering memo – which reads 'Jeremy has brought him [Lex Greensill] in to work a [*sic*] pro-bono in the Cabinet Office' – was part of a document that had nothing to do with the appointment decision, and which was sent over four months after Katharine Davidson had signed her appointment letter.

The rest of the draft report was written in a similar way, selectively choosing evidence to place as much blame as possible on Jeremy. In some cases, it went further, and was factually inaccurate. For example, it claimed that the 'first documented engagement between civil servants from the Cabinet Office and Mr Greensill, when he was employed at Citibank, was an email exchange and meeting with Lord Heywood … in August 2011', even though the documents showed that Greensill had met Francis Maude and Cabinet Office officials in July 2011 and engaged with Katharine Davidson before his meeting with Jeremy.

I spent a frantic weekend preparing a detailed rebuttal of the draft findings, which I sent on Tuesday morning. In this I said I was 'horrified by the way in which these extracts have been drafted in order to reach a pre-ordained conclusion against my late husband and deeply distressed by the lack of accuracy and fairness'. I then went on to list a series of allegations that were *uncorroborated* (like the accusation that Jeremy had introduced Greensill to the Treasury); were *uniquely and unfairly focused on Jeremy* (like the allegation that Mr Greensill had only made his plans to leave Citibank clear to Jeremy, when there was abundant evidence that he'd had meetings with multiple people in government during which this possibility was raised); *ignored evidence* that I'd given in my meeting with Nigel Boardman (for example, the suggestion that Lex Greensill and Jeremy had worked together in Morgan Stanley, which I'd stated was inaccurate); deliberately sought to minimise the involvement of others (like Maude's role in Greensill's appointment); or *relied on post-hoc testimony* (like Katharine Davidson's post-hoc assertion that the supply chain finance work was not core to the ERG's agenda or a priority for Lord Maude, which was in direct conflict with emails she'd sent at the time – for example, an email she wrote on 11 August 2011 to Jeremy in which she'd said she was 'very keen to work on how supplier finance can be improved').

Since I knew there was little chance of Nigel Boardman changing his report, I'd already started to make the flaws in his process, and his many conflicts of interest, public.* I was sadly right to assume that little would change because, when the report was published in an indecent rush on 21 July as Parliament prepared to rise, and only a day after I'd submitted my comments, little of substance had changed. The Cabinet Office's briefing then predictably minimised the actions of both historic and serving government ministers in the lobbying scandal while trying to focus on Jeremy's role in appointing Greensill ten years earlier. Despite all my attempts to make the report more balanced, it stands as a masterclass in how to use evidence selectively to support a predetermined conclusion.

---

* I also submitted a freedom of information request to the Cabinet Office asking it to declare Nigel Boardman's conflicts of interest and to say how they were being managed but, when it responded to this on 27 August, all his conflicts had been redacted from the documents, as had any mitigating actions. In response to a follow-up FOI request, it responded on 25 October to say that answering my question about Boardman's conflicts of interest would be too expensive.

PACAC, the parliamentary committee that had been looking into the same events, had continued to work throughout this period and, unlike Boardman, had welcomed (and made public) my written evidence. Coincidentally, it published its interim report ('Propriety of Governance in Light of Greensill') on the same day as Boardman but came to very different conclusions. It noted that Jeremy's role in supporting Greensill's appointment appeared to have been 'in accordance with Government policy on Supply Chain Finance at the time' and pointed out that 'Whilst the then Minister for the Cabinet Office and Prime Minister may have given the impression that they were not involved in its [supply chain finance] development, both gave speeches endorsing it at the time.' The committee concluded – again in marked contrast to Boardman – that both David Cameron and Francis Maude had 'formally authorised Lex Greensill's appointment' and that there hadn't been any 'obvious conflicts of interest' during Greensill's time in government.*

This whole experience taught me a lot about human nature. On the positive side, I was encouraged by the general derision with which the Boardman review was received when it was published and was touched that so many people came out in Jeremy's defence. Alex Allan, who'd been the Prime Minister's adviser on propriety, deplored Boardman's patently unfair process; Angela Rayner, Labour's deputy leader, underlined Boardman's many conflicts of interest, which are all the more glaring given that his report focuses on the need to seek out such conflicts; and Gordon Brown emphasised the deeply flawed nature of Boardman's conclusions. On the negative side the Boardman review had clearly been a determined, cynical and coordinated attempt to distract attention from some real, current issues by trying to blame someone who is no longer with us for matters that required no such blame. Any fair and reasonable assessment would conclude that the Lex Greensill who was appointed in 2012 had none of the significance he gained when his company went bankrupt

* The committee was also highly critical of the government's 'unacceptable' decision to try to prevent it from carrying out a legitimate inquiry by blocking the head of propriety at the time of Greensill's appointment from testifying before it.

many years later. But appointing someone with clear conflicts of interest to create and try to pin blame on a dead man conveniently allowed others to distract attention from a row about ministerial lobbying.

I hope that this government, and later governments, will now let Jeremy rest in peace. He gave his life to public service and died while still serving the Prime Minister of the day. While he would be the first to admit his own imperfections, he was a man of huge integrity, who deserves to be treated better both now and in the future by the institution and politicians he served with such dedication.

Epilogue

Theresa May came up to me during the reception after Jeremy's funeral, a beautiful though immensely sad affair. After commiserating with my loss, she paused.

'I think people will look back and notice when he stopped,' she said.

I looked at the Prime Minister and hoped it wasn't true. Jeremy would have done anything to support her in the battles he'd known she would face over Brexit. But I didn't just share her fear because of Brexit. I also worried about the other gaps that Jeremy had left behind – all those policies he'd championed, his ability to engage people from across the public and private sectors when issues needed resolving, and the civil servants he'd supported when things became tough. I hoped that, as he'd intended, Jeremy had done enough to strengthen the Civil Service so that it could continue to be innovative, be commercial, value diversity and find those solutions even without him there.

In June 2019, six months after Jeremy's funeral, we held a memorial service to commemorate his life. He would have been honoured by the fact that Tony Blair, Gordon Brown, David Cameron and Theresa May all spoke, as did Nick Clegg and Gus O'Donnell.* Each of these leaders had brought their own set of policy challenges – Tony Blair's determination to create a more 'modern' style of govern-

---

* Transcripts of their tributes are contained in the appendix.

ment and to transform public services, Gordon Brown's battle to address the financial crisis, David Cameron and Nick Clegg's endeavours to tame the deficit, David Cameron's referendums and Theresa May's struggle to implement Brexit. Jeremy had respected all of them. Of course he'd seen their flaws and mistakes – together with his own – but each had intended to make our country better and he was proud to have served them.

Like many of his colleagues, Jeremy worked long hours in public service. I know he never regretted that, and nor did we as a family – he was always also part of our world at home, we knew he loved us, and it was what he wanted to do. Sadly, Jeremy is only one of a number of hugely talented civil servants that we have lost in recent years. Others who also stepped across these pages include Paul Jenkins, Charles Farr and Chris Martin. We owe them and their colleagues huge thanks. The work they do makes our Civil Service the envy of the world.

I spent two years following Jeremy's death finishing this book, including completing the final interviews with his colleagues, many of whom have told me how much they miss his guidance on thorny issues of public policy. But for me, and for our children, the far greater absence is of a father, a husband and a friend; someone who cherished and supported us in everything we did. We will miss him for the rest of our lives.

Appendix 1

Memorial speeches

Jeremy had gifts, which as I grow older, I realise are rare. He wasn't born, of course, the finished article but he did become it.

He could inspire loyalty and give it. Find his way to a solution out of any thicket of problems.

He was calm in crisis, indifferent to rank in courtesy, his fellow staff adored him and as for us, his supposed Masters, the best tribute I can pay is that, when he was with me, I depended on him, and when he was gone, I felt his absence like an ache.

He was a negotiator of genius, weaving his way through the labyrinthine corridors of Whitehall with consummate skill. He also of course negotiated between TB and GB – not always easy – and once he negotiated with Cherie and survived.

For Jeremy, the Civil Service was not a tribe but a mission, a cause, to demonstrate what a top rate, well-functioning administration could be, seeing in it not the dull manoeuvrings of a desiccated machine of bureaucracy, but a vibrant instrument of governing, capable enough to guide a nation through turbulent times, creative enough to change the status quo not merely manage it, whilst staying true to its doctrine of impartiality.

Jeremy didn't simply believe in such a Civil Service. He represented it. Lived it. Advocated it and defended it in the face of politics high or low.

We feel his loss keenly. But also, his impact. And above all his example. If you're a young person thinking of a career in public service, study Jeremy Heywood.

The words Civil Servant seem too dry to describe greatness. But Jeremy was a great man whom I look back upon with a sense of pride in what he achieved and a sense of privilege in having achieved at least some of it together.

Tony Blair

I want to address my words directly to Jonny, to Lizzie and to Peter. Your father was not just a good father, he was a great man. I never met a public servant who day in, day out achieved so much in so little time.

He was not a 'yes Minister' man. He was more likely to say 'no Minister' and add 'I have an alternative that may be better' and it usually was. And he brought that creative genius in the thick of it every day to the task that all the thousands of brilliant public servants assembled here today are dedicating their working lives to – building a more decent world.

A collapsing pound, stock exchange crash, leaks, scandals, sackings, banks going under, capital flight, sometimes all in the same morning. Jeremy didn't need crisis, but crisis needed him.

Such was his work rate that he was probably the only person outside the Treasury who ever read every word of that twenty-three-volume study that in 2003 decided the fate of the euro.

And I will never forget how he and the brilliant team he assembled, all here today, worked around the clock and against the clock to shape agreements that prevented a global depression. Work that was praised in every continent, reinforcing in this dark, peacetime hour the already immense reputation of the British Civil Service as simply the best, the finest, the most dedicated public service to be found anywhere in the world.

So in May 2010 I left a handwritten note for David Cameron saying something like 'the country is in good hands: Jeremy is running it'.

Jonny, Lizzie, Peter. Quite often he spoke of the time he spent with you as the quality time that he valued most. He lives on not just through you but through the influence he has had on all of us. And we also see it in you and what you will become.

So to you and to Suzanne I say, 'we are thinking of you. We are here for you to call on. You only need ask and we will be there.'

It is what, with his unselfish generosity and humanity, Jeremy would have done for each of us. We will do no less for you.

Gordon Brown

Jeremy's tenacity, that semi-permanent half smile he always used to have, his svelt intellect, and his preternatural appetite for finding agreement in a sea of disputes were, in many ways, qualities that were tailor made for Coalition Government.

Because Coalition Government – even more than a single party Government (most of them) – is a non-stop process of conflict and compromise, conflict and compromise, for which resolve, creativity and an inexhaustible ability to chuckle at the absurd were all necessary.

And Jeremy had all those strengths in abundance.

I will never forget how – in our regular catch ups in my office – Jeremy would nod in sombre agreement and I thought full agreement as I railed furiously at some potty idea from my then Conservative Coalition colleagues, vowing I would never accept any of it, only to find an hour later around the Cabinet table that Jeremy would, without batting an eyelid, set out an exquisitely crafted compromise blending policy components in perfect harmony from both sides of the Government. And I – if a little dumbfounded – would invariably go along with what he suggested.

And I will also never forget hearing that, the day after the 2015 General Election – when it was obvious that I was not returning to Whitehall but Jeremy had a new Government to serve – the first thing he did was to go to my office and ask the team of civil servants who had loyally worked for me for half a decade how they were feeling and to reassure them that they would be well looked after.

That, in a nutshell, says it all. Not only about Jeremy the man but about the values of decency in public service which Jeremy held so very dear.

Nick Clegg

Jeremy was not just a great man, as has been said, but he was a 'good man' in every sense of the word. Loyal. Incredibly hard working. A team player. And with a deep, moral sense of right and wrong.

Possessed of a huge brain, he devoted it to public service. And the nation should be grateful. I know that I am.

Faced with an intractable problem … or an unresolvable conflict … or even an impossible colleague … there was no one you would rather have working by your side.

And never, ever dour. Even in the darkest moments, he would smile – and make you smile. And he was no Sir Humphrey. He was a radical, creative thinker and an innovator.

The picture I keep in my mind's eye of Jeremy is not the moment in 2010 when I walked through the door of No 10 Downing Street to see his familiar and welcoming face. Nor is it of our last meeting, as I could see him fighting so valiantly against the cancer that would take him.

It is of our first meeting. 1992. There he is – in his twenties – sitting on his desk in the ante room of the Office of the Chancellor of the Exchequer. Sleeves rolled up. Tie slightly undone. Mop of blond hair. Whippet thin. And he is holding court.

Surrounded by papers, he knows how to despatch every one. Beset by problems, he's finding a way through all of them.

There's the big cheeses of the Treasury – the Burns, the Budds and the Bostocks – all beating a path to the Chancellor's door. And half their age – less than half their age – he is dealing with all of them, without a scintilla of doubt or hesitation.

I am looking on in awe.

His was a confidence born of genuine ability, talent and brain. We were so lucky to have him.

David Cameron

I have many memories of Jeremy in the office – but I find it difficult to remember a time when he wore a jacket. That may sound a trivial thing to say but to me it summed him up. Because Jeremy was a man who quite literally came to work with his shirt sleeves rolled up.

Not just an extraordinary adviser, but an extraordinary do-er. Endlessly intellectually curious. Always looking for the answer. Never stopping until he found the solution to the knottiest of problems. Whatever the issue was, Jeremy would sort it. And time after time again, he did.

Such was his depth of dedication that, even when he was ill, he would stop at nothing if he thought that government might falter.

I would hear, 'Jeremy has sent an email'.

Jeremy sent lots of emails. And when emails weren't enough, and Jeremy couldn't come to you, you went to Jeremy.

Prime Ministers past and present, officials and advisers from across Whitehall and beyond, all queued up for their moment with him.

At first it caused a bit of confusion in their street in Clapham. The neighbours couldn't understand why all these people were coming to Suzanne's house. Because Jeremy was also a humble man and he hadn't really told them the magnitude of what he did or who he was. To them he was just Jeremy. But to us he was so very much more.

Calm, practical, pragmatic, forensic, creative and witty too. Some would say, the very best of Sir Humphrey, with none of the downsides. But I would go further. Surely the legend of our brilliant Civil Service should no longer be the fictional story of Sir Humphrey but the true story of Sir Jeremy. The greatest public servant of our time.

Theresa May

The first time I met Jeremy was at the Treasury over thirty years ago. He was working for me, well in theory at least. I remember being impressed by his intellect, his interests and of course his love of Manchester United, which we shared.

He was devoted to the three Ps: policy, politics and parties. We got on so well that when I departed for a spell in our embassy in Washington, Jeremy and friends moved into our house in Clapham. The parties continued, I am told, and judging by the state of our house when we returned, they were very good parties.

Despite this we remained great friends. Shortly after my return we were engaged in handling Black Wednesday. Jeremy loved finding a way through crises, seeing them as an opportunity not just a threat.

He worked closely with the then Chancellor, Norman Lamont, to build the inflation targeting regime which to this day lies at the heart of our monetary policy arrangements. Norman described him as the perfect private secretary – which actually is just as well since Jeremy went on to have similar jobs, managing multiple crises throughout his career.

The then permanent Secretary of the Treasury, Terry Burns, asked Jeremy to carry out a fundamental review of the department. This enhanced Jeremy's knowledge of the Treasury, but perhaps more importantly, introduced him to Suzanne, who went on to become his wonderful wife.

His knowledge of No 10 and No 11 Downing Street helped him to act as a trusted broker between the neighbours – we have heard that already – a skill that served him well throughout his career.

It came into its own over the question of whether to join the euro. Jeremy had many a meeting with Ed Balls at the cafe across the road from the Treasury as the intricacies of the five tests were painstakingly explored in twenty-seven volumes, as the former Prime Minister said. A solution was found, and nobody resigned. Those were the days!

This was just one example of Jeremy's unique ability to be the perfect interface between ministers, special advisers and the Civil Service. He achieved this with politicians from all parties as we have heard so eloquently today. He would be particularly pleased to see David Cameron and Nick Clegg here today, reminding us that collaboration between parties, particularly at times of national crises, can work extremely well.

When he took over from me as Cabinet Secretary the transition was seamless. But Jeremy was reluctant to take on the role of head of the Civil Service as he had never run a department. This humility, as has been mentioned, was another feature of Jeremy's character.

Of course, he later became head of the Civil Service and made his considerable mark, not only in improving policy-making but also in championing diversity and inclusion and devoting considerable time to making the service both more commercial and more digital. That so many colleagues are here today from all departments is a testament to his belief that improvments in these areas would make for a better Civil Service all round.

I have thought a lot recently about what Jeremy would think about the current impasse on Brexit. I know he would want to reassure the next Prime Minister of the resolve of the Civil Service to implement as effectively as possible whatever decision is made. In return, I know he would hope that Ministers show their support, and respect, for our brilliant, impartial Civil Service, the institution he so loved and championed and as the current Prime Minister, the former Prime Ministers and Deputy Prime Minister have spoken about so eloquently today.

And that is how Jeremy's family should remember him too. Not just as a wonderful father and devoted husband, but as an outstanding servant of this country who leaves behind a Civil Service ranked officially number one in the world.

All of us who had the privilege to work closely with him are still mourning the loss of a loyal friend who would brighten up our days, fix our problems and was always up for the next challenge.

He lorded it over Whitehall for so many years, it is truly fitting that we are here to say farewell, not to Sir Jeremy, but to Lord Heywood of Whitehall.

I miss him as a true and trusted friend.

We all miss him, and the country is poorer for his absence in public life, but his legacy lives on in the form of a stronger, more agile and truly impartial Civil Service.

Gus O'Donnell

Appendix 2

Interviewees and other contributors

Andrew Adonis, Stephen Aldridge, Alex Allan, Ken Anderson, Camilla Ashforth, Conrad Bailey, Ed Balls, Michael Barber, Owen Barder, Edward Barker, Toby Barnard, Philip Barton, Tam Bayoumi, Emily Beynon, Gita Bhatt, John Birt, Tony Blair, Kim Blanton, Alastair Blundell, James Bowler, Hugh Bredenkamp, Paul Britton, Gordon Brown, Terry Burns, Nick Butler, David Cameron, Alastair Campbell, David Campbell, Melissa Carrington, Stephen Carter, Simon Case, Louise Casey, Nick Catsaras, Matt Cavanagh, Will Cavendish, Suma Chakrabarti, Jeremy Clarke, Ken Clarke, Nick Clegg, Ronnie Cohen, Martin Collins, Dan Corry, Jeremy Cowper, Jon Cunliffe, Alistair Darling, Ara Darzi, Gareth Davies, Kathryn Davies, Mervyn Davies, Melanie Dawes, Robert Devereux, Andrew Dilnot, Helen Dudley, Tom Ellis, Amelia Fawcett, Rachel Fenton (now King), Simone Finn, Tom Fletcher, Justin Forsyth, Richard Freer, John Gieve, Carrie Gracie, Sarah Gracie, Bernard Gray, John Gray, Paul Gray, Sue Gray, Gerry Grimstone, Raji Gurumurphy, David Halpern, Sarah Healey, Simon Heywood, Fiona Hill, Rachel Hopcroft, Andy Hornby, Andrew Hudson, Jeremy Hughes, Anji Hunter, Joe Irvin, Michael Jacobs, Robin Janvrin, Bernard Jenkin, Barbara Judge, Gavin Kelly, Stephen Kelly, Tim Kelsey, David Kennedy, Bob Kerslake, Andrew Kilpatrick, Ian King, Reyahn King, Simon King, John Kingman, Paul Kirby, Norman Lamont, David Landau, Richard Layard, Stephanie Leonard, Oliver Letwin, Leigh Lewis, Simon Lewis, Simon Linnett, Ed Llewellyn, Stephen

Lovegrove, Helen MacNamara, Brian Magnus, Peter Mandelson, John Manzoni, Jeremy Marlow, Ciaran Martin, Francis Maude, Simon McDonald, Nick Macpherson, Theresa May, Tony Meggs, David Miliband, Ed Miliband, Calum Miller, Sally Morgan, Jennifer Moses, David Muir, Geoff Mulgan, Kris Murrin, David Normington, David North, Gus O'Donnell, Dick Olver, George Osborne, Sue Owen, John Parker, Nick Pearce, Brian Penman, Alice Perkins, Franck Petitgas, Craig Pickering, Jonathan Portes, Jonathan Powell, Henry Pugh, James Quinault, Paul Rankin, Charles Rice, John Rimington, Olly Robbins, Simon Robey, David Robinson, Steve Robson, Dan Rosenfield, Jill Rutter, Philip Rycroft, Gila Sacks, Jeff Saunders, John Scarlett, Tom Scholar, Anthony Seldon, Minouche Shafik, Adam Sharples, Nigel Sheinwald, Ray Shostak, Rohan Silva, Andrea Siodmok, David Soanes, Lord Sterling, Simon Stevens, Rowland Stout, Clare Sumner, Stefan Szymanski, Peter Thomas, Jon Thomson, Andy Tighe, Nicholas Timmins, Nick Timothy, Andrew Turnbull, Adair Turner, Andrew Tyrie, Shriti Vadera, Simon Virley, Keith Wade, Cathinka Wahlstrom, Rob Warlmsley, Ian Watmore, Stephen Webb, Ed Whiting, Nigel Wicks, Stuart Wood, Chris Wormald, Stephen Worthy.

Index